Buying Audiences

Scholars typically emphasize the importance of organized networks and long-term relationships for sustaining electoral clientelism. Yet electoral clientelism remains widespread in many countries despite the weakening of organized parties. This book offers a new account of how clientelism and campaigning work in weak party systems and in the absence of stable party-broker relationships. Drawing on an in-depth study of Peru using a mixed methods approach and cross-national comparisons, Muñoz reveals the *informational* and *indirect* effects of investments made at the campaign stage. By distributing gifts, politicians buy the participation of poor voters at campaign events. This helps politicians improvise political organizations, persuade poor voters of candidates' desirability, and signal electoral viability to strategic donors and voters, with campaign dynamics ultimately shaping electoral outcomes. Among other contributions, the book sheds new light on role of donations and business actors and on ongoing challenges to party building.

Paula Muñoz is Professor of Social and Political Sciences at the Universidad del Pacífico, Peru. Her research focuses on Latin American politics, political parties, and clientelism. Her dissertation received the 2014 Juan Linz Award for Best Dissertation in the Comparative Study of Democracy in the Comparative Democratization Section, American Political Science Association.

Buying Audiences

Clientelism and Electoral Campaigns
When Parties are Weak

PAULA MUÑOZ

Universidad del Pacífico

CAMBRIDGE
UNIVERSITY PRESS

CAMBRIDGE
UNIVERSITY PRESS

University Printing House, Cambridge CB2 8BS, United Kingdom

One Liberty Plaza, 20th Floor, New York, NY 10006, USA

477 Williamstown Road, Port Melbourne, VIC 3207, Australia

314–321, 3rd Floor, Plot 3, Splendor Forum, Jasola District Centre, New Delhi – 110025, India

79 Anson Road, #06-04/06, Singapore 079906

Cambridge University Press is part of the University of Cambridge.
It furthers the University's mission by disseminating knowledge in the pursuit of education, learning, and research at the highest international levels of excellence.

www.cambridge.org
Information on this title: www.cambridge.org/9781108422598
DOI: 10.1017/9781108525015

First published 2019
Printed and bound in Great Britain by Clays Ltd, Elcograf S.p.A.

A catalogue record for this publication is available from the British Library.

Library of Congress Cataloging-in-Publication Data
NAMES: Muñoz Chirinos, Paula, 1977– author.
TITLE: Buying audiences : clientelism and electoral campaigns when parties
are weak / Paula Muñoz.
OTHER TITLES: Campaign clientelism in Peru
DESCRIPTION: Cambridge, United Kingdom ; New York, NY : Cambridge University
Press, 2019. | Revision of author's thesis (doctoral)—University of Texas
at Austin, 2013, titled Campaign clientelism in Peru : an informational
theory. | Includes bibliographical references.
IDENTIFIERS: LCCN 2018038596 | ISBN 9781108422598 (hardback)
SUBJECTS: LCSH: Patronage, Political—Peru. | Patron and client—Peru. |
Political campaigns—Peru. | Political culture—Peru.
CLASSIFICATION: LCC JL3481 .M86 2019 | DDC 324.70985—DC23
LC record available at https://lccn.loc.gov/2018038596

ISBN 978-1-108-42259-8 Hardback

For my mom, Edda, who, among many other things, taught me to be perseverant.

Contents

Figures

Tables

Acknowledgments

This book started with my doctoral dissertation research and has come a long way since. The story of this research project is indeed very entangled with important stages of my professional and personal life. As soon as I returned to Peru from the United States to start conducting fieldwork for my dissertation, my mom's cancer relapsed and she passed away a few months later. I postponed the date of my first field trip outside Lima for as long as I could, and made the best use I could of the Dissertation Fellowship (and, later on, of two Summer Research Fellowships) I was generously granted by the Department of Government at the University of Texas at Austin. When I went back at UT-Austin and started writing my dissertation, I soon had to accept that there was no escaping cervical spine surgery to deal with a painful problem in my neck and arm that were preventing me from typing and generally from living normally. My full recovery from this process took much longer than the doctors had expected and accompanied me throughout my dissertation writing process. After defending the dissertation in May 2013, I started along a new path in my professional life by joining the Universidad del Pacífico faculty in Peru. Coming back home and facing the challenges of a new job slowed down my progress with the book project. Nonetheless, winning the 2014 Juan Linz Best Dissertation Award from the Comparative Democratization Section of the American Political Science Association convinced me to invest more time and energy in the book project. A couple of years later, I managed to send the book manuscript to Cambridge University Press for revision from the maternity work-room (literally) hours before my son Ignacio was born. My baby and other professional obligations distracted me more than I expected, so I had to make a special effort to find the time and energy to revise the manuscript in order to address the reviewers' criticisms and suggestions in 2017. But, although my progress was slow, I finally made it. The very last stage of this book project came along with more amazing news: a new pregnancy. I clicked the "send" button on my message to Sara Doskow, my editor, the final manuscript attached, when the onset of nausea, exhaustion, and other first-trimester symptoms convinced me I *had* to "finish finishing" revisions and send out the final manuscript. If everything goes well with the editing schedule, I thought, my book will see the light of day this year, after my baby daughter is born. This acknowledgment recognizes the different individuals and institutions that supported me in various ways and during the different stages of this long process, thus helping me successfully push through it.

The financial support for this project came from different sources. It was possible in the first place thanks to grants and fellowships provided by the Department of Government and the Lozano Long Institute of Latin American Studies at UT-Austin. I would also like to acknowledge the Instituto de Opinión Pública – Pontificia Universidad Católica del Perú (IOP) for their genuine interest in supporting academic research in Peru, in particular my colleagues David Sulmont and Vania Martínez who were working there at the time. The IOP included (pro bono) several items related to my research in their 2012 national survey, without which finishing the first stage of the research project would have been infeasible. Finally, the support of the Centro de Investigación de la Universidad del Pacífico (CIUP) was crucial during the later stages of the book. Their institutional funds afforded me the time and assistance I needed to expand my research and finish the project. In addition, a collaborative effort in 2017 with *Proética*, aimed at designing and conducting a survey on perceptions of corruption and sponsored partially by our *Vicerrectorado de Investigación,* allowed me to include the most recent empirical data available. Thus, without the Universidad del Pacífico's support, this book project would not have come to fruition.

I am extremely grateful for the generous intellectual support of Raúl Madrid and Kurt Weyland, my dissertation co-supervisors. Since I started working on my dissertation proposal, Raúl and Kurt were great at providing me detailed, prompt, and constant feedback. Throughout all the stages of this intellectual process, my supervisors were extremely supportive and pushed me to keep working and making improvements. And they continued doing so even after I graduated. Thank you both for your mentorship. I could not have asked for more accessible and engaged advisors and colleagues. The other members of my dissertation committee – Henry Dietz, Wendy Hunter, Javier Auyero, and Ken Greene – also contributed to the development of this project. The comments, criticism, and suggestions they provided during my dissertation defense were exceptional and helped give me focus for my book project. As a good friend of mine, also a political scientist, used to tell me, I had *un comité de lujo* (a "deluxe committee"). I am particularly grateful to Javier, whom I also met several times while I was conducting field work and during the writing process. His experience in studying poor people's politics in Latin America, as well as his intellectual generosity, were extremely helpful in clarifying my ideas.

Besides my chairs and the dissertation committee members, many other colleagues also gave me their insights, suggestions, and criticism at different stages of the project. I thank the participants of the Latin American Faculty–Student Group at UT-Austin for their constructive comments and criticisms of my work. Eduardo Dargent, my colleague and husband, has accompanied me throughout the entire project, giving me wise and useful advice (more on this later). Two very good friends and generous colleagues, Austin Hart and Ezequiel González-Ocantos, encouraged me and gave me insightful suggestions to improve my project during the most challenging stages of the research process. Daniel Nogueira-Budny read my first draft chapters and accompanied me very closely during the final stage of the dissertation writing. I am also indebted to Steve Levitsky, who discussed several dissertation-related products with me during his visiting year in Peru. I am likewise grateful to the participants and discussants at the Universidad de Los Andes-Bogotá seminar and the Latin American Studies Association (LASA) Conference. Moreover, I was very lucky to have a book workshop dedicated to my first manuscript at the Red de Economía Política Para América Latina (REPAL) 2016 Conference, planned by Ben Schneider, the host at MIT, and by Juan Pablo Luna and María Victoria Murillo, as program chairs. The generous criticism and comments I received there from two excellent and generous discussants, Juan Pablo Luna and Alisha Holland, encouraged me to push through the last stage of the book project.

I must also recognize the expertise and generosity of Ernesto Calvo who, without knowing me, shared the documents he used to conduct and analyze the networks estimation technique I replicate in Chapter 3. I am also grateful to José Luis Incio, now studying for his PhD at Pittsburgh University, who let me contribute to the design and discussion of The Peruvian Voter survey while working at the *Jurado Nacional de Elecciones*, a project that informed my research. My friend and colleague Arturo Maldonado attended the IOP's survey design meetings in 2012 and gave me great feedback for the design of my first survey experiment. In addition, I want to acknowledge Samuel Rotta's interest for including more academic-driven questions in the design of Proética's National Corruption survey in Peru and inviting me to help with two survey designs.

While working in the book project, critical research assistance (and friendship) were provided by Yamilé Guibert, Viviana Baraybar, and Madai Urteaga. I am particularly indebted to Vivi, who assisted me throughout the manuscript's final revision process as well as with very tedious details in the book editing process. Without her help and her smiling face, I would have gone crazy and postponed finishing this book even longer. I also want to express my gratitude for the great feedback and suggestions I received from two anonymous reviewers who certainly helped to make this book better. Finally, I recognize that I have been very lucky to have Sara Doskow as my editor. She has been professional, supportive, and effective throughout the revision and editorial process.

While conducting fieldwork, many people opened doors for me. Numerous politicians, experts, journalists, and citizens kindly shared their opinions and experience with me. This book would have been unthinkable without them. I cannot go on without singling out Sergio Sullca, Marco Zeisser, Roberto Romero, and Mario Carrión in Cusco, and Luis Loja, Elizabeth Rodríguez, and Rodrigo Urbina in Piura, for their help in the field. My work in Piura would have been extremely difficult without the generosity and kindness of Ceci Trelles and Raúl Aragón, my host family. I got to know the Aragón family circumstantially, but they became like a real family to me and made my stay in Piura unforgettable. I will always remember my conversations with Fernando, who sadly left us before I got back to Peru.

Other friends also made life more enjoyable throughout this research project. My friends Austin Hart, Laura Field, Erin Byrd, Ilana Lifshitz, Daniel Nogueira-Budny, Luis Camacho, Mary Slosar, Manuel Balán, Rodrigo Nunes, Sandra Botero, Rachel Sternfeld, and Kate Bersch made my stay at graduate school nicer, as too did other friends in Austin such as Carla, Solange, Lissette and Huáscar, Nora, María José, Isabel, Omar and Belén, Nino and Paola, Pucho and Kris, among others. My colleagues at the Universidad del Pacífico these past few years have also accompanied my academic progress with interest, caring advice, and friendship, particularly Cynthia Sanborn, Martín Monsalve, and César Guadalupe.

Finally, I cannot finish without thanking my closest family and friends for their emotional support and companionship during these years. My mom, Edda Chirinos-Gratta, was super strong during the time we were apart while I was pursuing my doctoral studies, which coincided with the relapse of her cancer. Despite this, she never stopped encouraging me to finish my dissertation and graduate. Mirella and Hilda, my mom's close friends, as well as Inés, all accompanied me in their own ways during the hardest time of my life. Ada, Matt, Noah, and Sofía made my final stay in Austin enjoyable. Felipe and Gabriela Dargent from Canada always kept in touch, as did my father, Jorge, from Chile. My parents-in-law, Leti and Yayo, have been extremely supportive, encouraging, and loving during all these years. Leti and Yayo also welcomed and took care of our "baby" dogs, Lucas, and more recently Kusi and Wayra, when we were not able to do so. My friendship with Pepa, Lorena, Alejandra, Elisa, and Zuly, my "sisters," only grew stronger during these years. Alberto and Miné were always there too. After coming back to Lima, I was welcomed into a group of friends at the university, the self-styled "*Tallas*," a new (and growing) family to us now. I was also able to meet more regularly with my godmother Dina and my godfather Chiqui, who left us last year but was always enthusiastic and proud of my professional accomplishments. I also want to thank Mónica and Lidia who lovingly helped me take care of Ignacio and the house this past year, making it possible for me to concentrate fully on my book project. Finally, and most importantly, I want to thank Eduardo Dargent, my loving husband, friend, and colleague. Eduardo has helped me in so many ways during these years that this book would have been impossible without him. For one, he has been the "hidden" advisor in this academic project: Eduardo has been patient enough to (endlessly) listen to me while trying to clarify my ideas and has given me extensive comments on tons of dissertation/book-related documents. Besides his intellectual generosity, Edu's lust for life, strength, love, and care helped me get through the many hardships that coincided with the project. And the happiness that we share with our son Ignacio, soon to be extended to our daughter, Agustina spurred me on to finish the book.

Introduction

You must have a wide variety of people around you on a daily basis. Voters will judge you on what sort of crowd you draw both in terms of quality and numbers. The three types of followers are those who greet you at home, those who escort you down to the Forum, and those who accompany you wherever you go. (Quintus Tullius Cicero)[1]

In recent decades, the distribution of gifts to voters during election campaigns has become the norm in Peru. While campaigning, candidates and their supporters give away all sorts of perks, including the likes of free alcohol and meals; food staples such as rice, flour, milk, or fish in coastal areas; T-shirts and caps bearing party logos; pots, pans, and cups; cookers and gas tanks; household appliances; cement bags and other construction materials; wheelchairs; and even sums of money to be raffled among participants at campaign events. A list experiment conducted after the 2010 local elections, estimated that around 12.8 percent of voters were offered a benefit in exchange for their vote during the 2010 subnational campaign (González-Ocantos *et al.* 2012a). Moreover, conventional surveys corroborate this finding, showing that at least 12 percent of Peruvian voters are regularly offered goods during campaigns in exchange for electoral support (Faughnan and Zechmeister 2011).

Gift distribution is particularly notable during subnational elections, but it is also commonplace during candidate visits and campaign events in presidential and congressional races. For instance, during the 2011 presidential election, multiple allegations were made against *Fuerza Popular*,

---

[1] Cicero 2012.

the *Fujimorista* party, for intensive distribution of freebies while campaigning.[2] In the southern region of Ayacucho, *Fujimoristas* even distributed the so-called "Keiko-kit" made up of several *Fujimorismo*-branded items for personal and domestic use – a bracelet, a scarf, a T-shirt, a large notebook, a plastic food-container, a breakfast mug, a box of matches, a pen, a cap, a poster and a *Keiko Presidente* bag – to convince voters from low-income sectors and rural areas to support their presidential candidate.[3]

This distribution of gifts became so pervasive that in 2015 the Congress unanimously approved a bill prohibiting the practice during electoral campaigns. An exception was made for those goods regarded as valid in the context of electioneering (pens, calendars, key chains, and others), which could not exceed 0.5 percent of the statutory tax unit (approximately 5.5 US dollars) per item. The implementation of this law during the 2016 general election campaign resulted in the expulsion of a presidential candidate and several congressional candidates from the race. Despite these draconian sanctions, experts believe that, given the limited state capacity throughout the territory, the law will not be enough to counteract such a ubiquitous electoral strategy, particularly during subnational elections in which thousands of lists compete for office.

To be sure, candidates of all stripes engage in this type of electoral strategy, even political *outsiders* with no party affiliation who compete for the first time and do not have previous experience of electioneering. Peruvian politicians know that they *have to* deliver goods in order to run effective campaigns. As one campaigner puts it, "You need to know how to invest. You have to hand out construction materials, cement, calves, beer. It is an investment. If you don't deliver, you are done: someone else will come and give away more."[4] However, because candidates are not backed by stable organizations, these handouts cannot guarantee voters' support at the polls. And politicians are well aware of this: "People receive handouts, but they do not commit. 'Let him spend his money,' they say."[5] Another politician is even more direct: "All candidates give

---

[2] Alberto Fujimori was president of Peru between 1990 and 2000. He was well-known for having used intensively clientelistic and pork-barrel strategies to garner political support.

[3] *Janampa, Tycho, "Campaña fujimorista despliega plan 'Merchandising' en Ayacucho"*, *Noticias SER*, May 18, 2011. In: www.noticiasser.pe/18/05/2011/ayacucho/campana-fujimorista-despliega-plan-%E2%80%9Cmerchandising%E2%80%9D-en-ayacucho. See also *"Keiko Fujimori repartee comidaentre los pobres a cambio de votos"*, El Mundo, May 6, 2011, in: www.elmundo.es/america/2011/05/06/noticias/1304691775.html.

[4] Personal interview with campaign manager Jorge Nuñez. Puno (June 12, 2010).

[5] Personal interview with Jorge Martorell, former candidate and political advisor to the mayor of Cusco (May 17, 2010).

away goods ... If they offer you something, you accept. But you vote for whichever candidate you prefer."[6]

Under prevailing theories of electoral clientelism, this widespread distribution of goods would be considered unlikely in the context of effective ballot secrecy (e.g., Auyero 2001; Stokes 2005; Kitschelt and Wilkinson 2007; Schaffer 2007a; Díaz-Cayero *et al.* 2007; Nichter 2008; Finan and Schechter 2012; Stokes *et al.* 2013; Lawson and Greene 2014; Zarazaga 2014, 2016). But these theories are inadequate in explaining the prevalence of electoral clientelism in countries with loose political organizations. Conventional wisdom among political scientists holds that in the absence of traditional bonds of deference, electoral clientelism requires well-organized political machines.[7] Clientelistic practices, it is argued, require extended organizations and enduring political relations, in part because of the problem of monitoring. Given that politicians usually deliver benefits such as food or cash before election day, voters could potentially "receive the benefit with one hand and vote with the other."[8] Politicians, therefore, need local agents to target distribution and enforce the clientelistic bargain. According to this logic, it would be foolish to engage in clientelistic distribution during elections in developing democracies without the support of a dense grassroots infrastructure.

Nonetheless, electoral clientelism persists in weakly organized political contexts throughout the developing world. Despite a growing trend of party deinstitutionalization in Latin America (Mainwaring 2006; Gutiérrez 2007; Sánchez 2009; Morgan 2011; Luna and Altman 2011; Dargent and Muñoz 2011; Seawright 2012; Roberts 2015; Ronsenblatt forthcoming) electoral clientelism remains a widespread phenomenon across the region. Indeed, the assumed positive relationship between party organization and vote buying is not borne out empirically in the region. There is no significant statistical association between the frequency of reporting vote purchases and the organizational strength of the party system. Moreover, although not significant, the direction of the association is in fact negative.[9] As can be observed in Figure 1.1, reports of politicians offering material benefits during campaigns are common

---

[6] Personal interview with Edmundo Gatica, campaign manager of Fujimorismo. Cusco (September 6, 2010).

[7] See, for example, Kitschelt (2000: 849–50); Brusco, Nazareno, and Stokes (2004: 85); Stokes (2005: 317); Kitschelt and Wilkinson (2007: 8–9, 17); Magaloni et al. (2007: 185).

[8] Argentine politician quoted by Mariela Szwarcberg in an unpublished manuscript written in 2001. Reference taken from Stokes 2007a.

[9] The Pearson coefficient is −0.2566 and its significance level is 0.3202.

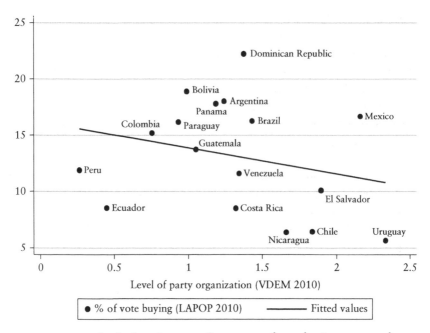

FIGURE I.I. *Latin America 2010: Percentage of vote-buying attempts by level of party organization*
Sources: LAPOP (2010); VDEM (2010)

in countries with loosely organized parties. Although Peru is an extreme case of weak party organization, in clientelistic terms it lies quite close to other countries with weak parties, such as Colombia, and Guatemala, as well as those with more organized machines such as Venezuela or El Salvador. Similarly, Bolivia, another country without well-organized parties, scores higher in vote-buying frequency than do more organized systems, such as Mexico and Argentina. But despite this phenomenon, most studies on electoral clientelism in Latin America focus mainly on cases with stronger local party organization, the latter two countries.

Peru's barely organized politics might be much more representative of the region today than the strong and well-organized party system in Mexico, or the Peronist Party in Argentina. Therefore, in this book, I use Peru as a deviant case study for theory building and testing purposes. Electoral clientelism persists in Peru's democracy even though parties have remained inchoate since their collapse twenty years ago (Levitsky and Cameron 2003; Tanaka 2005a), while political brokers lack long-term party affiliations (Levitsky 2013; Tanaka and Meléndez 2014; Levitsky and Zavaleta 2016). Why do candidates continue to employ clientelistic strategies in countries like Peru where, in the absence of political machines, they lack effective tools for enforcing the clientelistic bargain? And more generally, how do politicians campaign without organized parties?

Existing approaches do nothing to solve this puzzle because, as I argue, they concentrate only on the direct effects of clientelistic investments and fail to take competition and campaigning into account. Their theories have exaggerated the importance of organized networks and long-term relations in sustaining electoral clientelism. As discussed in depth in the second chapter, scholarly approaches focused on monitoring, reciprocity, or the conditional loyalty of clients all conceive electoral clientelism as an iterated relation backed up by political organizations. Consequently, these theories cannot account for short-term clientelistic transactions in unorganized settings. While recent theoretical studies (Szwarcberg 2012b; Holland and Palmer-Rubin 2015; Kramon 2016) address some of the shortcomings of this scholarly consensus and show that electoral clientelism can have an informational role in Latin America, they are still subject to inadequacies: some fail to tackle the paradox of how electoral clientelism persists without machines, while others do not fully develop the theoretical implications of their approach to explain how politicians campaign and establish varied political linkages in the absence of organized and enduring parties. This may be related to the fact that the literature on clientelism overlooks the presence of segmented and mixed electoral strategies (Luna 2014).

To deal with this conundrum, I propose an informational approach that stresses the indirect effects that investments in electoral clientelism early on in campaigns have on vote choice. From this perspective, electoral clientelism is a campaigning tool. In this chapter I begin by presenting my core arguments. Then, I discuss the theoretical relevance of this novel addition to the literature on electoral clientelism, campaigns, and party-voter linkages. Subsequently I present my research design. I conclude the chapter by providing an overview of the book.

THE ARGUMENT IN BRIEF

Prevailing approaches to analyzing clientelism as an electoral strategy assume that the main goal of politicians who distribute particularistic goods during campaigns is to buy votes, turnout, or abstention *directly* on election day. Consequently, electoral clientelism is portrayed as a campaign strategy aimed at influencing electoral results at the margins, contributing to victory only in tight races. Scholars who espouse this approach maintain that politicians distribute selective incentives close to or on election day, as this – along with other strategies – helps them reduce the likelihood of commitment problems. In summary, scholars continue to assume that the only effects of electoral clientelism are direct ones.[10]

In contrast to existing approaches, my theory highlights the unfolding dynamics of the campaign itself and stresses the *indirect* effects that early investments in electoral clientelism have on electoral choices. I contend that the clientelistic strategies used during campaigns generate and transmit valuable information that is utilized by strategic actors to make electoral decisions. Electoral clientelism shapes who becomes a viable candidate – the "supply" from which voters choose the most desirable option. Simultaneously, it also shapes the demands that voters make of candidates. By influencing competition, preferences, and the dynamics of the race, electoral clientelism affects vote choices. From this perspective, electoral clientelism is not, by any means, just a marginal tool to obtain votes.

I argue that politicians may engage in clientelism not *once they have* a viable political machine, but *because they lack one* – that is, they may distribute gifts during elections in order to attract voters' attention and influence unattached voters while campaigning. Electoral clientelism, thus, affects vote choices through two mechanisms. First, clientelism during campaigns is crucial to establishing candidates' electoral viability. From early stages of the race onward, politicians induce voters, often mostly poor ones, to show up at rallies and other campaign events by offering them rewards. Moreover, the distribution of material rewards allows candidates' campaign teams to make an impression, convey information, and signal to donors and the general public that they are *electorally viable candidates*. Actors' beliefs about candidates' prospects of winning are based, among other factors, on the perceived level of public support. By turning out large numbers of people at rallies, candidates establish and demonstrate their electoral prospects to the media, donors, benefit-seeking activists, and voters. In this way, politicians induce more and more donors and voters to support them strategically.

Second, candidates can use electoral clientelism to persuade voters while campaigning. Politicians buy voters' participation as a means of getting their attention. But though the distribution of gifts buys participation

---

[10] An exception is the recent study by Schaffer and Baker (2015), which analyzes clientelism as a persuasion-buying of opinion-leader's epicenters in informal conversation networks. The authors explore how politicians forge indirect linkages with voters by targeting relatively few individuals who work as social multipliers.

at campaign events, it may not necessarily be translated into support from voters at the polls. Indeed, without stable political attachments, most voters are opportunistic. Therefore, politicians need to work hard to transform the temporary hold they have on participants' attention into a firm electoral commitment. To this end, politicians deploy a series of mixed campaign appeals aimed at going beyond clientelism to forge political linkages with voters. First, during campaign events, politicians particularize their messages and promise particularistic benefits (local public goods) to specific constituencies. These events are also privileged opportunities to interact with poor voters and convey a candidate's personal traits. Indeed, personalistic campaigning becomes crucial to building credibility and trust in the eyes of unattached voters. Politicians can also expect to influence voters' choices by generating a positive "buzz" in the audience. In short, by providing citizens with valuable information at campaign events, politicians help clients, often mostly poor voters, form their preferences and make their political choices. They do so by combining campaign strategies and forging different types of political linkages.

My informational theory is well-suited to explaining electoral clientelism in loosely organized polities. Informational deficits are particularly severe in countries with weakly institutionalized parties (Moser 2001). Moreover, in contexts where political parties are poorly organized, and voters do not have lasting political attachments, elections are highly contested and there is greater uncertainty among politicians about their prospects of winning than in organized settings. As has been documented elsewhere (Bartels 1988), in races in which there is less information, substantive predispositions matter less in defining vote choices because voters give more weight to candidates' electoral chances.

Moreover, within loosely organized polities, the informational value of electoral clientelism can also vary for different types of elections. Strategic actors usually contrast the different sources of electoral information available, including turnout figures. In developing democracies, more information is usually available for national elections than for local elections. In the case of presidential elections, candidates need to have substantial name recognition before running successful campaigns. Likewise, national media and citizens are generally more attentive to presidential races. Opinion polls, in particular, tend to be conducted more frequently in presidential elections and become a primary source of information in defining electoral viability. Electoral surveys have a role that complements that of campaign rally turnouts, but this role is more important in national elections. Campaign clientelism should, thus, be more effective in local campaigns than in national ones. Consequently, the informational approach, better explains the effects of electoral clientelism on candidates' trajectories in local elections than in national ones.

Similarly, where party systems are institutionalized, the levels of information and the associated electoral uncertainty can also differ substantially between primaries and general elections. Therefore, the indirect effects of electoral clientelism on vote choices also function differently in each type of election; while signaling viability may matter more in defining primary races, influencing undecided voters may be more important during general elections. Thus, my theory may also aid our understanding of electoral clientelism in more organized political settings.

Finally, electoral rules may be instrumental to influencing the form of electoral clientelism that prevails (Hicken 2007, Gans-Morse *et al.* 2014). Particularly in the case under analysis, mandatory voting could be central to why goods are mostly distributed early as part of campaign clientelism, and not on election day to mobilize turnout at the polls. As Gans-Morse *et al.* argue, with higher abstention costs, compulsory voting has the effect of boosting turnout and, consequently, the number of weakly opposed or indifferent voters who will probably vote. Within a context of scarcely organized political machines in which politicians do not have the means to reliably identify voters' preferences and deal with non-compliance, these voters will most likely be the target of campaign clientelism rather than of vote buying attempts.

A NOVEL FOCUS ON CAMPAIGNS

This book makes several theoretical contributions to the study of electoral clientelism, political linkages, and campaigns. To begin with, in the informational theory that I propose here, political organization is not a prerequisite for electoral clientelism. In contrast to prevailing approaches, my informational approach portrays electoral clientelism as a complex game that takes place *throughout* the campaign and not just on or near election day. That is, electoral clientelism can in fact also be understood as a campaigning tool; once campaigning is taken into account it, the reasons why electoral clientelism can actually persist in contexts of low political organization become clear. Distributing resources helps overcome the challenges of campaigning, without the backing of a party machine because it helps politicians improvise political organizations, persuade indifferent clients, and signal their electoral viability to strategic actors. In other words, electoral clientelism can be an appealing campaign strategy precisely *because of* the absence of stable political parties, since it generates valuable information for strategic competition.

In addition, my approach takes campaign competition seriously since I do not assume that a single incumbent buys votes, nor do I focus only on cases in which machines are dominant and competition is negligible. Indeed, under this informational theory – most candidates, and not just powerful incumbents, can distribute minor consumer goods or cash during campaigns using private resources – candidates compete *through* electoral clientelism. Electoral clientelism can, thus, be associated both with political dominance and volatile electoral contexts. Moreover, while analyzing the tactics of elites, the informational approach also emphasizes the strategic logic of clients during campaigns. Thus, in making electoral choices, clients consider the changing electoral prospects of contending candidates in addition to their preferences. In contrast, most studies of vote buying assume that clients vote sincerely and underrepresent the degree of client opportunism and actual power that is found empirically.[11]

Moreover, instead of pitching in with an increasingly narrow discussion among specialists, my approach – by integrating important insights about political competition, strategic behavior, campaign styles, and party–voter linkages – opens up a broader dialogue with other strands of the literature on parties and sheds new light on existing debates. On the one hand, the core idea of my informational theory is that information about the electoral prospects of different candidates influences voters and elites to behave strategically in response to electoral incentives (Cox 1997). Sustained campaign clientelism is, therefore, important because it helps to generate this valuable information, which will then be used by strategic donors, activists, and voters. On the other hand, my informational approach shows how candidates *combine* different types of appeals to rally and persuade indifferent and unattached voters. Candidates use campaign clientelism to buy an audience, which they then try to persuade through particularistic and personalistic tactics. As research shows – and contrary to the assumptions of the conventional party–voter linkage framework – campaign strategies that involve segmenting (Luna 2014) and/or mixing (Boas 2016) are routine among parties and candidates in developing democracies.

My approach also confirms that the increasing mediatization of campaigning in Latin America – highly television-dependent, poll-driven, and consultant-based – has not so much supplanted traditional methods of

---

[11] See Nichter and Peress (2017) for a piece that bestows more bargaining power to clients.

campaigning as blended with them, resulting in the coexistence of old and new on the campaign trail (Swanson and Mancini 1996; Waisbord 1996; Plasser and Plasser 2002; De la Torre and Conaghan 2009). Through campaign clientelism, political marketing meets street politics. As in the past, when candidates demonstrated political strength by mobilizing partisans and supporters to the plazas, I show here that large-scale and visible mobilization still matters (De la Torre and Conaghan 2009; Szwarcberg 2012b). At least in low-organization settings, characterized by high uncertainty and electoral volatility, head counting is still a powerful cue for assessing appeal and electoral viability. In addition, I highlight how the media amplifies the informational cues of on-the-ground rallies. Candidates record and broadcast their mass rallies, or else the press covers them, disseminating turnout figures or pictures. Moreover, the expansion of the internet and social media over the last few years stands as a new, alternative route for the transmission of turnout informational cues, and this should be explored further in future research.

Finally, this research has normative implications. If electoral clientelism works as my informational theory predicts, it may be less problematic for democratic accountability in weakly organized polities than some scholars have suggested is the case for countries with entrenched partisan machines (e.g., Fox 1994; Stokes 2005, 2007b); poor citizens may sell their participation at campaign events, but this is not to say that they necessarily sell their votes. They decide whether to lend their vote to the buyer based on their tactical preferences, and so candidates must still convince clients of their electoral desirability. Hence, in scarcely organized contexts, these pragmatic voters are neither passive citizens subject to perverse accountability (Stokes 2005), nor diminished citizens who do not evaluate their governments or engage in public deliberation (Stokes 2007b). Nevertheless, campaign clientelism still raises normative concerns. Voters can be misled when public perceptions of electoral viability are manipulated by politicians. Moreover, in the absence of long-lasting clientelistic relations, electoral clientelism can result in the entrenchment of corruption and the monetization of campaigns, thus, reinforcing social inequality. I will further develop these issues in the concluding chapter.

RESEARCH DESIGN

I use Peru as a case study that deviates from the conventional understanding of clientelism; that is, it is a country in which electoral clientelism thrives without organized parties. But even if Peru is a deviant case in theoretical terms, it is still consistent with the ongoing trend of party and party-system deinstitutionalization in Latin America (Seawright 2006; Gutiérrez 2007; Sánchez 2009; Dargent and Muñoz 2011; Morgan 2012). To be sure, the scarcely organized politics of today's Peru are much more representative of the region, as a whole, than the strong and well-organized parties in Mexico, or the Peronist Party in Argentina. Yet as we have noted, studies on electoral clientelism in Latin America have focused exclusively on cases of strong local party organization such as these examples (for Argentina: Brusco *et al.* 2004; Stokes 2005, 2007a; Nichter 2008, 2010; Weitz-Shapiro 2008, 2014; Szwarcberg 2012b, 2015; Scherlis 2013; Oliveros 2016; and for Mexico: Fox 1994; Shedler and Manríquez 2004; Magaloni *et al.* 2007; Hilgers 2008; Lawson and Greene 2014; Díaz-Cayeros *et al.* 2016). Consequently, their conclusions are biased in favor of the prevailing approaches. Thus, studying a deviant case such as Peru may be helpful in refining the theory.

Peru is a country in which politicians actively invest in electoral clientelism during campaigns. As in other Latin American countries, relational clientelism was important in Peru in the past (Cotler 1967, 1969; Coronel *et al.* 1998). Long-lasting clientelistic relations, however, eroded progressively from the 1950s onward. Moreover, amidst profound economic and political crises, the Peruvian party system collapsed in the early 1990s, and subsequent party-building efforts have been unsuccessful. Indeed, Peru's political system in the 2000s was characterized as a case of "democracy without parties" (Levitsky and Cameron 2003; Tanaka 2005a), and the under-institutionalization of its party system, has even inspired the new concept of "party non-systems" (Sánchez 2009). Moreover, no state-apparatus-based machine currently substitutes for the absence of decentralized party organizations, as was the case during the 1990s under President Fujimori. The Peruvian case, therefore, offers a unique opportunity to examine electoral clientelism in the absence of organized political parties.

This study utilizes a mixed-methods research strategy to capture the dynamics of clientelism during Peruvian elections (2010–11). It draws on a wide variety of original data: (1) nationally representative surveys; (2) an original survey experiment; and (3) intensive qualitative field research on campaigns, including participant observation, interviews, and focus groups. First, nationally representative surveys allow me to obtain national-level estimates of the prevalence of different types of behaviors and attitudes. Meanwhile, I use the experimental data generated through a survey experiment to test one of the causal mechanisms postulated by my theory: that electors decide their votes by considering the number of people mobilized by candidates during campaigns.[12] Finally, qualitative data is crucial for understanding the political context in which electoral clientelism takes place and examining the causal mechanisms behind these transactions.

I use several survey datasets to increase the number of observations (King *et al.* 1994) and provide evidence of behaviors and attitudes that can be generalized to the national level. In particular, these quantitative data allow me to test some of the implications of the conventional approaches. If the conventional wisdom holds even under these very unfavorable contextual conditions, Peru would stand as a crucial testing ground for reassuring us of its leverage. To conduct such an analysis, I designed a set of questions for inclusion in two surveys with nationally representative and multistage random samples.[13] To reduce the possibility of any social stigma associated with clientelism distorting the answers (González-Ocantos *et al.* 2012b), I formulated questions that ask respondents about their attitudes toward electoral clientelism rather than their actual experiences.[14]

In turn, I gathered additional observations through the survey experiments conducted in 2012 and in 2017, allowing me to provide systematic evidence with which to test a crucial part of the casual claim of my informational theory. Given that these experiments were included in nationally representative surveys, they also provide the basis for external validity and the generalization of its results to the national level.

Finally, I use different types of qualitative data with theory-testing purposes, particularly for examining the causal mechanisms implied by the theories. Though Peruvian parties are weak in a comparative perspective, variation in levels of party organization does exist within the country, across both political groupings and electoral districts. Consequently, I rely on a subnational comparative method and conduct a completely

---

[12] The first experiment was included as part of the Political Representation and Social Conflict Survey, conducted by the Instituto de Opinión Pública (IOP) – Pontificia Universidad Católica del Perú (PUCP) in October 2012. For more details, see Chapter 4. A second experiment was included in a market survey conducted by Ipsos in October 2017.

[13] I work with a nationally representative survey conducted by Ipsos APOYO in 2010 for the Peruvian Electoral Tribunal (Jurado Nacional de Elecciones) and a post-electoral survey conducted by IOP in June 2011).

[14] "If a candidate or party official offered YOU or your family a benefit for YOUR vote, would you: a) Take the benefit and vote for him/her, b) Take the benefit and vote for the candidate of your choice; c) Refuse the benefit and vote for a candidate of your choice; d) Unsure." Categories (a) and (b) distinguish dispositions about committing versus refraining from a vote-buying deal. A second version of this question asks the respondents what they would do if offered cash.

different system of research design. While controlling for a common set of nationally driven political incentives, such as electoral rules, that are expected to affect clientelistic strategies and electoral behavior (Müller 2007; Hicken 2007; Gans-Morse *et al.* 2014), I select very different cases and expect campaign clientelism to operate in similar ways despite these differences. Through a process-tracing method that engages in a parallel demonstration, I analyze two municipal and two regional campaigns in two very different regions of Peru: Cusco and Piura. I compare the clientelistic strategies displayed during campaigns in these regions, which differ from one another in many respects, including their levels of party and machine organization. Despite the particularities of each race and the contextual differences that stand out among the two regions and cities, I show that the general political logic and consequences of clientelistic investments during campaigns are similar.

To collect causal process observations, I engaged in participant observation in both regions, following campaigns activities that were part of the 2010 local elections. I visited each region before the campaign started, during the campaign, and after the results were known. I also conducted 185 semi-structured interviews with politicians (candidates, activists, and political brokers), journalists, civil society actors, and academics. This number also includes additional interviews conducted in Lima and Puno regions in order to help me compare and contrast observations gathered in the two case studies and determine how generalizable my findings are to other regions.[15] Finally, based on the initial findings, in 2011, I also conducted eighteen focus groups with poor citizens from Cusco and Piura to inquire about their perceptions of the clientelistic strategies that candidates used during campaigns. I complemented this in-depth information on Cusco and Piura with data from secondary sources from newspaper archives.

This subnational focus allows me to uncover the political logic of actual clientelistic electoral strategies. On the one hand, participant observation, media sources, and semi-structured interviews help me reconstruct the political logic that politicians follow when they engage in clientelistic mobilization during campaigns. On the other hand, participant observation, interviews, and focus groups allow me to reconstruct

---

[15] The city of Lima is closest to Piura in terms of political and demographic indicators. Moreover, as the nation's capital and home to a third of its electorate, Lima is the center of power in Peru. Interviewing Lima's political and social actors is, therefore, necessary to understand Peruvian politics. Puno, on the other hand, has a similar sociopolitical trajectory to Cusco and is currently the most fragmented and fluid electoral district in Peru (Muñoz and García 2011; Zavaleta 2014).

the perceptions and political calculations of poor citizens – the most likely clients – during campaigns.

A final note about the value of this research design, and its implications for studying clientelism, is in order. As I will show in the empirical Chapters, the use of various qualitative data-gathering techniques was crucial for studying a phenomenon as elusive as electoral clientelism. The political logic behind these types of clientelistic exchanges can only be fully grasped with in-depth knowledge of the political context. Moreover, a proper understanding of the phenomenon requires that attention be paid to the points of view of both sides of the exchange: patrons and clients. Thus, this book reaffirms what other authors have pointed out: understanding the complexities involved in clientelistic transactions would be difficult, if not impossible, through reliance on survey or experimental data alone.

BOOK STRUCTURE

This book is organized as follows. In Chapter 2, I provide a more comprehensive discussion about the limitations of existing theories of electoral clientelism. After defining the concepts to be used, I show how existing approaches assume that electoral clientelism requires an extensive local organization or long-lasting relations between patrons and clients. While recent theoretical refinements that have tried to address some of the shortcomings of prevailing thought, they fall short of fully theorizing the puzzle of clientelism without machines. Then, I present the main thrust of my informational theory and discuss in depth its two causal mechanisms: signaling electoral viability and persuading participants at campaign events about a candidate's electoral desirability. I conclude the chapter by articulating my expectations and summarizing the main points.

In Chapter 3, I give an introduction to Peru's non-party democracy and test the empirical implications of conventional approaches in the context of this loosely organized polity. I begin with a brief overview of the ways in which clientelistic linkages have been organized in Peru since 1980. Subsequently, I show that currently most clientelistic networks are not all that extensive in terms of organizational reach. I also discuss the types of distributive strategies that politicians use once they access subnational office. Then, I use survey data to evaluate conventional approaches at the individual level, particularly the monitoring hypothesis. I complement these findings with qualitative data and conclude that vote buying and turnout buying at the polls are not viable electoral strategies in Peru.

In Chapter 4, I test the first causal mechanism of my informational theory. I demonstrate how the distribution of particularistic goods during campaigns allows Peruvian politicians to buy the electoral participation of indifferent voters, access crucial campaign fields, and boost turnout at campaign events. In uncertain and volatile electoral settings, high turnout at rallies affects the dynamics of the race by establishing name recognition, maintaining electoral reputation, narrowing the field of viable contenders, and attracting strategic voters in the final rush. Media horserace coverage, in turn, amplifies the effects of high turnout at campaign events. In this chapter, I also present qualitative data and survey results to support these findings. One survey experiment also confirms that Peruvians do consider turnout figures at campaign events when deciding on their vote choices. The other one, confirms that providing information about a candidate who distributes gifts while campaigning does not affect voters' perceptions of electoral viability, and *negatively* influences the likelihood of voters voting for such a candidate, even among low-income groups. In summary, this chapter shows that distributing goods during campaigns is a solution for campaigning without parties.

In Chapter 5, I set out qualitative and quantitative evidence to support the second causal mechanism of my informational theory: persuading clients at campaign events through non-clientelistic means. In a context of low party identification, candidates need to do more than simply demonstrating their electoral strength if they are to keep voters' attention and gain their support. Personalized communication at campaign events provides candidates with the best opportunity to convince voters of their electoral desirability. Through campaign clientelism, candidates can target promises to particular constituencies and convey crucial information about their personal traits and mannerisms. In addition, peer effects during these rallies can further help clients rank viable candidates and make their electoral choices. As I will show, personalized communication at campaign events is particularly important to clients.

In Chapter 6, in turn, I provide empirical evidence to illustrate the ways in which the informational theory helps us understand the changing dynamics of specific races within uncertain political contexts. I analyze two municipal and two regional campaigns in two very different regions within Peru: Cusco and Piura. Despite the particularities of each race and the notable contextual differences, the political logic of clientelistic investments in both cases is similar. Both in Cusco and Piura, candidates compete *through* campaign clientelism. The races analyzed show how viability and desirability combine to explain voting patterns and make sense of electoral trajectories within uncertain electoral contexts. Both electoral viability and desirability are necessary for a successful electoral strategy. The two cases also shed some light on issues around the implications and scope conditions of my theory, which are discussed in the concluding section.

Finally, in Chapter 7, I conclude the book by beginning with presenting a summary of my findings. Then, I present preliminary evidence suggesting that my informational theory can help explain the logic of handout distribution during campaigns in other Latin American countries with weakened political parties. Subsequently, I identify and test some empirical implications of my informational theory for organized political contexts, using Argentina as a case. Finally, I discuss the scope of my information theory and elaborate on its broader theoretical implications.

2

An Informational Theory of Electoral Clientelism

There has been renewed interest among political scientists in studying political clientelism and other types of distributive political exchanges. Scholars have written and debated about conceptual issues (Stokes 2007a; Stokes *et al.* 2013; Kitschelt and Wilkinson 2007; Schaffer and Schedler 2007; Nichter 2014; Hicken 2011; Hilgers 2011; González-Ocantos and Muñoz 2018), the conditions that shape the likelihood of different types of non-programmatic distributive exchanges (Shefter 1994; Kitschelt 2000; Piattoni 2001; Brusco *et al.* 2004; Chandra 2004; Chhibber and Nooruddin 2004; Kitschelt and Wilkinson 2007; Schaffer 2007a; Díaz-Cayeros *et al.* 2007; Szwarcberg 2015; Weitz-Shapiro 2012, 2014; Holland and Palmer-Rubin 2015), the foundations and logic of clientelistic relations (Auyero 2001; Brusco *et al.* 2004; Stokes 2005, 2007; Nichter 2010; Dunning and Stokes 2008; Finan and Schechter 2012; Gans-Morse *et al.* 2014; Díaz-Cayeros *et al.* 2016; Lawson and Greene 2014; Zarazaga 2011; Stokes *et al.* 2013), and their consequences for democracy and its institutions (Kitschelt 2000; Kitschelt and Wilkinson 2007; Stokes 2005, 2007b; Desposato 2007).

While clientelism has been intensively studied in comparative politics from very different theoretical perspectives and angles, the literature has not thus far been able to explain why campaign-based electoral clientelism can even be seen in settings without well-organized political machines. In this chapter I show that current theories have exaggerated the importance of organized networks and long-term relations in sustaining electoral clientelism. Approaches focused on monitoring or reciprocity, as well as those emphasizing the conditional loyalty of clients, conceive electoral clientelism as an iterated relation backed up by political organization. In other words, all these approaches focus on the long term. For the academics advancing these approaches, it is difficult to imagine electoral clientelism within a fluid, unorganized political setting where both patrons and clients are extremely opportunistic and focused on the short term. Nevertheless, empirical data show that the distribution of gifts during campaigns also proliferates in loosely organized political contexts.

In contrast to existing approaches, I develop a theory that places electoral campaigns, competition, and the dynamics of the race at the center of analysis. Moving beyond other theoretical attempts to address the shortcomings of the literature, I provide a full-fledged informational theory that emphasizes the *indirect* effects that turnout buying at campaign events – an often ignored subtype of electoral clientelism – has on electoral choices. Politicians buy turnout at campaign events to attract the attention of donors and voters to their candidacies and convince campaign clients to support them through other types of appeals. Thus, my theory can explain how short-term-oriented actors engage in electoral clientelism despite not having stable political organizations and attachments. Taking into account the informational role of campaign clientelism solves the puzzle of electoral clientelism in the absence of machines, and the study of clientelism as a phenomenon becomes all the richer for it.

This chapter is organized as follows: first, I engage in the debate on what electoral clientelism is and define what I mean by campaign clientelism. Second, I review established theoretical perspectives about electoral clientelism and show how all of them assume that electoral clientelism requires dense organizational networks or long-term commitments to work, and, hence, that these perspectives cannot explain clientelism in the absence of machines. Third, I present new approaches to electoral clientelism in which I seek to address some of the shortcomings of prevailing theories while also pointing to some indirect effects of clientelism. I also briefly discuss how these new approaches fall short of explaining the dynamics of campaign clientelism under a weakly organized party system. Fourth, I develop the main argument and causal mechanisms of my informational theory. Finally, I conclude the chapter by comparing the empirical implications of conventional analyses with those of my informational theory. I will test these implications empirically in later chapters.

CONCEPTUALIZATION

Political clientelism was originally conceived as a particular type of dyadic asymmetrical relationship which involved the direct reciprocal exchange of (noncomparable but valued) goods and services between actors of unequal status or power (Powell, 1970; Scott, 1972; Kaufman, 1974; Graziano, 1976; Landé, 1977).[1] With the expansion of competitive elections around the world, more contemporaneous definitions maintain the central thrust of this original definition but stress the electoral and strategic character of the political transaction (Stokes 2005; Kitschelt and Wilkinson 2007; Piattoni 2001; Schaffer 2007; Hicken 2011; Stokes *et al.* 2013). Hence, these definitions specify that electoral support is the currency that clients use to pay back different types of favors and benefits offered by politicians.

To avoid conceptual stretching and facilitate the delimitation of clear boundaries between neighboring concepts, the mainstream literature on comparative politics has identified *contingency* as the core or defining property of the concept of clientelism (Stokes 2005; Kitschelt and Wilkinson 2007; Stokes *et al.* 2013; Hicken 2011). This means that clientelism involves the discretionary allocation of goods or services to individuals whereby the receipt of benefits is contingent on the individual's political support – that is, the client is expected to return the favor with their vote or other forms of political support. Consequently, benefits are not distributed according to universal criteria and are thus potentially excludable.

Having identified this core dimension, the literature suggests – appropriately – that political clientelism should be differentiated from other distributive strategies in which politicians use material resources to garner political support but which do not entail the same degree of contingency (Stokes *et al.* 2013). For instance, "pork barrel politics" is not as discretionary as electoral clientelism. In this type of strategy, politicians deliver "local public goods" – that is, goods that have some degree of jointness of supply, but which are limited or targeted to a small residentially or geographically defined community (Magaloni 2006; Hawkins and Rosas 2006; Díaz-Cayeros *et al.* 2016). In contrast to private goods, local public goods generate non-excludable and often irreversible benefits (Díaz-Cayeros *et al.* 2016). In other words, citizens outside the group boundaries can be excluded from the enjoyment of such benefits, but none inside the boundaries can be (Kitschelt and Wilkinson 2007: 11).[2] Consequently, politicians hope for unilateral gratitude, not reciprocal exchange, and expect that at least a certain number of grateful clients will vote for them.

---

[1] This section partly relies on ideas contributed by the author in González-Ocantos and Muñoz (2018).
[2] Kitschelt and Wilkinson use the term "club goods."

This reconceptualization strategy has been a useful contribution to the empirical literature, but it has not come without its problems. First, the strategy has led scholars to confuse (and equate) conceptualization with explanation. The contingency requirement has become progressively equated to one particular rational-choice approach to explaining the microfoundations of the clientelistic exchange: the monitoring thesis. Consider, for instance, the definition of clientelism by Stokes *et al.* (2013):

> In other settings, the party offers material benefits only on the condition that the recipient returns the favor with a vote or other forms of political support. The voter suffers a punishment (or reasonably fears that he or she will suffer one) should he or she defect from the implicit bargain of a benefit for a vote; not (just) good will, but fear of punishment, turns distributive largess into votes. We call nonprogrammatic distribution combined with conditionality clientelism. (Stokes *et al.* 2013: 13)

Note that the first line, which lays down the core dimension of the definition, is followed by a specification of the causal mechanism that explains how and why clients commit to the clientelistic deal, which becomes part of the definition. Hence, the mainstream literature on clientelism excludes, by definition, the possibility of alternative causal explanations about how clientelism works, even though in-depth qualitative research has questioned the assumptions made for model cases of the monitoring theory, such as in Argentina (Auyero 2001; Zarazaga 2014; Vommaro and Quirós 2011).[3]

Defining clientelism as a contingent political exchange should not necessarily lead scholars to conclude that clients comply with the clientelistic bargain out of fear of punishment. In fact, the contingency principle was already implicit in original definitions which used the term "reciprocal" to characterize this asymmetric, but mutually beneficial, political exchange. By reciprocal, the authors meant that in order for the clientelistic bond to exist as a relationship, *both* actors engaged would have to give something in exchange for what they received.[4]

Furthermore, if applied rigidly, this concept could hinder the analysis as is to be expected when scholars provide very stylized but unrealistic case descriptions of clientelism that exclude more extensive and empirically

---

[3] Even Szwarcberg (2015), while adopting a monitoring framework to analyze the Argentine case, recognizes and documents that local brokers do not exclusively use monitoring and threats of punishing as the only mechanism to buy political allegiance.

[4] Theoretically, most of these first-generation scholars preferred to focus on trust bonds and the norm of reciprocity as causal mechanisms to explain the maintenance of clientelistic ties between unequal actors.

relevant instances of the phenomenon under study (Luna 2014: 24). And, as a side effect, this literature effectively biases us to study only those empirical referents that match their stylized theoretical referents. If monitoring and punishing clients require an organized local machine to be in place, a significant number of empirical cases will go unstudied in which politicians are willing to dispense clientelistic side payments despite not having such an organizational structure to effectively monitor clients, as is the case in Latin American countries such as Peru.

When applying this conceptual demarcation rigidly, scholars should invest a great deal of effort in proving that a given case empirically fulfills the necessary condition to be classified as clientelistic (Luna 2014: 24). In other words, they ought to offer extensive empirical evidence to show that in all cases under study an enforced contingent exchange is in place between candidates, their brokers, and their voters. However, because providing this evidence would be extremely demanding, many researchers in practice do not do so and simply "invoke" the presence of a party machine to show that the contingency of the exchange condition is met. This can often be seen, for instance, when scholars analyze survey results and take as a given that all accepted offers of gifts for political support are in fact "complete" – that is, contingent – clientelistic bargains. Thus, conceptual rigidity largely exists only on paper, but still predisposes us to focus our attention on those cases that can be expected to fit with the stylized depiction of a dense political machine, even though these cases might not be entirely representative of how politics is conducted in the region.

Beyond this widespread consensus on focusing on contingency as the core dimension, clientelism remains a contested concept. A number of issues, such as the appropriate level of analysis, the timing and duration of the relationship, and the definition of higher-level clientelism, are still subject to debate (Gonzalez Ocantos and Muñoz 2017). Of these issues, one is of particular importance to this book: the duration of the clientelistic exchange. When defining clientelism, academics from the older generation conceived of the duration of the clientelistic relation as a *variable* dimension (and not a defining property of the concept) to be documented empirically and explained (Landé 1977; Lemarch and Legg 1972; Powell 1970; Scott 1972). More recently, however, some scholars have identified iteration – the existence of a long-term clientestic link – as another core attribute of the concept of clientelism (Auyero 2001; Hicken 2011; Hilgers 2011; Schaffer 2007), or else implicitly assume that iteration is a necessary condition for the exchange to take place (Kitschelt and Wilkinson 2007; Stokes 2005; Stokes *et al.* 2013). Although there is not the same consensus around the importance of duration as a defining property of clientelism as there is for contingency, this approach likewise potentially hinders the analysis of real-world problems. Again, exchanges of gifts/favors for political support in contexts where particularistic distribution is more sporadic, and politicians lack first-hand knowledge of their clients, would fall outside the scope of the concept (Gonzalez-Ocantos and Muñoz 2017). Indeed, scholars adopting this definition would not classify instances in which candidates buy participation at campaign events as clientelism when these are short-term exchanges that do not last over time or become a permanent relationship. This exclusion would encompass an increasing number of developing countries with weak party systems and less-rooted machines where engagement in short-term particularistic exchanges is prevalent during campaigns.

In the light of these discussions and limitations, I adopt a definition that specifies clientelism as a contingent, asymmetrical political exchange, but I do not equate the contingency dimension to the existence of monitoring. I broadly define electoral clientelism as a strategy of electoral mobilization in which a politician offers private benefits (e.g., money, goods, or services) to individuals during electoral campaigns in return for electoral support, broadly construed (their vote, public display of political support, participation at political rallies, work as party representatives at elections, etc.). In turn, I classify "campaign clientelism" (or turnout buying at campaign rallies) as a subtype of electoral clientelism in which politicians buy the *participation* of poor voters at rallies and other campaign events by distributing private goods. I distinguish this subtype of electoral clientelism from others considered in the literature, such as "vote buying" (strategies in which politicians offer selective benefits in exchange for votes), "turnout buying" (strategies in which politicians offer selective benefits to immobilized supporters in exchange for turnout *at the polls*) (Heckelman 1998; Nichter 2008, 2014; Gans-Morse *et al.* 2014), and abstention buying (strategies in which politicians offer selective benefits to indifferent or opposition voters in exchange for not voting) (Cox and Kousser 1981; Cornelius 2004; Gans-Morse *et al.* 2014).[5]

This concept of campaign clientelism meets the contingency requirement. The particular form of electoral support demanded by campaign

---

[5] I do not define "turnout buying" as a strategy designed to mobilize only loyal as opposed to indifferent voters (Nichter 2008, 2014; Gans-Morse *et al.* 2014). Whether politicians buy loyal or indifferent voters may vary empirically and should not be defined a priori. For example, in contexts where political loyalties are in flux and most voters are indifferent, such as in Peru, these distinctions do not make much sense.

clients is turnout at rallies and other campaign events, not a vote for the party in exchange for side-payments – it is not a vote-buying deal. Since benefits are usually distributed *in situ* while campaign activities are taking place, clients receive the goods offered by politicians only on the condition that they attend the event. Thus, monitoring is not really an issue, since it is not strictly required as a clientelistic tactic.[6] This, however, is not to say that politicians will not identify and monitor attendees if they have the organizational resources to do so and they see it as conducive to maximizing their political gains. But monitoring attendance is not a necessary prerequisite for this subtype of clientelistic exchange to take place. Thus, campaign clientelism requires neither a consolidated on-the-ground political organization nor the monitoring of voter behavior.

On the question of the duration of the relationship, the subtype of electoral clientelism that I call campaign clientelism is characterized by short-term exchange. Following other authors (Nichter 2014; Kitschelt 2011), I distinguish electoral clientelism from "relational clientelism," a more durable type of political clientelism where there is a prolonged relational exchange that goes beyond an election season. These ongoing relations usually involve problem-solving networks (Auyero 2001) or the procurement of more "expensive" and long-lasting benefits such as public jobs (Oliveros 2013, 2016). Relational clientelism can be seen as a feature of machine politics as conventionally understood, whereas electoral clientelism can flourish in the absence of firm organizations.[7] Although electoral clientelism is occasionally combined with forms of relational clientelism that entail more frequent interactions beyond a single campaign season, it is important to make an analytical distinction between them (Nichter 2014: 325).

The case for studying campaign clientelism as a subtype of electoral clientelism is based on empirical grounds, both to reflect its importance

---

[6] As we will see in Chapter 3, there are certainly other instances in Peru in which politicians distribute side-payments after campaign events, monitor the attendance of clients, and threaten to withhold benefits to which clients are entitled if they do not show up at campaign events, as is reported, for example, by some women on the *Vaso de Leche* nutritional assistance program. However, these strategies are open only to local incumbents and are by no means the only forms of campaign clientelism exchanges that occur during election periods.

[7] Machines are "political territorial organizations that provide voters with solutions to everyday problems in exchange for political support" (Szwarcberg 2009: 6). Similarly, for Wolfinger (1972) "'machine politics' is the manipulation of certain incentives to partisan political participation: favoritism based on political criteria in personnel decisions, contracting, and administration of the laws. A 'political machine' is an organization that practices machine politics."

in weakly organized party systems and address its neglect in the literature as a departure from the theoretical orthodoxy. Indeed, campaign clientelism is a practice employed even in more organized political settings (Auyero 2001; Szwarcberg 2012b, 2015; Banégas 2011: 40; Vommaro and Quirós 2011: 74). As I will explain later on in this chapter, politicians *need* a large turnout at campaign events in order to inform as many voters and donors as possible about their electoral potential. As we will see, the ability to point to well-attended campaign events is the key to influencing vote choices and campaign contributions. Politicians need their campaign events to be seen as a "success," with large and vocally supportive attendances, and it is precisely this kind of success that politicians pursue. Thus, politicians engage in campaign clientelistic tactics even when they do not have a consolidated on-the-ground political organization, or when they cannot be sure they will be able to lock these clients into long-term clientelistic relationships. In order to understand the logic of electoral clientelism, then, attention must be paid to the all of the strategies used to mobilize voters over the course of the electoral campaign, and not just to vote or turnout buying at the polls. Before doing so, I will review the existing theoretical perspectives about electoral clientelism and show how all of them assume that electoral clientelism requires dense organizational networks or long-term commitments to work.

ELECTORAL CLIENTELISM REVISITED

Why do politicians invest in clientelism during electoral campaigns? In particular, why would they do so when they lack the appropriate organizational apparatus to guarantee that these efforts pay off? While political clientelism has been studied intensively in comparative politics from very different theoretical perspectives, the established literature has not been able to answer these questions.

Many influential studies on political clientelism have sought to explain the persistence of clientelistic linkages over long periods of time – that is, of relational clientelism. These include scholars adhering to socioeconomic modernization theory (Powell 1970; Scott 1969, 1972; Lemarchand and Legg 1972; Graziano 1973), historical institutionalism (Shefter 1994; Piattoni 2001), as well as political economy approaches (Chubb 1981; Kitschelt 2000, 2007; Lyne 2007; Weitz-Shapiro 2014). These different approaches have, without doubt, contributed significantly to our understanding of the conditions that affect the maintenance and demise of party-citizen clientelistic linkages. Nevertheless, because they are concerned with explaining long-term processes of change, these studies do not pay attention to *how* clientelism works during electoral campaigns. Moreover, these scholars are interested in clientelistic linkages that go beyond one election season, and so they do not address the question of how, and why, politicians invest in electoral clientelism in contexts where there are no long-lasting clientelistic relations and organizations in place.

In turn, many contemporary researchers focus primarily on the mechanisms that sustain clientelism, paying more attention to its electoral rationale (Auyero 2001; Brusco *et al.* 2004; Stokes 2005; Kitschelt and Wilkinson 2007; Schaffer 2007; Díaz-Cayeros *et al.* 2016; Finan and Schechter 2012; Lawson and Greene 2014; among others). These academics are particularly interested in analyzing the micro-foundations of clientelistic exchanges and in making predictions about the type of citizens whom clientelistic parties should target with material inducements (Brusco *et al.* 2004; Stokes 2005; Díaz-Cayeros *et al.* 2016; Cox 2007; Dunning and Stokes 2007; Nichter 2008, 2010; Gans-Morse *et al.* 2014; Finan and Schechter 2012; Lawson and Greene 2014; Zarazaga 2011, 2016; Stokes *et al.* 2013).[8]

Although these scholars disagree on the specific mechanisms that sustain the clientelistic exchange and their models make differing predictions about the type of voters that clientelistic parties target, they all assume either that electoral clientelism requires an extensive local organization – the machine – to work or that it entails an enduring relationship.[9] In other words, they contend that electoral clientelism can only work in a long-term perspective and, conversely, that electoral clientelism cannot be sustainable in an organizationally fluid political context in which actors are extremely opportunistic and focused on the short term.

Based on the causal mechanism that the authors propose as an explanation for clients' commitment to the clientelistic bargain, existing theories

---

[8] These scholars developed their models by extending and/or criticizing the insights developed by formal theorists interested in distributive politics, such as Cox and McCubbins (1986), Lindbeck and Weibull (1987), and Dixit and Londregan (1996).

[9] In this literature, a hierarchical political machine is the organizational foundation of electoral clientelism. Machines are headed by political bosses who command brokers on different levels (locally embedded agents) in a pyramidal fashion. In turn, brokers are local patrons: voters organized by the brokers representing each machine receive benefits from them on a regular basis. The literature commonly portrays these machines as partisan (e.g., Stokes 2005). However, machines can also be candidate-based, as is the case in Japan where most national-level Liberal Democratic Party politicians maintain personal support organizations (Scheiner 2007: 279). It should be noted that even in this case, the literature centers on the iterated interactions that constitute the machines (Auyero 2001; Stokes 2005: 318; Kitschelt and Kselman 2011: 4, 6; Hicken 2011: 292–3).

of electoral clientelism can be grouped into three broad categories. A first group of scholars proposes that clientelistic transactions are enforced *externally* by local brokers who monitor clients' behavior and threaten punishment for noncompliance. The second and third groups of academics both stress the *self-enforced* character of clientelistic relations. The second group is composed of rationalist scholars focused on the long term. They argue that patrons and clients' long-term interests are aligned and that, consequently, clients are loyal supporters. The third group proposes the norm of reciprocity as the causal mechanism that sustains electoral clientelism. Scholars working within the reciprocity framework contend that clients honor their part of the bargain because they feel obligated to repay favors or benefits they have already received. While rationalists who focus on the long term emphasize clients' future expectations, scholars working within the reciprocity approach focus mostly on clients' retrospective evaluations. In the rest of this section I will discuss each of these approaches, and their limited usefulness for understanding short-term clientelistic transactions in loosely organized and fluid political contexts.

First, two versions of the monitoring hypothesis can be discerned. A "hard" version is represented by scholars who argue that politicians enforce the clientelistic exchange by monitoring actual vote choices (Brusco *et al.* 2004; Chandra 2004, 2007; Stokes 2005, 2007; Kitschelt and Wilkinson 2007). From this perspective, clientelistic machines keep voters from reneging on the clientelistic bargain by threatening them and monitoring their votes, rewarding their support, and punishing defection (Stokes 2005: 317–18). To monitor individual voters, parties can use a variety of practices and techniques to violate the secrecy of the ballot on election day, or to at least give the impression to voters that they can do so (Stokes 2005; Kitschelt and Wilkinson 2007; Chandra 2007: 90). Analysts also argue that machines can penetrate voters' social networks to infer how voters voted with a high level of certainty (Stokes 2005, 2007a; Kitschelt and Wilkinson 2007). From this perspective, voters comply only if vote buying is externally enforced by a network of political operatives that monitors voters' actions and makes credible threats of sanctions against those who do not fall into line. Thus, these scholars assume that clientelism *requires* dense organizational networks to work (Brusco *et al.* 2004; Stokes 2005; Kitschelt and Wilkinson 2007).

The workability of effectively monitoring individual voting behavior when the ballot is secret, however, has been called into question (Krishna 2007; Nichter 2008; Zarazaga 2011, 2014, 2016). Consequently, contemporary scholars have backed away from this stringent assumption in favor of "softer" hypotheses of how patrons keep track of clients. Some, for instance, have pointed out that monitoring groups of voters by analyzing disaggregated voting results and opinion polls is more efficient and less costly than monitoring and rewarding individual voters (Chandra 2004, 2007; Kitschelt and Wilkinson 2007; Scheiner 2007). Similarly, Kitschelt and his collaborators on the Political Accountability in Democratic Party Competition and Economic Governance project focus on how different types of local organizations and monitoring methods influence the *effectiveness* of electoral clientelism (Kitschelt and Kselman 2011; Kitschelt and Rozenas 2011, Kitschelt and Altamarino 2015). So, although these academics no longer see organizations as necessary for clientelistic exchanges, in their framework, electoral clientelism is still externally enforced by local brokers who guarantee the electoral effectiveness of clientelistic investments.

Other scholars working from this "softer" viewpoint argue instead that monitoring turnout at the polls – that is, monitoring *whether* individuals who had received clientelistic benefits showed up to vote – is more feasible and thus should be considered as a more rational clientelistic strategy in the context of secret ballots (Heckelman 1998; Nichter 2008, 2010; Schaffer and Schedler 2007: 25).[10] Building on this observation, some scholars working from this approach have developed formal models in which a machine chooses to distribute rewards to voters who differ based on two dimensions: their propensity to vote or abstain, and their electoral preferences (Dunning and Stokes 2007; Gans-Morse *et al.* 2014; Nichter 2010; Stokes *et al.* 2013).[11] But while these new models incorporate important caveats, all of them still rely on some sort of monitoring assumption – i.e., that the political behavior of interest is either observable or at least partially observable. In other words, they still assume that politicians need a dense network of local operatives for electoral clientelism to work.

---

[10] Nichter (2008) develops a formal model of turnout buying.

[11] Dunning and Stokes' (2008) model predicts two strategies: "persuasion" (buying the votes of swing and opposition voters) and "mobilization" (buying turnout among loyalists). Gans-Morse *et al.* (2014) and Nichter (2010) contend that political machines frequently combine several of the following plausible strategies: "vote buying" (rewarding opposing or indifferent voters for switching their vote choices), "turnout buying" (rewarding immobilized supporters for showing up at the polls), "double persuasion" (rewarding indifferent or opposing nonvoters), "negative turnout buying" (rewarding indifferent or opposing individuals for not voting), and "rewarding loyalists" (rewarding supporters who would vote for them anyway). Stokes *et al.* (2013) extend previous work to provide a model of broker-mediated distribution.

In summary, scholars who propose softer versions of the monitoring thesis still assume that politicians *require* a grassroots organizational infrastructure to sustain electoral clientelism and to make sure it is electorally efficient. In these approaches, clientelism without organization remains a paradox.

Another group of academics develop a long-term rationalist explanation that resembles Hirschman's (1970) theory of loyalty. The key factor emphasized by these scholars is that machine clients are loyal voters who have no incentives to defect as long as they continue receiving benefits: voting for the machine's candidate is in their own best interest (Magaloni *et al.* 2007; Díaz-Cayeros *et al.* 2016; Calvo and Murillo 2008; Zarazaga 2011, 2012a, 2015).[12] However, for this perspective, clients' loyalty is *conditional* on future expectations. Patrons "risk eroding or even losing the loyalty of their core supporters when they attempt to build broader coalitions by delivering transfers to other social groups" (Díaz-Cayeros *et al.* 2007:11). Consequently, it is rational for them to continue targeting these loyal voters. In this approach, networks of local brokers function primarily as selection mechanisms, to accurately identify voters' preferences, and the lowest level of benefits needed to secure their votes, with precision (Díaz-Cayeros *et al.* 2007: 112–13; Calvo and Murillo 2008: 8; Zarazaga 2011: 3, 2016). So, although these rationalist scholars eschew the monitoring thesis, they still assume that electoral clientelism requires dense organizational networks to function.

Finally, another group of scholars resurrect insights from older generations (Gouldner 1960; Powell 1970; Lemarchand and Legg 1972; Scott 1969, 1972; Graziano 1973) to posit that voters comply with vote-buying exchanges due to feelings of personal obligation and gratitude engendered by the receipt of material benefits or services. Clients, unable to reciprocate in kind, vote for their political patrons. Thus, this internalized norm of reciprocity assures clients' compliance (Wang and Kurzman 2007; Schaffer 2007; Finan and Schechter 2012; Lawson and Greene 2014). For some academics working within this approach, networks of local brokers provide parties with perfect information about voters' preferences and levels of reciprocity (Finan and Schechter 2012: 867).[13] Alternatively, other scholars who are close to the reciprocity framework

---

[12] This approach is analogous to studies that stress that the incumbent's electoral success relies on public employees' self-interest (Robinson and Verdier 2003; Calvo and Murillo 2004; Oliveros 2016).

[13] Lawson and Greene do not make such a bold claim. Although they cite the importance of local networks in clientelistic relations, they do not explicitly argue that networks

place more emphasis on the long-lasting character of the clientelistic relation as a problem-solving network for the poor (Eisenstadt and Roniger
1984; Auyero 2001; Vommaro and Quirós 2011). In summary, this group
of scholars also sees electoral clientelism developing in the long term,
as a "network of reciprocities" (Lemarchand and Legg 1972: 153). And
for these scholars too, clientelism without organization or reciprocal
exchanges that take place over time would also be a surprise.

In conclusion, conventional approaches, in all their forms, cannot
account for the puzzle of widespread distribution of benefits during campaigns in politically unorganized, inchoate settings. Scholars have theo-
rized electoral clientelism based on the experience of cases with strong
local partisan organization, such as Mexico and Argentina.[14] In contexts
with solid political organization one can find relational as well as electoral
clientelism. As a result, the conclusions of these scholars are biased in
favor of conventional approaches that associate distribution with organizational density. Nevertheless, in practice, electoral clientelism proliferates
in many developing democracies besides Peru that lack the support of
organized political machines (Van de Walle 2007; Krishna 2007; Kramon
2016, 2017). As I will go on to show, my informational theory can solve
this apparent paradox and explain how and why clientelistic transactions
work in "machine-free" contexts populated by short-term-oriented actors.

NEW APPROACHES TO ELECTORAL CLIENTELISM

In the past few years scholars have begun exploring new avenues of
research to deal with the shortcomings of the conventional approaches.
For instance, Szwarcberg (2012a) focuses on the informational value of
turnout buying at rallies. Expanding her original research (Szwarcberg
2011, 2012b, 2015), Szwarcberg argues that rallies are still important in
the mass- and social-media era because they provide information to different members within and outside the party machine. First, rallies offer
party bosses information with which to monitor brokers' capacity to
mobilize voters. Second, they give party brokers the opportunity to show
their patrons that they can mobilize voters, with a view to promotion

---

are necessary for vote buying to take place. However, they do not specify an alternative
mechanism by which politicians can get information on individual levels of reciprocity.

[14] For example, Magaloni *et al.* (2007), Díaz-Cayeros *et al.* (2007), and Lawson and Greene
(2014) research on Mexico. In turn, Brusco *et al.* (2004), Stokes (2005), Weitz-Shapiro
(2014), Nichter (2008, 2010), and Szwarcberg (2015) study clientelism in Argentina.

within the party. Third, by turning out at rallies, machine clients can show their willingness to fulfill their part of the clientelistic agreement. Finally, building upon research on dominant parties and competitive authoritarianism, Szwarcberg contends that turnout at rallies provides the opposition with information about the electoral strength or weakness of the incumbent's power based on the public display of its voter-mobilization capacity. In this way, rallies contribute to strategic coordination.

Szwarcberg's latest study significantly advances our understanding about the informational value of rallies for political competition. As I will discuss in the Electoral Viability section, my theory builds on her contribution by looking at the importance of informational effects of turnout buying at rallies. But despite these breakthroughs, her theoretical model still only considers the informational value of clientelistic mobilization in contexts with organized partisan machines. Thus, she does not fully theorize the indirect effects of campaign turnout buying. My theory, on the other hand, illuminates these indirect effects in unorganized settings, while in the conclusion I briefly discuss the effects in organized settings.

In turn, Holland and Palmer-Rubin's study (Holland and Palmer-Rubin 2015) makes a crucial contribution to the study of distributive politics by theorizing the role of collective social actors and organizational brokers in clientelistic exchanges. They develop a typology of brokers and a framework for incorporating interest associations into the study of clientelism. In their view, brokers balance three possible sets of interests, generating different types of principal–agent problems – partisan interest (P), rent-seeking interest (R), and social interest (S) – which diverges from partisan or personal goals (Holland and Palmer-Rubin 2015: 10–11). Brokers, in turn, can be classified into four types depending on how much weight they place on these interests and their relationships with parties and interested organizations. They may be, on the one hand, embedded or not embedded in a social organization, and on the other hand, they may mobilize voters for a single party or for multiple parties. Based on this typology, the authors synthesize different *modes* of clientelist exchange documented in different case studies across Latin American countries.

In addition, their typology of brokers includes the subtype of "independent" brokers, who lack organizational ties with interest associations and, given their weak party commitments, mobilize voters for several parties at the same time. In other words, these independent brokers mostly follow their personal/rent-seeking interests while mediating clientelistic exchanges. This subtype flourishes in contexts with deinstitutionalized party systems and weak social organizations, such as in Peru.

In this study, Holland and Palmer-Rubin make a new and worthwhile contribution by broadening the scope of brokerage relationships that can sustain particularistic exchanges and treating political organization (brokers' stable political affiliation) as a variable rather than a constant. However, in common with the rest of the literature, they stop short of explaining *how* clientelistic relationships play out in contexts with scarcely organized political parties or clientelistic machines, and how (or whether) such relationships have an impact on electoral results. Indeed, like Szwarcberg, the authors still assume that the main mechanism sustaining clientelistic exchanges is the presence of brokers who monitor clients' behavior (Holland and Palmer-Rubin 2015: 3, 12–13).

Finally, Kramon's novel proposal is that candidates build credibility as future patrons while distributing handouts (Kramon 2016, 2017). Kramon argues that in the institutional context of Kenya, candidates for congress distribute money and gifts as a means of conveying information to poor voters – that is, they seek to demonstrate that they care about poor people and that they have the willingness to distribute resources to them in the future. Distributing cash and material resources during a campaign thus conveys information to voters about a candidate's *credibility* in these areas. At the same time, politicians distribute money to signal that they are electorally viable and to attract strategic support from voters, who seek to side with the winner so as to gain access to resources in the future. The expectation is that politicians who distribute private goods during campaigns are evaluated more favorably by poor voters than are otherwise identical candidate profiles who do not dispense handouts. From this perspective, then, vote buying is a self-enforced exchange and not a transaction that must be monitored.

Kramon's insights and experimental evidence are certainly an important contribution to the literature on clientelism. To be sure, he pays more attention to campaigns than do other scholars and he shows that distribution itself can inform voters. In fact, his theory complements mine and supports the informational approach and its potential to explain electoral clientelism in less-organized political settings.

But despite the similarities, our theories differ with regard to the causal mechanisms that link the distribution of private goods during campaigns to the electoral support they elicit. As will become clear in the next section, my theory departs from that of Kramon in four ways. First, our approaches differ in terms of why voters care about electoral viability. Kramon stresses that siding with the winner is important because voters want to be sure they will gain access to resources in the future. In turn,

I emphasize a more general, strategic (or psychological) approach to electoral viability. Strategic actors have no interest in wasting their ballots on hopeless candidates, because they want to affect political outcomes. Second, and related to the previous point, I – unlike Kramon – focus on the informational role that electoral clientelism has, not just for strategic voters but also for attracting strategic donors who can help fund the campaign. Third, our approaches take different views on the type of information that is transmitted and its effects on the choices of strategic actors. For Kramon, the key informational component is the distribution of gifts or money *per se*. In his argument, the distribution of electoral handouts is effective in winning votes – that is, a voter who hears that a candidate is distributing money will be more likely to support him or her at the polls. In contrast, in my informational theory, I identify turnout figures as the form of information that most affects the electoral fortunes of political candidates. It is this more than distribution of handouts that helps candidates to establish electoral viability vis-à-vis their opponents. Finally, and most importantly, Kramon does not specify a mechanism for understanding how voters decide between candidates that use the same electoral strategy (investing in campaign clientelism) – a scenario that is very likely in competitive and unorganized political settings. If many candidates distribute handouts while campaigning, how do voters decide who to support? Kramon is silent on this point. The main empirical evidence he cites in support of his theory are survey experiments in which he compares an imaginary candidate who distributes money with another otherwise identical candidate who does not. In theory, one might assume that an implication of his theory would be that if more than one candidate distributes money while campaigning, voters – seeking to engage in a future clientelistic relationship with a candidate in order to access further resources – will support the one who distributes more. In contrast, in my theory I develop a second mechanism that explains how campaign clients decide who to choose between competing clientelistic candidates by establishing other types of non-clientelistic political linkages. I show how politicians use clientelistic tactics while campaigning to attract potential clients to the rally and, then, persuade indifferent clients to support them through non-clientelistic means. In other words, candidates use mixed electoral appeals while on the trail.

Thus, while more recent theoretical studies address some of the shortcomings of conventional approaches, they either still do not solve the paradox of how electoral clientelism can persist without machines or do not fully develop the theoretical implications of their approach to explain how politicians campaign and use mixed electoral strategies in the absence of organized and enduring parties. Thus, I go beyond these partial theoretical refinements to develop a full-fledged informational theory that can explain electoral clientelism in competitive, unorganized settings. In the next section I provide an in-depth discussion of my main argument, the causal mechanisms I propose, and the advantages my theory has over existing approaches.

AN INFORMATIONAL THEORY OF ELECTORAL CLIENTELISM

The theory I propose stresses the indirect effects that investments in electoral clientelism have on vote choices. Rather than assuming that the effects on electoral choices of distributing material benefits are principally direct, as prevailing approaches do, I instead stress the indirect effects occasioned by material investments during campaigns. I contend that electoral clientelism generates valuable *information* that strategic actors use to form their preferences and make electoral decisions. By informing various types of observers about candidates' relative electoral viability and desirability, electoral clientelism *indirectly* affects electoral preferences and thus the outcome of elections.

Buying participation at campaign events allows candidates to overcome two fundamental hurdles to their election. First, campaign clientelism allows candidates to draw attention to themselves in two ways: by getting people to show up at their campaign events and by demonstrating their ability to mobilize. Candidates buy turnout to assure themselves of crowded campaign rallies, thus demonstrating their electoral viability to the wider audience of strategic actors (voters and donors) who watch these events or learn about them through other means, such as by word of mouth, radio, television, and newspaper reports. Second, campaign clientelism is crucial to helping clients form their electoral preferences, persuading them about candidates' electoral "desirability." By directly communicating with clients at campaign events through non-clientelistic appeals, candidates try to turn the fleeting hold they have on voters' attention into a longer-lasting commitment that will carry them through to election day. In other words, while attending campaign events, indifferent clients access information that helps them make their electoral choices and establish other types of political linkages. Together, changes in viability and desirability throughout the campaign shape candidates' electoral fortunes.

In my informational theory I place electoral campaigns, competition, and the dynamics of the electoral race at the center of analysis. I do so, first, by highlighting the importance of electoral clientelism as a *campaigning tool* and foregrounding an often-overlooked form of electoral clientelism: campaign turnout buying. By distributing minor consumer goods and favors, politicians buy the *participation* of poor voters at rallies and other campaign events. "Campaign clientelism," which I have already identified as a subtype of electoral clientelism, does not require a consolidated on-the-ground political organization or the monitoring of voter behavior. Quite the opposite, it is easy to put into practice even in contexts of low political organization. In fact, it is all the more crucial to establishing viability in unorganized settings, and to allowing candidates to persuade clients of their desirability through non-clientelistic tactics.

In contrast, most scholars apply a very narrow definition of electoral clientelism as "vote buying," which implies the treatment of campaigns as one-shot deals (e.g., Stokes 2005; Schaffer and Schedler 2007). Most definitions of vote buying emphasize that holding these clientelistic exchanges "are not only ex ante in that benefits are distributed prior to voting, but also that exchanges occur on or soon before Election Day" (Nichter 2014: 317). Thus, scholars often interpret any data about the distribution of material benefits during campaigns as efforts at vote buying.

Moreover, even those scholars who attempt to focus on electoral participation more broadly and distinguish different subtypes of electoral clientelism do not consider clientelistic strategies used *throughout* the campaign. For instance, "turnout buying" and "abstention buying" are subtypes of electoral clientelism in which payments are made close to election day (Cox and Kousser 1981; Heckelman 1998; Nichter 2008, 2010; Gans-Morse *et al.* 2014). In summary, most scholars limit the empirical referent of their theories only to what happens near election day.[15] In so doing, they miss the broader picture and the electoral rationale of other clientelistic strategies, especially in countries without organized machines such as Peru.

Second, my informational theory sets itself apart from existing approaches in that it takes competition under conditions of uncertainty as its core. While competition and uncertainty are present in – and essential for – any democracy, they are particularly accentuated in contexts that lack organized political affiliations. When voters do not have stable party attachments, it is much more difficult for them to coordinate and vote together. To be sure, informational deficits – and, thus, uncertainty – are

---

[15] Important exceptions are Auyero (2001), Szwarcberg (2009, 2011, 2012a, 2012b, 2015), and Vommaro and Quirós (2011) who do explicitly analyze turnout buying at rallies.

particularly acute in countries with weakly institutionalized parties (Moser 2001, Moser and Scheiner 2009).[16] Moreover, without institutionalized parties or machines, the number of competitors entering the race tends to be greater. Thus, competition is very intense and unpredictable.

As I have already shown, existing approaches cannot account for short-term clientelistic transactions in fluid, unorganized political settings. Indeed, most scholars have not only left short-term strategic clientelistic interactions untheorized, they also ignore electoral competition.[17] Most studies of electoral clientelism either assume that only the incumbent's machine buys votes (Stokes 2005, 2007a; Dunning and Stokes 2007; Stokes *et al.* 2013; Nichter 2008, 2010; Gans-Morse *et al.* 2014) or concern themselves only with cases in which clientelistic machines are consolidated and inter-party competition is limited (Auyero 2001; Wang and Kurzman 2007; Szwarcberg 2015, 2012a; Vommaro and Quirós 2011). In some theories, machines may react to competition insofar as they diversify their strategies (Díaz-Cayeros *et al.* 2016). But overall, electoral clientelism is seen as a viable strategy for machine incumbents and not for competitors. To a large extent, this has to do with a prevalent assumption: that today, electoral clientelism is mostly carried out using public resources.

Effectively, the role of private financial contributions has been downplayed and understudied. My theory, however, highlights the role of private actors in funding electoral clientelism. Although public resources are frequently used to finance the distribution of handouts during campaigns, private donations finance a sizable share of this distribution in several contexts.[18] Moreover, given that campaign clientelism is very sporadic and temporary and thus not all that costly, it is a strategy in which private actors may be willing to invest resources. In contrast, long-lasting clientelistic relations involve the continued delivery of private benefits for prolonged periods, which far fewer private actors will be willing to fund.[19] Moreover, campaign clientelism is also inexpensive in comparison with

---

[16] Or in elections such as primaries, in which partisan identification is not a decisive predictor of choices.

[17] Finan and Schechter (2012) and Zarazaga (2011, 2016) are important exceptions.

[18] See, for instance, Vicente 2014.

[19] Thachil (2014) studied a non-clientelistic strategy in India through which elite parties win poor voters' electoral support by privately providing them with basic social services on a regular basis via grassroots affiliates. Barrenechea (2014) studied the exceptional case of *Alianza Para el Progreso* (APP), a party that had used private resources to build up lasting clientelistic linkages in northern Peru. On APP's party-building limitations, see Muñoz and Dargent (2016).

alternative campaign strategies, such as media advertising. Therefore, it is an option that is open to opposition candidates as well as incumbents.

So, besides the state, who pays for campaign clientelism? First, candidates themselves may foot the bill. Relatively wealthy individuals can invest their own resources or savings to finance this form of electoral mobilization. Second, businesspeople make donations to candidates who establish electoral potential and whom they deem worthy of their support. They may do so to gain interest representation or to extract rents or obtain public contracts once the election is over. Finally, in countries with low state capacity such as Peru, both legal and illegal interest groups can easily fund campaigns and, thus, the goods that are delivered in campaign rallies. Financing campaign clientelism may also be beneficial for illegal organizations. With their investments, they can buy future influence on favorable new regulations or the nonenforcement of existing arrangements (Holland 2017). Additionally, they can access public contracts in order to launder money.

My informational theory differs from existing approaches in a fourth way: it incorporates campaign dynamics (time) to a much greater extent. Campaigns are more decisive in contexts of weak partisan cues and organizations than they are in established democracies (Lawson and McCann 2005; Baker *et al.* 2006). By emphasizing competition under conditions of uncertainty, I place much more importance on the campaigns themselves. I do so by stressing that voters will be affected by information about what other voters are doing during campaigns (Popkin 1991: 11). For my theoretical approach, information cues received *during campaigns* will be crucial for electoral choices.

Finally, my theory departs from other theories of clientelism by showing how, in a country with weak parties, candidates *combine* different types of appeals to rally and persuade indifferent poor voters: they use campaign clientelism to buy audiences and then issue mostly particularistic promises and personalistic appeals to gain their electoral support. In contrast, existing approaches to clientelism implicitly follow the conventional party–voter linkage literature for the analysis of electoral strategizing and thus neglect the study of mixed or segmented campaign strategies. Except for recent contributions (Luna 2014; Boas 2016),[20]

---

[20] While Luna (2014) and Boas (2016) both make excellent contributions to the study of party-voter linkages and campaigns, they nevertheless miss some elements that are needed to explain the paradox of electoral clientelism as an electoral strategy in the absence of organized political organizations. On the one hand, Luna studies how parties or candidates deploy segmented linkage strategies in unequal democracies; that is,

scholars studying electoral mobilization tend to characterize parties and even party systems as either "programmatic," "clientelistic," or "personalistic" (Kitschelt 2000; Kitschel and Wilkinson 2007; Kitschelt *et al.* 2010). They do so because they take the trade-off assumption for granted (Luna 2016). This thesis posits that parties can only successfully pursue one type of linkage strategy at a time due to system equilibrium dynamics (Kitschelt 2000), budget constraints (Díaz-Cayeros *et al.* 2016), plausible fiscal imbalances, or moral disagreements (Weitz-Shapirto 2012). In contrast to these approaches, I argue that campaign clientelism helps politicians mix electoral strategies while electioneering.

In addition, by highlighting the importance of electoral clientelism as a campaigning tool that helps candidates display mixed electoral strategies on the trail, my theory stands as an important contribution not just to the literature on clientelism, but also for the understanding of local campaigns in developing democracies. The literature on electoral campaigns is predominantly focused on advanced democracies and the few available campaign studies on Latin America, such as Boas' innovative piece, focus on presidential campaigns (Angell *et al.* 1992; Mayobre 1996; Waisbord 1996; Silva 2001; Tironi 2002; Rottinghaus and Alberro 2005; De la Torre and Conaghan 2009; Boas 2016). Indeed, my research shows that it is, in fact, possible to observe the phenomenon of success contagion (Boas 2016) in local elections despite limited organization continuity, and that this strategy has not been legitimized by successful terms in office. Candidates adopt campaign clientelism because it has proven to be an effective campaign strategy for signaling viability, establishing direct linkages with poor voters, and persuading them through particularistic and personalistic appeals.[21] In other words, candidates engage in campaign clientelism precisely because they lack organizational structures.

---

distinct appeals (i.e. symbolic, material-public oriented, material-particularistic) that are targeted at different constituencies. However, he does not consider the possibility that politicians under certain conditions might combine appeals that are targeted at the same constituency. I argue that this is indeed the case. On the other hand, Boas both conceives of, and effectively analyzes, the use of mixed electoral strategies in presidential campaigns in new democracies. Although this contribution is particularly important to discerning important nuances in presidential campaign strategies, Boas does not consider clientelistic appeals as part of his analysis. Indeed, he misses the point that in weakly organized settings such as in Peru, many of the direct strategies he characterizes as personalistic could in fact be carried out in combination with campaign clientelistic tactics.

[21] In fact, Boas misses the point that in Peru floating activists offer services and organizational support to all candidates and parties, not just to neo-populist outsiders. See Boas (2016: 174). Moreover, his characterization of Peru as a case of partial system collapse can be contested on empirical grounds.

In the following sections, I further develop the logic of my informational theory by unpacking the two main causal mechanisms by which campaign clientelism indirectly influences electoral choices. I then conclude by explaining how the two mechanisms combine to shape the dynamics of the electoral race.

Signaling Electoral Viability

According to well-established literature on strategic coordination (Duverger 1954, 1986; Leys 1959; Sartori 1968; Cox 1997), political actors can be understood as instrumentally rational actors who care mainly about influencing political outcomes, such as the composition of the government. Preoccupied with this goal, these actors do not wish to waste their ballot or resources on unviable candidates who are unlikely access power and, thus, would not be able to influence governmental outputs.

From this perspective, information on the relative support of competing candidates is a precondition for voters and elites (candidates and donors) to behave strategically in reaction to electoral incentives (Cox 1997: 79). During elections, elites seek to avoid wasting resources and effort and thus tend to concentrate on candidates who are expected to fare better (Cox 1997, Boix 1999). Conversely, strategic voters are unwilling to waste their ballots on hopeless candidates. Thus, they frequently end up voting for candidates who are ranked second or lower in their preference ordering, but are better positioned in the polls (Cox 1997).

This general psychological mechanism, which explains why political actors care about electoral viability, was originally conceived from a programmatic-politics perspective only. As is the case with most of the literature on parties, scholars who work on strategic coordination assume that voters decide their vote exclusively on programmatic terms. In this conception, voters are preoccupied with policy outcomes, and so they are interested above all else in influencing the eventual composition of the government. In other words, they use their vote as an instrument to achieve preferred policy outcomes (Benoit, Gianetti and Laver 2006).

However, that political actors care only about policy outcomes is empirically inaccurate, particularly in developing democracies where clientelistic and personalistic linkages flourish and corruption is rampant. Indeed, there are other reasons why political actors might care about electoral viability. On the one hand, voters may believe it to be important to side with the winner so as to gain personal access to valued particularistic resources. Thus, these voters care about electoral viability because they want to maximize their chances of accessing divisible resources (clientelism, pork, among others) once the election is over. On the other hand, campaign donors care about electoral viability because they are concerned about the prospects of maximizing their returns in terms of favorable regulation or contracts in the future. These actors are still instrumental insofar as they care about electoral viability and act strategically because they seek to influence the composition of the government and affect future particularistic outcomes.

In contexts without organized machines such as in Peru, politicians will have a hard time distributing private resources *ex post* in ways that individually reward or punish those who participated in campaign events, as the mainstream literature on clientelism would expect. However, politicians and voters can still engage in other discretional but non-conditional exchanges, such as pork-barrel spending (Ames 1987, 2001; Samuels 2002) and forbearance (Holland 2017) which are very common in Latin American and do not require a strong organizational device to become effective political strategies. Moreover, candidates and business interests can negotiate other types of political malfeasance that do not require an on-the-ground organizational structure to be enacted, such as improper lobbying and corrupt deals.

In short, strategic actors care about electoral viability because they expect to affect political outcomes, whether programmatic or particularistic. Electoral viability becomes important for easing programmatic-strategic voting and particularistic-strategic voting, and for attracting donors who care whether the candidate who wins will assure them of contracts or favorable regulation.

But how do actors learn about candidates' chances of being elected? Actors' beliefs about the electoral prospects of candidates are based, among other factors, on the perceived level of public support. Party affiliation is thought to be one of the best cues of candidates' competitiveness (Moser and Scheiner 2009). Voters can employ the electoral history heuristic – whether parties have previously gained seats in a given district – in order to form their expectations (Lago 2008). Strategic actors also take cues from other sources of easily observable data, such as poll results and interest group endorsements (McKelvey and Ordeshook 1985).

But what is frequently overlooked is the valuable information that campaign clientelism produces for electoral competition (Muñoz 2014). This is especially important in fluid political settings where political organizations are weak and voters are unattached. The distribution of material rewards plays a big role in campaigns, I argue, because it allows candidates' campaign teams to convey information and signal that they are electorally viable. Aggregate turnout at electoral events serves as a source of electoral information because it is easily observable. The number of people a candidate can mobilize is used as a proxy of his or her popularity among voters.[22] As Kitschelt and Wilkinson contend, "public pledges, or the display of badges, party colors or signs" are more valuable to politicians than private promises of support (Kitschelt and Wilkinson 2007: 15). Buying attendance at campaign events is, therefore, electorally appealing for politicians.

Moreover, campaign clientelism has advantages over other subtypes of electoral clientelism (Muñoz 2014). First, it is relatively cheap. Candidates buy attendance at campaign events by offering inexpensive consumer goods and other selective incentives for poor voters. In addition, candidates promise future benefits to activists who help organize those events. By contrast, vote buying can be rather expensive in certain contexts.[23] Second, unlike other subtypes of electoral clientelism, attendance at rallies cannot be reneged on: "Even when voters can decide not to support the candidate whose rallies they have attended, they, nevertheless, contribute to make these events a success simply by turning out" (Szwarcberg 2009: 14). Thus, monitoring individual compliance is not necessarily an issue: politicians do not need to invest time and resources in monitoring individuals to assure the turnout of large numbers of voters at rallies.

In contexts with loosely organized political machines, campaign clientelism acquires special significance: it serves both to mobilize and convince voters, activists, and campaign financers to support the most promising candidates. By establishing candidates' electoral viability, campaign clientelism indirectly affects vote choices.

How do bought turnout numbers affect electoral choices? Donors and voters contrast the information obtained from observing turnout at campaign events with that obtained from assessing recent electoral history, the spread of street propaganda, the opinion polls that might be available, and candidates' appearances in the media, which are in turn

---

[22] In authoritarian contexts, turnout at rallies is informative of the incumbent's power (Cox 2009: 12–13) and disseminates a public image of invincibility that diminishes bandwagon effects in favor of the opposition candidates (Magaloni 2006: 9). The size of protest demonstrations has also been considered as an informational cue that signals a lack of public support for oppressive regimes. See, for instance, Lohmann (1994).

[23] For instance, estimates indicate that a typical legislative candidate in an urban area of Taiwan distributes up to US$3 million in cash, and that candidates gave out a total of US$460 million in cash to voters in the 2001 legislative elections in Thailand (Schaffer 2007: 4).

influenced by turnout. As scholars have noted, the media tends to focus more on candidates who have momentum (Bartels 1988: 32–5). High turnout at electoral events provides cues about this electoral potential. The media thus transmits and amplifies the importance of high attendance at campaign events.[24]

Evidently, electoral surveys play a substantial role during electoral campaigns in helping candidates establish their electoral viability, and I contend that observing the turnout at campaign rallies plays a complementary role. Polls weigh more as an influence on electoral results when they are conducted on a more frequent basis, as occurs during national campaigns in developing democracies. This does not always occur in local elections. All in all, campaign clientelism also matters in presidential campaigns, but it can be expected to be less effective than in local campaigns for establishing electoral viability, given the widespread availability of electoral surveys. Although some polls are conducted and published in the media during local elections in developing democracies, they are not conducted as often as in presidential ones. Moreover, some of these polls might not be particularly reliable. That said, voters and donors do consider electoral polling information when it is available for local elections. Contrasting the informational cues provided by turnout at rallies with polls helps these actors confirm which candidates are leading the campaign. Strategic actors look for consistent information. For example, if a poll shows a candidate to be a leading competitor but their campaign events are not well-attended, people will disregard the inconsistency of the information.

In weakly organized polities, politicians frequently engage in campaign clientelism from the initial stages of the campaign onward to attract attention to their candidacy and take advantage of bandwagon effects. Campaign teams work intensively to ensure their campaign events are perceived as being successful. The goal is to maximize attendance. The better attended the campaign events are, the more a candidate's reputation as a viable contender will increase and, in turn, the easier it will be to convince strategic donors and voters to lend their support.

Indeed, the increasing distribution of goods throughout the campaign enables the wider audience of voters and donors not yet engaged in the race to update their beliefs about the electoral prospects of the candidates.

---

[24] In countries without institutionalized parties, the media can also directly substitute for partisan organizations during electoral processes (Hale 2006). In such cases, competition may take place directly within the media. Thus, access to media coverage through other means, such as ownership or media corruption, may be more important than demonstrating mobilization strength by turnout numbers.

Particularly at later stages of a campaign, the distribution of goods (as well as the display of propaganda) signals to the general public which candidates are in the lead and thus have better chances of being elected.[25] In this way, a narrower set of viable candidates is identified. And all else being equal, these candidates increase their chances of convincing strategic donors and voters of their electoral viability. In contexts in which elites fail to coordinate candidates' entry into electoral competition, this dynamic helps reduce the number of viable contenders, although not as much as in a complete information setting.[26]

At this stage, a clarification is in order. I do not argue that we should expect to find much in the way of successful strategic voting in places without institutionalized parties, such as in Peru. But it is nevertheless possible to have a modest degree of strategic voting in deinstitutionalized party systems with multimember districts, despite an insufficient vote-concentration effect. Although scholars have not afforded it attention in multimember districts, strategic voting is a general psychological feature of elections beyond first-past-the-post systems (Cox 1997: 99). As Cox (1997), Leys (1959), and Sartori (1968) recognize, there is always a degree of strategic voting in any electoral contest. These authors are clearer than Duverger on this point and contend that different types of electoral systems provide different incentives and, thus, make successful strategic voting (and the expected vote-concentration effect) more or less likely.[27] When the information available is lacking in precision or there is a lack of available information in general, as is certainly the case in less-institutionalized party systems, strategic voting need not necessarily have a reductive impact or a vote-concentration effect because a non-Duvergerian equilibrium can arise (Cox 1997). In these cases, it might not be clear *ex ante* who will be the first- and second-placed runners-up in the race, with the result that neither suffers strategic defection from voters or donors and thus the number of viable candidates exceeds Cox's M+1 rule. In fact, in new democracies with less institutionalized party systems, there is less strategic defection (Moser and Scheiner 2012).

---

[25] In contexts in which financial endorsements are not publicly made, the amount and quality of goods distributed also convey information about candidates' ability to gather resources.

[26] Of course, electoral rules will influence the ease of strategic coordination. One advantage of conducting a case study of a unitary country is that it allows the impact of electoral rules to be held constant.

[27] Following this logic, Cox (1997) proposes a generalization of Duverger's Law for multimember districts that he calls the "M+1 rule."

Thus, I am aware of voters' limited ability to strategize in contexts of imperfect information under weak partisanship. Cues from rallies may help reduce the otherwise even larger number of viable contenders, but they are certainly not as precise as partisan heuristics (where institutionalized parties exist) or reliable electoral survey results published routinely by reputable polling firms, such as in presidential elections. Indeed, given the lack of party identification in these contexts, voters often do not even have fixed and ordered preferences, as the standard strategic-voting model assumes. In fact, without a party label as a relevant cognitive shortcut, voters make up their minds about their electoral preferences *during* the campaign. This makes electoral coordination harder to achieve and contributes to having a larger number of effective parties than would otherwise be observed in more institutionalized party systems.

Moreover, my theory does not imply or require the empirical detection of a high degree of successful strategic voting with a reductive impact (a vote concentration effect) to work. I propose that signaling electoral viability through campaign clientelism matters for influencing not just strategic voters, but also campaign donors. Candidates distribute handouts to generate a semblance of "party organization" that can mobilize voters. Signaling this power and electoral potential, they seek to influence strategic voters and strategic donors alike. Thus, recruiting new financers who can help them sustain their campaigning throughout the race is crucial because signaling electoral viability is not enough in itself to decide the race. I do not argue that voters automatically decide to support those who have better chances of being elected or those who distribute more gifts. As I will discuss in more detail in the next section, signaling electoral viability is a necessary but only an initial hurdle to being elected.

Persuading Clients

Political parties have long been considered important institutions that organize popular demands and socialize citizens into politics (Duverger 1954; Lipset and Rokkan 1967; Sartori 1976, among many others). Moreover, partisan identification has been recognized as a common information shortcut that helps voters make their electoral choices less cognitively demanding (Berelson *et al.* 1954; Downs 1957). That voters do not fully inform themselves about policy positions before making electoral choices has been extensively discussed by the literature on electoral behavior (e.g., Berelson *et al.* 1954; Downs 1957; Campbell *et al.* 1960; Converse 1964; Popkin 1991; Lupia and McCubbins 1998). According to this literature, most voters neither follow politics closely nor think much about it on a regular basis. Thus, their political belief systems tend to be scarcely developed in terms of scope, range of issues covered, and organization (Luskin 1987). In the absence of stable party organization, voters lack the partisan attachments that make it easier for them to become informed about politics. Thus, in these contexts voters may have even less motivation to acquire political information, and less support in processing it, than is usually the case in institutionalized democracies. In addition, voters also lack the symbolic collective attachments – such as party identity – that may assure political allegiance for some sectors of the electorate despite short-term campaign dynamics (Luna 2016: 26). In fluid political settings, therefore, politicians will need to make more of an effort to attract and retain voters' attention.

Campaign clientelism has the underacknowledged benefit of allowing politicians to mobilize indifferent voters who may otherwise not inform themselves about the available electoral options. In contexts with low levels of political organization, campaign events provide candidates with *unique* opportunities to capture voters' attention. Once politicians buy poor voters' participation, they can try to persuade this audience about their desirability in three complementary ways: promising local public goods, conveying personal traits, and generating a positive buzz that will outlast the event. Candidate–voter encounters are, thus, useful for establishing candidate desirability through other types of appeals beyond clientelism. Overall, then, by assuring poor voters' participation at rallies, campaign clientelism improves candidates' prospects of gaining the support of this large electoral constituency.

Unlike regular political advertisements or debates, rallies and other campaign events allow politicians to engage personally with citizens. Face-to-face interactions between candidates and voters can be important in several ways. First, personal communication during campaigns has been proven to be instrumental in increasing electoral turnout (Shaw 2006; Green and Gerber 2008) and persuading voters (Popkin 1991; Fenno 1996; Mahler 2011; Nielsen 2012). Second, personal traits are easier to convey and evaluate during face-to-face interactions than through the media and virtual networks. Finally, in contexts without stable party attachments, closer interactions between voters and candidates can help lessen problems of credibility and distrust.

In particular, interpersonal interaction can help resource-rich or well-connected candidates to bridge the social distance with poor voters, made explicit by turnout buying. Campaign clientelism at once requires and exacerbates the social distance between better-off candidates and less well-off clients. On the one hand, buying voters' turnout at rallies requires access to enough resources to finance distribution throughout the campaign. Thus, candidates must be personally wealthy or able to utilize connections with businessmen or women during the campaign. On the other hand, differences in individual income levels will affect the likelihood of agreeing to participate in campaign events in exchange for a handout: poor voters will value handouts more highly than better-off ones.[28] Thus, campaign clients are most likely to be poor voters. Through face-to-face interaction, candidates can attempt to "level" with poor voters and guarantee them representation despite their social distance. In short, by enabling interpersonal interaction, campaign events are crucial opportunities for candidates to make a more lasting impression on participants.

During these public gatherings, candidates can also influence poor voters through *complementary* means. First, given the spatial nature and small scale of campaign events such as rallies and candidate visits, politicians can particularize their message and promise local-level public goods to districts, neighborhoods, or civil associations. Just by making these proposals and promises accessible and salient to clients, campaign clientelism can actually increase the clients' likelihood of voting for the buyer candidate – a priming effect similar to that gained from advertisements (Gerber *et al.* 2011). Moreover, politicians will also have more time to explain details of certain policy proposals or promises that may be relevant to the interests of a particular constituency, so voters in general can learn more about the candidates' proposals. In certain types of campaign events, such as candidate visits to local associations and neighborhoods, candidates and citizens may even have the chance to negotiate the terms of their political agreements or make specific requests that the former, once elected, might fulfill (Nichter and Peress 2016).

Candidate–client encounters are thus useful for establishing candidate credibility for engagement in other types of particularistic relations beyond clientelism, such as pork-barrel spending. On the one hand, pork-barrel spending does not require such high-precision targeting or monitoring to work as clientelism does. In this sense, as a distributive tactic it is much more feasible than clientelism. On the other hand, the main purpose of pork-barrel spending might not actually be to generate electoral support through the delivery of public works, but to have a supply of contracts to give out to cronies and/or to pay back campaign donors

---

[28] Budget constraints limit the type of benefits that candidates can distribute.

(Samuels 2002). In contrast, in the absence of organized machines, it would be difficult for candidates to distribute private resources *ex post* in ways that individually reward or punish those who participated in campaign events, as the mainstream literature on clientelism would expect.

Second – and most important since all candidates promise to deliver local public goods – campaign events are the most effective way to convey and evaluate candidates' personal traits.[29] In this sense, they provide unique opportunities for candidates to outperform their rivals in situations of valence competition around performance.

In unorganized political contexts, personalistic strategies may be more important for deciding elections than in contexts of institutionalized parties. As Fenno points out, "personal campaigning may be most appropriate in locating and securing a solid primary constituency" (Fenno 1996: 155). Since most voters are capable of processing information and form opinions about candidates' personalities rather easily (Popkin 1991; Fenno 1996) and given that political sophistication affects candidate-centered voting (Peterson 2005; Lavine and Gschwend 2006; Slosar 2011), which tends to be inversely related to socioeconomic status, personally connecting with poor voters on the campaign trail should be a priority for candidates in loosely organized settings. Through social interaction and socialization, individuals learn to interpret other people's actions and gestures (Mead 1947; Goffman 1959; Berger and Luckmann 1967). Consequently, all voters, regardless of their political sophistication, have the requisite abilities to judge candidates' personalities. Meanwhile, making policy and performance evaluations are more cognitively demanding than making judgments about personal character.

By allowing for interpersonal interaction, campaign events such as rallies and personal visits are excellent opportunities for candidates to concentrate on their public presentation. Analogous to the dynamics of everyday social interactions with others (Goffman 1959), during their public performances candidates present their "selves" to voters (Mahler 2011). Therefore, campaign teams invest plenty of time, energy, and

---

[29] In the Latin American literature on elections, there is a tendency to equate personalism with populist (or neo-populist) electoral styles. However, this does not need to be the case (Boas 2016). Priming a political divide – be it cultural (Ostiguy 2009), political (Weyland 1996, 1999; Roberts, 1995), or socioeconomic (Knight 1998, Sachs 1989, Conniff 1982, Donbusch and Edwards 1991, Collier and Collier 1991, De la Torre 2000) – is not the only way to make personalism count for electioneering and vote choice. As such, my theory follows the distinction made by Boas (2016) by focusing on personalistic electoral strategies as those in which candidates usually combine limited policy focus, direct linkages with voters, and minimal cleavage priming.

resources into planning campaign events and worrying about the result-ant public perceptions (Mahler 2011).

According to Fenno (1996), on a campaign trail there are three candidate-centered attributes that are linked to success: authenticity, con-sistency, and good character. Authenticity is related to the transparency of the political persona: the candidate must be "believable"; voters should not perceive him or her to be "faking it" (Fenno 1996: 324-325). Second, the presentation of the self to citizens is expected to be consistent over time (Fenno 1996: 325). Finally, a candidate must have "good character" – that is, desirable personal traits for an elected authority.

During these public gatherings, clients can closely observe the candi-date's mannerisms (the way they talk, the way they treat poor people, their response to competitors' accusations, etc.). Despite the intensive planning that goes into these events, they provide more room for spon-taneity; unlike advertisements or news reports, campaign events, by their very nature, are not edited. Therefore, citizens have a better chance to assess the candidate's skills, reactions, and personal trajectories, and to find out who the candidate's allies are.

The campaign trail is also an opportunity for candidates to demon-strate to indifferent clients that they truly know and understand the local needs. Come the day of the campaign event, candidates must show clients that they are aware of what they need (T-shirts and caps for work, food, etc.),[30] what they enjoy (music, meals, drinks, etc., during the event), or how much they expect to be paid to campaign as compensation for time off work (as in the case, for example, of motorcycle taxis and cars that join motorcades). The way benefits are distributed (Auyero 2001) – that is, how distribution is personalized – may be just as important as what or how much is distributed.

Finally, campaign events potentially generate a buzz around candi-dates and participants at campaign events can examine both the viability and desirability of candidates by observing their peers' reactions to them. In general, the more enthusiastic the public mood at campaign events,

---

[30] While a T-shirt or a cap with a candidate's name or party logo might be seen by some, especially middle to upper-class observers, as mere electoral merchandising, poor voters usually value the practical utility of these goods and thus understand them differently. They often regard them as potential job utilities that they can use or wear on a daily basis (and not just for campaign events). As such, even matchboxes or calendars are appreciated for their practical use despite their low economic value, even if it is not so clear that such low-value goods are perceived as valuable gifts by the majority of clients. Thus, it is here that I mark the limit for what I consider a campaign clientelistic good, and vice versa.

the better it will be for persuasion purposes. This is because the aim of persuasion is not only to make a good impression on participants, but also to get them to talk about the candidate in a positive way. Attendees at these rallies will often comment afterwards on the candidates and their proposals, so that mass attendance and general enthusiasm at these rallies becomes crucial for establishing a "buzz."

In summary, campaign events provide candidates with an ideal platform to convince voters of their electoral desirability; by attending political meetings after being offered certain selective incentives, clients get valuable information *in situ* that help them make their electoral choices.

Relations Between Mechanisms

Signaling electoral viability and persuading clients of electoral desirability are both necessary components of a successful electoral trajectory.[31] Although it may be theoretically plausible that a successful strategy based on just one mechanism could get a candidate elected, this possibility is unlikely in empirical terms. Any appealing candidacy needs to pass a viability threshold to succeed in the polls. Similarly, a candidate with good initial prospects needs to maintain momentum throughout the campaign. In this sense, neither electoral viability nor desirability may on their own be sufficient to explain successful electoral trajectories. But how do these causal mechanisms relate to each other?

Demonstrating electoral viability is a first step any candidate must take in order to be elected. Considering all candidates competing for office, signaling viability works as a first-stage *selection* mechanism, a competitive dynamic that helps reduce the viable number of contenders. Given the lack of alternative reliable shortcuts to assess candidates' electoral strength, such as party identification, strategic voters and campaign donors will concentrate further information-gathering efforts on

---

[31] A clarification is in order. Persuasion is not incompatible with strategic voting. Scholars interested in strategic voting assume that citizens already have a set of fixed partisan preferences (strict and ordered preferences). This theory does not predict that citizens will always vote for the frontrunner candidate, but that they may end up choosing their second or third preference if their first one does not have good enough electoral prospects. The identified mechanism of persuasion is thus a process by which indifferent clients can assess the "desirability" of different candidates *and form* their political preferences (or weakly identified clients can change theirs). After gathering information about candidates' electoral chances and forming their preferences, clients can decide how to vote.

a few candidates who are expected to fare well. Thus, demonstrating that mobilization capability during the campaign is a way of attracting the attention of the wider electoral audience. It also allows candidates to convey to campaign financiers they are serious candidates and worth supporting. Attracting additional donors is vital to assuring funds that will help candidates to continue financing their electioneering strategies throughout the campaign.

However, frontrunner candidates still need to convince rally participants of their desirability. Campaign clientelism serves to buy the presence of poor voters – that is, an audience – but this does not necessarily translate into support at the polls. Therefore, politicians need to create a link that even if such support does not outlast the campaign, it will at least endure through to election day. Candidates can thus further persuade participants through particularistic promises and by forming a personal connection with them. Final rallies and other events held near the end of a campaign may be crucial for cementing the vote of poor, undecided participants.

In other words, my informational theory does not imply a simple bidding process in which the candidate who offers more private benefits gets more electoral support, unlike what Finan and Schechter's (2012) model proposes for reciprocal voters and what Kramon's model (2017) seems to imply. Clients do not necessarily vote for the candidate who distributes the most benefits. The volume of goods being distributed may signal electoral viability and, provided it helps ensure crowded campaign events, will indirectly influence electoral decisions since voters consider electoral viability in making electoral choices; but as I have stressed, candidates' desirability affects vote choice as well.

Gifts are used to force interactions, after which voters evaluate non-clientelistic distributive promises and issues of authenticity and good character. Moreover, voters tend to reward candidates who show they understand local conditions and their needs.

Campaign clients also observe what others get and on this basis they can assess how much a candidate spends. Spending less than what is considered appropriate can be problematic because it may signal that either the candidate does not understand local needs or has not amassed the resources to afford to do so. But so, too, can blatant over-distribution of resources be counterproductive, potentially being seen by poor voters as inappropriate and even irking them. Indeed, exaggerated distribution can widen the social distance between the candidate and campaign clients, causing the candidate to be perceived as insensitive and arrogant.

Alternatively, exaggerated distribution may make voters suspicious of the candidate's true motives and ambition – winning merely to access and amass the spoils of office – without caring for the specific needs of the people. Either interpretation will impede a candidate's ability to establish an emotional connection with rally participants, which is crucial to attaining desirability.

In summary, both electoral viability and desirability are necessary for a successful electoral strategy. As will be shown later in the book, an examination of the strategies candidates use, and how viability and desirability combine, is needed to make sense of electoral trajectories and results.

EXPECTATIONS

Before concluding, in this section I briefly present the predictions of my theory. In an informational approach, considerable clientelistic efforts will be expected during elections, even in the absence of strong party organizations. In particular, this approach predicts that a significant volume of material benefits will be distributed at campaign events from the beginning and throughout the campaign. It expects clients to be predominantly poor people who turn out at such events to obtain handouts. Moreover, for my theory, challenger candidates and not just incumbents engage in campaign clientelism. In other words, to a great extent, campaign clientelism is carried out using private resources. Candidates may rely on local brokers to distribute goods, but they need not be part of an established vertical clientelistic network. The empirical implications of my theory are summarized and contrasted with conventional approaches in Table 2.1.

Table 2.2, in turn, specifies the main empirical observations I expect to find, and how these differ from those of Kramon's informational theory. Thus, although our theories are complementary in some respects, they differ in terms of the causal mechanisms linking electoral clientelism and vote choice.

CONCLUSION

In this chapter I have shown how existing, conventional theories have exaggerated the importance of organized networks and long-term relations to sustaining electoral clientelism. Conventional approaches are at odds on the particular causal mechanism employed to explain why

TABLE 2.1. *Empirical implications: Conventional approaches*

Dimension	Conventional approaches	Informational
Most frequently used type of electoral clientelism	Vote buying and turnout buying at polls	Turnout buying at campaign events
Timing of benefits distribution	Distribution on election day or very close to it	Distribution starts well before election day
Settings of benefit distribution	Distribution through established clientelistic networks of brokers (Private)	Distribution at campaign events (Public)
Most likely clients	Citizens who are part of clientelistic networks or who believe in the plausibility of monitoring	Poor citizens who are available to participate in campaign events

TABLE 2.2. *Empirical implications: Informational approaches*

Dimension	Kramon	Muñoz
Informational cue that influences electoral viability	Handout distribution	Turnout at rallies
Influence of handouts on prospective evaluations	Yes: Positive	None or Negative
Establishing candidate credibility	Handout distribution	Pork promises Personalistic appeals Buzz

Source: Based on Kramon (2017)

clients honor the clientelistic bargain, but all of them conceive of electoral clientelism as an iterated relation that is commonly accompanied by a political organization: a network of local brokers. By focusing on the long term, scholars do not expect electoral clientelism to take place in unorganized settings where actors are opportunistic and focused on the short term.

My theory incorporates some contemporary theoretical refinements that contemplate either the possibility of clientelistic transactions without established networks or the informational value of clientelistic tactics. However, I move beyond these new developments by providing a *full-fledged* theory that, first, emphasizes the information produced by buying turnout at campaign events; second, is able to explain how electoral clientelism takes place in unorganized political contexts; and, third, underlines how campaign clientelism creates fields of interaction between the candidate and voters, which are useful for establishing candidate viability through other non-clientelistic electoral appeals.

Politicians engage in campaign clientelism because of the indirect payoffs: raising contributions, recruiting benefit-seeking activists, attracting strategic voters, and persuading clients. Campaign clientelism affects electoral choices through two causal mechanisms: by signaling candidates' electoral viability to the wider electoral audience and by providing politicians with good opportunities to influence poor participants at rallies by convincing them of their desirability. Politicians distribute selective incentives in order to buy poor voters' participation at campaign events. This bought turnout allows them to attract clients' attention and further demonstrate their electoral strength to the general public. During campaign events, however, candidates need to make sure that they persuade clients to support them at the polls. They can do so through three complementary means. First, candidates can particularize their message and promise local public goods in crucial constituencies. Second, because campaign events involve face-to-face interactions between politicians and voters, they constitute the best way to convey and evaluate a candidate's personal traits. Finally, campaign events can help candidates generate a positive buzz that can amplify their attempts at gaining influence.

Now, having discussed the existing literature, set out my own theory, and contrasted the expectations of my theory with others, in the next chapter I will first provide an introduction to how politics works within Peru, a democracy without parties, and then test the empirical implications of conventional theories in this loosely organized polity. After showing the limitations of these approaches, I will proceed to demonstrate the soundness of my informational theory in Chapters 4–6.

3

Clientelistic Linkages in Peru and the Limits of Conventional Explanations

As discussed in Chapter 2, conventional approaches to the study of electoral clientelism would not expect to find much distribution of material benefits during elections in places that lack consolidated political organizations, such as Peru. Although they envisage different purposes for networks and differ in their explanations for voter compliance with clientelistic deals, these scholars generally assume that electoral clientelism *requires* extensive and stable networks of brokers at the local level. In addition, most of the existing literature focuses only on direct vote-getting strategies, such as vote buying, turnout buying and abstention buying. These scholars conceive these vote-getting deals as single-shot transactions that take place close to election day.

My informational theory, by contrast, would expect to observe intensive distribution of material goods for the entire duration of campaigns in contexts of low political organization. Rather than focusing on the direct effects of clientelistic investments, my theory instead emphasizes the indirect effects of these investments on vote choices. From this perspective, electoral clientelism affects electoral choices by shaping the dynamics of the race. Accordingly, politicians would be expected to invest in clientelism while campaigning, buying participation at campaign events in the hope of shaping the dynamics of the race in ways that translate into votes on election day.

In this chapter I have two main goals. First, I intend to provide a background to aid the understanding of the political context under study and to describe the scores of my dependent variable. Second, I test whether conventional approaches can explain how electoral clientelism takes place in Peru. In order to do so, I will proceed as follows. I begin by showing that Peru has a very low level of political organization, and that this has not been exaggerated by scholars. I present a brief historical overview of the gradual erosion of relational clientelism over several decades, and then I characterize the current state of political organization. I provide evidence to confirm that political parties or purely clientelistic machines are seldom organized or stable in Peru. Next, I discuss the types of distributive strategies that politicians use in this context of low organization. I contend that instead of building lasting clientelistic organizations, Peruvian politicians combine campaign clientelism with pork barrel spending and corruption. Finally, I use quantitative and qualitative data to test the implications of prevailing theories. To this end, I provide a description of how gifts are actually distributed during campaigns, focusing primarily on the timing and setting of distribution. I also consider the possibility that politicians have improvised a kind of monitoring system despite the absence of stable networks of local brokers. I conclude by summarizing my main findings: that conventional approaches cannot explain the type of electoral clientelism found in Peru. Then, in the subsequent chapters, I go on to show how my informational theory can account for these empirical observations.

THE DEMISE OF RELATIONAL CLIENTELISM IN PERU

The literature on clientelism has distinguished between traditional forms of relational clientelism and more modern forms based on partisan brokerage networks. Traditional clientelism differs from political machines because it is based primarily on face-to-face relations and bonds of traditional deference that tie clients and patrons together (Scott 1969). This type of clientelism is seen as more encompassing in its scope, in the sense that it covers virtually every aspect of people's economic, social, and political lives rather than just electoral politics (Archer 1990).

Peru had traditional clientelism before its democratization in 1980. This took the form of a clientelistic social system, in which political power was concentrated in the hands of a few families due to their social and economic wealth and, especially, their land ownership (Bourricaud 1966; Cotler 1967; Alberti and Fuenzalida 1969, Fuenzalida 1971; Guasti 1977). Society was organized into layers of hierarchical mediations with a high concentration of power at the apex (Alberti and Fuenzalida 1969: 67–8; Cotler 1978). This vertical societal structure also reproduced racial discrimination, in Andean areas particularly, the clientelistic system worked as an "ethnic administration" in which indigenous peasants were bound to landowners through a system of traditional authorities (*varayoc*) (Coronel *et al.* 1998). This "oligarchic" system eroded progressively with socioeconomic modernization and began to come under political attack during the 1950s and 1960s. But it was not until the agrarian reform, launched in 1969 by the reformist military government, that the system was ended for good (Lowenthal 1975; López 1997).

During the 1980s, with the return to democracy, some political parties used clientelism as a long-term strategy to drum up political support. Relational clientelism primarily involved providing jobs as patronage for partisans. While in power (1985–90), the *Partido Aprista Peruano* (APRA) used this strategy further than other parties, building a clientelistic machine that utilized social programs targeted at the urban poor, such as *Programa de Apoyo Directo* (PAD) and *Programa de Apoyo de Ingreso Temporal* (PAIT) (Parodi Trece 2000: 236–8; see also Blondet 2004: 42 for PAD). Party favoritism was particularly pervasive in the implementation of PAIT (Graham 1991, 1992). However, campaign-clientelistic behavior campaigns had yet to reach its fullest extent. Despite the use of food aid for party-political ends, electoral mobilization in the 1980s was increasingly programmatic. The failure of military corporatist rule spurred the rise of urban social movements that promoted an ethics of rights and egalitarianism (Stokes 1995). The result was a rift in the political culture of the urban poor in the 1980s, with the emergence of rival clientelistic and radical/leftist mentalities.

Clientelistic linkages radically changed after political outsider Alberto Fujimori (1990–2000) unexpectedly took the presidency in the wake of the 1980s crisis. Fujimori erected a corrupt, competitive authoritarian regime (Cotler and Grompone 2000; Marcus-Delgado and Tanaka 2001; Levitsky and Way 2002; Carrión 2006; Murakami 2007) and engaged in a state-building process that allowed him to regain control over the national territory (Wise 2002; Burt 2007). He also recentralized administrative power and resources in the executive branch (Planas 1998; Contreras 2002; Zas Fris 2005), while simultaneously weakening regional and provincial politicians and strengthening district municipalities (Tanaka 2002), particularly rural ones (Muñoz 2005). One of the effects of these changes was to make both pork-barrel and clientelistic strategies feasible for Fujimori.

Lacking a party organization, Fujimori used the state apparatus to distribute pork extensively, thus, increasing his chances of being reelected (Roberts 1995; Weyland 1998; Graham and Kane 1998; Roberts and Arce 1998; Schady 2000). Although the lack of party backing meant

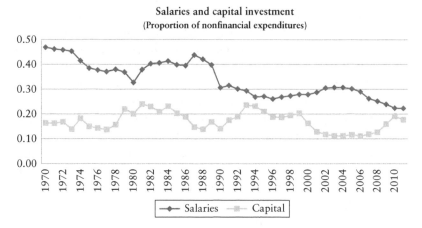

FIGURE 3.1. *Salaries and capital investment in Peru (1970–2011)*
Source: MEF, Banco de la Nación, and Banco Central de Reserva del Perú

job patronage was not as prolific as in the 1980s, this time it was selective and linked to the construction of a state-based machine. Fujimori used this machine to expand and institutionalize clientelistic ties to the poor through social programs such as Programa Nacional de Asistencia Alimentaria (PRONAA) (Rousseau 2009; Boesten 2010). Additionally, electoral clientelism took off, given Fujimori's use of public funds to buy turnout at rallies and campaign events so as to overcome his lack of party organization (Conaghan 2005: 164–6).

The construction of this authoritarian state-machine occurred alongside the permanent collapse of Peru's traditional party system. Fujimori's control of the state apparatus allowed him to deliver goods and services that the now extremely weak political parties were no longer able to provide, either at the national or subnational level.[1] Moreover, Fujimori got rid of many partisan cadres working in the state by implementing radical pro-market reforms (Gonzales de Olarte 1998; Weyland 2002). Among other measures, these reforms included an aggressive program to privatize public enterprises (which had been used as a source of patronage), as well as the dismissal of a large number of state employees. As an illustration of this, Figure 3.1 shows the substantial decrease in spending on salaries from the 1990s as a proportion of the central government's nonfinancial expenditure.

[1] Fujimori replaced elected regional assemblies with appointed executive authorities and modified subnational transfers to benefit district over provincial municipalities, where most party strongholds had their organizational bases.

But, in spite of so many reforms on other fronts, Fujimori did not engage in party building while in power (Tanaka 2001, 2002; Levitsky and Cameron 2003; Roberts 2006; Murakami 2007). Organizationally, Fujimori's "parties" "were empty vessels that served at the whim of their autocratic founder" (Roberts 2006: 139). Therefore, the technical structure of the state was free of partisan patronage.[2] To mobilize poor voters at government rallies and during campaigns, Fujimori's government relied on a network of paid political brokers organized by Absalón Vásquez, a former *Aprista* and expert in political mobilization who served first as Minister of Agriculture (1992–6) and then as a presidential advisor. Most of these brokers were former cadres from the left and APRA (Grompone 2000: 138). In Cusco, for example, the government hired former cadres from leftist parties such as *Vanguardia Revolucionaria*, *Partido Comunista del Perú (Patria Roja)*, and the Maoist *Partido Comunista del Perú (Puka Llacta)*, an offshoot of Patria Roja.[3] Former leftist politicians interviewed in Piura and Cusco also acknowledged that left political cadres, including themselves, worked for Fujimori's government.[4]

Apristas themselves acknowledge their losses to *Fujimorismo*. For instance, Carlos Armas, APRA activist and former congressman, confirmed that several activists left the party and joined Fujimori's government, albeit these were cadres without much power and leadership within the party.[5] Alberto Chumacero, APRA's secretary of organization in Piura, agrees, pointing out that Vásquez took with him many middle-ranked political cadres as well as local brokers.[6] These and other politicians attributed this shift of allegiance mostly to financial incentives: during what were very harsh economic times, these cadres did not have a stable income to support their families.[7] According to another ex-Aprista who was one of Vásquez's closer associates, in 1994 they recruited approximately 70 percent of APRA's former network of local brokers in Lima in

---

[2] Personal interview with Pierina Polarollo, technocrat and expert in public employment (Lima, September 30, 2009).

[3] Personal interview with Washington Román, union leader and journalist (May 17, 2010), Adolfo Mamani, former Puka Llacta partisan (Cusco, August 31, 2010), and Carlos Paredes, former member of Vanguardia in Cusco (Lima, November 7, 2009).

[4] Personal interview with anonymous political operators in Piura (November 15, 2010) and Cusco (August 2, 2010).

[5] Personal interview (Lima, August 3, 2010).

[6] Personal interview (Piura, November 24, 2010).

[7] Politicians also point out that Fujimori's government threatened many radical leftist cadres with prosecution on terrorism charges. The government offered to drop the charges on the condition that they agreed to work for the Fujimori administration. Personal interview with Adolfo Mamani (Cusco, August 31, 2010).

order to assure Fujimori's first reelection in 1995.[8] He also explained in detail how they used certain programs, such as PRONAA and *Programa Nacional de Manejo de Cuencas Hidrográficas y Conservación de Suelos* (PRONAMCH), to build this network of political support and mobilization for Fujimori.

After democracy reemerged in 2001, however, institutional factors and political competition made the consolidation of a state-based machine unlikely. A combination of institutional constraints (technocratic controls, transparency procedures, and the decentralization of social programs) and increasing social awareness (created by media and civil society organizations) limited the executive's latitude to use state resources for clientelistic ends.[9] In addition, despite the reinstatement of regional governments, subnational incumbents today do not have as much leeway with which to engage in clientelism as they do in other countries. National regulations play an important role in a still-centralized unitary body and constrain subnational incumbents. The three levels of subnational government also lack any legal authority or financial control over one other (Muñoz 2005, 2007), impeding the construction of political machines with territorial reach.

In summary, relational clientelism has diminished considerably in Peru. Traditional clientelism based on the *hacienda* system was replaced by partisan clientelism in the 1980s, which depended largely on the distribution of patronage (public jobs) to activists. With the collapse of the party system and the consolidation of a competitive authoritarian regime, however, partisan clientelistic linkages eroded significantly. Lacking a party, during the 1990s Fujimori used the state apparatus, and public resources, as a machine substitute to mobilize poor voters. Since 2001, this road to clientelism has been closed; under democracy, there are a series of institutional constraints on the kind of use to which Fujimori put the state as a clientelistic machine.

---

[8] Personal interview with anonymous political operator (Lima, February 17, 2010).

[9] Personal interviews with Guido Lucioni (Fujimorismo), Lima, February 5, 2010; Carlos Roca (APRA), Lima, April 6, 2010; Fritz Du Bois (former chief advisor for the Ministry of Economy and Finance and current editor of the newspaper Perú21), Lima, August 13, 2009; Javier Abugattás (former vice-minister of economy and finance), Lima, September 18, 2009; Víctor Caballero (former chief of PRONAA), Lima, October 23, 2009; Cecilia Blondet (minister for the advancement of women and human development, and current president of the NGO PROETICA), Lima, November 6, 2009; Lorena Alcázar (research director and senior researcher at the Grupo de Análisis para el Desarrollo, GRADE) (Lima, June 9, 2010). For more details about the power of technocrats in Peru, see Dargent 2012.

Today, relational clientelism, both in its party- and state-based versions, is difficult to sustain in Peru. As I will demonstrate in the next section, most political parties have not reorganized since democratization, but nor have state-based machines been consolidated. I will go on to show how the structure of political competition without stable partisan affiliations affects politicians' distributive strategies in ways that make the consolidation of clientelistic networks even less likely. Rather than building clientelistic networks, politicians with extremely short time horizons engage principally in corruption and pork-barrel politics while holding office.

POLITICS WITH LOW POLITICAL ORGANIZATION

Scholars have characterized present-day Peru as a "democracy without parties" (Levitsky and Cameron 2003; Tanaka 2005a; Levitsky 2013). With the exception of APRA (Cyr 2012, 2017), parties are weakly organized at the subnational level in Peru; they have few established committees and linkages with local brokers. Most registered national parties are in fact mere legal artifacts that do not even have much to offer promising local candidates (De Gramont 2010; Levitsky 2013; Zavaleta 2014). The main point I want to stress here, is not how few political cadres there are at the local level, but that these cadres are not linked within or across electoral districts with any degree of permanence; they change their political allegiances and labels constantly. Indeed, "parties" are created anew for each electoral campaign in Peru. Office-seeking politicians either create their own personalistic vehicles or renegotiate their "partisan" affiliation close to the launch of electoral campaigns. The result is a proliferation of ad hoc coalitions of independent candidates who band together at each election and dissolve soon after (Zavaleta 2014).

Without political parties to check and channel politicians' personal ambitions, politics becomes extremely short-sighted (Levitsky 2013). Short-term and improvised electoral alliances make politics unpredictable, producing a very fluid and unstable political system. Because elections in this context are highly volatile, politicians have a hard time securing reelection.[10] In fact, this absence of parties has resulted in both the end of

---

[10] Indeed, reelection rates in Peru are comparatively low, between 1995 and 2008 the country's legislative reelection rate of 20 percent pales against those of other Latin American countries such as Brazil (51 percent), Argentina (52 percent), and Chile (63 percent) (Tanaka and Barrenechea 2011). Percentages calculated by Legislatina, the legislative observatory for Latin America: http://americo.usal.es/oir/legislatina/reeleccion.htm.

many political careers and the spread of amateur and semi-professional politicians (Levitsky 2013: 23–4). As one experienced political operator notes, inexperience and improvisation are so pronounced in Peruvian politics that in many cases it is the printing house rather than the campaign team that selects the slogans for fliers and posters.[11] Consequently, he adds, candidates end up communicating a confusing and often contradictory mix of ideas and slogans during an election.

In the absence of stable political organization, national candidates' alliances with local candidates become crucial to effective campaigning that takes advantage of reverse coattail effects.[12] Improvised electoral groupings look for local personalities with some type of public reputation – colloquially called *"candidateables"* – to occupy candidacies for congress, mayor, and councilors.[13] Media outlets also play an important role in campaigning, in some cases standing in for the lack of organizational infrastructure. Thus, it is not rare to see television and radio journalists getting elected as authorities, for example, such as the former regional presidents Hernán Fuentes in Puno (Muñoz 2007; Zavaleta 2014) and Carlos Cuaresma in Cusco (De Gramont 2010; Zavaleta 2014).

Finally, candidates increasingly hire political entrepreneurs – known as "political operators" (*operadores políticos*) – to help them run their campaigns. Operators are semi-professional politicians who perform roles and tasks usually taken on by party structures in other contexts.[14] They specialize in political strategy, electoral law, media politics, and mass mobilization. Operators – or at least most of them – are not, however, local brokers. In fact, they are in charge of contacting and, ideally, recruiting local brokers for a campaign. With the exception of those who work for APRA, operators are not really partisan loyalists but "free" agents who switch affiliation at each election.[15]

---

[11] Personal interview with Adolfo Mamani (Cusco, August 31, 2010).

[12] Presidential elections are concurrent with congressional elections. And, since 2002 (when regional elected bodies were created), regional elections are concurrent with municipal elections.

[13] Often, these potential candidates begin marketing themselves as promising candidates many months or even years in advance of an election. For instance, posters and graffiti appeared in the streets of Cusco city several months before the 2010 local election, advertising just the name of a candidate. The same phenomenon was observed in Puno in July 2010.

[14] Some of these political operators were former local party cadres – mainly from the left and APRA. Many others started participating in politics in the 1990s or the 2000s without partisan affiliation and learned the arts of politics by trial and error.

[15] Extensive evidence supporting this claim will be provided in Chapter 4.

ESTIMATING POLITICAL NETWORKS IN PERU

Following the methodology of Calvo and Murillo (2013), I conducted a survey to estimate the size and structure of political networks in Peru, the results of which provide additional support for the claim that, with the exception of APRA, the country today lacks organized parties. This survey methodology relies on interviews consisting of a series of count questions (e.g., "How many X's do you know?"). Using these count questions as input, the method allows for the indirect measurement of political networks through the simultaneous estimation of each respondent's personal network, and of each respondent's predisposition to establish ties with particular political groups.[16]

The survey included a battery of questions intended to measure the size of each individual's personal network (questions about voters' common names and vital statistics; that is, population frequencies known through census data), as well as items to estimate networks of interest (questions about the number of activists and candidates in different political organizations, and about the number of public employees of different sorts that each survey respondent knows personally). To maximize the chances of a reliable estimate, the questionnaire included only questions about political parties that, as at 2010, were represented in Congress and had won the national executive office after 1980. Only four political parties met these requirements: *Acción Popular*, APRA, *Fujimorismo* in its different manifestations, and *Perú Posible*. In addition, the survey included a generic question about the number of candidates and collaborators from regional or local movements[17] that the respondent knows personally. This was intended to provide a rough estimate of the near-countless regional and local entities that have competed in elections since the collapse of Peru's party system.

The results of this method confirm, firstly, that APRA is still by far the largest party in Peru. As described in Table 3.1, the network of APRA activists is the biggest political network in Peru, with a prevalence of 0.611 percent. This network is almost three times bigger than that of *Perú Posible* (0.220 percent), more than double that of Acción Popular (0.270 percent), and almost double that of *Fujimorismo* (0.353 percent).

---

[16] Calvo and Murillo's method relies on recent developments in network analysis to estimate hard-to-count populations and uncover network structures from individual-level data (McCarthy *et al.* 2001; Zhen *et al.* 2006). For more details, see the appendix. For the estimation procedure used, see Calvo and Murillo (2013).

[17] According to Peruvian law, political organizations that stand candidates on the regional or local level are known as "movements."

TABLE 3.1. *Political networks by sizes*

Share of respondent's personal network	
Candidate for *Acción Popular*	0.093
Candidate for *Perú Posible*	0.106
Candidate for *Fujimorismo*	0.123
Candidate for regional or local movement	0.159
Candidate for APRA	0.176
Activist for *Perú Posible*	0.220
Activist for *Acción Popular*	0.270
Activist for *Fujimorismo*	0.353
Collaborator in regional or local movement	0.372
Activist for APRA	0.611

Source: Ipsos APOYO/JNE (2010)

The second largest political network after APRA is that of collaborators in regional and local movements (0.372 percent), which captures the myriad political operators who help run subnational campaigns, closely followed by *Fujimorismo* activists (0.353 percent). The fact that one of the most important national parties, which almost won the two last national elections (2011 and 2016), ranks third *after* this unarticulated group of political operators is symptomatic of the high level of political disarticulation in Peru.

The survey method employed by Calvo and Murillo (2013) provides us with, not only, a way to estimate the size of political networks, but also with procedures that allow us to say something about the structuring principle of political networks at the system level. Figure 3.1, for example, illustrates the relationships and hierarchies between the different political clusters. The figure shows that political networks in Peru are clustered horizontally (across political parties) more than vertically (within political parties). This means that knowing an activist for a given party makes it more likely that one will know another party's activist rather than a candidate for the same party. In the first political cluster, for example, knowing an APRA candidate is correlated with knowing a candidate for *Fujimorismo*. In turn, respondents who know a candidate for APRA or *Fujimorismo* are also more likely to know a candidate from *Perú Posible*. This whole cluster is closely related to *Acción Popular's* candidates and activists, the only intra-party cluster. In the second big political cluster, respondents who know more APRA activists also know more

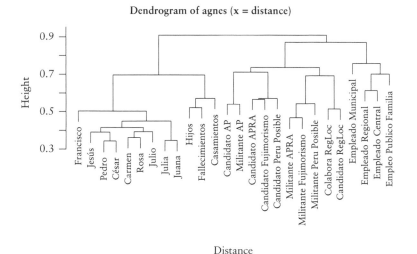

Distance

Agglomerative coefficient = 0.45

FIGURE 3.2. *Dendrogram describing the structure of networks in Peru*

Fujimorismo activists. Overall, these respondents also know more *Perú Posible* activists and, to a lesser extent, more politicians from regional and local movements. Finally, respondents who know more collaborators in regional and local movements also tend to be closer to candidates who run for these organizations. However, as I have mentioned, the estimates for "regional and local movements" include rather diverse political entities. In short, Figure 3.1 shows the lack of a clear structuring principle governing political networks, attesting to the fluidity of the Peruvian political system. If anything, the two big political clusters distinguish themselves by grouping, on the one hand, mostly candidates and, on the other hand, political operators and local brokers. Thus, the lack of partisan structuring in Figure 3.1 reflects the fact that Peruvian politicians frequently change allegiance among "parties."

This lack of political differentiation across organizations can also be seen in Figure 3.2, which graphs inter-group correlations. Darker squares denote a stronger correlation between networks. Partisan patterns of integration should appear as series of dark small triangles with vertices in the activist and candidate categories for each party.[18] As can be observed,

---

[18] For instance, Calvo and Murillo (2013), see the figure that plots Argentina's structure of political networks.

no clear dark pattern corresponding to the political networks of interest emerges on the center-left side of Figure 3.2. Instead of various small dark triangles, only a big light-colored triangle appears, starting in the vertex of *Acción Popular* candidates and ending in the vertex of candidates for regional or local movements. Within this big triangle, the only black square corresponds to the correlation between APRA and *Fujimorismo* activists.[19] One can contrast this lack of partisan clustering with the dark triangle shown in the lower-left section of Figure 3.2, which expresses the inter-correlation of personal networks.

In summary, Calvo and Murillo's method shows that there are in fact plenty of political cadres in Peru, but that most political networks do not relate to each other in a consistent way. In other words, it demonstrates the fluidity of Peruvian politics, reflected in the absence of a clear pattern of partisan articulation: politicians switch affiliations constantly. Not even APRA, the largest political party, shows a pattern of vertical integration – that is, a strong intra-party correlation between networks of militants and candidates. In fact, the only party that appears integrated to any extent is *Acción Popular*, a traditional party that been unable to recover in electoral terms since the collapse of the party system in the 1990s (the party did not even run its own slate in the 2011 national election). These survey results, thus, confirm that the qualitative characterizations of Peru's political system as somewhat fluid and unarticulated are not, in fact, exaggerated.

Up to this point, I have shown that present-day Peru does not have organized political parties. And, as I will demonstrate in the rest of this section, Peruvian politicians rarely build political machines while governing either.

As noted previously, since the collapse of Fujimori's authoritarian regime, the national state apparatus is no longer used as a substitute for a machine. Neither the *Perú Posible* (2001–6) nor APRA (2006–11) governments were able to successfully exploit the state to foster clientelistic linkages with the poor.[20] Indeed, despite achieving outstanding macroeconomic outcomes, neither of these parties presented a presidential candidate in the successive election. In particular, APRA's poor electoral

---

[19] This strong correlation between APRA and Fujimorismo activists would appear to corroborate the account given in the previous section about Fujimori's government buying APRA activists with a view to building a clientelistic network and securing his reelection and may explain this otherwise unexpected finding.

[20] Interviews with the mentioned politicians, technocrats, and researchers confirm this claim.

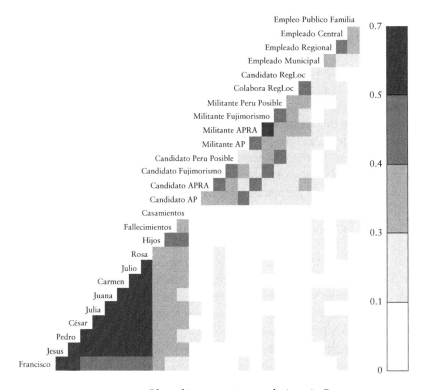

FIGURE 3.3. *Plot of inter-group correlations in Peru*

performance in the 2011 election illustrates the difficulties of using the state to build organized clientelism in present-day Peru. APRA is currently the only national party with the organizational resources necessary to become a successful clientelistic machine. In fact, APRA has been the closest Peru has come to having a party machine in recent history. Nonetheless, while governing (2006–11) the party was unable to systematically manipulate the national executive branch to solidify clientelistic linkages with the poor. This was primarily because transparency procedures, administrative systems, such as, the Integrated Financial Administration System (SIAF),[21] and the decentralization of crucial programs such as PRONAA made it difficult to do so. In addition, given APRA's and President Alan Garcia's earlier conduct in office in the 1980s, the media was particularly watchful for any signs of corruption and politicization of the state this time around. And with very few subnational governments (two out of

[21] *Sistema Integrado de Administración Financiera.*

twenty-five regional governments and 16 out of 194 provincial municipalities), APRA was unable to assert territorial control. Thus, instead of
systematically engaging in machine clientelism, the APRA government
invested heavily in pork and manipulated transfers to subnational governments, in order to buy off mayors and regional presidents.[22] However,
this strategy failed miserably; after an apparently successful term marked
by high growth rates and investment in infrastructure, the party barely
passed the electoral threshold in the following national contest, winning
only four seats in the Congress. Not even Carlos Arana, national secretary of organization and García's main political operator, was able to get
elected to Congress despite having led important infrastructure programs
such as Agua para Todos and FONCODES.

APRA's pork-barrel strategy was, therefore, not enough to activate the
goodwill of Peruvian voters. According to experienced political operators, this was due to the escalation of corruption during the construction
of public works.[23] As Absalón Vásquez puts it, "corruption was notori-
ous in the public works they delivered, people knew it ... Corruption has
gone way up ... Politicians lose their mind, they get blinded by ambition
and disconnect from the people."

Moreover, the existence of organized machines at the subnational level
is the exception rather than the rule in Peru. In the literature, "the notion
[of a machine] connotes the reliability and repeatability of control that
a political party or group exercises within its jurisdiction" (Menéndez-
Carrión 1985: 18). Thus, machine consolidation is expected to result
in stable local party systems and lower levels of electoral volatility
(Szwarcberg 2015: 69). Peru, however, has few consolidated machines
that have proven capable of maintaining control of government. In fact,
subnational politics is characterized by high levels of political fragmentation (with an average of 5.5 active parties over the three last elections)
and electoral volatility (a median of 40.5 percent for the 2002–10 period)
(Vera 2010; Muñoz and García 2011).

The absence of consolidated machines is also reflected in the comparatively low reelection rates for subnational offices. Only 33 percent of
incumbent provincial mayors and 27 percent of incumbent district mayors who ran as candidates in 2010 were able to secure reelection (Córdova

---

[22] The government also distributed patronage jobs to APRA's activists in the national state
structure. However, most of these activists were not patrons of territorial machines
reaching out to the poor.

[23] Personal interview with an anonymous political operator from Fujimorismo (Lima,
February 17, 2010) and Absalón Vásquez (Lima, December 12, 2012).

and Incio 2013).[24] Indeed, in contrast to what frequently occurs in other polities, municipal incumbency in Peru constitutes a *disadvantage* (rather than an advantage) when running for reelection (Córdova and Incio 2013). By contrast, for instance, since Argentina's democratization in 1983, the Peronist Party (*Partido Justicialista*, or PJ) – a well-known partisan machine – has won 207 out of 247 (84 percent) mayoral elections in its stronghold, the Conurbano Bonaerense, and currently governs thirty of its thirty-three municipalities (Zarazaga 2014).

What tends to be observed in Peru at the subnational level is quite different. First, clientelistic networks are not as extensive as implied by the machine model. Subnational clientelistic networks in the country have limited territorial reach. Most incumbents at this level distribute patronage jobs only to restricted cliques of close collaborators; for instance, one experienced political operator states that in general terms, very few local brokers manage to get a job in the municipality after campaigns.[25] Nepotism – elected officials hiring their family members – is, in contrast, much more common. Given that the law penalizes nepotism, in some places politicians have even come up with exchange systems: one mayor hires another mayor's parents and vice versa.[26] As economic technocrat Fritz Du Bois explains, the "coalition of opportunists" that governs is usually a small "coalition of close friends and relatives."[27] Moreover, even when patronage jobs go to political activists who helped candidates campaign, these beneficiaries do not regularly build their own clientelistic followings at the local level. Thus, as we will now see, local brokers are subject to criticism when they get a job in the municipality.

In Peru, leaders of local associations, known as *dirigentes sociales*, are what the literature would consider local-level brokers (Tanaka 1999; Ansión *et al.* 2000). In contrast to what can be seen in countries with consolidated clientelistic machines, where local brokers are appointed by politicians rather than elected by the people, *dirigentes* are elected community leaders. Their role as mediators with the state is, thus, vested by the people and not by political officials. This means that *dirigentes* are primarily accountable

---

[24] This reelection rate decreased in the 2014 elections in which only 17 percent of incumbent district mayors and 10 percent of incumbent province mayors secured reelection (Aragón and Incio 2014).

[25] Personal interview with Wilfredo Verano, political operator (Santiago, Cusco, September 7, 2010).

[26] Personal interview with Víctor Salcedo, journalist, newspaper La República Gran Sur, newspaper (Cusco, September 1, 2010).

[27] Personal interview (August 13, 2009).

to their association members and not to a political boss. Indeed, despite being elected, they tend to come in for considerable criticism from their bases (Ansión *et al.* 2000); usually, if they accept a public job in the municipality or regional government, they are expected to quit their position as *dirigente*[28] or else they are accused of taking advantage of their association and pressed to resign. As one *dirigente* from Cusco puts it:

The *dirigente* who gets a job in the municipality discredits himself with the people because local authorities do not allow them to be autonomous ... When the *dirigente* colludes with the mayor, he surrenders his power and people get angry. (Ricardo Pezo, president of the *Frente de Defensa de Huancaro*, Cusco, September 2, 2010)

A political operator from the same municipality agrees with this local broker, explaining that,

There have been *dirigentes* who have used their position to get a job with the elected mayor. But they have ended up branded as traitors, as being a twisted *dirigente*. Being steadfast and consistent is important for people's opinion about *dirigentes*. In this case, the *dirigente* has utilized the organization [to get a job]. (Wilfredo Verano, Santiago, Cusco, September 7, 2010)

Moreover, *dirigentes* are not professional politicians in the sense that they do not make a living from politics. *Dirigentes* usually have a nonpolitical occupation and carry out their brokering duties in their free time. Some are employed formally (as construction workers or teachers, to name but two known examples), but many others work independently (as street sellers or self-employed bus drivers, for example). Some *dirigentes* are hired by local authorities to work for the incumbent's campaign, but usually begin no earlier than just a few months before the campaign begins.[29] Many more receive a "tip" for allowing candidates to campaign in their neighborhoods, and for helping them organize campaign events.[30] One former councilor was critical, "*Dirigentes* sell themselves to the highest

---

[28] Many of the *dirigentes* interviewed pointed this out.

[29] Personal interview with Marco Antonio Huamán, President of the Frente de Defensa de los Intereses de la Zona Noreste de Cusco (Cusco, September 7, 2010); Carlos Moscoso, candidate running for mayor of Cusco city (Cusco, December 18, 2010); Elizabeth Rodríguez, political operator (Piura, July 24, 2010).

[30] Personal interview with Edmundo Gatica, Fujimorismo political operator (Cusco, September 6, 2010); Rolando Rozas, political operator, Partido Nacionalista (Cusco, September 3, 2010); Víctor Villa, political operator (August 31, 2010); Elizabeth Rodríguez, political operator (Piura, July 6, 2011); Rodrigo Urbina, political operator (Piura, July 8, 2011).

bidder. They rent themselves out. They are mercenaries."[31] Thus, although *dirigentes*' busiest time is during campaign season, their role as activists is mostly *temporary*.

There is another important characteristic distinguishing *dirigentes* from machine-affiliated brokers: *dirigentes* perform brokering functions, but they are not local patrons. *Dirigentes* mobilize their external contacts, in order to attract collective benefits for their communities or organizations; in particular, this form of brokering public works helps *dirigentes* build a reputation and legitimize themselves in the eyes of their bases (Ansión *et al.* 2000: 14). However, most *dirigentes* have no ready access to a source of private benefits they can distribute regularly to their association members in exchange for political support. The only exception may be those *dirigentes* who administer the *Vaso de Leche* program at the neighborhood level,[32] since this program provides milk or other food products that the *dirigentes* distribute to the registered beneficiaries for free on a daily basis.[33]

Besides this system of *dirigentes*, Peru's local-level politics are set apart from consolidated machines by the lack of institutionalization of political networks, even when they are organized and extend deep into the grassroots. As we have noted, *dirigentes* do not have stable partisan affiliations and are free to switch allegiances from campaign to campaign – and sometimes even within the same campaign. Indeed, as we will discuss further in Chapter 4, *dirigentes* often cheat political brokers and politicians during campaigns by working for more than one at the same time. Indeed, it is not for nothing that Peruvian politicians complain so much about *dirigentes*. For instance, former congresswoman Carmen Losada (*Fujimorismo*) denounces most of them as *"pseudo-dirigentes"* who believe that they are representative when in fact they are not, in her view, most *dirigentes* "sell themselves" and "prostitute politics." She adds, "They fill their headquarters with pictures. But the next day or in two hours they post the pictures of another candidate."[34]

---

[31] Personal interview with Julio Gutiérrez, former councilor for Santiago district, Cusco, May 24, 2010.

[32] Vaso de Leche is a nutritional assistance program aimed at pregnant and lactating mothers and children up to six years old. It is funded by the national government and administered by municipalities. See Suárez Bustamante (2003), Alcázar *et al.* (2003), Alcázar (2007).

[33] Despite the potential clientelistic character of this program, Vaso de Leche beneficiaries are not necessarily vote-selling clients, a point that will be further demonstrated and explained in the next section.

[34] Personal interview with Carmen Losada (Lima, April 8, 2010).

In summary, Peru lacks not only organized parties, but also consolidated machines. With the partial exception of APRA, candidates switch electoral affiliations often or form their own personalistic vehicles, in order to compete in elections. These politicians do not form lasting links with local brokers and look to them only when campaigning. Moreover, while governing, most incumbents do not build lasting clientelistic networks using public resources. In such a fluid political context, what type of distributive electoral strategies do politicians use? In the following section I address this central question.

POLITICIANS' DISTRIBUTIVE STRATEGIES

When you act without thinking about the future, it doesn't work. (Adolfo Mamani, political operator, Cusco, August 31, 2010)[35]

So far I have emphasized the fluidity of Peruvian politics and the lack of organized machines. In this section, I will explain how the lack of enduring organizations affects politicians' distributive strategies.[36] If electoral clientelism is a political strategy used heavily in campaigns, how do politicians govern once they are elected in regional and local positions? As we have seen, machine clientelism is not the norm in Peru, since politicians do not usually establish linkages of clientelistic accountability (Kitschelt 2000; Auyero 2001; Díaz-Cayeros *et al.* 2007). Although most incumbents do not routinely invest in delivering clientelistic goods and services outside election periods, they start doing so when a campaign approaches. And once elected, politicians tend to "forget" their voters again. As one citizen puts it:

Politicians only give stuff away during campaigns. Only during campaigns, every week or each time they go out. (Female focus group, Sucsu Auccayle Community, Cusco)

Challengers as well as incumbents start distributing gifts to the poor as soon as the campaign approaches. But such sporadic investments in selective inducements make politicians look very opportunistic. As several poor citizens point out, politicians "remember" the needy only when an election approaches, leading to their popular characterization as "migratory birds."[37] The following excerpts from focus group discussions illustrate this point well:

---

[35] "Cuando no actúas pensando en el futuro, no funciona."
[36] This section draws heavily from Muñoz (2016).
[37] *Aves de paso.*

P1:	Politicians give us T-shirts, cups, to campaign for them and once they get elected they forget us ...
P2:	In my opinion, all politicians are liars. They never accomplish what they promise ... What we have achieved we have achieved by protesting. (Female focus group, Females Los Polvorines settlement, Piura)
INTERVIEWER:	You told me that politicians give away gifts during campaigns. Once they get elected, do they remember you? Do they continue supporting you?
EVERYBODY:	No! [Laughter]
PARTICIPANT 1:	He does not remember us anymore ...
PARTICIPANT 2:	They forget us [More laughter]
INTERVIEWER:	Do they continue bringing presents?
EVERYBODY:	No!
PARTICIPANT 3:	They forget everything. Once the campaign is over, everything is over, forgotten ...
PARTICIPANT 4:	If a congressman comes to visit, he no longer recognizes you. On the contrary, he expects you to greet him. He barely looks at you. They are already earning money in Congress. At the municipality they are sitting, safely earning money for four years. (Male focus group, Occoruro community, Cusco)

In general, Peruvian politicians do not invest in party building – either programmatic or clientelistic – and when they do, their prospects of success are limited (Levitsky and Zavaleta 2016; Muñoz and Dargent 2016). There is a system equilibrium that reinforces politics without organized parties; the structure of political competition without stable partisan affiliations and organized parties has given rise to widely dispersed informal institutions and, consequently, has made the collapse of the party system self-reinforcing (Levitsky and Zavaleta 2016). Indeed, most politicians believe with some justification that they can succeed electorally without established parties. And since this is true of most who are elected, once in power they do not deem it necessary to invest in organization building, whether programmatic or clientelistic.

Moreover, although less risky in electoral terms (Díaz-Cayeros *et al.* 2016), relational clientelism is more expensive in relation to other distributive strategies available such as the delivery of pork-barrel works. Indeed, a clientelistic machine is a comparatively expensive form of political organization (Kitschelt and Wilkinson 2007: 9). Relational clientelism is costly in terms of both monetary and organizational resources. On the one hand, long-lasting clientelistic relations involve the continual delivery of private benefits over extended periods. On the other hand, they also require the bankrolling of a network of brokers who can target clients, distribute these goods, and constantly mobilize political support. And the relative autonomy of brokers adds problems related to commitment similar to those already pervasive in the case of voters (Stokes *et al.* 2013; Swcarberg 2016). Thus, the typical view among politicians in Peru is: why invest in a costly strategy such as clientelistic network-building when they were elected without any such organizational structure in place, and could theoretically repeat the same electoral strategy again?

But what do politicians do when they access office? Instead of building lasting clientelistic networks, the majority of elected politicians prefer to allocate public resources to pork-barrel projects – that is, to the delivery of "local public goods" to crucial constituencies (Magaloni 2006; Hawkins and Rosas 2006; Díaz-Cayeros *et al.* 2016). They do so because, first, as aptly suggested by Samuels (2002), politicians trade pork for money. By investing in pork, incumbents are paying back campaign contributions and signaling to the business community that they are willing to continue to do so in the future. As noted by various interviewees, elected authorities "compensate" their generous donors with public contracts once in office.

Given Peru's low rates of reelection and the widespread pattern of incumbency disadvantage (Córdova and Incio 2013), a high percentage of incumbent candidates regularly finance their campaigns entirely through private means. In fact, although incumbents also make use of public resources to invest in electoral clientelism, the private sponsorship of electoral clientelism in Peru is increasingly important.[38] Hence, the pork barrel is appealing because it helps politicians raise funds from private interests to fund campaign clientelism, among other things.

Second, and related to the previous point, pork-barrel politics is also appealing to incumbents because it allows them to engage in corruption and, thus, extract and appropriate public resources. Indeed, the distribution of local public works, is the perfect complement to corruption. Public works provide incumbents with several opportunities for extracting resources, both during the bidding and the construction stages. During the

---

[38] As pointed out, in post-Fujimori Peru it has become difficult to divert public resources openly, since media attention and central government controls make it harder to abuse incumbency resource advantages. Obviously, incumbents still engage in this practice, but are much more cautious than before and it is easier to divert public resources to finance campaign clientelism, for example, in rural areas with limited media access.

former stage, incumbents offer to grant firms public contracts in exchange for kickbacks. Similarly, during the latter stage, overvaluation of construction materials and other budgetary manipulations in government direct investments can provide incumbents with additional sources of income. As one very experienced political operator from Cusco explains,

The mayor makes a deal with a milling company ... Millers, businesses, office supply stores, and councilors finance campaigns ... All local authorities make secret deals.[39] Hardware retailers, for example, give up to 20% to the mayor. In the case of *Vaso de Leche* suppliers, they give 10%. The mayor also gets tons of money from construction projects. That is why everybody "plants cement;" they build cement works because this is where they get the money from. (Alfredo Mamani, Cusco, August 31, 2010)

In fact, in a context such as Peru in which politics is highly discredited and resources are abundant – due to the fiscal boom – politics is frequently seen as a quick way of making money and establishing business connections. Moreover, Peru's fluid organizational context and the dearth of lasting political parties has shortened politicians' time horizons, rendering them extremely short-sighted and opportunistic (Levitsky 2013). Whereas institutionalized parties, as collective organizations, constrain individual politicians' self-interest and enlarge their time horizons – parties must serve the needs of their different members across districts and electoral cycles[40] – personalistic vehicles are created to pursue individual goals in the short term. Consequently, they spur individualism and undermine coordination around strategies focused on collective or future benefits (Levitsky 2013: 22).

Since the odds are generally against political survival in Peru, the short-term maximization of personal wealth becomes an important motivation for entering electoral politics.[41] Incumbents with very low prospects of reelection are often tempted to "get what they can" during their period in office (Levitsky 2013: 26). A widespread view is that politicians "think about serving themselves rather than serving the people."[42] As a former

---

[39] *Tratos por lo bajo.*

[40] In a study on the political ambitions of legislators in Latin America, Vera finds that party institutionalization is in fact directly associated with reelection ambitions: "Independent of the attractiveness of office and the odds of winning, old parties are better at motivating incumbents to seek reelection" (Vera 2014: 23).

[41] All politicians interviewed agree that this trend is increasing, although most state that it does not apply to them.

[42] Personal interview with Rosario Peralta, *Partido Humanista Peruana* activist (Cusco, May 17, 2010).

mayor of the province of Anta (Cusco) notes, "[When they gain office] politicians think they have won the lottery. It's an opportunity to seize the booty."[43]

The majority of politicians who gain executive office divert public resources to enrich themselves rather than reinvesting these funds in party building. In this context of weakly institutionalized parties, with an open-list electoral system in the national legislature, we would certainly expect to find less party-based corruption (oriented toward political advancement) than personal corruption (oriented toward personal enrichment or of a small group) (Gingerich 2013). One former APRA activist, involved in organizing a regional movement composed of *dirigentes* in Cusco, complains that "after attaining power, politicians steal and forget to build organizations. They have money but no organization. Power is disarticulated."[44] An experienced political operator adds, "Politicians are not interested [in building organizations]. They just want to spend some time [in office]. They will be in office for only four years."[45]

The existence of the informal institution of *diezmo* reveals the widespread practice of corruption in Peru. The term *diezmo* was originally used to refer to a mandatory tax (10 percent) collected by the Catholic Church in Spanish colonies. Currently, it is used colloquially to refer to a specific type of graft: a 10 percent commission, a contractor pays to a politician or functionary after gaining a public contract. The practice of *diezmo* is ubiquitous, particularly at the subnational level,[46] and all politicians interviewed for this study attested to this.

Corruption remains pervasive in Peru.[47] However, instead of being managed from the apex of power, as was the case during the 1990s,

---

[43] Personal interview with Wilber Rozas (Cusco, May 24, 2010).

[44] Personal interview with Víctor Villa (Cusco, May 25, 2010).

[45] Personal interview with Adolfo Mamani (Cusco, August 31, 2010).

[46] During the last decade, the budgets of regional and municipal governments have increased considerably (Pro Descentralización 2006; Grupo Propuesta Ciudadana 2007; Arellano 2008; Asamblea Nacional de Gobiernos Regionales 2012). This monetary expansion is driven for the most part by an exponential increase in mining revenues accruing from the mineral price boom. This flow of resources to subnational governments has been so vast that it has prompted some scholars to warn about the economic and political consequences of the emerging "subnational resource curse" (Arellano 2008).

[47] Unsurprisingly, Peru has been heavily impacted by the fallout from the Odebrecht corruption scandal, with one former president remanded in custody, one with an extradition order against him, and another under investigation. Meanwhile, Peru's sitting president has also been accused of undue dealings with Odebrecht while previously serving as finance minister, and the main opposition leader has also been accused of receiving undeclared campaign donations from this firm.

corruption is now diffused throughout the different levels of the state apparatus, including subnational governments (Tanaka 2005b, 2005c; Muñoz *et al.* 2016). In a press conference in 2014, the anti-corruption attorney reported that 92 percent of the 1,841 mayors nationwide were under investigation for alleged acts of corruption, including embezzlement, misappropriation of funds, abuse of office,[48] and collusion.[49] In addition, 429 former provincial mayors and 1,326 former district mayors were under investigation for crimes of the same type. He further stressed that the state was suffering "incalculable" economic losses due to the recurring allocation of multi-million works to companies chosen on the basis of *diezmo* payments.[50]

Another appeal of the pork barrel in the Peruvian context is that it allows politicians to build legitimacy on the basis of performance. By distributing small projects to certain neighborhoods, communities or associations, politicians hope to generate gratitude that translates into electoral support in the next electoral cycle. Thus, they can deliver their campaign promises by distributing something visible, memorable, and easy to evaluate retrospectively.

However, distributing pork to territorial constituencies may not be enough to secure reelection.[51] There is an electoral trade-off between spending public resources on distributive politics or extracting it through corruption. Corruption should not spiral out of control or be so blatant as to damage the incumbent's reelection prospects.[52] A good "balance" between public works and corruption can help incumbents build a reputation based on their performance in office. Just like corrupt incumbents who consistently deliver to their clientelistic networks (Manzetti

---

[48] Known in Spanish law as *negociaciones incompatibles*.

[49] *Radio Programas del Perú* (July 16, 2014), "*Procuraduría: 92% de alcaldes del Perú son investigados por corrupción*". Available at: http://rpp.pe/politica/actualidad/procuraduria-92-de-alcaldes-del-peru-son-investigados-por-corrupcion-noticia-708399.

[50] *Radio Programas del Perú* (July 16, 2014), "*Procuraduría: 92% de alcaldes del Perú son investigados por corrupción*". Available at: http://rpp.pe/politica/actualidad/procuraduria-92-de-alcaldes-del-peru-son-investigados-por-corrupcion-noticia-708399.

[51] As Weaver's (2017a, 2017b) ongoing research shows, good performance in office and the delivery of local public goods seems to be insufficient to guarantee the reelection of Peruvian municipal incumbents.

[52] This trade-off also manifests itself in a context of organized clientelism. If a machine fosters corruption, it has to do so carefully in order to continue maximizing electoral returns (Scott 1969: 1144). As Scott puts it, "Whereas non-machine corruption often has a random and sporadic character or aims only at the consolidation of narrow elites who control wealth or armed forces, the machine must remain popular to survive and must consequently meet the demands of a broad stratum" (Scott 1969: 1154).

and Wilson 2007), an incumbent who is effective in delivering public works demanded by the population, can become popular even if they are suspected of engaging in corrupt acts. The popular saying *roba pero hace obra* ("he steals but gets things done") encapsulates this trade-off well. This mentality is also exemplified by Luis Cáceres Velásquez, a former congressman and mayor of Juliaca (Puno) and of Arequipa, who readily admitted in an interview that he earned commissions from public works while governing, on the grounds that this practice is "normal" in Peru. "Who does not steal in this life? ... They used to say, 'He steals but delivers' and that filled me with fondness. You have to steal with decency."[53]

Unlike the now-retired Cáceres, many of the short-sighted politicians of today no longer seem to honor this electoral trade-off. Indeed, several incumbents prove incapable of delivering projects in good shape, and corruption spirals out of control to the point of affecting public works. Thus, *public works* are either never finished, even when "on paper" they are recorded as having been delivered to their beneficiaries, or, alternatively, they are delivered in substandard conditions because too many resources are diverted through the corruption chain. The widespread perception of the proliferation of corruption (Carrión *et al.* 2015) may be partly related to this, in that voters can often see with their own eyes how public resources are squandered in unfinished or defective projects.

Whether or not an incumbent's competence, or lack thereof, in providing goods can influence the effectiveness of electoral accountability for corruption is, however, still open to debate. Indeed, while some authors in the experimental literature find that voters penalize corrupt politicians and that the notion of *"roba pero hace obra"* is a myth (Winters and Weitz-Shapiro 2013), others argue that voters ignore corruption when there are side benefits to it (Fernández-Vásquez *et al.* 2016). Fortunately, survey experimental research conducted by Vera (2017) in Peru yields mixed and interesting results. Although voters punish corruption electorally regardless of the competence of the candidate and the prevalence of corruption in the environment, their sanctions are less severe for those politicians who deliver more public works to their district. The cost of punishing corruption is higher under the condition of high goods provision, she argues, because voters prefer not to run the risk of getting an incompetent leader in place of one who "steals but gets things done."

[53] In Spanish: *"¿Quién no roba en esta vida? ... A mí me decían 'Roba pero hace' y a mí eso me llenaba de cariño. Hay que robar con decencia." La República-Gran Sur* (January 31, 2010).

When corrupt practices spiral out of control, as has often seemed to be the case in Peru during the last few years, the potential electoral pay-off of delivering public goods can diminish, and so too can the welfare benefits that may associated with them – especially when compared to clientelistic transfers (Díaz-Cayeros *et al.* 2016). Besides the multi-million economic losses to the state that corruption causes, unfinished or defective works can harm citizens' opportunities and even result in losses of life. Take for example the case of the defective sewage system built in the city of Iquitos (Loreto) during Governor Iván Vásquez's tenure. The project's initial budget was 460 million soles, but it ended up costing 734 million soles and indebting fifty-one district municipalities, seven provincial municipalities, one university, and one development institute that had co-subsidized the project, under the charge of the regional government (Melgar 2017). Besides this tremendous waste of public resources, the sewage system as delivered is so deficient that Iquitos gets flooded with wastewater each time it rains heavily, something that happens not infrequently in this Amazonian city.[54] The economic losses stemming from this malfunctioning public work, besides the public health problems it will cause or aggravate, are difficult to imagine.

Of course, widespread subnational corruption further discredits politics and politicians and affects their reelection prospects. In an original household survey conducted by Weaver (2017a), with 1,061 respondents across eighteen urban, peri-urban, and rural municipalities in the region of Cusco, a large majority (68.71 percent), disagreed that mayors should be entitled to run for reelection. Weaver also asked the following question: "Imagine that a mayor in this municipality did a really great job in his/her first term in office, then he/she is re-elected. How likely is it that he/she will do a good job in his/her second period?." Interviewees were subsequently asked why they rated the prospect as likely or unlikely. Among those who answered Unlikely/Very unlikely,[55] "the top reason (53.4 percent) was that '[mayors] learn how to be corrupt in the first period, so they are more corrupt in the second'" (Weaver 2017a: 27).

---

[54] Útero.pe (July 7, 2014), "*¡Inundados! Iquitos y el caótico alcantarillado*". Available at: http://iqt.utero.pe/2014/07/07/inundados-iquitos-y-el-caotico-alcantarillado/. El Comercio (November 10, 2015), "*Iquitos: alcantarillado y planta de tratamiento funcionan mal*". Available at: https://elcomercio.pe/peru/loreto/iquitos-alcantarillado-planta-tratamiento-funcionan-mal-240817.

[55] Only 40.5 percent of her sample responded "Very likely" or "Likely." In turn, 22.9 percent answered "It depends," and 35 percent said it was "Very unlikely" or "Unlikely."

Thus, short-term politicians who invest mostly in campaign clientelism, pork barreling, and resource extraction through corruption may foster a vicious electoral circle (Muñoz 2016). The prominently negative perceptions about reelection found by Weaver, may unintendedly encourage corrupt behavior by undermining mayors' electoral incentives to perform well while in office and contribute to the extension of a municipal electoral disconnection (Weaver 2017a, 2017b).

One last point on this matter is worth stressing: the prevalent combination of campaign clientelism, pork barreling, and corruption should be clearly distinguished from the clientelistic machine model.[56] The reproduction of corruption and pork barreling does not require organizational infrastructure on the same scale that relational clientelism does; and nor does campaign clientelism. Hence, despite the lack of organized machines, short-term clientelistic investments during campaigns are widespread. During the last subnational and national elections, for instance, journalists in different parts of the country highlighted how candidates were actively distributing bags of food, mugs, pans and other kitchen supplies, natural gas containers, construction materials, and even cash to voters.[57] Empirical evidence beyond this study confirms that the distribution of material benefits during campaigns is "normal politics" in Peru. Estimates from a survey list experiment conducted after the 2010 local elections indicate that around 12.8 percent of voters were offered a benefit for their vote during the 2010 subnational campaign (González-Ocantos *et al.* 2013). Conventional national survey studies back this up, indicating that around 12 percent of Peruvian voters are regularly offered goods during campaigns in exchange for electoral support (Table 3.2).

In short, Peruvian politicians distribute gifts while campaigning despite the absence of established political organizations. This goes against the conventional wisdom; traditional approaches would not expect to find clientelistic distribution without extensive and relatively stable networks of brokers. So, *how* do Peruvian politicians manage to distribute material benefits? Can politicians, for example, rely on existing local brokers to *select* voters who will be more responsive to accomplishing clientelistic bargains? Alternatively, despite the fluidity of this political system, can

[56] Public works can provide the incumbent with patronage in the form of jobs to distribute. However, public works alone cannot sustain an extensive machine in the long term, due to the transitory character of the jobs they create.

[57] For example, "*Candidato APP a región Ayacucho hace su campaña regalando dinero*" in La República, May 31, 2010; "*Keiko Fujimori reparte comida entre los pobres a cambio de votos*" in www.elmundo.es/america/2011/05/06/noticias/1304691775.html.

TABLE 3.2. *Clientelistic offers during electoral campaigns*

Survey	Response	Number of responses	Percent of total
LAPOP (2010)[a]	Often	44	2.99
	Sometimes	131	8.91
	Never	1,295	88.1
	Total	1,470	100
IOP-PUCP (2011)[b]	Many times	47	3.34
	Few times	123	8.74
	Never	1,237	87.92
	Total	1,407	100

[a]In recent years and thinking about election campaigns, has a candidate or someone from a political party offered you something like a favor, food, or any other benefit or thing in exchange of your vote or support?
[b]During the last campaign, has a candidate or someone from a political party offered you something like a favor, food, or any other benefit or thing in return for your vote or support?
Source: LAPOP (2010) and IOP-PUCP (2011)

candidates rely on local brokers to *monitor* voters' electoral choices? The next section addresses these questions.

TESTING CONVENTIONAL APPROACHES

Given the sporadic character of distribution in Peru, it is unlikely that perspectives emphasizing *prospective* orientations can account for electoral clientelism.[58] These perspectives take citizens' commitment to the vote-buying deal as a given, as long as the party continues delivering benefits. That is, they focus on conditional loyalty: without regular and consistent distribution, poor citizens have no reasons to continue supporting the party. Moreover, as I will explain further in Chapter 5, politicians' promises of future support lack credibility, and poor voters are highly distrusting of them. Thus, only a very small cliques of candidates' close friends and extended family can be expected to act according to prospective orientations.

But what about the other approaches? Can they account for the way in which electoral clientelism is employed during campaigns in Peru?

---

[58] This section draws heavily on Muñoz (2014).

It is certainly possible that politicians have found some sort of system that allows them to gather relevant information at the local level, or to closely follow their clients' behavior. In this section, I provide evidence to explore these possibilities, before discarding the conventional wisdom as an explanation for what is observed in Peru.

Then, how does clientelistic distribution take place in Peru? Are empirical observations about the way goods are distributed consistent with the conventional wisdom to any extent? First, against standard expectations, monitoring vote choices in Peru is in most cases impossible (Muñoz 2014). To begin with, the secrecy of the vote makes it difficult to monitor individual vote choices. Candidates, political operators, and local brokers all agree on this point. For instance, one candidate explains this conundrum as follows:

The *dirigente* is the nexus between the state and the people. *Dirigentes* paint propaganda in the neighborhood. They motivate, persuade voters, and are in charge of the logistics. They open the doors to the candidates, so we can campaign ... They set the scene for you. But they cannot guarantee the vote. (Sergio Sullca, candidate for mayor, Santiago, Cusco. May 25, 2010)

Similarly, an APRA activist and local broker concedes that she does not know who most people voted for in her neighborhood. "The vote is secret," she explains.[59]

More importantly, the secret ballot means that poor citizens do not fear any reprisals from politicians. For example, these focus group participants made it clear that they have no concerns about politicians finding out their vote choices:

PARTICIPANT 1:	If I have decided to accept the gift, he [the candidate] is not going to see my vote.
PARTICIPANT 2:	Because it is already a gift, it's done. He comes and says 'Here is a little gift but give me your vote ...' 'Alright,' we say. But as he [another participant] says, it is a personal decision.
INTERVIEWER:	Nobody can tell who you vote for?
ALL:	No! Nobody!
PARTICIPANT 2:	I can say I am going to vote for you but at the end only I know who I'm voting for. (Female focus group, El Indio settlement, Piura)

[59] Personal interview with Francisca Chasquero, general secretary, Base Ciudad del Niño, Castilla. Piura, November 25, 2010.

TABLE 3.3. *Attitudes toward vote buying by belief in the secrecy of the vote*

What would you do if a candidate offered you a benefit in exchange for your vote?	Do you believe that politicians violate the secrete vote?	
	Yes	No
Honor it	12.37% (81)	16.22% (170)
Renegez	16.49% (108)	15.17% (159)
Reject the offer	65.04% (426)	64.22% (673)
Don't know	4.39% (46)	6.11% (46)
Total	100% (655)	100% (1048)

Pearson chi^2(3) = 6.9066; Pr = 0.075.
Source: Ipsos APOYO/JNE (2010)

Survey analysis confirms the limitations of applying conventional monitoring/vote-buying approaches to the Peruvian case. As Table 3.3 indicates, there is no significant statistical association between the belief that politicians can violate the secret vote and how citizens would react if offered a vote-buying deal.[60]

Moreover, as can be seen in Table 3.4, voters who are threatened by politicians are no more likely to honor the vote-buying deal. On the contrary, such voters are actually significantly more likely to renege on the vote-buying deal (that is, take the benefit and vote for another candidate of their choice).

Monitoring individual behavior in general is difficult in Peru, given that in many cases politicians and operators do not know the clients. In fact, 48 percent of respondents who reported having been offered a clientelistic deal during the 2010 and 2011 campaigns specified that it was the first time they had seen the person who offered them the benefit.[61] In some cases, however, politicians do know the clients and have some leverage over them. Incumbents, for example, sometimes ask the beneficiaries of social programs to support them and threaten to take away their social benefits if they do not. This often occurs for example, with poor women enrolled on the *Vaso de Leche* program. Nonetheless, interviews and focus groups show that even in these cases, citizens turn out

[60] Regression analyses not reported confirm these bivariate findings.
[61] IOP 2011.

TABLE 3.4. *Attitudes toward vote buying by experience of threat*

What would you do if a candidate offered you a benefit in exchange for your vote?	Respondent threatened by a politician	
	Yes	No
Honor	15.38% (20)	12.05% (161)
Renege	41.54% (54)	22.16% (296)
Reject the offer	38.46% (50)	61.53% (822)
Don't know	4.62% (6)	4.27% (57)
Total	100% (130)	100% (1336)

Pearson chi^2(3) = 30.34; Pr = 0.00.
Source: IOP (2011)

at campaign events but vote for their preferred candidate anyway given their confidence that the vote is secret. According to one regional movement activist in Piura:

Mónica [the mayor] went to the local *Vaso de Leche* committee to demand support; if [she didn't get support], she threatened to take away the milk ... She confused people; people felt under pressure. They said that they were going to Mónica's rallies but that they would vote for [another candidate]. (Nancy Tinoco, El Algarrobo settlement, Piura, November 23, 2010)

Politicians not only lack the strong organizational resources required for monitoring individuals, but they are also unable to monitor how groups vote. Because voting precincts are not organized territorially, disaggregated electoral results are not available for politicians to examine (Chandra 2004; Kitschelt and Wilkinson 2007; Scheiner 2007). Within each electoral district in Peru, the distribution of voters into polling precincts is organized according to the date each individual's identity card was issued or renewed. For this reason, voters living within the same house usually end up voting at different polling stations (usually schools) and within them, in different booths. This makes it impossible to know how different neighborhoods or communities voted within a district, and thus, to engage in group monitoring. As APRA's secretary of organization in Piura affirms, "to get the vote tally by neighborhood is impossible." Or, in the words of a local broker:

It is not possible to know for sure how people vote in the neighborhood. Many residents have come from somewhere else, they have changed their address. There is only one school in the southern zone of the city [where his shanty town is located], but many neighbors vote in other schools. They are dispersed. (Joel Pulache, APRA general secretary at Antonio Raymondi settlement. Piura, October 2, 2010)

In other words, financial inducements and threats are effective as a *campaigning* tool (to assure participation at campaign activities) but they are not so effective at changing vote preferences at the polls.

Second, the timing of goods distribution during campaigns does not match standard expectations. As noted in Chapter 2, the conventional wisdom assumes that the main clientelistic strategies associated with the distribution of material goods during elections are vote-buying deals, turnout buying, or abstention buying (Brusco *et al.* 2004; Stokes 2005; Cox 2007; Stokes 2007a; Schaffer 2007; Nichter 2008, 2010; Gans-Morse *et al.* 2014). Moreover, as noted by Nichter, in most studies of vote buying, benefits are expected to be delivered on or just before election day (Nichter 2014: 317). Similarly, those authors emphasizing the importance of mobilization define turnout buying as a subtype of electoral clientelism taking place *on* election day (Cox 2007; Nichter 2008; Nichter 2014).

But, in actual fact, the distribution of material benefits in Peru takes place throughout the entire campaign (Muñoz 2014). Respondents in interviews and focus groups cite the importance of early distribution as part of *campaigning* efforts among poor sectors.[62] As one citizen explains during a focus group conversation,

Candidates distribute gifts during the campaign. When they start campaigning, whichever place they visit, they *have* to bring presents with them. During the whole campaign they have been giving away gifts. (Mixed-sex focus group, Compone Community, Cusco)

It is worth calling the citizen's statement quoted in the previous section, indicating that politicians distribute presents only while campaigning, almost every week, and they do not do so during nonelectoral times. Distribution is certainly stepped up as election day approaches (particularly in the last month), but it is by no means confined to this period. One former candidate running for district mayor stated that candidates give away items during the whole campaign but "three days before the election day, the madness intensifies."[63]

---

[62] Indeed, as I will explain further in Chapter 4, voters receive gifts principally while attending campaign events.

[63] Personal interview with Sergio Sullca, Santiago (Cusco, May 25, 2010).

Finally, politicians who work with local brokers are not usually very selective when it comes to distributing gifts during campaigns. Politicians do not have much reliable information about the electoral preferences of individual voters, as most of these voters switch allegiances repeatedly and only decide their vote close to election day.[64] Moreover, as I will show in Chapter 4, local brokers and poor voters are quite opportunistic during campaigns and often fool candidates and political operators. And as discussed, local brokers cannot be certain about voters' actual choices either.

Discussions held in focus groups with poor voters portray the distribution of gifts during campaigns as being very indiscriminate and improvised. Candidates and their followers regularly distribute presents to as many voters as they can, without differentiating among them. As the following citizens explain:

PARTICIPANT 1:   During the last campaign the presidential candidates brought a lot of clothes: T-shirts, underwear, even brassieres. They distributed these presents to the people, organizing them in lines. Of course, everybody in the community lined up, so both supporters and non-supporters received the gifts.

INTERVIEWER: Does the same happen in other communities?

PARTICIPANT 2:   Politicians come to our assembly and the candidates themselves distribute the gifts. But I have never seen them organize people in lines to distribute gifts, only during the assemblies. (Male focus group, rural Cusco).

One experienced electoral observer has the same impression. He notes that, "generally, politicians give away gifts by location: candidates go to a certain place and give away stuff to as many people as they can. There are no lists or an organized system."[65] Indeed, references to poor voters "piling up"[66] trying to get a gift during campaigns were quite frequent in interviews and focus groups. Thus, it seems highly unlikely that these improvisational politicians are effective at gathering precise information or in targeting particular types of voters during campaigns.

In short, conventional expectations are not met in Peru. In general, vote buying is not a viable clientelistic strategy in Peru. With few exceptions,

---

[64] For a more detailed explanation about this point, see Chapter 5.

[65] Personal interview with Juan Aguilar, *Asociación Civil Transparencia* (Piura, July 19, 2010).

[66] las personas se amontonan.

given low levels of partisan identification and scarce information about voters' preferences, turnout buying at the polls is virtually nonexistent. Moreover, because voting in Peru is mandatory and enforced, turnout buying is not even an appealing electoral strategy for politicians since politicians can assume that most citizens will vote anyway.[67] This being the case, why do politicians distribute goods so profusely in Peru? Are they irrational? Or do they know something that we, political scientists, do not? I will address these questions in Chapter 4.

CONCLUSION

In this chapter I sought, first, to clarify my dependent variable and show empirically that Peru is a case in which both political parties and machines are neither well organized nor stable. To this end, I began with a brief historical introduction about the progressive demise of relational clientelism. I showed how relational clientelism changed over time (from traditional clientelism to partisan machines to a state-based machine) to ultimately erode considerably.

Since the collapse of Fujimori's authoritarian regime, politicians have been unable to manipulate the state structure to the point where organizing clientelism is viable. Moreover, as I have demonstrated, political parties have not managed to recover since their effective demise in the 1990s. With the partial exception of APRA, political parties in Peru are ephemeral personalistic vehicles created solely for electoral purposes. Indeed, as the replication of Calvo and Murillo's method demonstrates, political networks are not articulated in a consistent way. While political cadres abound, most of them are new to politics and do not have stable political affiliations. This political fluidity is also reproduced at the local level, where most subnational incumbents likewise do not invest in building clientelistic machines. Local brokers in Peru are not, in fact, local patrons; while most *dirigentes* perform brokering functions, they are only political part-timers who do not command the allegiance of regular and long-term followers.

Having demonstrated this absence of stable political organizations, I went on to describe the strategies politicians pursue while governing. I contend that this fluid organizational context shortens politicians' time

---

[67] In 2006, Congress passed a law reducing the fine for abstention, with steeper reductions for voters registered in poorest districts. However, the new law was not publicized in the media. Consequently, knowledge about the reduction was not widespread at the time of the 2010 municipal election (León 2017).

horizons; given their short-sightedness, most Peruvian politicians prefer to engage in pork barreling when in office, instead of investing time and effort in building parties or clientelistic structures. The pork barrel is organizationally and financially less demanding than relational clientelism and is appealing for three further reasons. First, it allows incumbents to pay back campaign contributions, used to finance campaign clientelism and other electoral tactics. Second, pork provides plenty of opportunities for extracting resources for personal gain through corrupt means. And third, if combined with "reasonable" levels of corruption that do not endanger the benefits citizens get from public works, delivering projects can help politicians build legitimacy based on performance. Although voters disregard electoral sanctions for incumbents who deliver pork effectively (Vera 2017), widespread corruption seems to have a negative effect on voters' beliefs in reelection and electoral accountability (Weaver 2017a).

In this chapter I also demonstrated that, despite this fluid political context, candidates invest heavily in electoral clientelism during campaigns. After providing data about how gifts are actually distributed during campaigns, I concluded that conventional explanations cannot account for most of the electoral clientelism that takes place in Peru. First, prospective-oriented explanations are discarded because of the absence of long-lasting clientelistic relations. As shown, Peruvian politicians engage in clientelism during electoral campaigns only, and most recipients of gifts do not continue to receive benefits after the electoral process is over. Second, after showing that the distribution of goods in Peru is rather indiscriminate, I raised doubts about the capacity of politicians to make accurate estimates of voters' electoral preferences or to target the right kind of voter. Finally, I presented substantial empirical evidence to show that monitoring both individual and group electoral choices is in fact impossible in Peru. I concluded that direct clientelistic vote-getting strategies (vote buying and turnout buying at the polls) are, in fact, unviable clientelistic strategies in Peru. In the next chapters I will, in turn, empirically evaluate the ability of the informational theory to account for this theoretical puzzle.

4

Convoking Voters and Establishing Electoral Viability

Political organization in Peru is weak. With the exception of *Partido Aprista Peruano* (APRA), present-day politics is populated by coalitions of independent politicians that are formed to compete for power and dissolved after the elections are over (Zavaleta 2014). Such a situation means that Peru not only lacks organized parties, but political machines as well. This means that subnational clientelistic networks are typically not all that dense or extensive; thus, they cannot assure subnational incumbents of territorial political control. In addition, the national state apparatus can no longer be mobilized extensively for clientelistic ends, as President Fujimori did in the 1990s.

Despite these low levels of political organization, candidates actively distribute material benefits during elections. This distribution of handouts does not follow the expectations of the conventional approaches. As discussed in Chapter 3, distribution takes place from the initial stages of the campaign onward and is often not very selective. Indeed, vote buying and turnout buying do not seem viable strategies in this loosely organized context. Thus, in a setting so seemingly unpropitious, why do politicians distribute goods during campaigns? In this chapter, I address this question.

My informational theory explains electoral clientelism in Peru. Here, I provide evidence to supporting my first causal mechanism; namely, that Peruvian politicians distribute handouts in order to buy the electoral participation of poor voters as well as to access crucial constituencies. Above all, campaign clientelism allows candidates to demonstrate their electoral potential to the broader electoral audience. By mobilizing large numbers of people at campaign events and rallies, a candidate can persuade strategic donors, activists, and voters that they have a good chance of winning an election. These clientelistic strategies are especially important in Peru's political context. Short-term and improvised alliances mean that electoral politics, in this polity with low political organization, are highly uncertain. Many citizens are indifferent and do not decide their vote until close to election day. In the absence of political organization, electoral clientelism is crucial to contacting voters and establishing a candidate's electoral viability.

This chapter is organized as follows. First, I explain why electoral clientelism takes place during campaigns in Peru. I provide evidence about candidates buying *participation* and *access* to electorally decisive poor constituencies in quite a diverse variety of settings. The informal institution of the *portátil* – a group of "portable people" – is indicative of the prevalence of this type of clientelistic strategy. Second, I demonstrate that politicians distribute handouts to assure large numbers of people at rallies, as they are well aware that turnout at campaign events is crucial to influencing the public perception of their electoral viability. Third, I present the results of two survey experiments to provide evidence to support the causal mechanism associated with my theory. The first experiment demonstrates how, all other things being equal, Peruvians decide their votes by taking into account the number of people that candidates mobilize during campaigns, which shows that politicians are right to worry about turnout at rallies. In turn, the second experiment shows that information about a candidate distributing gifts while campaigning does not affect voters' perceptions of electoral viability and *negatively* influences the likelihood of voting for such a candidate, even among low-income voters. Thus, Kramon's (2017) informational theory does not find empirical support in Peru. Subsequently, I illustrate the ways in which campaign clientelism allows candidates to influence the dynamics of the race, raise campaign contributions, and bolster their electoral prospects. In the penultimate section I briefly show how media politics does not so much substitute as *amplify* the effects of street politics and mobilization. Finally, I conclude the chapter with a summary of the propositions advanced.

CAMPAIGNING WITHOUT PARTIES

Although Peruvian politicians cannot buy votes directly, they *do* distribute goods throughout the campaign. Why would they do so? My research indicates that in this context of low organization, politicians hand out benefits precisely *because* they lack established local networks. Electoral clientelism is primarily a solution for campaigning in the absence of organized parties. First, Peruvian politicians use inexpensive consumer goods to attract poor and otherwise indifferent voters to *attend* campaign events and meet the candidate. Second, politicians distribute material benefits in order to *access* crucial constituencies such as poor neighborhoods and villages. Third and most important, Peruvian politicians distribute goods to *boost turnout* at campaign events and rallies, and thus, induce strategic behavior such as strategic voting, strategic giving, and strategic withdrawals from competition by rival politicians. Donors and voters observe turnout at campaign events and use the magnitude of the turnout (or reporting about it) as a proxy for perceived electoral viability. As a result, strategic actors find candidates that invest in campaign clientelism more appealing. In summary, politicians expect a large turnout to indirectly affect electoral choices.

In a context of low party identification, politicians use campaign clientelism in order to attract the attention of poorer and indifferent voters and expose them to the candidates. And politicians hand out goods at campaign activities because otherwise few people will attend. According to IOP's 2012 nationally representative survey, during the 2010 and 2011 election processes, 35 percent of Peruvians attended campaign events in which politicians distributed gifts to participants. Tables respondents' list of priorities when and 4.2 provide interesting information about predisposition by class toward attending rallies where gifts are distributed. Although the small sample sizes mean that no firm conclusions should be made about whether socioeconomic classes C and D/E behave differently, the results do show that poorer and middle-income respondents attended more events of this nature than wealthier ones (Table 4.1). In addition, as Table 4.2 indicates, relatively more poor voters answered that they attended these events just to receive the gifts being distributed. In turn, middle class and poorer voters responded in similar proportions that they attended both to receive the gifts being distributed *and* to listen to the candidate's proposals.

It is likely that these responses are negatively affected by desirability bias, which would lead some respondents – in particular, poor voters who are usually criticized for their willingness to receive handouts – not to disclose that they are motivated to attend this type of campaign event in order to receive goods. In any case, in this sample, receiving material incentives in exchange for electoral participation seems to be important to survey respondents in the middle and, particularly, the lower categories of the Socioeconomic status (SES).

TABLE 4.1. *Campaign clientelism by respondent's SES*

As part of their campaigns, some candidates distribute gifts to participants at their campaign events, such as food, drinks, and T-shirts, as well as raffle and bingo prizes. During the last municipal and presidential campaigns, did you attend a campaign event, such as a rally or a candidate visit to your neighborhood, at which politicians distributed this type of gifts?

	A/B	C	D/E	Total
Yes	26.85%	36.26%	37.78%	34.97%
	(69)	(132)	(218)	(419)
No	73.15%	63.74%	62.22%	65.03%
	(188)	(232)	(359)	(779)
Total	100%	100%	100%	100%
	(257)	(364)	(577)	(1198)

Pearson chi^2(2) = 9.7276; Pr = 0.008.
The socioeconomic stratum indicator in Peru distinguishes among five groups, ranging from richest (A) to poorest (E).
Source: IOP (2012)

TABLE 4.2. *Reasons for attendance by SES*

For participants only: Why did you attend these campaign events? (percentage)

	A/B	C	D/E	Total
To receive what was being distributed	1.95%	3.29%	6.37%	4.49%
	(5)	(12)	(37)	(54)
To receive what was being distributed and listen to the candidate's proposals	6.23%	10.96%	8.95%	8.98%
	(16)	(40)	(52)	(108)
Others[a]	91.83%	85.75%	84.68%	86.53%
	(263)	(313)	(492)	(1041)
Total	100	100	100	100
	(257)	(365)	(581)	(1203)

Pearson chi^2(4) = 14.3020; Pr = 0.006.
[a]Others include: "To get to know the candidate and their proposals" and "To show my support for that candidate."

Qualitative evidence gathered through interviews with politicians, brokers, and focus groups with citizens, confirms that low-income voters are a category that politicians frequently target through campaign clientelism while electioneering. As one focus group participant in Piura explained, providing goods in exchange for poor voters' participation at rallies makes sense because most of them are uninterested in politics and would not attend and listen to the candidates otherwise:

When you ask if the politician distributes goods in order to attract people or to assure votes, [it's] definitely not to assure a vote. What happens is that bringing these [gifts] is the best option a candidate has, because this is the communication between the politician and the people. The politician wants to make sure that the people listen to his message or project ... He could do it in the media but not everybody listens. (Male focus group, Males, Los Polvorines settlement, Piura)

Similarly, another participant in the Piura focus group acknowledged:

It is not a good way to campaign ... But, what would have happened if you did not bring your sodas? [Everybody laughs] See, even you think in the same way, you realize ... [More laughter] Because a full belly makes a happy heart.[1] If you come to present a project here, nobody goes ... And those who attend [would think] 'I have already heard that ...' and they go away. If you order more sandwiches and drinks, we can continue discussing [Laughter]. (Male focus group, Los Polvorines settlement, Piura)

Second, candidates distribute private goods as a sort of condition of *access* to regular meetings of local associations (such as *campesino* communities, shanty towns, soup kitchen organizations, etc.) as a means of introducing themselves, talking to the participants, and trying to win their support.[2] As Washington Román, a union leader, journalist, and former candidate for Cusco's regional presidency, points out, "Today people ask you 'What have you brought us?' If you haven't brought anything, they do not listen to you."[3] Providing these goods is the "price of admission."[4] In this vein, one former candidate states that:

People play the candidates. People ask the candidate "what have you brought us?" "Five pushcarts, tools, and three containers of beer." "Let them in," and they greet him. They end up with their storehouse packed ... They do not receive some candidates [at their assemblies], particularly if there is a councilor or a mayor who did not keep his promises. (Sergio Sullca, candidate for mayor of Santiago district, Cusco, May 25, 2010)

---

[1] *Barriga llena, corazón contento*, a popular saying in Spanish.
[2] These meetings usually take place over weekends, so candidates plan their visits ahead.
[3] Personal interview (Cusco, May 17, 2010).
[4] In addition to distributing handouts to the participants at these meetings, candidates also promise and sign commitments to give collective benefits to communities or associations who support them, if elected. This point is further discussed in the next chapter.

Similarly, a political operator working for a Congresswoman representing Piura explains that:

Nowadays, if you do not take something with you, people do not even receive you. The candidate arrives and voters ask 'What have you brought us?' If you do not have something with you, they all make up an excuse and go back home. (Ana Lilian Vilela, Lima, July 2, 2010)

Distributing goods during campaigns is a way for political movements without permanent organizations to reach voters. As a candidate in Piura puts it, "Politicians do not have a permanent organizational structure to reach the citizenry ... There are no alternative mechanisms to reach people than through these types of benefits and offers."[5] Politicians distribute goods to poor voters in quite diverse settings and at different types of campaign events. The specific modalities, change but the ultimate goal is the same: to attract poor voters to campaign events or to access organizational constituencies. In their references to the organization of bingos or raffles, a form of campaign clientelism that is spreading in Piura, the participants in another Piura focus group attest to this:

INTERVIEWER:	What types of distribution of gifts have you observed here?
PARTICIPANT 1:	One is that they give away bingo cards, house by house. They give you one or two bingo cards and they publicize the prizes to amass people at the *plaza*.
PARTICIPANT 2:	... they do that, for example, when they are going to present their candidate, in order to attract people who, hoping to win the bingo, line up there. 'All these people support me,' they think; and people go because of the bingo [Laughs] ... They fall for it hook, line, and sinker.[6] (Female focus group, El Indio settlement, Piura).

Politicians provide goods at campaign events in part because their rivals do so, and clients have come to expect it. In the words of an experienced politician, "It's a *fiesta*! The more rural the voters, the more profitable the campaign *fiesta* is ... The voter has realized that it is the only time politicians come by."[7]

---

[5] Personal interview. Piura, July 7, 2011.
[6] *Es un anzuelo, prácticamente caen los pececitos.*
[7] Personal interview with Rodrigo Urbina, political operator working then for APRA's regional government. Piura July 23, 2010.

In addition, this competition triggers a reinforcing mechanism. One candidate, who claimed to be ideologically opposed to this practice, conceded "You cannot campaign otherwise ... they wipe you out."[8] Given this competitive pressure, even the most organized political movements and parties are forced to distribute gifts to attract nonaffiliated poor voters to their campaign events. For instance, APRA's local brokers in Piura explained that they distribute donations (such as backpacks, school supplies, pans, fish, bananas, medicine, etc.) to the needy, both partisans and non partisans.[9] As I will discuss in depth later, this competition also leads to the increasing use of goods in campaigns over time.

Attracting poor voters and accessing crucial constituencies is important for candidates. But the third, and most important, reason why politicians distribute goods at campaign events and rallies is to assure a large turnout. As one participant at a focus group in Piura explained:

Definitively, these gifts have taken place only to assure attendance; to assemble people for the picture ... Goods were handed out as a hook, so everybody will go there. (Male focus group, Los Polvorines settlement, Piura)

Politicians employ this strategy consciously; they are aware that they must get a large turnout at their political activities, and are willing to spend campaign resources to do so. For instance, a political operator, currently a congressman representing Cusco, notes that distributing gifts is a form of "paternalism" that is part of the campaign's "sensationalism."[10] An NGO expert working for many years with local governments in rural areas of Piura agrees, stating that:

Candidates organize their feast, they give away little things. It is not a tradition, it is a political strategy: people go to rallies because they can get something there, such as food. (Manuel Albuquerque, CIPCA. Piura, July 21, 2010)

But why do politicians invest so much resources and efforts into buying the attendance of poor voters at campaign events? As my informational theory predicts, high levels of attendance at campaign activities are crucial for establishing and maintaining the public perception of candidate

---

[8] Interview, Piura, July 21, 2010.
[9] Personal interviews with Kelly Coronado, general secretary of APRA's Los Olivos local committee and candidate to the Council (Piura, September 28, 2010); Joel Pulache, general secretary of APRA's Antonio Raymondi local committee (Piura, October 2, 2010); and Jaime Bejarano, general secretary of APRA's La Florida local committee (Piura, November 23, 2010).
[10] Personal interview with Rubén Coa. May 25, 2010.

viability in Peru. Lacking stable party identifications, indifferent citizens are free to choose from a menu of improvised personalistic vehicles, and often do so very close to election day. Peruvian electoral campaigns often go through dramatic swings as some candidates soar and others crash.[11] Politicians utilize campaign clientelism to help create the public perception that they are strong candidates who are known and welcomed everywhere.

The size of campaign rallies can affect strategic considerations by donors and voters: large turnout allows strategic actors to identify the frontrunner candidates. An experienced political operator explains this rationale as follows:

Vote choice is not informed but strategic ... The distribution of food and cash, organizing *fiestas* is becoming more common; it has increased. The candidate has to arrive with food and presents, and to party. He has to make donations ... The voter sees how much support the candidate has, who mobilizes more people, which candidate is more promising. (Rodrigo Urbina, Piura, July 23, 2010)

Campaign turnout serves as an especially important signal of electoral viability to donors and voters because the dearth of party organization means that there are few alternative sources of electoral information on the strength of candidates. As the following candidate clarifies, distribution of goods and turnout are related, and together they have an electoral impact:

People always talk about the distribution of gifts. It does happen. For example, the distribution of food, T-shirts, small gifts, toys and little things for the children ... Why do they give things away? Everything is about your image, because you can mobilize these people to your rally.[12] When you organize motorcades it is the same: people believe that the candidate who mobilizes more people in these motorcades is the one who is doing better in vote intention [laughs]. There are not many polls, not reliable ones. Consequently, what you convey matters a lot: to appear as if you are effectively supported. (Candidate for regional vice president. Piura, July 20, 2010)

Results from IOP's survey confirm the intuitions of politicians. As shown in Table 4.3, voters mentioned the number of people mobilized at campaign events as one of the main cues they take into account when assessing candidates' electoral potential in municipal elections, tied in

---

[11] See, for instance, Levitsky's account of the 2011 presidential election.
[12] The Spanish word he uses is *"mediático."*

TABLE 4.3. *Cues to evaluate electoral viability (2012)*

How do you know that a candidate for a district municipality has a good chance of winning the election? (three choices)

The candidate appears in the media	858	26.29
The number of people mobilized at campaign events	709	21.73
Lots of propaganda	676	20.72
Poll results	514	15.75
The quantity of gifts distributed	445	13.64
Other	61	1.87
Total	3,263	100.00

Source: IOP (2012)

second place with the amount of propaganda displayed.[13] Voters even take the amount of goods distributed at such rallies as an indicator of electoral viability. Together, the number of people mobilized and the quantity of gifts distributed make up 35 percent of the responses. The only informational cue that trumps campaign mobilization is the candidate's appearance in the media. Media coverage, however, is partly dependent on large rallies. Also notable is the relatively low number of respondents who depend on polls to assess electoral viability.

It may be surprising to observe that the quantity of gifts distributed is very low on the respondents' list of priorities when assessing candidates' electoral viability. However, in a more recent national survey, conducted by Ipsos in October of 2017, this informational cue is seen to be more important, making it clear that campaign clientelism can be an appealing strategy for manipulating public perceptions of electoral viability and, thus, influencing the race.

Candidates are well aware that large attendance at rallies is important, and fear the consequences of only a few people showing up. Indeed, nothing is worse for a politician's campaign than a poorly attended rally (*una plaza vacía*). As one former mayor says:

The rally was pretty important. I was terrified but it is a tradition: the entire town expects the best rally ... You hand out gas vouchers to ensure taxis and motorcycle taxis participate in your parade. How many vehicles you gather is a measure of your candidate's "success." You organize a parade, a motorcade with

---

[13] A difference-in-proportions test shows that they are not statistically different from each other.

TABLE 4.4. *Cues to evaluate electoral viability (2017)*

How do you know that a (district) municipality candidate has good chances of winning the election? (three choices)	Freq.	%
The candidate appears in the media	659	21.52
The number of people mobilized at campaign events	592	19.33
Lots of propaganda	690	22.53
Poll results	496	16.20
The quantity of gifts distributed	581	18.97
Other	44	1.44
Total	3,062	100.00

Source: Ipsos (2017)

[party] badges and crowd the plaza. You hire a band. I was able to gather a crowd 50 meters long and 200 meters wide. It was a total success. (Former mayor of Oxapampa-Junín, October 10, 2009)

Likewise, a party activist in Puno also vouched for the importance of drawing a crowd when he noted that, "One has to pay 5 soles to motorcycle taxi drivers so they crowd the plaza. If not, it looks empty and we are going to be criticized" (Fujimorismo activist, Puno, June 10, 2010).

In most cases, the use of clientelistic tactics during campaigns is not controlled by the candidates themselves. Instead, *movilizadores,* political operators in charge of organization and street propaganda activities, are usually the ones who decide when and how to use clientelistic strategies in campaigns. As a former mayor and councilor of Carabayllo district in Lima remarks, "Operators get paid during campaigns: a certain amount for a rally, a certain amount for painting propaganda. They at least assure a market where you can sell your plan. They summon an audience for you."[14] These *movilizadores* are crucial to the campaigns. As one journalist has written, "There's a key character in every campaign who is not the presidential candidate: the *movilizador.* His job is a sort of 'mandatory political service' which consists of crowding plazas for speeches."[15]

Movilizadores master a series of techniques to count heads and, thus, measure the relative success of an event and compare it with those of a candidate's adversaries. One such technique is to place four individuals per square meter, then measure the number of square meters occupied

[14] Personal interview with José Távara (Lima, March 2, 2010).
[15] "Los hombres de la portátil," *La República* (April 2, 2006).

by the crowd and multiply it by four.[16] Moreover, they divide the crowd space by district of origin, so they can count how many persons each local base has mobilized.[17] *Movilizadores* also organize rally participants in such a manner as to ensure that the media will capture images of a crowded gathering.

Peru under Fujimori's government exemplifies the most pragmatic and systematic enactment of turnout-buying strategies targeted to a mass public. It was precisely during these years that the institution of the *portátil* came into being. In Peruvian political jargon, a *portátil* consists of a group of poor people mobilized to show public support for a politician in exchange for material rewards. *Portátiles* emerged as a way of engaging in political campaigning in the absence of organized parties.

One senior political operator then working for Fujimori referred to the mobilization of these *portátiles* as part of the "psychosocial operations" (*los psicosociales*) they conducted, which he deemed important to generating favorable public opinion trends during campaigns.[18] As an example, he describes how they used *portátiles* in local markets during the municipal campaign of 1995.[19] They took five buses packed with (paid) women carrying shopping bags, and gave each of them two or three soles to buy something and, thus, appear to be regular customers. These women were strategically placed at hotspots around the market. When Jaime Yoshiyama, the *Fujimorismo* candidate, passed by, they cheered and threw confetti in each aisle of the market. One of the women gave him flowers, the same bouquet that was being rotated from aisle to aisle.

These market operations were complemented by frequent personal visits by the candidate to local shanty towns, during which the candidate was instructed to warmly greet people and eat with them. The *movilizador* I spoke to contends that these strategies allowed Yoshiyama to turn around a poor start of 2 percent and rise in voting intention to almost 42 percent. Since then, such organizational devices have risen in popularity and are now utilized in many different types of campaigns.

Without party identification to guarantee loyalty, campaign clients are highly opportunistic. They go to multiple rallies and accept goods

[16] Personal interview with political operator working for *Unidos Construyendo* (Piura July 23, 2010).

[17] This allows *movilizadores* to assess how well a candidate is doing in different neighborhoods or districts. The practice, thus, serves as a sort of political thermometer.

[18] Personal interview (Lima, February 17, 2010).

[19] In the 1993 municipal elections, Fujimori had noted that he was unable to translate his national-level popularity into support for his municipal candidates.

from different candidates.[20] In the words of one political operator, "The *portátiles* mobilize [people] according to the candidates' budgets ... During electoral times voters receive from all movements and decide their vote only after many mobilizations."[21] Certainly, people receive benefits, but they do not commit to candidates. Politicians are fully aware of this. "'Let them spend their money,' the people say after they accept the goods," explains a political advisor.[22] Some clients even make a point of "collecting" T-shirts and other supplies from different organizations.[23] "'A T-shirt, a T-shirt!' The T-shirt itself is a big thing," a politician commented ironically.[24] What happens nowadays, a journalist remarks, is that "the people are taking advantage of the candidates and not the other way around."[25]

Politicians often complain about this kind of opportunism, because on many occasions the same *dirigentes* who help them organize visits to neighborhoods do the same for other contenders. As one focus group participant in Cusco acknowledged:

[The candidates] always come and we have to wear the T-shirt they give away and wait for them during the campaign. For example, San Román arrived to Chacabamba with journalists, so they gathered us there to amass a crowd and they made us cheer in groups "San Román! San Román!" Afterwards Coco Acurio came. Similarly, first we changed T-shirts, and we started cheering because he brought presents such as pencils, erasers and we also demanded modern irrigation and a health center. He answered "Yes, I will do that, this mill will become the leading one, I personally will take charge of its implementation." He promised all this so we noted it down in our log book. Given that they distributed many gifts we started cheering "*Coco Presidente! Coco Presidente!*" as we did with San Román, and they filmed us and the reporters interviewed us. (Male focus group, rural Cusco)

Some *dirigentes* even betray politicians who they have been working with for long periods. For example, Carlos Moscoso, a lawyer who has been a candidate for mayor of Cusco three times, narrated how, during the last campaign, he sought out a group of *dirigentes* he had been advising for

---

[20] Participant 1: People have got into the habit of looking for candidates' gifts. Participant 2: Yes [...] and they go to different rallies successively to receive something [...]" (Female focus group, rural Cusco).

[21] Personal interview with *Fujimorismo* political operator Edmundo Gatica (Cusco, September 6, 2010).

[22] Personal interview with political advisor Mario Martorell (Cusco, May 17, 2010).

[23] Male focus group, rural Cusco; female focus group, El Indio settlement, Piura. Also, personal interview with former candidate (Piura, July 7, 2011).

[24] Interview with Javier Barreda (APRA) (Lima, September 6, 2012).

[25] Personal interview with reporter Rocío Farfán (*Cutivalú Radio*) (Piura, July 22, 2010).

six years.[26] Three months before the election day, he explained, the provincial municipality hired these local brokers as promoters and they never again returned his calls, instead campaigning for the mayor's reelection.[27]

Most *dirigentes* are, in fact, "political adventurers" who "are with one candidate after the other."[28] Some of them "vote crossways" (campaign for a mayoral candidate from one political movement, and for a candidate for the regional presidency from another) but others even "play both sides" – that is, they work for two candidates at the same time.[29] Indeed, I was able to uncover a case of playing both sides. On the recommendation of a political operator, I contacted and interviewed a *dirigente* who (supposedly) had been working with the *Obras+Obras* political movement in Piura. He received me in the community hall of the shanty town where he operated, which still had a hand-made banner hung on the wall that read "Welcome Congressman Carrasco Távara."[30] During our conversation, the *dirigente* mentioned that he used to be an *Aprista*, but gave up his membership because, he said, there was too much corruption in the regional government. Later in the same campaign, he said, he switched his support to *Unidos Construyendo*, posting propaganda on behalf of Javier Atkins's candidacy for regional government and Óscar Miranda's run for the mayoralty in Piura. However, later on he conceded that he was also campaigning for a mayoral candidate from *another* movement at the same time, having forgotten by that stage in the conversation that it was a political operator *Obras+Obras* (which was running its own candidate for mayor, Ruby Rodríguez de Aguilar) that had recommended him to me.

Not even the most organized parties can monitor local brokers effectively during campaigns. In Piura, one of APRA's strongholds, the party was unable to distinguish between reliable and unreliable brokers during the last subnational election.[31] As the candidate for regional vice-president explains,

---

[26] Personal interview with candidate Carlos Moscoso (Cusco, December 18, 2010).

[27] See Chapter 6.

[28] Personal interview with APRA's political operator César Tume (Piura, November 26, 2010).

[29] The expression used in Peruvian Spanish is *jugar a dos cachetes*. Personal interview with *Unidos Construyendo*'s local broker Roberto García (Piura, November 23, 2010).

[30] Carrasco Távara was at that time one of APRA's congressmen for Piura. APRA also had a candidate running for mayor.

[31] This inability to evaluate the reliability of local brokers lies behind the difficulties the party had in assessing its true reelection prospects.

It is difficult to be sure if local brokers are working for you. We don't have a political culture. I distribute breakfast to poor people – a tradition in the party. But if tomorrow another candidate arrives with toys, several of the brokers that have been with me will be with the other candidate. 'Don't trouble yourself and accept! We have to take advantage,' they say. Many of these *dirigentes* are not *Apristas*, they are not registered with the party. (Luis Ortiz Granda, APRA's candidate for regional vice president. Piura, July 23, 2010)

Most candidates do not even try to monitor clients at rallies in Peru. At most, they count the approximate number of people from every sector or district to assess (however imprecisely) their popularity in different areas.[32] At the same time, since politicians can safely assume that most participants at the rallies will show up on election day, mandatory voting makes it even more tempting for politicians to buy attendance at rallies in an attempt to persuade uncommitted voters. If the vote were voluntary, many of these indifferent constituents might, instead, abstain.[33] Rather, the key issue for candidates is to assure a large turnout because it helps them signal their electoral potential. Additionally, as I will discuss in depth in Chapter 5, clients' attendance at campaign events also constitutes an opportunity to use persuasion.

In summary, politicians distribute material goods during campaigns to substitute for the absence of stable political organizations. Material benefits allow politicians to attract poor voters, who may not attend otherwise, to their campaign events. Distribution of gifts also allows politicians without local networks to access crucial constituencies. In exchange for the goods given out, local associations let these politicians introduce themselves and their projects during their regular scheduled meetings.

---

[32] Personal interview with *Unidos Construyendo* political operator Gregoria Muro (Piura, July 23, 2010).

[33] León combined a field experiment with a change in the electoral laws in Peru that reduced the cost of fines for abstention, to identify the effect of monetary incentives on turnout (León 2017). He took advantage of the fact that the passage of the law in 2006 remained largely unpublicized. Informing voters about the fine reduction through the field experiment did have the effect of reducing turnout. However, contrary to what Gans-Morse et al. (2014) report, the reduction in the fine for abstention did not affect the incidence of what he calls "vote buying" – the proportion of respondents who reported having accepted cash or a gift from a political operator (León 2017: 3, 23). In their article, the authors quote a previous version of León's paper in which he states that the cost of abstention reduced the incidence of vote buying by 20 percent. However, León's published papers estimate a reduction effect of 0.2 percent, which is not statistically significant (León 2017: 40). Hence the distribution of gifts during campaigns may remain an attractive electoral strategy in Peru even after the reduction in fines. This is because, as I argue, votes are not bought or influenced directly through the distribution of gifts.

More importantly, the distribution of gifts allows politicians to gather crowds for their campaign events. Such mobilization of large numbers of people during campaigns is important because strategic donors and voters use the size of turnout as a proxy for perceived electoral viability. In the next section I present experimental evidence to support this argument.

TESTING THE CAUSAL MECHANISM: EXPERIMENTAL EVIDENCE

In this section I present the results of two survey experiments that provide further evidence for my claim that turnout at campaign events actually influences voting behavior. This theoretical claim, I propose, accounts for why politicians invest in campaign clientelism despite a lack of established political organizations.

The randomization of subjects into experimental groups provides the basis for causal inference and internal validity. The survey experiments were included in nationally representative survey samples in Peru conducted by prestigious local polling firms. This representative sample of the general population helps lessen concerns regarding the external validity of the experiment. That these experimental findings help explain behavior in real-world settings can be also verified by considering the consistent qualitative information included in this book.

The first experiment was included as part of the Political Representation and Social Conflict Survey conducted by the polling firm IOP in October 2012. The survey utilized a multistage random probability sample that represented adults (18+) across the nation. For the experiment, I designed a vignette with the portrayal of a candidate running for mayor. This profile was intended to "travel" well across different audiences. Past election results and my own knowledge of municipal campaigns helped me elaborate this "ideal" profile. For instance, taking into consideration the anti-partisan predispositions and distrust for politicians exhibited by Peruvian voters, the candidate was presented as an outsider who had recently formed a political movement. Similarly, I chose Peruvians' preferred profession (economist) for candidates (JNE 2010) and the predominant gender of real-life mayors (male) (Muñoz and García 2011). I assigned the candidate one of the most common first-names for males in Peru (José), a name that does not connote any specific racial or socioeconomic origin. Overall, the candidate's proposals and personal traits were designed to attract a broad constituency encompassing both middle- and lower-class constituencies. He promised to deliver public works and deal with pressing problems, such as crime and education. In addition, the profile shown to respondents also specified that the candidate showed real concern for the poor during the campaign. The text is the following:

Imagine that José were a candidate for mayor in your district for a recently created political movement. José is 45 years old and is an economist. This is the first time he has participated in politics but he has a renowned professional trajectory. José has no known criminal record. During the campaign, he demonstrated social awareness and willingness to "get his hands dirty" while visiting poor people to present his proposals. His plan emphasized the need to develop people's quality of life by delivering public works in the district and to invest in road infrastructure. He also promised to coordinate with the Ministry of Education to improve the quality of education and with the police to assure public security.[34]

All respondents were shown the same candidate profile. After this sketch, I randomized three versions of the questions.[35] For the *control* group, the experimental question did not provide any additional text and asked each interviewee about the likelihood that they would vote for José for district mayor if the elections were held next Sunday.[36] In the *low turnout* treatment group, before asking this question, the interviewer read out a primer that said, "Members of the community say that José's campaign events did not attract many people. Neighbors comment that José's final rally was attended by approximately 100 people."[37] Finally, in

---

34 The original Spanish wording is: "*Imagine que José es candidato a alcalde de su distrito por un movimiento político de reciente creación. José tiene 45 años y es economista de profesión. Es la primera vez que participa en política pero tiene una trayectoria profesional reconocida. No se ha sabido que José tenga antecedentes judiciales. Asimismo, durante la campaña demostró tener sensibilidad social y vocación por 'ensuciarse los zapatos' visitando pueblos humildes para dar a conocer sus propuestas. Su plan de gobierno ha enfatizado que trabajará para sacar adelante obras importantes para mejorar la calidad de vida en el distrito y va a invertir en mejorar la infraestructura vial. También ha prometido trabajar en forma coordinada con el sector educación para mejorar la educación en el distrito y con la policía para mejorar la seguridad.*"

35 IOP provided the researcher with the identification number of the questionnaires, including the ID numbers assigned to each interviewer. These ID numbers were randomly assigned into three groups corresponding to the three versions of questionnaires using a Statistical Package for the Social Sciences (SPSS) routine following a uniform probability distribution. The interviewers were instructed to conduct the survey respecting the order of versions assigned by this randomization. The balance tests are included in Appendix 2.

36 The original Spanish wording is: "*Imagine que las elecciones municipales fueran el próximo domingo. ¿Qué tan probable sería que votara por un candidato como José para alcalde de su distrito? A) Muy probable B) Probable C) Poco probable D) Nada probable.*"

37 The original Spanish wording is: "*Los vecinos dicen que las actividades de José durante la campaña no reunían mucha gente. Los vecinos dicen que en su mitin de cierre José logró convocar alrededor de 100 personas.*"

TABLE 4.5. *Probability of voting for candidate by turnout (dichotomous)*

	Low turnout	Control	High turnout	Total
Likely	194	216	235	645
(Very likely/Likely)	50.26%	56.54%	60.41%	55.75%
Unlikely	192	166	154	512
(Somewhat likely/ Unlikely)	49.74%	43.46%	39.59%	44.25%
Total	386	382	389	1,157
	100.00%	100.00%	100.00%	100.00%

Pearson chi^2(2) = 8.2414; Pr = 0.016.
Source: IOP (2012)

the *high turnout* treatment group, before asking this question, the interviewer read out a primer that said, "Members of the community say that José's campaign events attracted a lot of people. Neighbors comment that José's final rally was attended by approximately 1,000 people."[38] In all versions, the experiment was located at the end of the questionnaire.

Table 4.5 presents the cross-tabulations of voting intention for the imagined candidate by the experimental groups. In line with the expectations of my informational theory, those respondents in the low-turnout treatment group were less likely to vote for the made-up candidate than respondents in the high-turnout group. Although the descriptive statistics show a positive association between the experimental groups and vote intention, the treatments are not statistically different from the control group.

Overall, as Figure 4.1 illustrates, voting intention is in fact conditional on the public perception of campaign mobilization. Peruvian voters seem to be more willing to vote for a mayoral candidate when they are primed about his good performance at mobilizing large numbers of voters while campaigning. Moreover, after hearing that a candidate is not able to attract many voters at rallies, respondents seem less likely to vote for that candidate.

Hence, the experimental evidence provides additional support for the causal explanation identified by my informational theory of electoral clientelism. Peruvian voters do indeed condition their electoral choices on

---

[38] The original Spanish wording is: *"Los vecinos dicen que las actividades de José durante la campaña reunían mucha gente. Los vecinos dicen que en su mitin de cierre José logró convocar alrededor de 1000 personas."*

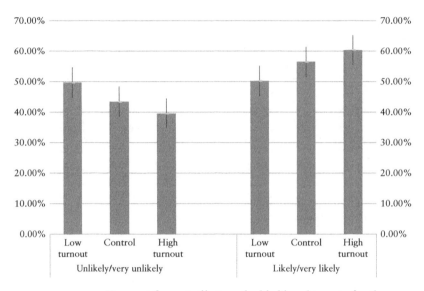

FIGURE 4.1. *Turnout figures' effect on the likelihood to vote for the candidate*
Source: IOP (2012). For the table with the result of the analysis, see Appendix 3

the perceived level of turnout: all other things being equal, they prefer to vote for a candidate who can mobilize larger numbers of voters at campaign events and defect from one that is not able to do so. Campaign clientelism can, thus, affect the strategic-voting considerations of all citizens. Politicians, as well as donors, are aware of this strategic voting. And this awareness explains why candidates invest in campaign clientelism despite a lack of established organizations; by influencing the public perception of electoral viability, campaign clientelism *indirectly* affects voting intention in Peru. As I will explain in the next section, high turnout at campaign events allows candidates to influence the dynamics of the race, raise campaign contributions, and bolster their possibilities of election.

But, what of the alternative explanations? How, in empirical terms, do I distinguish my informational theory from that of Kramon (2016, 2017)? It should be recalled that for Kramon, candidates distribute gifts and cash to demonstrate that they care about poor people and that they have the willingness to distribute resources to them *in the future*. Distributing private benefits during the campaign conveys information to voters about a candidate's *credibility* in these areas. In addition, in Kramon's theory, distribution also allows politicians to signal electoral viability and attract strategic voters who seek to side with the winner in order to assure themselves of future access to resources. In my theory, in contrast, prospective calculations are not a central mechanism, so I do not have specific expectations about how the information about a candidate engaging in campaign clientelism will influence voters' perceptions about candidate's behavior in the future. Rather, I propose that candidates distribute gifts, first, to gather audiences, which they will then try to persuade of their electoral desirability through non-clientelistic appeals. Second, candidates distribute gifts to turn out large numbers of voters at campaign events. For them, turnout is the key informational cue, important not only to assess electoral viability and influence strategic voting, but also to attract strategic donations.

I decided to conduct a second survey experiment in order to test some of the empirical implications of our theories. For one, it might be the case that the distribution of handouts itself also influences electoral viability and strategic calculations in Peru. I would not expect this to be true in direct terms (or at least not to a great extent), because desirability bias against the distribution of handouts may decrease the direct effect that the distribution of gifts might have on electoral prospects and calculations.

The second experiment was embedded in a survey conducted by Ipsos in October 2017. This survey used a multistage random probability sample of 1,083 citizens from cities in all departments of Peru. This time I randomized two versions of the experiment.[39] Again, I designed a vignette portraying a candidate running for mayor, to be read aloud in the control group. The text was as follows:

Imagine that José were a candidate for mayor in your district for a recently created political movement. José is 45 years old and is an economist. This is the first time he has participated in politics but he has a renowned professional trajectory. During the campaign, he visited various poor neighborhoods to present his proposals for increasing the quality of life in the district.

The treatment group received the same vignette, with the following addition:

In addition, neighbors say that many gifts were distributed to the attendees during José's rallies, such as T-shirts, cups, and groceries, while household appliances were raffled.

---

[39] Two groups were randomly selected. The survey was administered in person, using tablet computers. The balance tests are included in Appendix 2.

The vignettes were followed by questions related to voting intention, electoral viability, and prospective perceptions about the candidate's performance in office, similar to those that Kramon included in his field experiments.[40] First, I asked respondents how likely they would be to vote for a candidate like José for mayor in their district. In Kramon's theory, the distribution of handouts would be expected to affect vote-choice decisions. Moreover, his theory expects to find that information about a candidate's engagement in the distribution of handouts should be especially electorally effective with poor voters. In contrast, I do not expect information about a candidate's distribution of gifts while campaigning to increase the likelihood of voters voting for that candidate, not even among the poorer segments (Hypothesis 1).

Second, I asked respondents how likely it would be for a candidate like José to win the election in their district. With this question, I sought to approximate the effect on a candidate's perceived electoral viability of information about their distribution of gifts while campaigning. Unlike Kramon, I do not expect to find that all voters, poor and wealthy alike, would perceive this clientelistic candidate as more electorally viable. Since the relevant informational cue is turnout figures, information about the distribution of gifts should not affect electoral viability directly (Hypothesis 2).

Third, I have no specific expectations regarding voters' prospective evaluation of the candidate. In my theory, candidates distribute gifts not to generate positive expectations of their future performance and willingness to distribute resources to the poor, but because in the absence of partisan structures they have to do so in order to campaign. Consequently, information about a candidate's engagement in campaign clientelism should not generate positive expectations about this candidate's future performance in office, not even among the poor (Hypothesis 3).

Fourth, I do not expect that the delivery of campaign clientelism, per se, will generate candidate credibility. As I explained in Chapter 2 and will go on to empirically demonstrate in the next two chapters, it is through personal interactions that candidates are able to persuade voters about

---

[40] The original Spanish wording is: "*En una escala del 1 al 7, donde 7 es muy probable y 1 es muy improbable, ¿qué tan probable es que … 1. Usted vote por un candidato como José para alcalde de su distrito. 2. Un candidato como José gane la elección en su distrito. En una escala del 1 al 7, donde 7 es muy probable y 1 es muy improbable, ¿qué tan probable es que al asumir la alcaldía un candidato como José: 3. Haga las obras que el distrito necesita; 4. Ayude a gente que vive en pobreza 5. Vaya a ser corrupto; 6. Vaya a cumplir sus promesas de campaña.*"

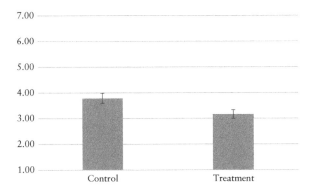

FIGURE 4.2. *Likelihood to vote for the candidate*
Source: IPSOS (2017). For the table with the result of the analysis, see Appendix 4

their electoral desirability. But this is not to say that information about a candidate engaging in campaign clientelism will fuel the belief that the candidate will uphold campaign promises (Hypothesis 4).

The experiment results confirm most of my expectations. First, as Figure 4.2 shows, not only does information about a candidate engaging in campaign clientelism fail to make voters more likely to vote for the candidate, but voters in the treatment group actually punish the candidate electorally. More important, and in contrast to Kramon's findings, hearing about a candidate engaging in campaign clientelism does not make poor voters more likely to vote for the candidate either (Figure 4.3). On the contrary, similarly to what is found for other socioeconomic groups and the sample as a whole, respondents of lower socioeconomic status who get information about a candidate distributing handouts while campaigning make them less likely to vote for that candidate.

Second, the results also confirm that information about a candidate engaging in campaign clientelism does not affect respondents' perceptions about electoral viability (Figure 4.4). Although the direction of the average treatment effects (ATEs) varies across socioeconomic classes – it is negative in the middle and upper-income groups and positive in the low-income category – they are not statistically significant in any subgroup. Hence, information about the delivery of electoral handouts is, thus, not an effective means of conveying candidates' electoral viability.

Third, information about campaign clientelism does not have a positive impact on prospective expectations about the delivery of benefits to the poor either. On average, respondents in the treated group believe that the candidate will be *less* likely to help people living in poverty

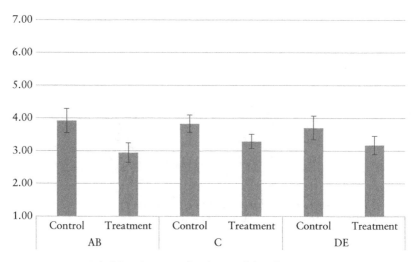

FIGURE 4.3. *Likelihood to vote for the candidate by socioeconomic status*
Source: IPSOS (2017). For the table with the result of the analysis, see Appendix 5

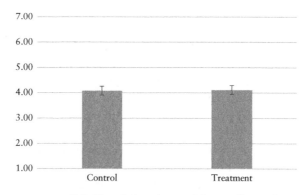

FIGURE 4.4. *Likelihood that the candidate will win the race*
Source: IPSOS (2017). For the table with the result of the analysis, see Appendix 6

(Figure 4.5). The ATE is −0.37 and its *p*-value is 0.006. These negative prospective expectations among the treated respondents also hold within subgroups of socioeconomic classes. However, while the direction of the trend is consistent with the results for the whole sample in that treated respondents within the low-income subgroup also believe that this candidate will be *less* likely to help people living in poverty, the ATE is only statistically significant among middle class respondents (Figure 4.6). The magnitude of ATEs among the poor are smaller (−0.22) and not significant (*p*-value = 0.37).

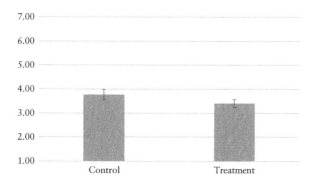

FIGURE 4.5. *Likelihood that the candidate will help poor people if elected*
Source: IPSOS (2017). For the table with the result of the analysis, see Appendix 7

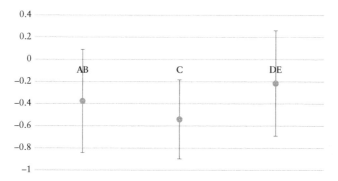

FIGURE 4.6. *Likelihood that the candidate will help poor people if elected by socioeconomic status (ATE)*
Source: IPSOS (2017). For the table with the result of the analysis, see Appendix 8

The respondents were also asked about the likelihood that a candidate like the one presented in the vignette would deliver the public works that the district needed. With this question as the dependent variable, the treatment also generates *negative* prospective expectations among respondents. Across the whole sample, respondents who received information about a candidate engaging in campaign clientelism answered, on average, that this candidate would be *less* likely to provide the public works needed: the ATE is −0.35 and its p-value is 0.005. Again, the direction of the ATE remain negative within class sub-groups, but, as can be observed in Figure 4.7, while the treatment is in fact significant among upper and middle-income respondents, it is not significant among poor voters – its p-value is 0.587. Interestingly, when asked about the

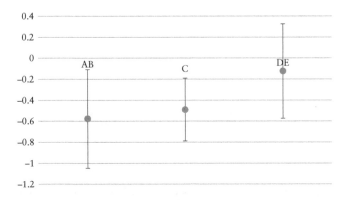

FIGURE 4.7. *Likelihood that the candidate will deliver the public works that the district needs if elected, by socioeconomic status (ATE)* Source: IPSOS (2017). For the table with the result of the analysis, see Appendix 9

likelihood that the candidate will deliver public works, the magnitude of the ATE among the poor is lower (–0.12) than when asked about the likelihood of the candidate helping the poor after accessing office (–0.22).

One question raised by these results is whether respondents are being influenced by social-desirability bias when answering; particularly those within the low-income sub-group. Poor voters may feel socially pressured to answer that a candidate who distributes electoral handouts will *not* deliver the public works that the district needs, even if they actually believe the candidate might do so. This may be the case, because these voters are often criticized for supporting candidates accused or suspected of corruption by receiving handouts from them during the campaign, or because they are influenced by the *roba pero hace obra* leitmotiv. However, social-desirability bias does not wholly explain why, on average, voters believe that this clientelistic candidate may not in fact help the poor upon arriving to power. Moreover, it does not make sense that the prospective expectations of poor voters about this clientelistic candidate's willingness or ability to deliver public works will be less negative than their expectations about his willingness to help the poor. At the same time, although many of the ATE within class sub-groups are not significant,[41] they do vary in magnitude: the low-income category exhibits ATE that are of smaller magnitude than those from the two other socioeconomic groups in relation to the questions about public works and helping the poor, and

---

[41] Splitting the simple into sub-groups reduces statistical power.

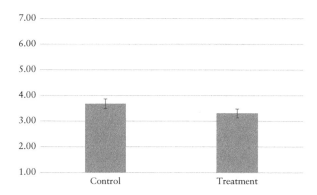

FIGURE 4.8. *Likelihood that the candidate will fulfill his campaign promises if elected*
Source: IPSOS (2017). For the table with the result of the analysis, see Appendix 10

one that is bigger (and positive) for the question about electoral viability. Thus, it may indeed be the case that social desirability is biasing the lower income responses, and that poorer voters' perceptions may, in fact, be more influenced by a candidate distributing gifts than they are willing to admit. However, as will be seen in Chapter 5, this does not seem to be the case. Poor voters appear indifferent (or even proud) about admitting that they receive gifts at campaign events and they assure that they decide their vote based on other factors. What is subject to strong social desirability bias is vote buying: the idea that a voter would vote for the candidate after receiving a gift.

In summary, although we cannot conclude that campaign clientelism impacts prospective evaluations about the future delivery of particularistic benefits among the poor, we can conclude that the ATE remains negative and is of a lower magnitude among poor voters than among their more affluent counterparts.

Finally, the experiment results also show that providing respondents with information about a candidate engaging in campaign clientelism does nothing to boost the candidate's electoral credibility. On the contrary, the ATE (−0.38) indicates that voters believe a clientelistic candidate will be less likely to fulfill campaign promises (Figure 4.8). It may be the case that, as my theory predicts, candidates know this and try to build credibility by other means, such as by personally interacting with voters during campaign events.

In summary, the survey experiments provide leverage for my informational theory. Peruvian voters do condition their electoral choices on the perceived level of turnout: all other things being equal, they prefer to vote for a candidate who is able to mobilize larger numbers of voters at campaign events and will defect from one who is not able to do so. In contrast, providing information about a candidate who distributes gifts while campaigning does not affect voters' perceptions of electoral viability, and *negatively* influences the likelihood of voters voting for such a candidate, even among low-income groups. At the same time, the results do not allow us to conclude that information about campaign clientelism impacts prospective evaluations about the future delivery of works to the poor. Information about a candidate engaging in campaign clientelism does affect prospective perceptions about their willingness to help the poor in the sample as a whole, but in a negative way. Likewise, information about the distribution of electoral handouts affects not only perceptions about the probability that a clientelistic candidate will be corrupt, but also negatively affects both the candidate's credibility regarding fulfillment of campaign promises and their likelihood of delivering public works.

Now, having provided experimental evidence to support the first causal mechanism of my theory, in the next section I will illustrate how high turnout at campaign events allows candidates to influence the dynamics of the race, raise campaign contributions, and bolster their possibilities of election.

CAMPAIGN CLIENTELISM AND THE DYNAMICS OF THE RACE

As the evidence has shown, politicians engage in campaign clientelism because they expect it to influence their electoral fortunes. By signaling electoral prospects, campaign turnout shapes the dynamics of the race: it establishes name recognition, marks one candidate as a frontrunner, and attracts strategic actors in the final rush. These factors exemplify the importance of maintaining clientelistic activities *throughout* the campaign and not just near election day, as conventional approaches to vote buying propose.

During the initial stages of the race, crowded campaign events can be crucial in prompting surges in voter intentions. In Peru's fluid political system there is always room for outsiders to rise, gain momentum, and, in many cases, win elections. Fujimori in 1990 and Toledo in 2000–1, for example, were both outsiders who emerged as serious contenders during the campaign and ultimately won the presidency. Similarly, another outsider, Ollanta Humala, emerged as a competitive candidate during the

2006 campaign and almost won the presidency. Politicians are keenly aware of the volatility of electoral preferences and use campaign clientelism expressly to generate and influence electoral fluctuations. For example, one political operator interviewed in Piura explained to me how he achieved name recognition for his candidate, a young individual with no previous political experience. He did so by organizing a bingo event with cash prizes as part of the candidate's first political rally. The operator went house-to-house handing out bingo cards and did not widely disclose the fact that they were given away for free (the cards had a face value of two soles). Thus, when around 6,000 people showed up at the first bingo/rally, many political rivals, who had assumed that the recipients had actually bought their cards, were left surprised by the apparent popularity of the candidate. This operator organized another three events on a similar premise and with similar turnouts, and in so doing helped make this previously unknown candidate a widely recognized figure. He described these practices as an innovation in political marketing.[42]

Because individuals judge how well a candidate is doing in part by attendance at campaign events, continued "investment" in campaign clientelism is crucial. If their campaign events draw only meager crowds, candidates risk abandonment by strategic donors, activists, and voters. Voters care for electoral viability because, as the literature on strategic coordination had long argued, they want to maximize the chances of their vote counting (Cox 1997). In one focus group conducted in Piura, I asked why politicians distributed goods if they could not be sure that the recipients would vote for them. "They get a pay-off, psychologically," a female participant responded, "Because the psychology is where there are lots of people. Voters say 'We have to vote for that candidate.' If they see more cars [they think] 'Oh! She is going to win! Give your vote to her'" (Female focus Group, El Indio settlement, Piura). In turn, other voters might instead care about voting for an electorally viable candidate in order to increase the chances of extracting particularistic benefits in the future (Kramon 2017). However, as discussed in the previous section, there is not enough consistent empirical evidence to support this alternative claim.

As I pointed out in Chapter 3, campaign clientelism in Peru is financed in large part by private resources. Therefore, amassing a large turnout at rallies is also important to demonstrate viability to strategic donors: campaign contributors want to make sure that their investments yield

[42] Personal interview with Mariano Huamanchumo (Piura, July 21, 2010).

returns, so they try to assess whom to support. That is why is very important for candidates to appear as if they are well supported:

And, to transmit that image, you have to give things away and you have to look for money, and you have to commit to whomever can contribute and pay for this. (Candidate to regional vice president. Piura, July 20, 2010)

Businesses are interested in financing viable candidates because this increases their chances of gaining public procurements once the election is over.[43] Private interests also finance viable candidates in the expectation that this can buy them nonenforcement of existing regulation perceived as being against their interests. For instance, in Pucallpa, illegal loggers finance regional election campaigns to avail themselves of allies in power and thereby, gain control of wood extraction (Canseco 2016: 39). A similar phenomenon can be observed in Madre de Dios and Puno with illegal gold miners (Uribe 2014; Baraybar 2016), while drug-trafficking interests also get involved in financing subnational elections in several departments of Peru. For instance, according to a Congressional Report on narco-politics, 133 candidates for regional and municipal office in 2014 were investigated on drug trafficking allegations, three of whom were ultimately elected as regional governors, one as a provincial mayor, and eleven as district mayors (Congreso de la República 2016). The report also found that one of the most common ways through which drug traffickers get involved in politics is through the formal incorporation of companies that then fund campaigns or help candidates launder money in exchange for corrupt practices.

Thus, as the campaign advances, business, and illegal interests will support the strongest candidates, usually betting on the frontrunners.[44] Given the high electoral volatility and turnover rates in most electoral districts, donors commonly spread their electoral investments. Consequently, local businesses "marry" the three leading candidates.[45] Once a candidate achieves momentum, donors "swarm like flies," as a candidate explained to me:

---

[43] As I explained in Chapter 3, strategic donation will later translate into corruption.

[44] Unfortunately, no systematic and reliable data about campaign donations is available in Peru, particularly at the subnational level. As a politician who wished to remain anonymous explained to me, there is an important informal connection between businessmen and politicians, and local businesses regularly finance campaigns to assure proximity to power; but nobody will openly admit this (Personal interview in Lima, March 20, 2014).

[45] Personal interview with political operator Adolfo Mamani. Cusco, August, 31, 2010.

The principle is: people are going to join up with the one they believe will win. Then this becomes a snowball. Even contributions are made based on this principle. Contributors realize the way it is going and they decide to provide more [funds to a frontrunning candidate]. (*Unidos Construyendo* candidate, Piura, July 11, 2011)

Such strategic donations are also known to take place in national elections in Peru. During one interrogation by public prosecutors in Río de Janeiro as part of the ongoing investigations into corruption allegations associated with his firm's activities in Peru, Marcelo Odebretch declared that his standing policy was to finance the presidential candidates who had the best chances of being elected and, thus, claimed that Odebrecth made financial contributions to Ollanta Humana *and* Keiko Fujimori in the 2011 election.[46] But in presidential elections, they mainly use polling results to assess viability. In summary, donors look for informational cues as a means of assessing electoral viability before making campaign contributions. And in subnational elections where alternative credible informational cues such as polls results do not abound, turnout figures are often used in their stead.

Voters, in turn, judge the prospects of candidates partly by the amount of money they spend on propaganda displays and the distribution of gifts (see Tables 4.3 and 4.4). As an APRA activist stressed, "When you give things away, you demonstrate power. People say, 'this is not just any candidate, he can win; he has power.' People recognize the candidate that comes with a big crowd, his people and his cars. Only after that, they start listening to you."[47] Another experienced political operator thinks similarly. For him, "giving things away is a matter of marketing. If you don't do so, you are Mr. Nobody."[48]

The public's point of view on this issue is also relevant. At a focus group in Cusco, I asked participants what people said about candidates who do not distribute gifts:

---

[46] RPP, November 10, 2017, "*Odebrecht dijo que aportó a todos en 2006 y 2011, pero que le pregunten los detalles a Barata*". Available at: http://rpp.pe/politica/judiciales/ odebrecht-dijo-que-aporto-a-todos-en-2006-y-2011-pero-que-le-pregunten-a-barata- noticia-1087862. Odebrecht and other Brazilian firms that are currently under investigation on corruption allegations involving financial contributions that were later paid back in the form of public contracts with subnational governments in Ancash, Cusco, San Martín, and Callao, See the study conducted by IDL-Reporteros, available at: https:// idl-reporteros.pe/los-contratos-de-odebrecht-en-peru/.

[47] Personal interview with Javier Barreda, APRA, September 6, 2012.

[48] Personal interview with Rodrigo Urbina. Piura, August 7, 2011.

PARTICIPANT 1:   Everybody gives things away! At least a match box [...]

PARTICIPANT 2:   People say that candidates who distribute fewer gifts do not have enough of a budget, that they are not being supported. And about those candidates that give away a lot, [they say] that they have many people who are financially supporting them. (Female focus group, Sucsu Auccaylle community, Cusco).

Similarly, in a focus group in Piura, a female participant argued that "The candidate who gets the most money wins because she thrusts the campaign into voters' eyes everywhere: the radio, television, newspapers, houses" (Female focus group, El Indio settlement, Piura). Politicians are, thus, accurately anticipating citizens' perceptions and behavior.

Furthermore, campaign turnout also signals the frontrunning candidates to benefit-seeking activists who expect to get a job once the candidate gains office in exchange for their campaign services.[49] Activists, including hired brokers, will frequently defect from candidates who do not surge in the polls and instead offer their services to the leading candidates. Thus, during the last weeks of a campaign, candidates who are at the head of the pack begin receiving large numbers of volunteers at their headquarters. For instance, the leading movement in Piura's 2010 regional elections had to open two new makeshift campaign centers to be able to deal with this sudden and expected burst of volunteers. Longer-serving activists viewed the newcomers with distrust and regarded them as opportunistic.[50] The candidate's closest aides, however, welcomed this sudden explosion of interest in their project because it meant it was already perceived as a sure bid.

In summary, through continuous observation of turnout figures at campaign events, strategic donors, voters, and activists can tell which candidates will be the frontrunners in the race. These figures are usually contrasted with poll results that come out during the last two months of

---

[49] According to my interviews, this is a common expectation of activists that often goes unmet, at least for most of them. This, in turn, usually leads to legitimacy problems and splits within regional movements and even national parties that act as electoral vehicles. One such example is *Unidos Construyendo* after it won the 2010 election in Piura (Personal interview with former Regional Vicepresident, August 11, 2014). See also the *Partido Nacionalista* after Humala won the presidency, in Muñoz and Dargent (2016).

[50] Observation notes and personal interviews with *Unidos Construyendo* activists (October 2 and November 31, 2010).

the campaign. Although I do not argue that polls have no effect on influencing perceptions of electoral viability in subnational elections, these poll results are partly shaped by earlier gains made in influencing electoral viability through campaign clientelism. Moreover, polls are available only for regional elections and municipal contests in some provinces and urban districts, but not in rural areas and smaller towns and cities. And even when they are available, poll results from different firms sometimes contradict one another, as I will discuss in Chapter 6. Thus, campaign turnout remains a powerful informational cue for strategic actors in subnational elections.

The campaign turnout commanded by viable contenders typically comes to a crescendo in the last few days before an election. Final rallies are particularly important since they offer voters the last piece of information with which to judge the viability of a candidate before deciding their vote.[51] According to one political operator in Cusco:

The election is decided, basically, during the last week. During the last two weeks people say 'this one,' 'no, this one.' What does that depend on? On the size of the crowds you can mobilize. On the quantity of propaganda you can display … Not organizing a final rally would be the worst political suicide ever because the media would say 'this party organized a rally with approximately 2,000 people, this other one with 500, that with 200' … Whoever organizes the best final rally wins. (Adolfo Mamani, Cusco, August 31, 2010)

A female participant at a focus group in Cusco described the final rallies and their importance in similar terms:

For the campaign finale each party organizes a party. They hire a band, the candidates walk around the plaza … they prepare grills, fried chicken, *chicha*,[52] and arrive carrying the food and drinks as if it were a traditional feast. Then the bands play and people dance, they party, and they join the candidate who has the most people, thinking that he is going to win. (Female focus group, Anta, Cusco)

A successful rally partly depends on previous work in shaping electoral viability, gaining name recognition, being signaled as a frontrunner, and, consequently, getting more donors to continue financing electoral mobilization through campaign clientelism. Thus, more goods are distributed

---

[51] Until 2011, electoral law prohibited the reporting of poll results during the last week of the campaign. In addition, electoral laws forbid any sort of political propaganda or rallies within three days of election day. Thus, the final rally is the last legal campaign activity allowed.

[52] A traditional alcoholic drink in Peru prepared using corn.

as election day approaches. Then, on election day, candidates send trucks to pick up voters from *campesino* communities and villages, particularly in small rural towns and villages with no media coverage. They openly distribute food, alcohol, and even cash, often hidden inside match boxes. But even in these apparently direct vote-buying attempts, there are some very interesting bidding dynamics among front runners who attempt to signal electoral strength to voters. According to one female focus group participant in Cusco:

Because there are a lot of vehicles, people wander around the cars. It is there that the *compañeros* ask them to get in and give them a matchbox [with money inside]. Then, seeing this, a lot of people struggle to get into a car, and as a lot of people gather, they start saying 'this party is going to win.' And, since in other cars politicians do not distribute cash, only two or three persons get in. (Focus group, females, rural provinces, Cusco)

Similarly, an APRA activist in Piura noted that:

On election day there is a contest about who brings more people to the polls. The candidates arriving first have the best chance ... When they arrive they take people to houses where there is food and alcohol. Wherever you find the best food, the candidate is the strongest.

As these quotes make clear, voters are not so much selling their votes as looking for a candidate with good chances of winning.

Indeed, the amount or quality of the food on offer, the number of cars (if candidates provide transportation), the occasional distribution of cash, and the number of people mobilized on election day are all used as cues to assess which candidates are in the lead. For instance, a focus group participant in rural Piura describes how transportation on election day works:

Each party delivers transportation for voters. During presidential elections, people go to vote alone but during municipal elections they expect candidates to bring a car to their doorstep. They give away to a greater or lesser degree. There, they pay voters 30 soles, 40. It depends. They paid 50 soles per family ... They tell us who to vote for. Now we are the ones who decide the vote ... There are candidates who do not offer [transportation]. Because they are low in voting intention, they do not arrange for transportation. (Female focus group, Alamor village, Lanconces, Sullana, Piura)

This anecdote reaffirms my informational theory: voters are not partisans being mobilized to the polls but opportunistic clients trying to guess who will win.

In summary, campaign clientelism helps politicians influence the dynamics of the race. By signaling electoral prospects, high turnout numbers at the early stages of the campaign can help candidates without organized parties to establish name recognition. Moreover, mobilizing large numbers of people allows some candidates to distinguish themselves from the rest of the field. Thus, a smaller number of candidates are marked out as frontrunners, attract strategic donors, and compete to attract voters in the final rush. Making sure that voters receive information about turnout is, thus, decisive for increasing the chances of getting elected. In the next section I address this issue.

TRANSMITTING TURNOUT FIGURES

To maximize the chances of influencing vote choices, politicians need to guarantee, that the cues sent out by turnout at campaign events are conveyed effectively to different constituencies. Turnout is, certainly, highly visible (Szwarcberg 2015). In Peru candidates visit commercial areas, particularly markets and plazas, while campaigning. In these settings, many people who do not participate at these campaign events can observe or learn of the candidate's mobilizational capability. Also, during campaigns, candidates go on intensive tours of poor neighborhoods and rural villages, particularly during weekends. These visits frequently end with rallies at public spots in which campaign clientelism is usually employed. Those who attend these rallies or pass by when they are taking place have the chance to directly evaluate the candidates' performance in terms of mobilizing numbers.

Furthermore, in urban centers, motorcades are an effective means of conveying information. They allow candidates to reach large areas of the city or town and engage voters' attention relatively quickly. Moreover, voters from different socioeconomic strata can easily and directly observe the number of people and cars mobilized by candidates. Thus, campaign teams invest considerable time and resources adorning vehicles with propaganda and, ideally, packing them with people that will cheer for the candidate. In most cases, candidates "buy" the participation of vehicles, giving the owners money for the fuel as well as a tip. Thereafter, the number of cars mobilized will serve as an informal indicator of the candidate's monetary power and potential electoral strength.

In addition, all those who observe a candidates' mobilizational strength will later act as informal sources of information through word of mouth. A variety of informal social mechanisms such, as political discussions or chats at work, at family gatherings, or with neighbors serve as channels for transmitting information about candidates' turnout at campaign events. Political information is disseminated through social interaction and constrained by voters' social context (Huckfeldt and Sprague 1987). Thus, the findings of Schaffer and Baker (2015) are, in fact, complementary to my informational theory. In relation to this, one political operator noted how interpersonal communication is decisive during campaigns because "people tend to believe more in those who surround them day-to-day [than in radio reporters]: the good neighbor, the good merchant ... They function as a transmission belt ... The media are important but they do not determine an election."[53] Moreover, politicians know that rumors about their mobilizational capacity will affect the public perception of their electoral strength. This is part of the reason why they spend a considerable amount of time doing street campaigning rather than relying solely on the media. This also explains why politicians might target citizens as opinion-leading epicenters, who can, thus, create a social multiplier (Schaffer and Baker 2015).

If direct observation and anecdotal accounts play a part in informing voters about candidates' mobilizational strength, the media also has an important role for conveying the electoral potential of candidates. Rather than substituting for traditional campaigning, media coverage *amplifies* the effects of mobilization at campaign events. As in other polities, the media in Peru covers elections as if they were horse races, identifying which candidates are in the lead and giving more space and time to the frontrunners' events (Bartels 1988).

One piece of information that influences media reporting in Peruvian elections is the number of people that candidates are able to attract to campaign events. The regional media size the crowds that candidates mobilize, particularly at final rallies. For example, the *El Tiempo* newspaper of Piura included a picture of *Obras+Obras'* final rally on the front page of its September 29, 2010 edition. In the picture, the rally looked packed. Moreover, the accompanying article noted that people occupied "an area that spanned the stage of the Cathedral atrium to the downtown branch of Interbank." In addition, photographers usually wait until rallies are at their peak before taking their pictures,[54] so political operators work hard to display people in ways that suggest a crowded rally.

---

[53] Personal interview with Marco Torres Paz (*Fujimorismo*; Lima, February 5, 2010).

[54] Interview with Luis Poma, head of archives at *La República* newspaper (October 25, 2012). This is the reason why it was difficult to find pictures of rallies taken from different points (with an empty plaza and a crowded one) in time for the experiment. Given this difficulty and pressures of time, I decided to use vignettes alone for the experiment.

During national elections in Peru the media frequently use nationally representative poll results to evaluate the electoral potential of presidential candidates. Given that polls are not conducted in many districts, or at least not with any frequency (or credibility) during subnational elections,[55] media coverage follows local campaigns to evaluate candidates' electoral potential. While national and regional media (particularly TV and press) do not always cover candidates' activities in detail, local broadcasters and radio stations usually do. And all media outlets will report on the number of participants at campaign activities, particularly at rallies. In addition, most districts and provinces in Peru have at least one local radio or television station that closely follows campaign activities. Moreover, many shantytowns and villages have their own communal stations that broadcast propaganda and information about campaign activities organized in the area. At least one dweller, usually a *dirigente*, has a megaphone, which is used to inform neighbors about local matters and call them to meetings. During campaigns, candidates persuade (or pay) megaphone owners to disseminate propaganda and information about campaign events.

In those parts of the country with well-developed local television markets, candidates campaign directly on TV stations more often than not. They will, for example, devote time to appearing on popular chat shows, news shows, and televised debates. Investment in TV advertisements will also make up a larger part of campaign expenditure. But even in such contexts where candidates campaign directly on television, campaign clientelism remains an important strategy. For instance, campaign clientelism is commonplace in Cusco and Puno, both of which have developed broadcasting companies.[56] In Cusco city, most candidates must work closely with journalists who double up as political operators and have connections with the local media. One of these media political operators explains that during campaigns he follows the *movilizadores* "who mobilize everything: the motorcades, the *portátil*, graffiti."[57] During political events he takes pictures and afterwards writes up a press release to distribute to his contacts in the media.

Why, then, does campaign clientelism persist even when the media market is more developed? The politicians and political operators interviewed explain that to reach and campaign among poorer constituencies, street politics and traditional campaigning are still fundamental. For instance, a

---

[55] See previous section.
[56] On Cusco's regional and municipal 2010 election, see Chapter 6.
[57] Personal interview with Oliver Delgado (September 1, 2010).

political operator campaigning in Piura for a regional movement argues that "95% of campaigning among low-income sectors is 'traditional style' politics, a grassroots effort."[58] Candidates use the media primarily to reach middle and upper-class constituencies. Poor voters, in contrast, do not follow media campaigns consistently,[59] and generally tend to be less informed than the better-off sectors. Moreover, as I will explore further in Chapter 5, for poor constituencies it is important to evaluate candidates' traits personally. This necessity explains why many candidates invest considerable time visiting poor neighborhoods and villages.

In short, having diverse channels in place to publicize and amplify the effects of high turnout is important for candidates; it is vital to improving their electoral chances. Direct observation of turnout, rumors, and media coverage all help politicians in achieving this goal.

CONCLUSION

In this chapter I provided empirical evidence that documents the first causal mechanism of my informational theory. In Peru, candidates without the backing of organized parties buy participation at campaign events because, otherwise, few people would attend. During the campaign, these candidates also distribute goods in order to access crucial constituencies with whom they have not established relationships. More importantly, politicians distribute handouts to increase turnout numbers at rallies and, thus, influence the public perception of electoral viability. Politicians engage in campaign clientelism because they expect it to influence their electoral fortunes. High turnout at campaign activities tells strategic actors (donors, activists, and voters) which candidates are in the lead. Also, given that other credible information outlets concerning electoral viability are scarce or not credible, turnout helps strategic donors and voters, coordinate, and identify a smaller number of viable candidates. Consequently, politicians can distribute goods in a rational and strategic manner without having established political networks, since mobilizing supporters during the campaign influences electoral choices.

---

[58] Personal interview with Gamaniel Ventura (Piura, July 26, 2010).
[59] According to LAPOP data (2010), in Peru, the frequency of news consumption is directly related to respondents' material wealth. LAPOP data (2012) confirms a direct relationship between the frequency of news consumption and interviewees' household income. Material wealth and interest in politics are also positively related to the 2010 Peru database. See also Chapter 5.

In conclusion, my evidence shows that electoral clientelism is widespread in Peru, not only in spite of the absence of political organization, but in many ways *because of* this absence. It is this lack of organization that allows for the tremendous fluidity and openness of electoral contests enabling candidates to rise, through "bought" turnout and forces them to continue buying turnout in order to collect donations and avoid a downward spiral in popularity. Distributing resources is, thus, a rational solution to the challenges of campaigning without parties and machines because it helps politicians to campaign and signal their electoral viability to strategic actors. This strategy is particularly helpful in races with few alternative sources of political information, such as frequent and credible polls. As a result, campaign clientelism plays a bigger role in subnational elections.

The quantitative, qualitative, and experimental data I have discussed in this chapter, combines to provide a more thorough empirical assessment of electoral clientelism in Peru. The quantitative data proved decisive in obtaining national estimates of the prevalence of different types of behaviors and attitudes. In particular, it was indispensable in revealing the widespread utilization of the hitherto understudied strategy of campaign clientelism and to identify informational cues that voters use to assess electoral viability. In turn, the qualitative data were crucial for understanding the political logic of campaign clientelism in Peru and documenting the causal mechanisms at work. Politicians and voters' opinions and perceptions served as a means of documenting the rationale for distributing material benefits during campaigns in the absence of organized machines. Finally, the experiments empirically tested the causal mechanism implie by my informational theory that links turnout at campaign events to electoral choices, while also discarding Kramon's alternative explanation about the importance of distributing gifts as an informational cue and its impact on poor voters' prospective expectations about the delivery of benefits. In this way, it provided systematic evidence to sustain part of the causal claim of my informational theory. In Chapter 5 I will explore the second causal mechanism that I propose: persuasion.

5

Persuasion from the Citizens' Point of View

Not everything [in campaigns] is about money. It's also about image. People are intelligent. (Absalón Vásquez, Fujimori's former political operator, Lima, December 12, 2012)

INTERVIEWER: What do people say about candidates who do not give gifts away?

PARTICIPANT 1: Cheap! [Laughs]

PARTICIPANT 2: Few people supported those candidates because you didn't see anybody at their rallies. That's the truth. People go when they have an interest, when they receive something in exchange.

PARTICIPANT 3: And to listen to the proposals. Let's see: one goes, gets the gifts and also hears the proposals and what he [the candidate] has worked on, his experience, observing him, his ability. (Female focus Group, Bellavista, Piura).

In Chapter 4 I showed that electoral clientelism is widespread in Peru because of the absence of political organization. Candidates distribute material benefits during elections to substitute for the lack of stable party linkages. During campaigns, politicians improvise organizations as electoral vehicles and visit poor neighborhoods and villages. They hand out goods such as food stamps or house supplies to gain access to local association meetings. They distribute material incentives to attract voters to their rallies. By bringing large numbers to their campaign events, candidates can further demonstrate their electoral viability to strategic donors and voters.

TABLE 5.1. *Persuasion at campaign events*

During these campaign events, did anything you heard or observed decide your vote?

	Freq.	%
Yes, it convinced me to support that candidate	157	40.9
Yes, it convinced me not to support that candidate	64	16.7
No, it did not convince me. I decided my vote afterwards	163	42.5
Total	384	100

Source: IOP (2012)

Campaign clientelism may guarantee presence at campaign events, but not support at the polls. Thus, there is a crucial second step that politicians must also take to assure themselves of this: they need to convince participants of their electoral *desirability*. Campaign events provide candidates with excellent opportunities to do so. In the IOP 2012 survey, those respondents who said they had attended campaign events at which candidates distributed or raffled material benefits during the last elections in Peru were then asked if this practice influenced their vote choice. As Table 5.1 shows, 57.6 percent stated that their choices were influenced by what they heard and observed; 40.9 percent said they were persuaded to support that candidate; and 16.7 percent answered that they were dissuaded from supporting them. In turn, 42.5 percent stated that what they saw and heard did not change their minds and that they only decided their vote afterwards.

Hence, the evidence appears to suggest that candidates do influence voters at campaign events. But what are the main mechanisms at work? How can candidates persuade campaign clients to support them? Do they do so through clientelistic strategies? In this chapter, I argue that two kinds of persuasion are crucial: persuasion via particularistic promises, and via personal performance and character. Candidates can take advantage of the localized character of campaign events to particularize their message so as to appeal to specific constituencies and promise them local public goods once elected – that is, they promise to engage in non-clientelistic distributive strategies. In addition, by conveying information about their personal traits and manners, a candidate can appeal more effectively to less politically sophisticated constituents. Finally, by presiding over enthusiastic rallies, candidates also hope that peer effects will persuade voters attending these events to support them.

In this chapter, I present empirical evidence to document the mechanism of persuasion. First, I briefly discuss the approach I took to analyze the qualitative evidence I obtained from focus groups, for the purposes of this chapter. Second, I describe the type of proposals and promises that politicians make at campaign events. I discuss why this information is relevant to clients' electoral choices, but also the limitations of relying on electoral promises alone to influence voters. Second, I present an account of the additional kinds of information that candidates transmit through personalistic appeals during their presentations at campaign events. I explain why personal information matters from the clients' perspective. Third, I briefly describe the ways in which peer effects (the "buzz") can convince undecided voters to support a given candidate. I conclude by presenting a summary of the chapter's main contributions.

FOCUS GROUP DATA ANALYSIS

I conducted a total of eighteen focus groups, nine in Cusco and nine in Piura, with a mean of 6.9 participants per group. Participants were recruited among residents of shantytowns, poor neighborhoods, and rural villages. They were each offered a sandwich and refreshments during the activity, but were not paid. I conducted six of these focus groups personally and entrusted the others to local assistants. In Cusco, I looked for speakers of Quechua who would be able to lead and then translate the contributions of *campesinos* for whom it was their first language. Except for a single case in Cusco, the focus groups were conducted with male- and female-only participants, respectively. I found no substantive differences between what women and men reported in the focus groups. Consequently, I do not make any sub-group comparisons.

The focus groups were designed to provide additional empirical evidence to test my theory and alternative explanations. I pre-tested the structured questionnaire with a pilot focus group involving young voters in Piura, which is not included among the eighteen analyzed here. The final questionnaire included a total of four modules (see Appendix 11). The first contained questions regarding participants' experience of electoral campaigns in their place of residence. The second contained a series of questions regarding the frequency and forms of gift distribution. The third explored participants' perceptions about gift distribution and asked about how they decide their vote. Finally, the last module included questions about gratitude and feelings of obligation to return favors as well as how politicians behave once in office.

TABLE 5.2. *Frequencies of codes across focus groups*

Code	Frequency	Percentage
Gifts help politicians amass people	13	83
Vote is for candidates with chances of winning the election	8	44
"Others" vote for the gifts they receive	11	61
Candidate's personal traits matter in deciding the vote	14	83
People evaluate candidates' proposals/promises in deciding their vote	14	78
People vote to support family/kin	6	33
Candidates build credibility as future patrons	7	39

I began my analysis of the focus groups by looking for evidence to test the implications of my theory regarding the frequency, timing, settings, and targets of gift distribution. I found a high level of agreement across focus-group answers (more than 90 percent) on this matter,[1] and discussed these findings in Chapters 3 and 4. Subsequently, I analyzed how participants (and people in their environs in general) decide their vote and how (and whether) the distribution of gifts impacts this decision. I formulated six codes, for which I selected quotes from each of the focus groups. Table 5.2 provides an overview of the frequency of responses pertaining to each code, per focus group. I assigned a code of one if participants referred to ideas related with the label in question on at least one occasion. It should be noted that this frequency does not assess the extent to which the subject is discussed collectively.

Before proceeding to the analysis, it is important to explain the general pattern of response that emerges while analyzing how people decide their vote vis-a-vis the distribution of gifts in campaign activities. As mentioned, the data confirms that politicians frequently engage in campaign clientelism when electioneering within low-income constituencies. Thus, the distribution of gifts is completely normalized for participants.

---

[1] Thus, for example, of all the localities where I conducted focus groups, I only found evidence of the plausible existence of relational clientelism in one rural district in Piura. In this small district, the mayor seemed to engage in relational clientelism with poor voters, continuously delivering benefits to cultivate strategic friendly relations (*compadrazgo*). In each of the other cases, participants said that the practice of distributing gifts was mostly limited to electoral times.

Moreover, many of them even admit that they attend rallies and other campaign activities in order to receive gifts. However, none stated that receipt of gifts equated to the sale of their vote. On the contrary, they specifically remarked that they evaluate candidates' proposals/promises (78 percent) and/or their personal attributes/behavior before deciding whom to support (83 percent). They stressed that voting decision is down to the voter's "conscience" and that politicians cannot tell for sure who they will support at the polls. I analyze this information to empirically support my arguments in this chapter. Although all of the quotes presented here are representative of these modal patterns, I selected the richest ones that I believed best expressed the complexities of voters' behaviors or beliefs.

At the same time, in most of the groups (61 percent) at least one intervention or discussion revealed that many participants *do* believe that a portion of the electorate – varying across groups: 3–70 percent – are in fact influenced by gifts and, thus, "sell" their votes. But the usual suspect in all cases is the "other" voter who the group participants intentionally distinguish themselves from. In all cases, this "other" voter was conceived as someone who, sociologically speaking, has a lower social status in Peru. Answers included references to "*campesinos*" (variously defined as persons from rural areas, *campesino* communities, or higher altitude areas, usually considered to be more "indigenous" in Cusco), the "illiterate" or the "least educated" voters, and "women" (who tend to be less educated in Peru). Thus, there is always an inferior who is "dumb" enough to be deceived by politicians and who sells their vote for a gift. In all conversations, these vote-selling "others" were looked down on by participants.

Some of these contributions regarding voters who sell their votes for gifts also included references to a logic akin to what Kramon's informational theory would expect to find: that these "others" sell their votes because they believe that the candidate will continue delivering material benefits in the future. But participants also commented on how naïve or mistaken these voters are given the high rates of broken promises by politicians who access office. Although we cannot rule out this alternative explanation entirely, I propose on the basis of the data collected to date that even if such behavior is present, subject to social desirability bias, and potentially underreported, it is not modal in Peru.[2]

In summary, it is evident that focus group participants have no qualms about admitting that they often receive gifts, but that they do not wish to be branded as vote sellers. This reaffirms my proposal that

---

[2] See also Chapter 4.

most voters who engage in campaign clientelistic deals decide their vote based on other considerations and not on the amount or quality of the gifts received. As explicitly stressed in some of these discussions, it would appear that, it is voters who dupe politicians and not the other way around. Indeed, it is the very characteristic dynamics of focus groups, which induce social pressures, groupthink, and social bias and lead to the emergence of consensus, that gives this method external validity (Cyr 2016: 1039). Moreover, as we will see, I triangulate data from interviews with politicians and operators and that from focus groups to empirically support my findings.

PARTICULARIZED PROPOSALS AND PROMISES

Giving things away also involves talking. (Javier Barreda, APRA, Lima, September 9, 2012)

    All candidates give things away. I don't think people vote for the gift received. All candidates go to convince: if someone offers you something you accept but you vote for the candidate that suits you the most. (Oliver Delgado, media operator, Cusco, September 1, 2010)

Poor voters often attend campaign events where politicians hand out material benefits to those present. As shown in Chapter 4, many low-income voters who participated in rallies during the most-recent electoral contests in Peru claimed that they did so in order to receive what the politicians distributed or raffled off (see Table 4.2). These survey respondents stated that they were not primarily interested in listening to the candidates' proposals or showing their support. This is not altogether surprising considering that poor voters in Peru tend to be less interested in politics than do wealthier ones. Both politicians and poor citizens acknowledged this fact during interviews and focus groups. Moreover, poll results confirm that there is an inverse association between how interested Peruvians are in politics and their socioeconomic status. As shown in Table 5.3, 57.39 percent of respondents from stratums A/B, the wealthiest voters, are uninterested or somewhat interested in politics. Meanwhile, 78.56 percent of the respondents in the poorest stratum (E/D) said they were not interested in politics.

    Indeed, according to IOP's survey, many underprivileged participants in campaign events are voters who are uninterested in politics. By contrast, relatively few of these participants who are uninterested in politics come from the higher SES. This pattern can be observed in the distributions plotted in Figure 5.1.

TABLE 5.3. *Interest in politics by SES*

How interested are you in politics?

	Socioeconomic status*			
	A/B	C	D/E	Total
Uninterested	20.78%	22.93%	28.65%	25.21%
	(53)	(83)	(163)	(299)
Somewhat interested	36.61%	42.27%	49.91%	45.36%
	(101)	(153)	(284)	(538)
Interested	28.24%	26.80%	17.40%	22.60%
	(72)	(97)	(99)	(268)
Very interested	11.37%	8.01%	4.04%	6.83%
	(29)	(29)	(23)	(81)
Total	100%	100%	100%	100%
	(255)	(362)	(569)	(1186)

Pearson chi^2(6) = 38.7519; Pr = 0.000.
*Where A is the highest socioeconomic status and E is the lowest.
Source: IOP (2012)

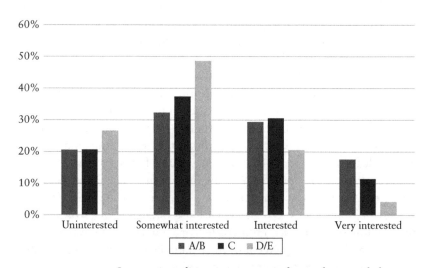

FIGURE 5.1. *Interest in politics among respondents who attended campaign clientelism events, by SES*
Source: IOP (2012)

In short, poor voters in Peru do not always attend campaign events in order to listen to the candidate, unlike wealthier voters. However, participants at these mass meetings *do*, nevertheless, get information about the candidate's proposals. Citizens receive material benefits when they participate in campaign events, where they are also exposed to the candidates' message. In addition, voters frequently receive print propaganda at these public gatherings. For instance, candidates often attend the assemblies and meetings of local associations and introduce themselves and their proposals to the attendees. In the words of one political operator:

We do not buy consciences. We offer breakfast to get people involved. Moreover, we present our political project there, our ideas. (Gregoria Muro, *Unidos Construyendo* political operator. Piura, July 23, 2010)

The account of this Quechua-speaking *campesino* confirms this claim:

Presidential elections take place every five years and regional and municipal every four. During those periods the politicians arrive and campaign [in the community], they campaign for three months before election day. They tell us what party they are running for, why they are running as candidates. They make us listen to their program and they distribute propaganda. We observe. In this way we get to know if they are old or new [to politics], what their trajectory is, if they are members of old parties, and so on. We analyze what they say, what works they will provide. By listening and analyzing such things we support whoever convinces us most. Consequently, on election day we have already decided and we enter (the booth) and vote for the candidate we like. (Male focus group, Occoruro community, Cusco)

An analogous scenario plays out at rallies. Besides other activities intended to entertain the attendees – music, singing, and dancing, raffles, and the distribution of prizes or donations – rallies always set aside some time (or periodic intervals of time) for the candidates' presentations. This exposes the voters attending the rally to the candidate's proposals, even those whose participation is primarily motivated by receipt of the politicians' gifts. This strategy is precisely what a woman participating at a focus group in Cusco explains:

For example, they go to a rally saying 'Well, I will drink the "O" punch,' for Ollanta. Or they go to Keiko's rally saying 'I'll get a bag,' like me, and then shout 'Bag! Bag!' [Laughs] In this way, successively they go to different rallies to receive something. Well, they get to listen to the proposals anyway and maybe receive a gift. And, if they don't like [the candidate], they don't vote [for them]. That is what people do: they go from one to the next; they go and listen to proposals. (Female focus group, Sucsu Auccaylle community, Cusco)

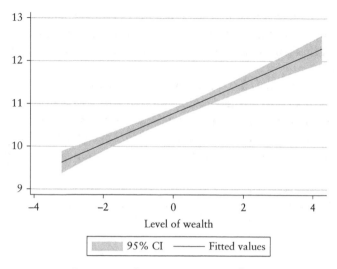

FIGURE 5.2. *Frequency of news consumption by material wealth*
(linear prediction)
Source: LAPOP (2010)

This and other accounts related in the focus groups show how campaign clients are exposed to candidates' proposals at campaign events.

It is important not to underestimate the relevance of transmitting electoral information in this way. Middle- and upper-class voters may have access to better or more accurate sources of information, but for many poor electors, these events *can* make a difference to their choice of candidate. Indeed, many low-income participants would not otherwise access any information whatsoever about candidates' proposals. This is because poor and indifferent citizens inform themselves about candidates more sporadically than wealthier voters. As Figure 5.2 indicates, wealth is a significant determinant of the frequency of news consumption.

In some ways, campaign clientelism might be considered as an extended political advertisement. When politicians buy attendance at campaign events, they gain a captive audience that is exposed to the candidates' message for a longer time than is the case with a conventional TV or radio advertisement. As a result, the chances that priming will work are greater than they are with media advertisements. In addition to being a more effective way to convey messages, this type of "advertising" is considerably cheaper than most media advertisements. This advantage remains even after accounting for the cost of the material goods to be distributed. Indeed, many of the products distributed or raffled at rallies are donations that would be more difficult to collect in cash. It is simply easier to convince a fishing company to donate seafood products to distribute at campaign events or a textile businessman to donate t-shirts than to persuade them to contribute cash to the campaign.

But what types of proposals do politicians expound while taking advantage of their investment in campaign clientelism? Rather than delivering general discourses about their political beliefs and what they would do in office, candidates adjust their messaging to appeal to the targeted constituency. When candidates visit social organizations or when they give speeches at rallies in poor neighborhoods, they make sure they transmit proposals they believe are of interest to the attendees. With this in mind, they try to present very specific proposals that convey local knowledge of people's needs. Thus, candidates' speeches commonly include specific (group- or locale-oriented) promises, often concerning the future delivery of club goods. In the following extract, a *campesino* describes how politicians offer specific promises to different groups while campaigning:

In the communities there are associations such as the dairy products association, the crafts association, the small animals' association. The candidates visit the different associations and they offer things. For example, to build sheds and bring improved breeding animals [for the small animals' association]. In the case of dairy products, they offer to find a market niche to sell their products. In the case of the cattle owners, they say they will take the cattle directly to Lima [with no intermediaries] to find better prices for producers. (Female focus group, rural Cusco)

The more targeted the proposals, the greater the chances of politicians influencing a particular constituency because politicians try to convey awareness of local needs. Consequently, campaign teams tend to ascertain people's main demands or concerns ahead of time so they can adapt the candidate's message to the local audience's needs and expectations. This strategy was explained by Gregoria Muro, who worked as a political operator with Javier Atkins' campaign in Piura both in 2006 and 2010. In her words, throughout the campaign they "studied" each district.[3] Before each campaign event, she sent a logistical team to gather information about the localities and prepare for the candidate's arrival. During the campaign, they ended up visiting all sixty-four of Piura's districts

---

[3] Personal interview with Gregoria Muro, political operator, *Unidos Construyendo* (Piura, July 23, 2010).

plus many villages located near the highways. Another political operator, with much more experience, explained to me that he keeps an up-to-date database with relevant information on many poor neighborhoods for the campaign: how many voters there are, what basic services they lack, if they have property titles, etc. His aim in doing so was to create a geo-referenced database that would help him sell his services to politicians more easily.[4] A shantytown dweller from Piura also confirms that campaign teams do some basic research in advance of their campaign events;

Generally, before going to a shantytown the candidate sends his team. They always look for the needs. "Let's go and let's see what we can propose in Los Polvorines. Let's see what we will propose in La Molina, what people need." The politicians carry out a study first. (Male focus group, Los Polvorines settlement, Piura)

Furthermore, campaign events are usually excellent opportunities for poor local communities to relay their demands to politicians. This happens frequently, for example, when candidates visit associations in poor villages and shantytowns. On these occasions *dirigentes* present their affiliates' needs to the candidate and explain what they would expect from him after being elected. Usually, *dirigentes* request permanent investments such as local public goods (a school, water and sanitation projects, electricity, a mill, a community hall, etc.), or the creation of jobs or income-generating projects for their affiliates. As a focus group participant from rural Cusco explains:

The candidates ask: "*Compañeros*, what can we do for you?" And we enthusiastically make our requests: "We want tractors, a community hall." And the candidate says, "All right, for sure I will do it." The candidate agrees to everything that the *comunero* asks for. (Male focus group, Males, rural Cusco)

More importantly, through campaign clientelism poor voters get information about different candidates. Whether opportunistic or just curious, voters attend several campaign events. After listening to several candidates, they have the chance to compare proposals and select the candidate who, in their eyes, is the most convincing. Thus, the information gathered through campaign clientelism helps poor voters to *form* their electoral preferences. Therefore, campaign clients should not be portrayed as avaricious or unthinking voters who mechanically react to the goods received and vote for the candidate without discrimination. As one

[4] Personal interview with *Fujimorismo* political operator (Lima, February 17, 2010).

citizen ironically remarks, poor voters are capable of thinking too, even if they do receive material goods during campaigns. In her own words,

PARTICIPANT 1:   I receive the gift anyway. Or will they [the candidates] know who I am going to vote for? ...

PARTICIPANT 2:   The vote is secret ...

PARTICIPANT 1:   The majority, at least in the city, we are aware and we know who we will vote for ... What do they think we are? ... Do they believe we don't think and that we are going to switch our vote [in exchange for a gift]? (Female focus group, Huancaro, Cusco).[5]

To believe otherwise is to underestimate underprivileged electors: they may not be fully informed, but they *do* make their own electoral choices.

Campaign clients are not passive political actors, as confirmed by many of the utterances of the poor voters who took part in the focus groups. During campaign events they listen to candidates' proposals, and then examine this information before deciding their vote. As a shanty-town dweller from Piura explains:

They compare all the candidates' proposals ... Then, another candidate arrives, with a new proposal. We compare them [and say] "No, this one is better," and we change our mind. Because we support whoever supports our shantytown's improvement. (Male focus group, EL Indio settlement, Piura)

Furthermore, often voters meet after candidate presentations to deliberate about the best electoral option for their community or association. The following focus-group extracts attest to this. The first is from a female *campesino*:

I have been able to see how in Salla community in Urcos, they receive all the candidates. Afterwards, during an assembly, they analyze the proposals each made by each candidate and see which promises can be accomplished. They discuss it with the *comuneros* and they reach a unanimous decision and agree to vote for a certain candidate. This is what I saw in Salla: after receiving all the candidates, they analyzed each proposal. In Huaro community they proceeded in the same way. (Female focus group, rural Cusco)

An analogous description is given by a participant of a focus group conducted in a poor neighborhood of Cusco City:

[5] Her reference to the prejudices and stigma associated with this practice are plain to see.

We analyze. Each candidate arrives ... we analyze what they offer ... they come here, to our assembly ... They arrive with their program of work and they offer us a lot of things. When this finishes we analyze and ask ourselves, "Who should we support?" But, finally, democratically, we leave the final decision to each member, so they can vote for the candidate they think can do best for us. (Mixed focus group, Villa Primavera settlement, Huancaro, Cusco)

Of course, the extent to which underprivileged voters will collectively deliver on these electoral choices hinges upon the cohesiveness and strength of community-level institutions (Baldwin 2015). Given that communal institutions are historically stronger in Cusco than in many other parts of the country, it is no surprise that comments of this type are made in focus groups conducted in that region.

Like any other type of advertisement, the direct announcement of specific proposals and promises at campaign events is not an infallible means of persuading voters. Indeed, it is subject to similar challenges as media-based advertising. Voters strongly distrust politicians in Peru because electoral promises are frequently ignored once authorities are elected. Consequently, most voters do not believe in the candidates' words. "*Menos palabras, más obras*" (literally, "fewer words and more public works") is a common expression used by Peruvians to question politicians. "*Las palabras se las lleva el viento*," which literally means "words are carried off by the wind," but might be compared with the English expression "actions speak louder than words," is another often heard adage in Peruvian politics. Indeed, as I discussed in Chapter 3, elected officials in Peru often invest intensively in public works with the primary aim of improving their political reputation.

During conversations in the focus groups, poor voters frequently reiterate this lack of confidence in politicians and stress how they are tired of listening to empty promises over and over again. Examples abound. The following excerpt, in which participants express their frustration with politicians' behavior after getting elected, is just an illustration:

PARTICIPANT 1   Once they win the elections, candidates do not recognize anybody despite the fact that our vote got them elected as mayor or councilor. They do not take us into account and they forget the promises they made during the campaign ...

PARTICIPANT 2   What my *compañeros* say is true. During the campaign we are their equals, their brothers and sisters. But once in office they don't remember the proposals

> they presented. That is, they don't deliver the public
> works and support they offered while campaigning.
> (Female focus group, rural Cusco)

Thus, a problem of credibility can undermine the effectiveness of directly communicating proposals at campaign events.

However, unlike media advertisements, personal contact with campaign teams allows poor voters to develop informal mechanisms that help them defend themselves against deception. For example, it is not unusual for local communities to ask visiting candidates to sign written statements confirming they will pursue their campaign commitments once in office. As one political operator recognizes:

There are other requests [besides gifts]: the memos. Everybody comes with their record book. People make the candidate sign. You *have* to sign. You have to sign and, if you win, they bring you a copy of the statement. (Jorge Nuñez, political operator, Puno, June 12, 2010)

The same strategy is explained by a participant in a focus group conducted in Cusco:

Candidates arrive in towns offering too many things. They promise so much that in the peasant communities, *comuneros* prefer to note the candidates' promises in their record book. Because during campaigns candidates promise many things but they forget them when they get elected. Then, *comuneros* visit the elected candidate and take with them their record book where the commitments were signed. They go to remind him of these offers, saying "During the campaign you offered to build us these projects. We are coming to remind you about that so you can execute it right away." (Male focus group, rural Cusco)

Moreover, poor voters make similar demands of several candidates during campaigns, and they ask for written commitments from each of them. These statements allow citizens to claim the fulfillment of campaign promises once the elected authority assumes office. Although the documents do not have legal validity, they can serve as focal points around which to articulate collective action efforts, and even protests, at a later date. The following excerpt from a focus group in urban Cusco illustrates the process:

PARTICIPANT 1: It's one way in which residents try to take advantage. They know that a candidate is going to come so they prepare a request for a given project. They ask the candidate to support it and they assure him 'We will support you but sign this document.'

PARTICIPANT 2:   People in need take advantage. They ask everybody
                   [to sign]! It is not just one candidate ...
PARTICIPANT 1:   Whoever wins, they already get it ...
PARTICIPANT 3:   Generally, if they are fly-by-night candidates,[6] they
                   will not accomplish their promises. But with the writ-
                   ten request we can go and protest. (Focus Group,
                   Females, Huancaro, Cusco)

In summary, after attracting participants through campaign clientelism,
candidates present specific proposals and promises for targeted constituencies. Conveying policy messages at campaign events works as an
extended political advertisement and is much cheaper than buying media
ads. Moreover, personal contact between candidates and voters helps
improve politicians' credibility. Nonetheless, the effectiveness of personal
communication is not solely reliant on the announcement of particular-
ized promises at campaign events. The conveyance of personal traits during public gatherings is also crucial to persuading clients of a candidate's
credibility and, thus, of their electoral desirability. I explore this second
informational channel in the next section.

A GOOD CANDIDATE

Politics is the art of gestures (Roberto Romero, political operator, Cusco.
December 17, 2010).

I paint [political propaganda], that's my job. I have painted propaganda for many
people. But if I support a candidate it is because he convinced me. I can paint for
many, but if one convinces me, I support him. If not, I can work for him but it's
different. It's another story ... For example, if I am a member of a sports association and a candidate donates T-shirts for the team. He donated, but I will not feel
pressured to vote for him. To vote for him, first he has to gain your trust. (Male
focus group, El Indio settlement, Piura)

Since the collapse of the party system in the 1990s, Peruvian politicians
have come up with different ways of making up for the absence of stable
political organizations. Reliance on the media for campaigning and communicating with voters is one path that has been taken. But media-driven
politics has not displaced street campaigning. As I explained in Chapter 4,

---

[6] Candidatos de paso.

the creation of *portátiles* and the investment in campaign clientelism are among the strategies devised to deal with this lack of permanent organization. Poorly prepared candidates can easily improvise canvassing structures and public gatherings for their speeches. One experienced political operator noted:

This is my conclusion: an organization is not enough [to campaign successfully]. You need a good candidate. A good candidate replaces a good organization. There is no organization in Peru ... The organization ends up being supplementary. (Abraham Parrilla, political operator, Piura. September 23, 2010)

In other words, (permanent) organization is not essential to running a successful campaign in Peru. A strong candidacy, however, is much more difficult to do without. Why might this be the case? In a context such as Peru where most voters do not identify with party labels and dislike political parties and politicians, a candidate's ability to effectively *connect* with voters can be decisive. A good candidate can make up for many other shortcomings exhibited by a political grouping, such as improvisation or inconsistency. In contrast, a bad candidate generally has fewer prospects of getting elected even if they are backed by strong organization. Indeed, while it is possible to play up a candidate's professional background, skills as a speaker, personal charisma, and ability to interact with voters from different socioeconomic backgrounds, this is only true up to a point. The Spanish proverb holds that *Lo que natura no da, Salamanca no lo presta,* which means that certain personal qualities are innate and cannot be learned; not even at a prestigious university such as Salamanca.

But what do a candidate's characteristics have to do with campaign clientelism? In what way is electoral clientelism connected with personalism in politics? In this section I show that a candidate's participation in campaign events is probably the best way to convey personal traits to voters. By gathering an audience, campaign clientelism provides the ideal opportunity for public performance and personalized political communication. Moreover, given that campaign clients tend to be less politically sophisticated than more affluent voters, the direct evaluation of a candidate's traits is more relevant for this group of voters. Consequently, a viable candidate's performance at campaign events can be crucial to attaining electoral success. When candidates are perceived as viable *and* desirable, they have better chances of getting elected.

There are several reasons why campaign events, such as rallies and candidate visits, are better for projecting candidates' personal information than propaganda and other types of events. Campaign events provide opportunities for face-to-face interactions. During electoral events, politicians interact directly with voters; candidates do not just rely on mediators but engage directly with voters, either individually or as a group. Without a doubt, "speeches at rallies and candidate-voter interactions ... are arguably the closest we can come to political communication without mediation" (Nielsen 2012: 13). As a Peruvian political operator contends, "the vote is emotional. Thus, interpersonal communication is more important [than relying just on the media] ... 'I believe in what I see, not in what they [the media] tell me,' people say."[7] According to a candidate for the regional vice-presidency in Piura, "people want to see the candidate and get to know him."[8] Many activities even provide opportunities for physical contact: voters have the chance to personally greet, kiss, hug, and touch the candidate. As the following quotation shows, poorer voters are often interested in such personal or physical contact with politicians:

Sometimes strangers come from other places or from Lima. They bring caps and other stuff. We come out from our homes to meet them. We are interested in finding out if they are warm or cold people. We touch their hands so we can know if they are warm or cold. We then gather and decide whether they have been cold or warm; or short ... In other words, we go out mostly to meet them, to find out what they are like. (Male focus group, Occoruro community, Cusco)

Moreover, candidates have numerous opportunities to interact spontaneously with attendees at campaign events. Even at the most carefully planned gatherings, there is always room for spontaneity. Candidates may receive comments or be the butt of a joke that catches them unawares; or something may not go as planned and candidates might be required to give explanations to the public or improvise a speech. Of course, campaign events are not edited like advertisements and news coverage. And voters who interact with candidates will be attentive to the candidates' responses and reactions during these unplanned moments, as they know that the way in which the candidates react will reveal much about their personal character. The 2011 Peruvian presidential elections provide a great example of how candidates are exposed to the unexpected at campaign events. During one of Pedro Pablo Kuczynski's visits to a poor neighborhood in the port of Callao, a woman expressed her appreciation of him by grabbing his genitals. Astonished, Kuczynski managed to smile

---

[7] Marco Torres Paz, *Fujimorismo* political operator and advisor in Congress (Lima, February 5, 2010).

[8] Personal interview. Piura, July 20, 2011.

and let her touch him. His reaction was positive – he did not become aggressive, and the moment was widely regarded as funny. The moment endured in the public memory long after it had passed. The candidate's reaction was perhaps so memorable because it was unexpected. Already in his seventies, Kuczynski is a businessman and former Minister of Finance who is seen as being more *gringo* than Peruvian (he lived in the United States for many years and held dual nationality at the time).[9] His reaction was seen to be very *criolla*, befitting of a "streetwise" Peruvian rather than from a wealthy and straight-laced businessman. Kuczynski's team immediately saw an opportunity in this spontaneous event; they took pictures of the scene and distributed them widely through the media and the internet. As a result, Kuczynski received invitations onto many TV programs, and the scene was imitated by comedy shows.[10] Without a doubt, this unexpected event and the candidate's reaction to it helped enhance his relatability and, therefore, his popularity.[11]

Finally, and perhaps most importantly, campaign events are performances – they are theatrical acts. Analogous to what happens in any other interaction in everyday life (Goffman 1959), candidates present their "selves" to voters during these events. That is, politicians try to manage the impressions voters receive while interacting with them. In this way, the candidate displays and communicates a political persona on the campaign trail (Fenno 1996: 324). Analyzing campaign events as performances means that *the way* in which candidates behave will be of vital importance in defining what their personal style and characteristics are from the voters' perspective. Indeed, during these public performances, candidates get exceptional chances to *connect* personally with the participants. As Mahler (2011) points out, achieving this connection can be crucial for actually winning support from voters. Thus, the public presentation of a candidate at campaign events can be crucial to persuading voters of that candidate's electoral desirability (or undesirability).

Aware as they are of the importance of electoral events, campaign teams deliberately plan for their candidate's public perception as a success. A very important factor for a campaign event to be considered successful is the number of people the candidate can mobilize. However, gathering large numbers of voters is not enough to make a rally effective in electoral terms. Politicians also need to make sure that the event

---

[9] Kuczynski was elected president of Peru in 2016. On this election, see Dargent and Muñoz 2016.

[10] For instance, see: http://trome.pe/actualidad/717153/noticia-le-agarraron-bolonas-ppk.

[11] Indeed, it worked so well that some journalists suspected it was staged.

creates a favorable impression – or better still, widespread public interest. Two elements are crucial to attaining those goals.

First, campaign teams must set the scene for the political show – the most "doable" stage of preparing a campaign event. It is the responsibility of the team, particularly of the *movilizadores*, to plan the logistics and assure everything will be ready on time. Setting the scene well requires expertise and resources. But it is something that can be learned (or even purchased).

Distributing material benefits during campaign events is an important part of this process since it helps assure a gratifying environment for attendees. Gifts or prizes work as selective incentives to attract poor voters and give them a reason for attending the event. Moreover, and as voters themselves acknowledge, distributing gifts is also another way for the political group to reach out to people:

On some occasions, the candidate himself gives away goods because it's a way to get closer to the people, to make yourself known. But there is also a committee of supporters who are distributing gifts at the other side of the event or from different sides. (Mixed focus group, Compone Community, Cusco)

However, setting the scene goes beyond distributing goods. The ambience should be attractive to people. A great deal of the campaign team's work, therefore, goes into decorating the venue and organizing entertainment. The stage is usually filled with balloons and flags in the party's colors, banners, and pictures of the candidates. Supporters wear the party T-shirts. Often, one person dresses up in a costume that represents the group's label, commonly an animal, a known character, or an object such as a star. In addition, campaign teams usually organize dance performances and singing acts. They also take bands to play – seeing a popular band can be another incentive to attend a campaign event. During visits, politicians take megaphones with them to play music and communicate political slogans. The aim of all this spectacle is to create a buoyant mood in the crowd: the "*fiesta electoral*" (electoral party) should induce a party atmosphere that everybody enjoys. Team members, thus, try to avoid boring the attendees while they all wait for the candidate to show up.

Organizing a campaign event, however, is not limited to preparing the physical setting. Second, and most importantly, advisors also work with the candidate to help deliver a strong public performance. In this regard, everything matters: the candidate's outfit, tone of voice and body language, use of words, sense of humor, ability to respond to questions and criticism, and how closely they interact with people. Political advisors work assiduously on the candidates' image, making a strenuous effort to minimize their negative characteristics and maximize their capacity to fulfill voters' expectations. And voters themselves are aware that the public presentation of a candidate involves some investment in political marketing. As an illustration, the reference this *dirigente* makes during a focus group in Piura is interesting:

Today there are more people who have a lust for power. Therefore, they have to invest ... And what is the way to invest in a campaign? To invest means to satisfy the voter. It also means to present yourself as generous, caring, and affectionate. I arrive with a gift, with a kiss. Candidates are transformed. Did you meet Javier Atkins before the campaign? Don Javier Atkins did not used to wear a straw hat ... Why did he begin wearing one? It was because people began to perceive him as the candidate who represented the rich. He wears the hat so that everybody will feel that they are in front of a candidate who is a real *Piurano*, a *paisano*. (Male focus group, Los Polvorines settlement, Piura)

Interacting with poor voters at campaign events and assuring a strong personal performance is particularly important for candidates. In all polities, poor citizens tend to be less politically sophisticated and to have less political information than their wealthier counterparts. Peru is no different (see Figure 5.3), and the challenge of acquiring and processing electoral information is exacerbated by the lack of stable partisan attachments and policy positions that can work as cognitive shortcuts. But poor

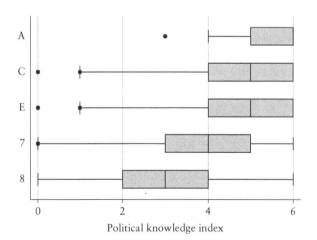

FIGURE 5.3. *Political knowledge by SES*
Source: Ipsos APOYO (2010). Survey conducted for the *Jurado Nacional de Elecciones*

voters are well versed in evaluating personal traits. Since they tend to be less politically sophisticated, when deciding their vote, low-income voters put more weight on personal characteristics than do wealthier ones (Slosar 2011). Indeed, their everyday experiences and socialization has taught them to garner insights into personal characteristics and behavior during social interactions. This in turn forms the basis of their judgment of a candidate's desirability. Therefore, the public performances of candidates at campaign events is particularly important for determining the electoral preferences of this constituency.

But what aspects of a candidate's performance at campaign events are important? What information do voters consider electorally relevant to them? The candidate-centered attributes of success (authenticity, consistency, and good character) identified by Fenno (1996) broadly coincide with the qualities recognized as important to poor voters in Peru, and the third appears especially relevant for deciding actual vote choices. Simply put, Peruvian voters look for a politician with "good" personal traits for an elected authority. Of course, the specific characteristics that appeal to voters may vary; but they are all personal skills and attributes rather than stances on policy issues.

To begin with, voters usually consider candidates' public and professional background. Thus, as electoral surveys show, 28 percent of Peruvian voters would prefer to have a mayor who is an economist or manager while 10 percent would prefer an engineer (JNE 2010). However, more than the profession per se, what most voters seems to look for is a candidate who has technical expertise and initiative – and, consequently, one who will be a good administrator who delivers public works and solves people's problems effectively. Thus, when asked about the main characteristics that a politician should have, 57 percent of respondents prioritized fulfillment of electoral promises, while 47 percent referred to the *ability* to identify problems. Hence, while campaigning it is crucial for candidates to show that they have the requisite abilities but also the willingness to address people's concerns effectively.

Second, voters prefer candidates who are likable and approachable. Some of the focus-group participants referred to this as "charisma." One voter from Cusco articulates these priorities as follows:

Compañeros, there are many candidates who want to access power. [To decide our vote] we take into account their qualities. For example, we want to make sure that, while campaigning, the candidate is an agreeable person ... We see if he is nice. Afterwards, we also evaluate his capabilities, if he is prepared to lead people or not ... We observe how the candidate talks, his attitudes, his willingness to work and his capacity to negotiate. Although we sometimes get it wrong, this is what decides our vote. (Male focus group, rural Cusco)

Bad candidates, in turn, tend to be exposed at campaign events. The following discussion provides another good illustration of how candidates' attitudes and performances while campaigning can hurt them electorally:

PARTICIPANT 1:   During the last municipal elections there was a candidate who did everything he could. He gave out gifts almost house by house ... He had run as a candidate two or three times [previously] but this year he did it forcefully. The people realized: where does all that money come from? And how is he going to retrieve it?

INTERVIEWER: Did he give away *that much*?

PARTICIPANT 2:   You should have seen the campaign trail. There was no wall without propaganda or not painted with his name ... It was too much! Over the top!

PARTICIPANT 3:   He already felt like the winner! But, in the end, he finished in around fourth place.

INTERVIEWER: So, people did not support him?

PARTICIPANT 1:   You know what happened? This gentleman [Mogrovejo] is a little arrogant. In one moment, he says 'brother ...' [i.e., he treated them well] But afterwards, someone approaches him and he stares at you. Arrgh! [He makes a derogatory gesture]. He is a despotic person. If he were mayor, how would he treat people?

(Mixed focus group, Villa Primavera settlement, Cusco)

Third, another trait that voters – especially poor voters – look for in candidates is a clear demonstration that they have local interests at heart. By interacting with voters, candidates must persuade voters that they understand and care about their needs. As Mahler points out:

[T]he practical challenge presented by the world of politics, at least from the perspective of politicians, is not simply that one must be-known-in-the-world-out-there in the guise of a celebrity or as someone who has simply been able to make a name for oneself by whatever means necessary. The challenge is just as much, if not more so, to connect with those-in-the-world-out-there – to be known as someone who is sympathetic with their causes and concerns; which is to say to be known as someone who knows and understands and is familiar with the-world-out-there. (Mahler 2011: 159)

In other words, the challenge for candidates is to be recognized for their knowledge of conditions and people's expectations.

Poor voters believe that someone who wants to represent them must be familiar with the places in which they live and work; otherwise, it would be difficult for politicians to understand people's needs and frustrations. From this perspective, only those who live in poverty or are close to it can understand this way of life. This thought process is reflected, for example, in the following focus-group comments:

INTERVIEWER: What would we need to change the way politicians behave [while in office]?

PARTICIPANT 1:   They need an advisor, but an advisor who lives in a place like Los Polvorines so he can communicate their people's need...

PARTICIPANT 2:   A small group of well-trained people that can explain the needs.

PARTICIPANT 3:   In the case of mayors, I believe that they should be present there [in the field] to see the problems and not to wait for an intermediary. (Female focus group, Los Polvorines settlement, Piura)

Campaigning personally and intensively, with continuous visits to poor neighborhoods and remote areas, therefore, helps candidates build credibility in the eyes of this population group. As Cánepa and Málaga note, in reference to political marketing strategies used in Cusco, "During the campaign, a candidate must be *everywhere*. This ubiquity provides him with legitimacy to speak, from his experience, about the region's and the city's problems" (Cánepa and Málaga 2011: 34).[12]

In addition, poor voters look for signs in a candidate's public performance that could affect the degree to which they are perceived as truly having local needs at heart. To begin with, the *way* in which turnout buying is carried out matters greatly. Indeed, there is certainly more to it than throwing around goods or money: candidates and their campaign staff must show that they *care* about assisting the needy. Therefore, they are expected to follow certain social codes (or at least pretend to do so).

---

[12] The original Spanish wording is: "*Un candidato, mientras dure su campaña, debe estar en todas partes. Esta ubicuidad le da legitimidad para hablar desde la experiencia sobre los problemas de la ciudad y la region.*"

Political operators are aware of this need and advise candidates to behave in certain ways. One politician explained this as follows:

They [political operators] want to sell the image that you are the good guy, you are a guy predisposed to giving stuff away, that you would give even your life and, of course, rice, oil. [He laughs] That you are willing to go and get your shoes dirty in the shantytown and spend a night there with people. That is the image you start to sell. (Maximiliano Ruiz, *Unidos Construyendo* candidate for regional vice presidency, Piura July 20, 2010)

Candidates also need to strike some sort of balance in the type and the quantity of goods they distribute. If they give away too little, they risk being perceived as inconsequential candidates who are incapable of collecting enough contributions. But giving away too much risks offending poor voters or sending out the wrong message – that is, they could be perceived as being arrogant and unscrupulous. As this political operator puts it:

You need to know how to invest, it is not just about giving away more stuff. For example, there was a case of an intermediary who sells meat at Yerbateros and who ran as candidate for mayor in Ilave. People call him "the bull." He has tons of money. During the campaign everybody called him padrino because he would give things away. But people asked him, let's say, for one meter of fabric and he gave four. Or they asked for one crate of beer and he gave four. People started saying that he was showing off too much [the candidate ended up losing] ... If you do that people will believe that you are investing that much because what you are really aiming to do is make it back while in power. So, the idea is to do something but not to go to extremes: not too much, not too little ... You need to know how to invest. (Jorge Nuñez, political operator, Puno, June 12, 2010)

The lengthy focus-group extract from the Villa Primavera settlement, also suggests that exaggerating while investing in campaign clientelism (and propaganda) can actually be electorally counterproductive. Participants in one group refer to a similar case in which a candidate, in their view, spent too much money and was not elected. This candidate, who was not able to fully convince voters of his desirability, ended up third, 10 percentage points behind the second-placed contender.[13]

---

[13] Something similar happened with Mario Vargas Llosa in the 1990 presidential election. The electoral alliance he ran for, the *Frente Democrático Popular* (FREDEMO), was seen to have spent too much money on advertising. FREDEMO was increasingly perceived as the party representing the wealthy. Many poor voters opted instead to support Fujimori, an unknown candidate who ran a campaign that stressed his humility and whose slogan was "*un president como tú*" (a president like you).

If the quantity of goods distributed matters, then so too does the type. Candidates need to distribute things that poor people like (such as certain types of food or drinks, and even music or other types of entertainment) or need (such as clothes, food stamps, or free dental visits and haircuts).

Going back to Fenno's typology, during campaign events voters also seek to assess the candidate's authenticity. Thus, citizens try to determine whether candidates are being truthful in how they present themselves, or whether they are "just faking it." But "faking it" should be distinguished from a willingness to learn how to behave while visiting poor neighborhoods, which is not necessarily seen as something bad and can be quite productive (as we saw in the Pedro Pablo Kuczynski anecdote). However, a candidate simply pretending to be nice and later letting the mask slip is detrimental. Voters examine not only how candidates treat them, but also how a candidate treats their staff. Thus, given the extent of the candidates' public exposure, it is relatively easy for them to tell if a candidate is faking being nice.

Finally, voters evaluate a candidate's consistency as well, particularly after they are elected.[14] Indeed, in the focus groups participants frequently complained about politicians' inconsistency, particularly, after they are elected. Numerous participants, for instance, spoke of how politicians often treat poor people differently after gaining power, adopting a cold manner or even failing to acknowledge citizens who visit their offices. Most elected authorities stop visiting local neighborhoods and villages, and are known to forget their promises. The following quote provides an illustration of such inconsistency:

PARTICIPANT 1:   In Ocongate district, candidates go to town. They talk with the *dirigentes*, they present the candidates for Council in the assembly, then the candidate running for mayor introduces himself ... But we see now, after the elections, that no candidate has come back to our communities, even though they committed to work with us. They said "we will work together because I am a *campesino* like you are, I wear *ojotas*[15] like you." And now they don't even get out of the pickups they drive ...

---

[14] Since they are not part of established parties, most candidates in Peru do not maintain a relationship with voters after the campaign is over. However, consistency can only be assessed with any degree of accuracy over time. In other words, it is only possible to evaluate these traits when elections are over, and only for those candidates who get elected, or who at least run on repeated occasions.

[15] *Ojotas* are traditional sandals made of rubber.

PARTICIPANT 2:   The councilor or the mayor is not the same anymore. They always change. When you greet them it's not like before. During the campaign they greet you using terms like "brother," "friend." And they come to the *faena*[16] and work with us; they carry the tools and work with us. But once he becomes mayor or councilman, he even changes the *ojotas* for shoes and is no longer the same. (Male focus group, rural Cusco)

Most elected authorities in Peru show inconsistency in their relationships with their constituencies. This may be part of the reason why few subnational authorities get reelected in Peru (Córdova and Incio 2013; Weaver 2017b).[17] Thus, it is precisely because poor citizens do not trust politicians that meeting them in person makes sense and is so important for these voters: direct interaction can help them examine candidates' traits and attitudes with precision. During campaigns, politicians must overcome this mistrust and build credibility by showing authenticity and good character, and campaign clientelism events provide them with an excellent opportunity to do just that.

However, investment in campaign clientelism also poses a dilemma for politicians: its excessive use exacerbates the social distance with poor voters. Buying poor voters' turnout at campaign events requires access to resources – either personally or via donations – to finance the distribution of goods. Thus, it is a strategy open to candidates who are themselves well-off or can build close connections to the wealthy during the campaign. But as we have seen, resource-rich candidates only buy poor voters' attendance at campaign events, not their support. Consequently, the big challenge they face is in trying to bridge this social gap while campaigning; candidates need to create an impression of responsiveness and commitment to people's needs, to show poor people that they are not members of the "elite" who cannot relate to them and will do little (if anything) for them. And personally interacting with voters provides candidates with the best chances to do this.

In summary, a candidate's public presentation at bought campaign events is crucial for persuading poor voters and reducing the social distance between candidates and the poor that is accentuated by campaign clientelism itself. As far as voters are concerned, campaign events such as rallies and candidate visits are ideal opportunities to interact with

[16] Mandatory community work.
[17] See also Chapter 3.

candidates and evaluate their personal characteristics. During these public gatherings, candidates perform and, thus, convey their political persona. Evaluating these personal performances at rallies is particularly important and helpful for poorer voters; this demographic, who are usually less informed and politically sophisticated, put more weight on personal traits in defining their vote choices. By getting the opportunity to evaluate candidates' attitudes and behavior in person, poor voters can decide which candidate will most effectively represent them and respond to their needs. Thus, they can *form* their electoral preferences and rank viable candidates according to their desirability. Campaign clientelism can, thus, spur personalistic voting among clients.

THE MASS MOOD AND THE BUZZ

As explained in Chapter 4, political information is conveyed through social interaction between peers; rumors about politicians' mobilization capabilities affect public perception of their electoral strength. This interaction explains why it is important for candidates to demonstrate their electoral viability to the general public by mobilizing large numbers of voters at rallies. But turning out large numbers of people is equally important for a second reason: it can help candidates persuade turnout clients and other participants at campaign events of their electoral desirability.

To be successful in their efforts at persuading voters, campaign teams must demonstrate that their candidate is both a viable *and* a desirable candidate to the people attending their campaign events. Voters' impressions about a candidate and the campaign event itself will be used to update their information about that candidate. The more enthusiastic the public mood during a rally, the better it will be for the purposes of influencing. An enjoyable, positive, and upbeat environment reassures participants that the candidate is liked by the majority and that they, in fact, have high electoral potential.

However, the goal is not only to make a good impression on participants at campaign events but also to get the attendees to talk about the candidate, hopefully in a positive way. If an event is enjoyable enough, it will give people something to chat about once it is over. A positive buzz can help a candidate to amplify the original message: that they are an electorally viable and desirable option. As one voter puts it, "Most people follow what the majority says."[18]

---

[18] Focus group participant, Villa Primavera settlement, Huancaro, Cusco.

Moreover, at campaign events it is apparent that participants examine and scrutinize their peers' reactions as well as the candidate. They actively interact with one other at gatherings, remarking on the proposals they like or dislike. If they strongly disagree with something a candidate said, they will make their feelings known to those around them, and some will even shout them out to the masses. At other times, participants do not talk but glance at one other and express their distaste with grimaces (see Figure 5.2). And if, on the contrary, rally participants like a particular proposal or promise, they will react by enthusiastically cheering the candidate. Indeed, at successful rallies, groups of participants compete with one other to cheer the most vigorously. Participants are, thus, exposed to their peers' reactions during these mass gatherings; one can sense when the public's mood is, negative, indifferent, or enthusiastic.

As an illustration, it will be useful to describe what I observed in 2010 during the final campaign rallies of the two leading candidates for regional government in Piura: César Trelles (APRA) and Javier Atkins (*Unidos Construyendo*). The rallies took place in a similar setting (on the same street in downtown Piura) on different days. *Unidos Construyendo*'s event seemed to have more participants: the area looked more crowded. APRA's rally may have taken up more space, but this was only because party activists made an effort to distribute participants over a wider area to create an illusion of higher turnout. However, both rallies were well enough attended. The difference in turnout could not be discerned easily from a distance and it was not emphasized that much in the press coverage.

Without a doubt, the greatest contrast between both events was the mood of each rally and the participants' interactions at either one. *Unidos Construyendo*'s rally was extremely enthusiastic and upbeat; people were happy and enjoying themselves, and it was immediately apparent to the observer that this was the case. The event was crowded because people were trying to get closer to the stage. In fact, many participants tried to catch the candidate's attention so that he would approach the front row and greet them. Moreover, the attendees' enthusiasm for the candidate and his wife seemed sincere, not faked. Delegations from different districts frequently cheered for them both, calling them by their first names (Javier and Sandra). Walking around the event, one could hear that the participants' comments about the candidate were overwhelmingly positive. In short, people were celebrating: the rally was a veritable electoral party. It went so well that attendees stayed to dance for a while longer after the event was over.

APRA's rally, on the other hand, was anything but a party. Walking through the crowd was quite easy because, as stated, participants were more scattered around the space than they were at the former event. APRA is the most organized party in Peru, and Piura is one of its historical strongholds. Party activists are disciplined. Therefore, many followed their leaders' instructions by showing up for the final rally. However, the public's mood was not enthusiastic at all; on the contrary, it was gloomy and skeptical. Although participants cheered the candidate, as instructed by the *Apristas* activists, they came across as reluctant and insincere. Many participants even looked disgruntled; one could see long faces everywhere. Ironic comments were heard, and so too were complaints about APRA's performance in government and the party's candidate for regional presidency, Trelles, whose speech drew a negative response. In summary, the rally served to confirm the candidate's non-desirability to voters.

Attendees also interact with one another at other types of campaign events. During candidate presentations at local association assemblies, for instance, participants often comment on the proposals the candidate makes and applaud those they like. Voters also chat and gossip about the candidate's attitudes, physical traits, and behavior. Most of the time, participants at these smaller gatherings even have the chance to speak to the candidate (and to one another). Besides relaying their demands, voters can also express their doubts or criticisms, or encourage the candidate to change a proposal or attitude.

In turn, candidates' walks through shantytowns are often tempestuous. Besides cheers and indifferent responses to candidates' presentations, I have witnessed some instances in which residents shout at a candidate they dislike, using terms such as "liar," "thief," or "corrupt."

Peer effects also influence vote intentions by giving participants something to talk about afterwards. They can create positive or negative "buzz," or word-of-mouth. In this way, participants can become effective transmission belts of electoral information, and an event's effects can be amplified through social interaction. Participants may acquire an anecdote to tell others, whether good or a bad one. On the one hand, attendees can disseminate a description of how charming the candidate was, how he danced or sang, how humble and honest he seemed, and, consequently, how credible his promises are. On the other hand, participants might gossip about how bad a rally was, what a disaster the candidate was, how he seemed arrogant and did not treat people well, how infuriated or despondent people were at the event, etc. In this way, the positive or negative buzz generated can reach and (hopefully, in the case of a successful event) persuade voters who did not attend the event or who were still undecided after attending.

Ultimately, all of these kinds of voter-to-voter interactions during and after campaign events will be weighed by the electorate when deciding whether a candidate is desirable. Interpersonal communication among voters at campaign events, therefore, is factored into voters' electoral considerations: by interacting with their peers, voters can receive reassurance about the impressions candidates leave. Furthermore, interpersonal communication can help candidates to amplify the impact of their appeal: participants themselves can become a source of electoral information and, thus, help other voters form their electoral preferences.

CONCLUSION

In this chapter, I provided empirical evidence to show how influencing clients at campaign events is crucial to attaining electoral success. In a highly volatile political context, candidates must do something beyond demonstrating their electoral potential to retain voters' attention and gain their support. To increase their chances of getting elected, candidates must persuade turnout clients of their electoral desirability. And they do so through non-clientelistic means. Personalized communication at campaign events provides candidates with the best prospects of accomplishing this goal.

There are three ways in which politicians can persuade turnout clients to support them. First, during campaign events candidates particularize and target their policy proposals in a much more effective way than they can through media advertising alone. Campaign events guarantee politicians a captive audience that will listen to them for extended periods of time. Campaign teams typically gather information about the needs of particular constituencies before an event takes place. Therefore, candidates can offer group-oriented proposals and promise to deliver local public goods. In turn, voters present candidates with their needs and requirements during these campaign activities. By listening to different candidates, voters can evaluate and contrast their proposals and promises. Some poor voters even state that they get together to deliberate collectively on which candidate best fits their organization or community's interests.

Second, and probably more important, campaign events and rallies provide candidates with perfect occasions in which to present themselves and their views to their public. Conveying personal traits is easier through direct personalized communication. Campaign events are performances, and politicians are aware of this. Campaign teams plan the logistics and set up the stage for the show ahead of time. The goal is to create an environment that is as interesting and entertaining as possible in order to engage the audience. During these events, candidates and turnout clients have the opportunity to interact directly and spontaneously. Poor voters will pay a lot of attention to the candidate's public performance: the way they speak, interact with people, their gestures, how reliable and trustworthy they seem. Since lower-income voters place greater emphasis on personal traits for their vote choices, candidates can take advantage of campaign events to "level" with poor voters and bridge the social distance that separates them. In general, creating a connection with the public at these events improves candidates' electoral prospects.

Finally, achieving a positive public mood at campaign events can help politicians reassure participants of their viability and desirability as candidates. Enthusiasm for a candidacy can be effectively conveyed through interaction with peers. Rallies and other mass events provide the ideal setting to develop a contagious mass environment. Participants are not passive consumers at these public gatherings. They chat and comment about the candidate's proposals, behavior, team, and many other details they deem important to evaluating their electoral choices. They also evaluate other participants' reactions to the candidate's presentation. If the event is interesting enough, participants will have something to talk about with their peers after the event. Word-of-mouth can, thus, be an amplifier of the event's success (or failure).

By attending multiple campaign events, opportunistic clients become more informed about electoral offers than they would otherwise be. Each event these clients attend allows them to update their electoral information and compare and contrast whatever elements may be most important for them: the particular proposals that candidates offer, the candidates' personal traits, and/or their peers' impressions and opinions about the candidates. Thus, through these various means, campaign clientelism allows undecided clients to learn about the different candidates' proposals and rank candidates according to their preferences.

In this chapter I also showed that campaign clientelism actually reinforces personalistic politics in Peru. More than anything, campaign events are ideal opportunities for engaging in personalized political communication. In a context with low partisan identification and high distrust in politics, candidates build credibility based on their personal trajectory, traits, and attitudes. Thus, for example, any sort of targeted promise will be more credible in poor voters' eyes if it comes from a candidate they deem reliable. Rather than being mutually exclusive electoral strategies (Kitschelt 2000; Stokes 2007), electoral clientelism and personalism can complement each other.

6

Analyzing Campaigns

In the previous chapters I tested the causal mechanisms of my informational theory. In Chapter 4, I showed how the distribution of handouts during campaigns in Peru allows politicians to buy the electoral participation of indifferent voters, access crucial campaign fields, and boost turnout at campaign events. Combining quantitative, qualitative, and experimental data, I confirmed how high turnout at rallies affects the dynamics of the race by signaling electoral viability, narrowing the field of viable contenders, and attracting donors and strategic voters during the final rush. Chapter 5, in turn, revealed how Peruvian politicians use campaign clientelism to buy captive audiences that listen to them for extended periods of time. Face-to-face interactions with these bought audiences allow candidates to particularize their promises and convey crucial information about their personal traits and mannerisms; in other words, to persuade voters through non-clientelistic means. In addition, peer effects experienced by clients during these rallies also seemed relevant in helping them form their preferences and make their electoral choices. Overall, campaign clientelism is a valuable tool for Peruvian politicians; it allows them to improvise electoral vehicles that resemble partisan structures and to campaign within a highly uncertain and fluid electoral context. Moreover, campaign clientelism generates valuable information, helping candidates signal that they are electorally viable and desirable contenders.

But how does campaign clientelism influence a specific campaign? How do these mechanisms play out in particular contests? In this chapter, I illustrate the ways in which informational theory helps us understand the changing dynamics of the race in uncertain political contexts, taking time as a relevant variable of analysis. To do so, I study the municipal (provincial) and regional campaigns in two very different Peruvian departments: Cusco and Piura.[1] The goal of this paired subnational comparison is to engage in a parallel demonstration and highlight the generality of the process by which campaign clientelism indirectly affects vote choices in very different contexts (Skocpol and Somers 1980). Despite the particularities of each race and the conspicuous contextual differences, the two departments are subject to a similar political logic of clientelistic investments. In both Cusco and Piura, regional and municipal candidates compete *through* campaign clientelism. To establish themselves as leading contenders in the race and attract the attention of strategic donors and voters, candidates are forced by competition to actively engage in campaign clientelism. Simultaneously, candidates take advantage of bought audiences to interact with voters and persuade them – through non-clientelistic tactics – that as contenders they are not only viable, but desirable. At the same time, this subnational analysis allows us to discern certain specificities within campaign dynamics that shed light on how campaign clientelism still works when organized machines are in place, and on what could happen when a candidate explicitly campaigns against the use of clientelistic tactics.

I organize the chapter as follows. The first section characterizes the two cases by describing the different values they take on and the dimensions that are relevant for the comparison. In the second section, I discuss the general political and institutional context in which the electoral races take place. In the third, I analyze the regional and municipal elections in Cusco and Piura. Finally, I conclude by summarizing and discussing the main findings.

THE CASES UNDER STUDY

In this chapter, I rely on process-tracing to compare the clientelistic strategies displayed during electoral campaigns, taking advantage of a comparative research design. I take a most-different-system approach, selecting two departments – Cusco and Piura – that differ from each other in terms of several variables, including the main theoretical variable under discussion: the degree of local political organization. Table 6.1 highlights this and other relevant features of both departments. It is important to recall

---

[1] Peru has two tiers of local government: provincial municipalities and district municipalities. Each province is made up of a varying number of districts. Provincial municipalities rule over the entire province and assumes the functions of the district municipality in each province's capital district.

TABLE 6.1. *Case selection variables*

Variables of theoretical interest	Cusco	Piura	
Degree of organization and longevity of political groupings	Low	High	
Level of organized clientelism (machines)	Low	Medium	
Political trajectory	Partido Aprista Peruano (APRA) influence	Leftist influence	

Other control variables

Political variables	Cusco	Piura	Departmental average/mode
Political trajectory	APRA influence	Leftist influence	–
Development of local broadcasting market	High	Low	–
Number of electoral districts (provinces)	13	8	7.8
Number of electoral districts (districts)	108	64	73.5
Regional reelection 2002–6	No	Yes	8%
Rate of local reelection 2002–6 (district)	34.62%	26.19%	35.27%
Rate of local reelection 2002–6 (province)	8.30%	50.00%	22.32%
Sociodemographics	**Cusco**	**Piura**	**Departmental average/mode**
Population 2010	1,274,742	1,769,555	1,178,477
Electoral population 2010	276,917	459,189	767,830
Rural population as % total	48.84	25.24	33.09%
Poverty rate (2007)	54.4%	45%	45.28%
Poverty rate (2010)	49.5%	42.5%	36.15%
Human Development Index (Position in Ranking)	13/24	17/24	–
Population with indigenous native tongue (2007) as % total	52%	0%	21.92%

Sources: 2007 National Census; INEI; InfoGob-JNE, Aragón and Incio (2014)

that given Peru's unitary structure, all departments share the same rules for electing their regional and municipal authorities.[2]

Although Peruvian parties are weak from a comparative perspective, there is some variation in levels of party organization across electoral districts. When I conducted this study, in 2010, Cusco and Piura differed considerably in their levels of local political organization. Cusco was a case of low political organization and low organized clientelism, at both the regional and the local level. In contrast, Piura stood out as one of the departments in which more organized national and regional parties were active. In addition, by 2010 it was known to have a clientelistic machine, organized from the regional (state-level) government.

To begin with, Cusco is closer to "normal" unorganized Peruvian politics than Piura (Muñoz 2010; Tanaka and Guibert 2011; Bellatín 2014; Zavaleta 2014). Until 2006 Cusco gave "hope" to some Peruvian scholars about the prospects of party reconstruction from the bottom up (Meléndez and Vera 2006). In particular, they keenly observed the experience of *Unión Por el Perú* (UPP), which won the regional presidency in Cusco and six out of thirteen provincial municipalities that year. However, it soon became clear that UPP was just the latest in a long line of failed party-projects.[3] Just like in many other departments, political parties (besides APRA)[4] and regional movements in Cusco do not have an organic life beyond election periods.[5] While APRA does have local cadres in the department (mostly in urban areas), it has not proven to be an electorally viable option in this historically left-oriented polity. Though the party has managed to elect representatives to Congress on the strength of coattail effects, it has been less successful at the regional and local level since the 1986 municipal elections.[6] In contrast, the other

---

[2] On the electoral rules, see the next section.

[3] The UPP splintered shortly after the 2006 elections, and during the ensuing governmental term, the regional and municipal governments led by the party were involved in several corruption scandals that weakened it still further. In the 2010 regional election, the UPP candidate won only 3.38 percent of the valid vote.

[4] On APRA's strength at the subnational level, see Cyr 2017.

[5] The Party Law (Law 28094) establishes different requirements for the registration of "political parties," "regional movements," and "local political organizations," respectively. Political parties hold a monopoly on political competition in national elections (congressional and presidential elections) but can also run candidates in subnational electoral processes. In turn, regional movements compete in both regional and municipal elections, while local organizations can only compete in the municipal elections in the jurisdiction for which they were registered.

[6] Indeed, the only occasion when APRA gained the Cusco municipality was in the mid-1980s when they invited a former *Partido Demócrata Cristiano* politician (Carlos Chacón

political organizations that compete in regional and local elections in Cusco are mostly coalitions of independents who join together only during election times (Zavaleta 2014), and, therefore, do not have stable agents (partisan cadres) at the local level.[7]

To be sure, Cusco has faced difficulties not only in organizing and consolidating political parties or regional movements, but in institutionalizing clientelistic machines more generally. By 2010, there were no institutionalized regional machines – that is, clientelistic machines vertically articulated by regional politicians acting as patrons. And there have been no known (or appreciably successful) attempts at building clientelistic machines at the local level either. When asked, none of the politicians, journalists, and experts interviewed in Cusco could identify the names of clientelistic local bosses. Instead, since 2002, when regional governments were introduced in Peru, Cusco has been marked by very unstable and crisis-prone regional politics, with numerous corruption scandals (Muñoz *et al.* 2016).

In this context, there are more visible cases of corruption in municipalities and regional governments than of organized, long-lasting clientelism. One can observe small interest groups that assume governance for the short-term benefit of private interests: they appropriate public resources for themselves or a small clique of friends or parents, rather than to build up networks of political followers. Moreover, instead of investing in the construction of clientelistic machines, most municipalities and the regional governments in Cusco seemed to privilege pork-barrel politics – that is, the delivery of local public works. Certainly, Cusco looks like a good example of the modal form of distributive portfolio in Peru, in which elected authorities mostly make pork-barrel investments, seeking to extract resources for repayment of campaign contributions (Samuels 2002) and personal gain, rather than re-investing them in building clientelistic machines (Muñoz 2016).[8] In summary, by 2010, Cusco was characterized by pork barrel politics and multiple corruption allegations, but limited organized political clientelism.

Galindo) to run for the APRA ticket as an independent (Personal interview with Chacón Galindo, mayor of Cusco between 1987 and 1989. April 16, 2010).

[7] An exception to this trend is the *campesino*-centered regional movement *Autogobierno Ayllu*. While *Autogobierno Ayllu* has grassroots activists in many provinces (mostly indigenous *campesinos*) and is more organized than most Peruvian parties, it still faces several limitations that prevent its successful competition at the regional level (Bellatín 2014).

[8] See Chapter 3.

Piura, on the other hand, stands out as a case of medium-high to high political organization at the local level (by Peruvian standards), at least as at 2010.[9] These higher levels of political organization are related primarily to the strengths of APRA in Piura, one of the historical strongholds of this long-lived party. As is also the case in other northern regions, *Aprista* identity is still meaningful and transmitted through family channels and political socialization through the party structure (Cyr 2012, 2017). Moreover, APRA is a political organization with a life beyond election times; it runs a permanent political office in each of the municipalities of Piura, although organization is stronger in the coastal areas and the larger towns and cities. According to *Apristas* interviewed, the party structure suffered a great deal during the 1990s.[10] Many activists, even some then major regional leaders, ended up working for Fujimori's machine.[11] However, after the democratic transition, regional leaders, such as César Trelles, worked hard to rebuild the party in Piura, to which García's (2001) comeback to national electoral politics certainly lend impetus. This renewed party structure allowed APRA to gain access to regional office when the first regional elections took place in 2002. By 2010, the party drew on a network of local grassroots activists who participated in party activities throughout the year.

Besides APRA, Piura had another organized local movement: *Obras + Obras* (O + O),[12] structured around the figure of its charismatic leader, José "Loro"[13] Aguilar. A former *Aprista,* Aguilar was elected mayor of Piura for that party in 1993. He secured his reelection in 1995 (with 56 percent of the vote), running this time as an independent representing his newly created O + O movement. His experience in APRA helped him organize local networks of supporters, and he built a local party that closely resembled a clientelistic machine. To this end, he trained youngsters to work as brokers, relaying poor people's demands.[14] While serving as mayor, Aguilar would tour the shanty towns and rural villages of

---

[9] After the 2014 subnational elections, it became clear that Piura was converging to the nationwide trend of disorganized politics, with the consequent prevalence of coalitions of independents (Muñoz *et al.* 2016).

[10] Interviews with APRA's legal representative in Piura, Miguel Talledo (July 23, 2010), and Alberto Chumacero, APRA's Secretary of Organization in Piura (November 23 and 24, 2010).

[11] Luis Ortiz, candidate for regional vice-president of Piura, APRA (July 26, 2010). Alberto Chumacero (November 24, 2010).

[12] Literally, "projects and more projects."

[13] "Parrot."

[14] Interview with Elizabeth Rodríguez, former O + O political broker, July 24, 2010.

Piura and respond personally to the assorted requests submitted through his network of local brokers, allowing him to be seen to be solving poor people's everyday problems.

O + O registered as a regional movement for the 2006 electoral process. They invited Javier Atkins, a bank manager with no previous political experience, to run as their candidate for the regional presidency. Aguilar was reelected as mayor of Piura for the third time with 45 percent of the vote (quite an accomplishment by Peruvian standards) and coattail effects carried Atkins to second place in the regional elections. While governing, Aguilar fell ill with cancer and finally succumbed to the disease in 2008. Since O + O was a personalistic organization, the death of its leader called its survival into question. The transfer of power within the municipality made this process harder, since the first councilor (legally bound to assume office as the new mayor) was not an O + O activist but an independent. However, by 2010 it was clear that at least part of O + O's local networks had managed to survive Aguilar's death by transferring their loyalty to his widow, Ruby Rodríguez, the movement's candidate for mayor of Piura that year.

Besides having a higher level of political organization, by 2010 Piura also exhibited greater levels of organized clientelism than Cusco. This was mainly due to the construction of a political machine from the regional government, held by APRA since 2002. The individuals interviewed clearly recognized the existence of a clientelistic apparatus with local bases driven by the regional government resources. Here, the distribution of public jobs (patronage) was related to party- and network-building. It was widely known that the regional government gave jobs to *Apristas*, who helped campaign for César Trelles.[15] As one APRA activist acknowledged, "with the consolidation of the party, the expectation of employment among the *compañeros* [APRA activists] has grown." Of the jobs distributed, a considerable number were given to local cadres who help organize party activities. In addition to supporting the party and campaigning for reelection in 2006, all beneficiaries were expected to "donate" 10 percent of their salary (the *diezmo*) to the party. With this money, the *Apristas* were able to buy a house for use as their office in Piura city (they used to rent a site) and make improvements to their

---

[15] Luis Loja (political operator, July 19, 2010) and Lili Guevara (*El Tiempo* newspaper, November 20), among other interviewees. 2010. Miguel Talledo, APRA activist and legal representative, also recognizes that there was an oversizing of the government during APRA's second term in office (November 17, 2010).

offices in other provinces.[16] And the number of *simpatizantes* the party had at its disposal only increased following APRA's victory in both the national and regional elections in 2006.[17]

Apristas also used regional public funds to prepare for their second re-election. An example of this can be found in the regional-government social initiative *Programa de Acción Social* (PAS); from 2009 (the year before the elections), the regional government used PAS funds to organize and finance several "civic campaigns," which consisted of scheduled visits to poor neighborhoods, particularly in remote provinces and rural towns. During these visits, PAS officials distributed private goods to the people they assembled, such as backpacks and books for children, and also provided free services to the citizenry, such as medical consultations and haircuts.

In Piura, some interviewees also had the impression that *Apristas* used certain state-provided programs, such as *Juntos* and *Construyendo Perú*, for political ends.[18] Other rumors also pointed to the political manipulation of the Interior Government structure – networks of governors and deputy governors, central-government representatives at the local level who are appointed by the Ministry of the Interior – to distribute private goods in poor and rural areas of the department.

In addition, corruption was commonly alleged against incumbents in Piura. For instance, APRA's regional government was subject to numerous corruption accusations, particularly during its second term, and so too were Municipal authorities including the mayor of Piura. However, in 2010, corruption scandals in the city of Piura were not as frequent as in Cusco city. Indeed, during the municipal term 2007–10, no mayor or councilor in the Municipality of Piura was removed from office on corruption charges, unlike in the Municipality Cusco.

As we have seen, Piura is a case of higher political organization, and its politicians also invested more in party building through clientelism than their counterparts in Cusco. Moreover, although corruption allegations are also common in Piura, they are less commonplace or consequential than in Cusco, at least in terms of the figures removed from office. Despite these differences, and as I will discuss in the next section, political actors competing in both electoral districts share the same set of electoral rules and a general context of electoral uncertainty. Competing electorally within this uncertain political context, they rely greatly on campaign clientelism.

[16] Miguel Talledo, APRA's legal representative in Piura (July 23, 2010).
[17] APRA did not opened inscriptions to the party in many years in Piura. They began accepting new activists already during the 2010 electoral campaign.
[18] In 2006 APRA won the presidential elections in Peru.

THE SUBNATIONAL ELECTORAL PROCESS IN PERU

Subnational offices in Peru are elected every four years. Elections for regional governments, provincial municipalities, and district municipalities are held simultaneously on the same day. Municipal councilors are elected on a single ballot alongside the mayor and deputy mayor. In 2010, the regional council elections were separated from the regional executive elections, and an electoral threshold of 30 percent plus one was introduced. Moreover, the new law established a mixed electoral system for electing the regional councils, with a plurality electoral rule for those provinces that elect one representative, and a proportional rule for those provinces with more than one representative.

In general, given the dearth of organized and enduring national parties, these legal provisions have engendered a bifurcated system of political representation in which national parties remain competitive at national elections but fail to successfully compete in subnational processes. Since 2006 political parties have lost ground to regional movements and face increasing difficulties in achieving party aggregation and the articulation of the political system (Vera 2010; Guibert and Tanaka 2011; Vergara 2012; Zavaleta 2014; Battle and Cyr 2014). Indeed, Peru – together with Ecuador and Venezuela – is one of the Latin American countries with the greatest degree of incongruence in the competition structure between the national and subnational (Freidenberg and Suárez Cao 2014).

Moreover, political disarticulation in Peru is a problem that affects not only national political parties, but also regional movements – most of which are not organized regional parties per se and, therefore, also struggle to assure an effective territorial presence at the local level and to articulate their respective regional political systems (Muñoz and García 2011; Tanaka and Guibert 2011; Zavaleta 2014). This incongruent multilevel structure of political competition goes hand in hand with other political phenomena, such as high levels of electoral fragmentation and high party and electoral volatility (Vera 2010; Muñoz and García 2011); frequent party switching and high numbers of political amateurs running for office (Levitsky 2013; Zavaleta 2014; Levitsky and Zavaleta 2016); as well as low subnational reelection rates and incumbent disadvantage (Córdova and Incio 2013). These characteristics make subnational electoral races highly uncertain processes in which it is extremely difficult to predict the alliances that local politicians will make, and who will win.

Given the lack of durable, organized national parties or regional movements, it is hardly surprising that improvisation predominates in subnational electoral campaigns. Incumbent subnational authorities, who are required by law to either resign or ask for leave to be able to compete for office, usually wait until the last minute to formalize their candidacy with the electoral authorities. Similarly, local politicians negotiate endless possible electoral alliances with registered regional or national tickets. Hence, both political parties and regional movements normally flood into electoral offices on deadline day to legally register their lists of candidates; In turn, this glut of last-minute applications results in congestion and delays, since the electoral authorities have to go over hundreds of records to check whether the submissions comply with the legal requirements asked of candidates (e.g., personal declarations, age, domicile, etc.), and lists (e.g., presentation of manifesto and fulfillment of gender, indigenous, and age quotas, etc.). In addition, after lists are accepted, Peruvian electoral law gives voters the opportunity to file an objection to a list or candidacy, providing parties with incentives to sabotage their adversaries' lists. Thus, even after the electoral authorities publish the list of registered candidates, they must still deal with an avalanche of objections.

Thus, these regulations and the highly fragmented electoral offering causes considerable delays in the processing of applications by electoral authorities. These delays translate into high levels of uncertainty, since voters are left unsure of which of the plethora of candidates to consider, or whether their preferred options will be able to legally compete.

In this context, strategic actors have a paucity of reliable electoral information with which to make their choices. Consequently, campaign clientelism becomes crucial for candidates, as they can use it to signal the viability of their candidacies from the beginning of the race and to attract the attention of donors and voters. As such, strategic actors compare and contrast electoral history heuristics, turnout rates at campaign events, and available poll figures in order to form their expectations about the electoral prospects of each candidate and, in turn, to make strategic choices.

In the remainder of this chapter, I utilize a process-tracing to compare the clientelistic strategies displayed during electoral campaigns and to analyze how the two causal mechanisms identified – signaling electoral viability and helping develop electoral desirability – play out in these dissimilar cases. In the next section, I analyze the regional and provincial races in Cusco, showing how electoral clientelism becomes important in making up for the unreliable electoral information available to strategic actors within an extremely fluid political context.

CUSCO'S RACES

Given its lower levels of political organization, Cusco more closely resembles the typical Peruvian department, with uncertain political dynamics, than Piura does. The Cusco case shows, first, that in a highly disorganized political context, campaign clientelism is a vital tool for candidates lacking in name recognition to attain electoral viability, and for better-placed candidates with firm electoral potential to maintain and increase that potential. However, the cases analyzed also corroborate that buying audiences with goods distributed during campaigns is not enough to guarantee clients' support at the polls and victory in the contest. This is not a competition to distribute the most gifts; being marked as a desirable candidate – in particular, being perceived as a good or likable candidate – is indispensable in setting a candidacy apart from the others and in persuading campaign clients, and other voters through word of mouth, that your candidacy is not only viable but worth supporting.

As can be seen in Table 6.2, the use of campaign clientelism is key for candidates to stand out in the election as viable contenders. However, the combination of perceived candidate viability and desirability configures varied campaign dynamics. On the one hand, in the regional election, two candidates stood out from an early stage in the contest as candidates with electoral potential, and effectively block the path for other contenders. Both used campaign clientelistic tactics intensively to mobilize voters. One was perceived as the most viable candidate at the beginning of the race. But the other candidate gradually edged ahead by drawing on campaign clientelism to electioneer heavily throughout the region. By the end of the race, the candidate who began second was positioned as the leading contender. Campaign clientelism not only helped him increase his perceived electoral viability, but also allowed him to personally interact with poor voters and distinguish himself as a worthy and authentic candidate who was prepared for the job (in terms of professional expertise and past performance) and understood local conditions and needs. By adroitly displaying personalistic strategies while visiting multiple localities, this candidate signaled himself as the most desirable of the two viable contenders and managed to win the race.

On the other hand, in Cusco province, the municipal election initially unfolded as a contest between two local incumbents with plenty of resources to invest in the race and who made intensive use of campaign clientelism as a tool for electoral mobilization. Despite starting out in a prominent position, one of them steadily lost momentum and eventually

TABLE 6.2. *Mechanisms at work in Cusco's campaigns*

Factors	Cusco region		Cusco province		
	San Román	Acurio	Cuzmar	Florez	Moscoso
Use of campaign clientelism	High	High	High	High	Medium
Electoral viability	Medium-maintained	Increasing	Increasing to decreasing	Increasing	Increasing
Desirable candidate	No	Yes	No	Yes	Yes
Likable (charisma)	No	Yes	No	Yes	Yes
Cares and knows about local needs	No	Yes	No	Yes	Yes
Technical expertise		Yes			Yes
Effective (delivered in past)		Yes	Yes	Yes	
Won the race	No	Yes	No	Yes	No

lost points in voting intention despite continuous campaign-clientelism electioneering. This candidate's terrible personal performance on the trail explained why he ultimately lost to the other incumbent (who was more successful in positioning himself as a good and effective candidate who truly understood local needs), as well as why he was outdone by a lesser-known but more personally appealing candidate who was unable to invest as intensively in campaign clientelism as he did.

Matched Viability, Differences in Desirability

Cusco started the 2010 campaign without organized parties or clientelistic machines, and no incumbent running for reelection. In this context, expectations were raised about the possible candidacy of Máximo San Román in the preelection year. San Román is an engineer and successful businessman from humble origins who began his political career in 1990, when he was elected vice-president and senator for Fujimori's *Cambio 90*. He became widely known for his opposition to the 1992 coup, in which Fujimori closed Congress. After this event he defected to the opposition, competing against Fujimori in 1995 and securing his reelection as congressman. He ran unsuccessfully for the Peruvian presidency in 2000 and as congressional candidate in 2006 for an alliance of different political entities. Also, in 2006, San Román ran for the regional presidency in Cusco for the first time; he was invited to lead the ticket of a regional movement, *Inka Pachakuteq*, which had finished fifth in the 2002 race with 8.5 percent of the vote. San Román finished second, obtaining 138,108 votes at a margin of 15.8 percent ahead of the third-placed candidate (Table 6.3); the contest was won by Hugo Gonzáles with 32.6 percent of the vote, second placed in the 2002 contest on 17.6 percent. Meanwhile, Marina Sequeiros, the candidate who ended up third in the 2002 regional election with 15.8 percent of the vote, ran this time as candidate for mayor of Cusco for a different ticket, and won. Moreover, Wilson Ugarte (APRA), who came fourth in the 2002 regional election with 15.2 percent of the vote, was elected congressman for Cusco in the 2006 congressional elections.

At the beginning of 2010, some analysts and politicians thought that, having finished second in 2006, San Román had the best chances of becoming regional president in the upcoming race. This expectation was boosted by poll results that were published in November 2009, almost a year before the race. San Román led the voting intention for regional president with 16 percent, followed some way behind by Jorge Acurio,

TABLE 6.3. *Cusco: 2006 regional elections results*

Political organization	Last name	Names	Valid votes	Percentage
Union Por El Peru	Gonzales	Hugo	1,635	32.60
Movimiento Regional Inka Pachakuteq	San Román	Maximo	13,8108	27.54
APRA	Villasante	Jorge	58,502	11.67
Restauracion Nacional	Ramos	Alipio	50,038	9.98
Partido Nacionalista Peruano	Carreño	William	44,416	8.86
Frente Independiente Moralizador	Cuaresma	Carlos	33,519	6.69
Agrupacion Independiente Sí Cumple	Suenaga	Carlos	8,296	1.65
Partido Movimiento Humanista Peruano	Quispe	Dante	5,047	1.01

Source: INFOgob – JNE

mayor of San Sebastián, a district of Cusco city, with 3.8 percent; and Carlos Cuaresma, former regional president (2002–6), with 2.8 percent.[19]

These showings of electoral viability allowed San Román to negotiate strong electoral alliances with promising local candidates in the region very early on in the race, recruiting them to his newly created regional movement, *Pan*.[20] As we saw in Chapter 3, local politicians usually seek to join tickets alongside front-running candidates with potentially powerful coattails.[21] Thus, for many local politicians, this time "San Roman appeared as a safe bet for the campaign. Joining him was logical."[22] Political operators and politicians also assumed that since San Román

[19] Centro de Educación y Comunicación Guamán Poma de Ayala, 2009. Poll results published by Revista Parlante, N° 102, December 24, 2009–January 2010, Cusco, 2009.
[20] *Pan* means "bread" in Spanish; San Román used this name, and the symbol of a loaf of bread, to represent the successful company manufacturing equipment for bakeries that he built up.
[21] See also Zavaleta (2014) and Levitsky and Zavaleta (2016).
[22] Interview with Sergio Sulca, candidate for mayor of Santiago (December 15, 2010).

was a businessman, he would have resources to invest in the campaign, as well as better prospects of collecting donations. Hence, when *Pan* was selecting municipal candidates in February, many people approached San Román asking for inclusion on his ticket.[23] This comparative advantage allowed San Román to recruit a new and promising candidate in La Convención province (a crucial electoral bastion in Cusco) as well as mayors running for reelection, such as Ciriaco Condori in Calca province and Eduardo Guevara in Urubamba; and former mayors with promising electoral prospects, such as Ricardo Cornejo in Canchis province (another crucial constituency). These candidates would work as local political operators, campaigning for San Román and mobilizing the vote in rural areas, which was crucial considering that *Pan* did not have an organized structure. Some of these figures, like Cornejo and Guevara, were well-known for investing heavily in campaign clientelism during campaigns, and 2010 was no exception.[24] San Román also invested in campaign clientelism during the campaign events he organized directly. For example, he delivered gifts and good while campaigning in the low-income district of Santiago, in Cusco city.[25] Thus, from early on in the race, San Román positioned himself as a front-runner with the potential to win.

However, San Román's early establishment of electoral viability was not enough to assure his victory. He had to face Jorge Acurio, a relatively unexperienced contender with great potential; Acurio was the mayor of San Sebastián district in Cusco city and ran at the head of the list for *Gana Cusco*, the regional ticket of the *Partido Nacional* (PN), the party governing the country at the time. By May of that year, the politicians, journalists, and analysts interviewed already saw San Román and Acurio as the leading contenders with the best prospects of being elected.

Acurio began his political career in 2002 when he ran as mayoral candidate in San Sebastián district for a regional movement, *Movimiento Democrático Juntos por el Progreso*, winning just 13.72 percent of the vote but still finishing second. In 2006, on the strength of his relatively strong showing last time out, the PN invited him to run for their ticket.[26]

---

[23] Interview with Aldo Estrada, *Pan* legal representative (December 20, 2010).

[24] Interviews with Rubén Coa (September 4, 2010) and Alberto Valcárcel, *Acción Popular*'s candidate for mayor in Urubamba province (August 30, 2010).

[25] Carlos Huilca, broker in Chocco settlement, *Margen Derecha* zone, Santiago district (May 13, 2010).

[26] In fact, many movements invited them to join their ticket for the same reason. Interview with Miguel Choque, councilman of San Sebastián municipality (May 20, 2010).

This time, under the nationalist's banner, Acurio took the municipality with 29.25 percent of the vote.[27]

During his term in office, and in a context of near-absolute distrust of subnational authorities, Acurio gained name recognition as an effective mayor in Cusco city.[28] However, he was not particularly well known outside Cusco city, and the PN did not have any organizational backup on its own. A few short months after the 2006 presidential election in which Humala won 73 percent of the Cusco vote in the presidential runoff, the PN performed terribly in the regional elections. After splitting with UPP, its former ally, the PN ended up *fifth* in the regional race, achieving less than 9 percent of the vote. And in the following years, the PN failed to strengthen itself organizationally. As one activist put it, in 2010 the PN was still "a complicated and messy sum of forces and individuals from all over."[29] Indeed, Acurio, a guest in the party, was nominated by national leaders as its regional secretary in 2010, triggering resentment in the local committees of several vital bastions such as La Convención, Canchis, and Chumbivilcas.[30] These quarrels made it difficult for the PN to recruit good local candidates in these areas.

Despite these limitations, joining the PN proved a shrewd decision for Acurio. After the party's disastrous showing in the 2006 subnational elections and looking ahead to the 2011 presidential contest, the PN looked to improve its electoral performance at the subnational level. Given that Cusco was one of Humala's strongholds – he won 73 percent of the valid vote in the 2006 presidential run-off there – the party staked everything on taking at least Cusco's regional presidency. After dealing with the numerous conflicts inside their loose regional coalition, the PN's national committee decided to invest heavily in turning Acurio's candidacy into a viable one. This included, of course, investing heavily in campaign clientelism.

Gana Perú, the movement alongside which the PN ran its ticket in Cusco, started renting a large house on a major Cusco avenue many months before the campaign began for use as its campaign headquarters. They displayed electoral propaganda all over the department from the beginning of the race in a bid to convey the strength of Acurio's

[27] The PN's head, Ollanta Humala, lost the 2006 presidential run-off by a small margin of votes. His support was particularly high in southern Andean regions like Cusco.

[28] As mentioned before, during the 2007–10 municipal term, several mayors and councilors in Cusco city were removed due to corruption scandals.

[29] Rubén Coa (September 4, 2010).

[30] Rubén Coa (September 4, 2010).

candidacy; for instance, they arranged *pintas* – hand-painted political advertisements – all over Cusco's major roads and avenues. Moreover, when the PN registered Acurio's candidacy, they mobilized numerous followers. As a result, the press reported that Acurio's registration was accompanied by a great popular demonstration of support.[31] As with *Pan*, they had the resources to invest in campaign clientelism from the initial stages of the campaign and they duly did so, as subsequent interviews, focus groups, and direct observations attested.

Gana Perú recruited a network of leftist former political operators to help them organize the campaign regionally, outside Cusco city, by recruiting activists and mobilizing voters to their campaign events. These operators planned an intensive mobilization campaign in which Acurio would visit each of the rural provinces more than once, and they practiced campaign clientelism. The operators interviewed stated that because voters expected candidates to distribute gifts while campaigning, especially in rural areas, they "had" to do so.[32] Indeed, for one political operator, investing in campaign clientelism is part of the "sensationalism" inherent to the race.[33] Another political operator working for Acurio, Rolando Rozas, said that although gift distribution is very common in rural areas, this does not mean that the practice equates to buying votes because rural voters are pragmatic and they do not "sell" their conscience. Rather, delivering means of transportation and food to rural voters is crucial for their effective mobilization to attend a candidate's rallies. For Rozas, this explains why there are several cases in Cusco in which candidates who deliver lots of perks still fail to win votes in decisive numbers.[34]

This intense campaign clientelism-driven activism seemed to attenuate an early round of negative crusading against Acurio, and helped him increase his name recognition outside the province of Cusco, particularly in the high-altitude provinces.[35] As we can observe in the overview of voting intention polls (Figure 6.1), Acurio gradually began to gain in popularity, catching up with San Román by August and going on to beat him up in the first round of the election. The other nine candidates for regional office never managed to climb in voting intention early on in the

[31] Diario del Cusco (July 6, 2010, p. 2, 9).
[32] Rubén Coa (May 25, 2010).
[33] Sensationalism in the sense of *producing* feelings and emotions or *impacting* the public with news and events.
[34] Rolando Rozas, political operator working for Acurio (September 3, 2010).
[35] Rubén Coa (September 4, 2010).

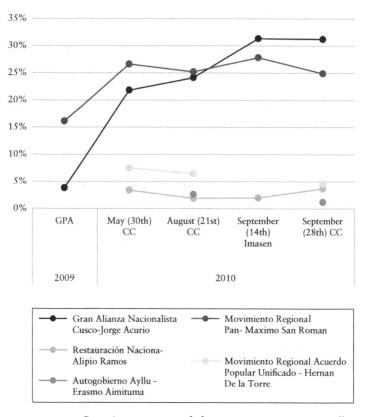

FIGURE 6.1. *Cusco's 2010 regional election: voting intention polls*
Sources: Guamán Poma de Ayala, November 2010; César Carranza,
May 30, 2010; Carranza, May 21, 2010; Imasen, September 14, 2010; César Carranza,
September 28, 2010

race, and once voters' attention was already concentrated on San Román and Acurio, it became difficult to break that trend.[36]

But as explained by Acurio's political operator, distributing lots of gifts is not enough to win a race.[37] Being signaled as a leading contender is just the

---

[36] Other candidates were identified as having some potential but still some way behind from two frontrunners were Carlos Cuaresma, the former regional president; Hernán De la Torre, mayor of La Convención province; and Carlos Valencia, former mayor of Cusco city and candidate for *Fujimorismo*. Two of these, Valencia and De la Torre, appeared in a poll conducted in May as the third- and fourth-placed contenders, with 9 percent and 7.5 percent of the vote, respectively (*Centro de Estudios e Investigaciones César Carranza*, May 2010). Available at: www.encuestascusco.com/encuesta-mayo-2010-elecciones-municipales-y-regionales-2010.

[37] Rolando Rozas, political operator working for Acurio (September 3, 2010).

first hurdle to overcome in the electoral race. As my informational theory contends, campaign clientelism is also used to attract voters to campaign events and create a field of interaction in which the candidate persuades the voters of his electoral desirability through non-clientelistic means.

In Acurio's case, personally campaigning across Cusco's electoral strongholds helped him persuade voters that he was a desirable candidate, worthy of support at the polls. As most candidates do, while campaigning he promised if elected to deliver the projects the different territorial constituencies needed. But what seemed to mark Acurio apart from other candidates were his personal characteristics and his great willingness to visit low-income localities and listen to poor people express their needs. While campaigning, Acurio showed "good character," the aggregate of several desirable characteristics for an elected authority. He is a politician with charisma, who easily connects with voters.[38] He is down to earth, and this made it easy for voters to identify with him.[39] In addition, Acurio conveyed technical expertise while campaigning; he convincingly impersonated the role of an architect who knows how to "get things done" and has experience building infrastructure projects. Indeed, his depiction of professionalism is what helped him get elected mayor in San Sebastián in the first place.[40] Moreover, during the campaign Acurio credibly conveyed an ability to effectively *deliver* on his promises, as he did while governing San Sebastián Municipality.[41] Finally, by traveling intensively across local communities in the department and listening to people's demands, he also showed he cared for local needs. Besides showing good character, Acurio's political persona seemed authentic. He was not perceived as someone faking it for the camera while on the trail. In general, Acurio's personal traits were strong and helped him offset the negative impact on his candidacy that Humala's ambivalent position about the "defense" of Cusco's natural resources had during the regional race in Cusco.[42]

In contrast to Acurio, San Román did not show enough interest in getting to know the people and their problems. And unlike his rival, San Román had a higher level of name recognition when the campaign began. Based on his electoral trajectory and business connections, many thought

---

[38] Councilor Miguel Choque (May 20, 2010). Rubén Coa (May 25, 2010).

[39] Rubén Coa (May 25, 2010).

[40] Councilor Miguel Choque (May 20, 2010).

[41] Rubén Coa (May 25, 2010).

[42] During the regional campaign, Cusco's media closely covered an ongoing conflict over water use with the neighboring region of Arequipa, as well as developments regarding the gas pipeline Humala was promising to build in his future government.

he was a sure bet for the regional presidency this time. Moreover, his local allies were meant to assure an easy victory in many important constituencies through inverse coattail effects, coupled with displays of electoral propaganda and voter mobilization through campaign clientelism. San Román's central campaign team trusted that their ally's campaign would be enough to sustain the candidate's initial popularity and win the race – or at least make it to the run-off.

But San Román gradually lost his electoral advantage. Overall, San Román proved not to be a good candidate. To begin with, he did not have the personal traits that are desirable for a politician; he was simply not charismatic enough and appeared more distant to voters. In contrast to Acurio, who everybody knew by his nickname "Coco" during the campaign, San Román was addressed by his professional title, *ingeniero*, even by his adviser.[43] Consequently, he had to work harder than Acurio to persuade voters about the personal desirability of his candidacy. And although he succeeded in establishing authenticity, he proved to be temperamental and failed to exercise self-control during the campaign, thus, making several mistakes that were evident to voters.[44] Political operators working for San Román believed that this happened because he was stubborn and did not want to listen to their advice.[45] For example, he did not accept a proposed alliance with Carlos Moscoso, a politician with great potential in the Cusco Municipality – who ended up second – preferring instead to team up with a political unknown who finished fifth. And he did so in February, when virtually everybody was desperate to join his ticket.[46] Many other mistakes followed, but the most-costly of all was that San Román did not express interest in local needs. Despite public denouncements of his desire to govern Cusco despite not living there, San Román spent relatively long stretches of the campaign outside the region.[47] In addition, he did not travel to rural areas enough, even though, as we have discussed, a candidate's personal visits are crucial to persuading Peruvian voters about that candidate's desirability. Noticing all these drawbacks, San Román's allies stopped campaigning in his favor midway through the campaign and decided to focus instead on their own candidacies.[48] Gradually, his share of the voting intention began to decrease.

[43] "Engineer." This was noted in the personal interview with his adviser, Estrada.
[44] Rubén Coa (September 9, 2010).
[45] Jorge Valcárcel (December 19, 2010).
[46] Jorge Valcárcel (December 19, 2010).
[47] Aldo Estrada, *Pan*'s legal representative (December 20, 2010).
[48] Aldo Estrada (December 20, 2010).

In addition to these problems related to San Román's political persona, the candidate did not raise as many funds for electioneering as Acurio did, at least according to his advisor.[49] Once on the trail, San Román did not convince enough donors about his potential to win the race, and he was outspent by Acurio's campaign. Acurio also had another advantage that he exploited well in Cusco city: he was a local incumbent and used this incumbency in his favor, channeling San Sebastián Municipality funds and logistical resources to campaign in the city.[50]

During the last ten days of the campaign, San Román tried to counteract these mistakes and imbalances by investing heavily in the race, in terms of both TV ads and campaign clientelism. For instance, his contenders reported that he gave away gas cookers manufactured by his company and stepped up a negative campaign against Acurio, conducted through third-party accusations of corruption.[51] But this came far too late in the race and not enough to persuade voters of San Román's electoral *desirability*, even if expectations about his electoral *viability* were largely maintained. On October 3rd, San Román lost the race to Acurio, who managed to gather more than 30 percent of the votes (Table 6.4).

When Non-Desirability Hurts Viability

The municipal contest in Cusco province, on the other hand, was quite different to the regional one and had an electoral dynamic all of its own. Illustrating the low levels of political organization, incongruence, and volatility of the regional party system, the three leading candidates in Cusco's municipal race ran for different tickets than the two frontrunners in the regional competition. Neither San Román nor Acurio recruited competitive candidates for their tickets in the most important electoral constituency in the region,[52] so coattail effects were scarce.[53] Ultimately, sixteen lists competed for Cusco's municipal office.

---

[49] It is not possible to be conclusive on this point. Peru's law does not effectively sanction political organizations that fail to submit financial reports of donations and expenditures. Consequently, most candidates simply did not submit this information in the races under analysis.

[50] Aldo Estrada (December 20, 2010).

[51] Rubén Coa (September 9, 2010).

[52] According to INFOgob-JNE, the province of Cusco amounted to 48.6 percent of the region's registered voters in 2010.

[53] *Gana Perú*'s candidate ended up fourth basically due to coattail effects – his candidacy did not stand out during the race at all.

TABLE 6.4. *Cusco: 2010 regional elections results*

Political organization	Last name	Names	Valid votes	Percentage
Gran Alianza Nacionalista Cusco	Acurio	Jorge	170,873	33.37
Movimiento Regional Pan	San Roman	Maximo	131,692	25.72
Restauración Nacional	Ramos	Alipio	45,987	8.98
Movimiento Regional Acuerdo Popular Unificado	De La Torre	Hernan	37,471	7.32
Autogobierno Ayllu	Aimituma	Erasmo	22,374	4.37
Tierra Y Libertad Cusco	Rozas	Wilbert	22,271	4.35
Perú Posible	Cuaresma	Carlos	20,451	3.99
Unión Por El Perú	Jurado	Florecio	17,315	3.38
Fuerza 2011	Valencia	Carlos	16,312	3.19
Others			27,332	5.34

Source: INFOgob – JNE

At the end of 2009, one survey identified Willy Cuzmar, mayor of Wanchaq, a middle-class district in Cusco province, and Luis Florez, sitting mayor of Cusco province, as having greater chances to win the mayoral race. The survey put Acurio in third place, with 4 percent of the voting intention.[54] Nonetheless, it should be noted that the estimated voting intention shares were quite low; 66.7 percent of the respondents did not have a preferred candidate at that stage. The three figures out on front were sitting mayors of two districts and of the province of Cusco, respectively. Two of them (Florez and Cuzmar) were successful businessmen with no party affiliation who had recently entered politics as independents, running for different tickets.

Luis Florez's route to the mayoral office was particularly fortuitous. He was elected Councilor of Cusco in 2006 for the 2007–10 term as the third-ranked candidate on the UPP ticket. For eight months between October 2008 and May 2009, three successive mayors, beginning with the democratically elected one, were removed from office by the electoral authorities on charges of nepotism. This period of turmoil and paralysis in the Cusco

[54] It should be recalled that at that point Acurio had yet to announce his candidacy to the regional presidency.

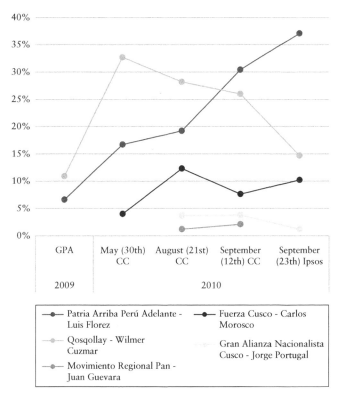

FIGURE 6.2. *Cusco's City 2010 municipal election: vote intention polls*
Sources: Guaman Poma de Ayala, November 2010; César Carranza, May 30, 2010; César Carranza, May 21, 2010; César Carranza, September 12, 2010; Ipsos, September 23, 2010

municipality ended with the appointment of Florez as mayor. During the following months, Florez, a successful entrepreneur and newcomer to politics, made a difference by resuming administration of the municipality and completing stalled projects. In a context of corruption scandals in the region, Florez stood out as an effective authority who proved capable of delivering the services and projects the citizenry expected. This helped him gain the name recognition he lacked before (Figure 6.2).

After Acurio announced his candidacy for regional office, media attention on the municipal race started focusing mainly around Cuzmar and Florez. As mentioned, both candidates had the advantage of being businessmen who could invest their own economic resources in the race. They also had connections with the business community, making it easier for them to collect donations during the race. But in addition to these advantages, by running as incumbents, they were able to draw on the municipality's logistical and human resources and institutional connections for their campaigns; for instance, they asked public employees to mobilize in their favor and hand out campaign publicity in their neighborhoods.[55] Moreover, their respective candidacies enjoyed media backing, thanks in Florez's case to the Municipality's institutional advertising; and in Cuzmar's case to connections with figures at the two most important television channels, who were running as candidates for his regional movement.[56] This was crucial considering how influential media outlets, particularly television, were in Cusco city. Cuzmar and Florez not only advertised heavily in the local media, but had easy access to different TV shows. However, it is interesting to observe that despite the extensive use by these candidates of local media outlets in Cusco city, it does not serve as an effective replacement of traditional electioneering. The different campaign teams actively organized motorcades as well as visits to markets, *campesino* communities, and poor neighborhoods. This is to say that rather than replacing street campaigning and mobilization, media advertising and coverage complemented it. Thus, the media's main role was in broadcasting or printing images and reports of campaign events.

Both Cuzmar and Florez made intensive use of campaign clientelism as an electioneering tactic. As a local leader from a rural part of Cusco province pointed out,

The Condor ticket [the *Qosqollay* regional movement] wasted a lot sending gifts and truckloads of food during their visits to *campesino* communities. In turn, *Papa* [another regional movement, "potato" in English] gave away small grain mills. There has been squandering. One could note at plain sight this excessive misspending (Víctor Raúl Noa Quispe, leader of the Agrarian League of Santiago district, December 22, 2010)

Florez also became known for giving away free gas to taxi drivers at the gas stations owned by his family. "For every 60 soles you spent, you got 10 more for free."[57] To be sure, Florez's lengthy motorcades through the city of Cusco were a common sight during the campaign.

In addition, both incumbents also mobilized the beneficiaries of social programs for their campaigns. Víctor Villa, a political operator supporting another ticket for office, contends that Cuzmar and Florez were not interested in assuring "the autonomy of the low-income sector. They relate

---

[55] Carlos Moscoso, candidate for mayor (December 18, 2010).

[56] Carlos Moscoso (December 18, 2010).

[57] Oliver Delgado, media advisor to Cuzmar (September 1, 2010).

to it through gifts and political operators."[58] In particular, Florez actively leveraged campaign clientelism to turn out beneficiaries of the *Vaso de Leche*[59] nutritional assistance program in support of his campaign events. That December, I had the chance to converse with several women registered to the program who were waiting to receive their Christmas presents at one of the municipal offices. They acknowledged that they campaigned for Florez and that they had been induced or coerced into doing so, either through the promise of additional incentives (such as an extra ration of milk) or threats – staff members told them that if they did not show up at a campaign event or rally, they would have their ration cut or delayed for a month.[60]

In fact, Moscoso stated that municipality officials prevented him from approaching and delivering gifts to these women on at least one occasion. In August, during the 30th anniversary of the *Vaso de Leche* program, he tried to greet and leave gifts for several beneficiaries who were attending a sports championship held as part of the celebrations. However, municipal officials stopped him from entering the stadium.[61] Moscoso also contends that the Florez administration bought the loyalty of many well-known *dirigentes sociales* (local brokers) by hiring them as social promoters when the election was approaching, so they could campaign for him and mobilize poor voters to his rallies.

Through this intense electioneering process, in which he actively invested in campaign clientelism and turned out people in numbers, Florez gradually distinguished himself as the most viable candidate in the race. For example, in early September, the *Diario del Cusco* reported that Florez received mass support from the citizenry during his weekend activities.[62] However, although by mid-September Florez was already leading the voting intention in the polls, many analysts still saw a tight election coming. For Vidal Pino, for example, the election of Florez "was a stroke of luck. He took advantage of a favorable situation with money: he could buy off the media and sell an image of efficiency."[63] But, if Florez had the money and connections, why didn't he just buy off the media to secure

[58] Víctor Villa, political operator supporting *Tierra y Libertad*'s list for Cusco (August 31, 2010).
[59] "Glass of milk," so-called because program beneficiaries tend to receive a daily ration of milk.
[60] Anonymous beneficiaries of Cusco's *Vaso de Leche* program (December 21, 2010).
[61] Carlos Moscoso, candidate for mayor (December 18, 2010).
[62] *Diario del Cusco* (September 6, 2010, p. 5).
[63] Vidal Pino, political analyst (December 21, 2010).

an image of popularity instead of bothering with campaign clientelism? That strategy would not have been successful since, as political operators explained, poor voters do not inform themselves as often and need to be reached through traditional engineering.

Indeed, many interviewees believed that what really helped Florez turn the race in his favor was his ability to personally communicate with voters, particularly compared to Cuzmar. Both had built legitimacy based on their performance in office, whereby they proved themselves to be effective and capable of delivering projects. But for the public, Florez exhibited good character while campaigning, and he came across as authentic in his interactions with voters. In contrast, Cuzmar's personal traits were not attractive enough. Roberto Romero, advisor to the mayor's office in Cusco Municipality, explained to me in August that "Florez has a good-natured, peaceful, and participatory character. Cuzmar, in contrast, is hard, he doesn't have the character for dialogue" (Roberto Romero, August 27, 2010). In turn, for Sergio Sullca, mayoral candidate for the district of Santiago for *Tierra y Libertad*, Florez had a very good public relations team that did a professional job of marketing the candidate. In his words, "it was devastating. The campaign caught him rising. Cuzmar's image, however, was one of a high-handed man."[64] Later, in December, appraising the race after it was over, Romero reaffirmed his earlier analysis, stressing how Cuzmar's deficient communication skills helped Florez win the race. As he put it,

Politics is the art of gestures. They [Cuzmar's campaign team] should not have made so many mistakes, they were a team of experienced [former] militants. But Cuzmar's character was a problem. While governing he was intolerant, people disliked him. The Turk [Cuzmar] was Florez's key campaign manager. (Roberto Romero, December 17, 2010)

To be sure, while a positive buzz among campaign-event attendees helped Florez bolster his candidacy, negative vibes sunk Cuzmar's: once on the trail, very few people liked him, and this perception spread among voters.

Effectively, Cuzmar's low desirability affected his candidacy. Florez was approachable, Cuzmar was not. This helped the former to persuade voters, while centering his campaign on taking local needs to heart. According to political advisor Roberto Romero, the identification of Florez with local customs was also important in establishing this linkage:

[64] Sergio Sullca, candidate for mayor of Santiago for *Tierra y Libertad* (December 12, 2010).

while Florez speaks fluent Quechua – he is from Calca province – Cuzmar, of Turkish origin, does not.[65] In turn, Ricardo Pezo, leader of the *Frente de Defensa de los Intereses del Distrito de Santiago* and well-known, explained that many *dirigentes* supported Florez's campaign because, as mayor, "Lucho" tried to vindicate the *dirigente* class by empowering them. After coming to office, Florez reached out to the *dirigentes* and gave them budgetary allocation powers to prioritize local projects during the participatory budget process.[66] Florez also showed an interest in listening and solving local problems by establishing a weekly session of public hearings. Citizens could come along and air their problems to the mayor in person. I attended one of these meetings in May, a couple of months before the campaign officially began.[67] In this hearing, I observed Florez interacting with citizens very closely. He patiently listened for hours on end to all their complaints, problems, and requests. He was very diligent and tried to tackle the issues raised right away, calling the officials in charge of the different policy areas to publicly inform them about the situation and address each complaint. Whenever it was not possible to deal with an issue immediately, he asked the officials to coordinate with the resident to help them in the following weeks. Something noticeable was that Florez also dealt with requests for new funding for local projects. In these cases, he explained to the residents that the budget had already been allocated for the year and that they should submit their proposals in time for the following year's participatory budget process. In one case, he offered to provide some water pipes to a social organization as a contribution to their collective effort at improving their water supply. In general, according to the Municipality advisor, those who attended Florez's public hearings saw a politician willing to listen and talk to them.[68]

Confirming this view about Florez willingness to identify and deal with local needs, the beneficiaries of the *Vaso de Leche* program stated that although they had been mobilized through campaign clientelism and threats, they supported Florez at the polls because they personally liked him and believed he was working well and delivering important projects to the city.[69] Thus, rather than turning out at rallies but ultimately voting for another candidate at the polls because they did not like the incumbent

---

[65] Roberto Romero (August 27, 2010). On this point, see also De la Cadena (2010).

[66] Ricardo Pezo (September 2, 2010).

[67] July 5 was the deadline for registering lists of candidates for the elections – that is, ninety days before election day.

[68] Roberto Romero (August 27, 2010).

[69] Anonymous beneficiaries of Cusco's *Vaso de Leche* program (December 21, 2010).

mayor – as women from the *Vaso de Leche* program reported in Piura – the Cusco beneficiaries interviewed were persuaded that Florez was a desirable candidate worthy of their support.[70] Cuzmar, in contrast, could not convince enough voters that he had knowledge of or interest in local needs and problems, especially those of poor people, beyond his middle-class district (Wanchaq).

Given Florez's financial advantage, greater campaign spending, and investment in campaign clientelism, as well as his capacity to personally connect with clients during his campaign events, it is no surprise that he won the election. Indeed, the real surprise was Carlos Moscoso's surge in the polls.[71] He managed to increase his vote share from the 4.09 percent he recorded when he ran for mayor in 2002, to 13.681 percent in 2010, finishing second and displacing Cuzmar. As can be observed, the 2010 municipal election results for second place were as good as tied (Table 6.5).

As we have seen, during the campaign, Moscoso complained about not being able to match, or indeed come close to, the spending of Florez and Cuzmar on electoral propaganda and campaign clientelism. These two candidates outspent Moscoso by some margin, and this was noticeable in their greater propaganda presence during the campaign. However, despite this disadvantage, Moscoso succeeded in reaching certain groups of voters through campaign clientelism. His voting intention share gradually increased during the two last months of the race. And having already amassed electoral viability, he was able to beat Cuzmar when it came to desirability. As already mentioned, Cuzmar did not have the right character. Despite his perceived viability at the outset, Cuzmar was not able to convince enough voters of his desirability as a candidate. In contrast, Moscoso stood out for his capacity to engage with poor voters during his campaign events. After this surprising electoral showing, Moscoso was finally elected as Cusco's mayor in 2014.

---

[70] *Vaso de Leche* beneficiaries are used to having municipal staff use both positive and negative inducements to mobilize them in support of the incumbent's official and campaign activities. They see these as "normal" municipal politics, since everyone else does it; that is, they see the clientelistic deal as turnout buying at rallies and campaign events, not vote-buying. Whether or not threats backfire on incumbents at the polls hinges on their ability to persuade the clients of their desirability as a candidate either by promising public local goods or establishing personalistic linkages. See Chapter 5.

[71] Moscoso was an activist of *Acción Popular* until the 1990s. He reentered politics in the 2000s as an independent, forming his own regional movement.

TABLE 6.5. *Cusco: 2010 municipal election results*

Political organization	Last name	Name	Valid votes	Percentage
Patria Arriba Peru Adelante	Florez	Luis	66,044	33.43
Fuerza Cusco	Moscoso	Carlos	27,028	13.68
Qosqollay	Cuzmar	Willy	26,877	13.61
Gran Alianza Nacionalista Cusco	Portugal	Jose	26,333	13.33
Movimiento Regional Pan	Guevara	Juan	17,955	9.09
Acuerdo Regional de Integracion	Infantas	Hernan	8,472	4.23
APRA	Chevarria	Franz	5,209	2.64
Others			19,637	9.94

Source: INFOgob – JNE

PIURA'S RACES

The 2010 races analyzed in Piura contribute important nuances to a better understanding of the implications and scope of my informational theory. On the one hand, and in contrast to Cusco, in Piura we see how the presence of a very organized party and a regional machine alters the dynamics of the regional race, but not the way in which campaign clientelism works. In César Trelles and APRA, there was an incumbent up for reelection for a second time, who availed himself of an experienced party and an organized clientelistic machine to distributed goods intensively among the poor. Moreover, during its second term the party's popularity plummeted amidst corruption allegations. Opposition candidates sought to vote out the machine, and two of them formed an electoral alliance to that end. Despite an uneven playing field – the incumbent party channeled public funds into intensive clientelistic tactics during the campaign – the joint ticket electioneered vigorously throughout the region, likewise mobilizing voters through campaign clientelism. Soon, they stood out as the most viable opposition ticket, attracting high levels of public support as a credible and feasible proposal for change, and, just

TABLE 6.6. *Mechanisms at work in Piura's campaigns*

Factors	Piura region		Piura province			
	Trelles	Atkins	Zapata	Rodríguez	Elera	Miranda
Use of campaign clientelism	High	Medium-high	High	High	Low-none	Medium-high (coattail)
Electoral viability	Decreasing	Increasing	Decreasing	Medium-maintained	Increasing	Sudden increase
Desirable candidate						
Likable (charisma + authenticity)	No	Yes	No	No carisma, but authentic	–	–
Cares about local needs	No	Yes	No	Yes	No	–
Technical expertise		Yes	No	No	Yes	Yes
Effective (delivers)			No	Yes		
Won the race	No	Yes	No	Yes	No	No

as important, because the candidate was likable and established an emotional link with poor voters while campaigning.

On the other hand, the municipal contest in the province of Piura shows two things. First, it reaffirms that distributing goods to turn out voters is not enough in itself to win a race. In Piura's municipal election at least two candidates intensively used campaign clientelism as a tactic to mobilize voters and signal electoral viability to the general public. However, while campaign clientelism helped one candidate to establish herself as the frontrunner, it did not help the incumbent to do the same. The local media was highly critical of the incumbent for not dealing with the city's most pressing problems and denounced her use of public funds for clientelistic electioneering. These alternative sources of information counterbalanced the effect that turnout figures alone could have as a signal of potential electoral strength. In addition, the incumbent did not persuade enough campaign clients that his candidacy was a desirable one. Consequently, high levels of participation at her events did not translate into support at the polls. In contrast, the other candidate used campaign clientelism effectively to signal her viability to the general public and donors, and to persuade her bought audiences that she understood local needs, cared for the poor, and would look after them if elected.

Second, the case of the municipal election in 2010 illustrates the electoral potential, but also the limits, of an electoral strategy that openly criticizes the use of campaign clientelism as an electioneering method in an electoral district where a sizeable minority of voters are middle class. Toward the end of the race, a candidate positioned himself as an electorally competitive option. He did so principally through intense exposition at public debates and in the media. Through his public appearances, he convinced a sector of the electorate that he had the professional trajectory and technical knowledge needed to solve Piura's most urgent problems. Thus, two candidates distinguished themselves as viable contenders at the end of the municipal race using different strategies: one made heavy use of campaign clientelism and local electioneering while the other privileged media appearances and policy-oriented debates. They targeted their electoral strategies to different socioeconomic classes, and fought vote by vote during the finale. While one was able to persuade principally middle-class voters of his desirability based on his professional expertise and policy-based discourse, the other did the same with poorer and rural voters by actively using campaign-clientelism tactics and personal interaction during campaign events. The election was finally decided by only 2,230 votes, which proved the efficacy of campaign clientelism

TABLE 6.7. *Piura: 2006 regional elections results*

Political organization	Last name	Names	Valid votes	Percentage
APRA	Trelles	César	174,114	24.71
Obras + Obras	Atkins	Javier	157,432	22.16
Alianza Electoral Unidad Nacional	Castagnino	Juan	147,379	20.75
Movimiento de Desarrollo Local	Vásquez	Isaías	86,434	12.17
Partido Nacionalista Peruano	Ruiz	Maximiliano	77,053	10.85
Others			66,475	9.36

Source: INFOgob – JNE

combined with public engagement as an electioneering tactic at the margins. Unexpectedly, the vote count also attested to coattail effects from the regional race, which were not anticipated from polls. And by turning out large numbers, the opposition joint ticket also convinced undecided voters to support them in the municipal contest.

Voting out the Machine

In contrast to Cusco's high electoral uncertainty – associated with the absence of organized parties and strong contenders – the regional campaign in Piura was marked by fear of APRA's dominance. Being an organized and incumbent party (at the regional government level), most candidates and political operators were afraid of APRA's capacity to mobilize enough voters to win by a small margin, despite increasing disapproval of the party's candidate, Trelles, as had happened in 2006. APRA's support in Piura has never been massive, but it was big enough to win the elections in 2002 and 2006 within a context of political fragmentation. In 2002, César Trelles won the regional presidency with 28.3 percent of the vote, 8 percent points ahead of the second-placed candidate. In 2006, although APRA was able to reelect Trelles, this time the margin was much tighter. APRA obtained 24.7 percent of the vote, followed closely by Javier Atkins (invited candidate of O + O) with 22.16 percent and Juan Castagnino (*Alianza Electoral Unidad Nacional*) with 20.75 percent (Table 6.7). Incumbency advantage played in APRA's favor, as they were able to mobilize regional government resources and logistics to campaign. In addition, APRA is well-known in Peru for its capacity to mobilize a great number of experienced representatives to the polling stations on election day, in order to effectively defend the party's votes and gain more than the unexperienced or inexistent representatives of other candidates, thus, changing popular will *en mesa*.[72] To be sure, after the 2006 elections, rumors spread in Piura about electoral fraud committed by *Apristas* in the province of Talara (APRA's stronghold within the region), which helped assure their reelection. Consequently, in 2010 many politicians and observers expressed concern that electoral fragmentation would again help APRA overcome increasing dissatisfaction with its rule and cling onto power.

Fear of APRA winning again prompted two former candidates to join forces and create *Unidos Construyendo* (UC) in a bid to defeat the APRA machine. This was an alliance between Javier Atkins, the business oriented (and supported) candidate who ended up second in 2006; and Maximiliano Ruiz, candidate from the leftist regional movement *Poder Regional* who finished fourth in 2006. The two candidates amassed 234,485 votes between them in that election, which accounted for 33 percent of the total share. Thus, in 2010, they had the potential to win the election outright or make it to the run-off. In the event, the electoral alliance worked well, despite the apparent ideological contradictions between the candidates. At the beginning of the race in early February, UC share of voting intention (10.7 percent) was already very close to that of APRA (15.4 percent). Apart from this particular effort at entry coordination, however, the options available in the 2010 regional election were very fragmented. The number of registered candidacies to regional presidency increased to thirteen from the seven on offer in 2006. This was due in part to the establishment of the electoral threshold of 30 percent and the run-off, which was seen by politicians as an additional opportunity to coordinate. All in all, the chances of APRA winning the election were still considerable.

In general, opposition candidates perceived that the race was partially unfair since they had to compete with an incumbent party that used the state power and resources they commanded in their favor. For instance, Abraham Parrilla, a political operator working for UC, explained that APRA had both an organizational structure and the regional government's logistics at their disposal. Parrilla also complained that besides

---

[72] "At the table," that is, to change the popular will while the votes are being counted.

this resource advantage, APRA bought off neighborhood gangsters to intimidate the opposition and prevent them from electioneering.[73] In turn, a political operator working for APRA said in an interview that July that he believed the race was going to be polarized around APRA and UC. But, he added, he believed UC did not actually have a chance of winning against APRA since they did not have an electoral machine in place and would not be able to improvise one in just three months.[74]

The opposition claims about APRA's tendency to use public resources and logistics for reelection electioneering was confirmed by the journalists interviewed.[75] They contended that APRA actively used regional government offices as campaign headquarters. *Apristas* stored propaganda there and even used the facilities to prepare sandwiches they would later distribute.[76] They also used the regional government's vehicles and staff for campaigning. For instance, for their final rally, they asked temporary workers to attend their rally, and to each take along between five and a hundred family members or friends.[77] In the Morropón province, officials working for the sub-regional office were seen distributing propaganda during office hours.[78] Trelles and Marco Tulio Vargas, the regional government's general manager and candidate, respectively, actively initiated small projects despite electoral law forbidding it.[79] The regional government also stepped up the organization of "civic campaigns" in poor neighborhoods and rural towns during the race, giving away backpacks and notebooks for children as well as offering free haircuts and medical appointments.[80] They conducted these clientelistic tactics particularly in rural highland areas where there are fewer journalists covering the campaign.[81]

Thus, APRA made intensive use of clientelistic tactics, including campaign clientelism, during the campaign. As we have seen, APRA had a clientelistic machine in place and ran it from the regional government. They actively invested public resources in patronage to hire local APRA

---

[73] This was also confirmed by Flor and Roberto García, local activists for UC in charge of the northwest sector of Piura (October 2, 2010).

[74] Rodrigo Urbina, former leftist activist working at that time as political operator for APRA's regional government (July 23, 2010).

[75] Karina Miranda, *La Hora* newspaper (July 22, 2010). Lili Guevara, *El Tiempo* newspaper (November 20, 2010).

[76] Rocío Farfán, *Cutivalú* radio station (July 22, 2010).

[77] Lili Guevara, *El Tiempo* newspaper (November 20, 2010).

[78] Karina Miranda, *La Hora* newspaper (July 22, 2010).

[79] Rocío Farfán, *Cutivalú* radio station (July 22, 2010).

[80] Karina Miranda, *La Hora* newspaper (July 22, 2010).

[81] Rocío Farfán, *Cutivalú* radio station (July 22, 2010).

activists to serve as campaign workers. In addition, as the only organized party in the region, APRA has local committees in place in most poor neighborhoods and villages. These local activist networks helped the party to organize events and mobilize voters during campaigns, but they also helped channel PAS resources to engage in campaign clientelism in the midst of the race. For instance, secretaries of local committees in the southern sector of Piura city asked the regional government for kitchen supplies such as cookers, pots and spoons for distribution among *Vaso de Leche* and *Comedor Popular* committees in the campaign. Moreover, they distributed free services and food to all party and non-party voters who participated in "social" campaign events.[82] Local cadres also helped to organize civic actions, schedule doctors' visits and deliver free medication.[83] These local agents also asked the regional government to execute small projects to benefit their neighborhoods or villages. When they obtained such projects, they also distributed temporary positions as construction workers among their neighbors. As a result, many people were willing to support them when they campaigned.[84]

However, it is important to clarify that even within this organized political context, voters in Piura still play candidates against one other during campaigns. As these local partisan cadres explain, "people receive goods from all candidates and, at the polls, the vote is secret so we don't know who they actually support. That is why it is important to know how to personally reach the voter."[85] Indeed, "people take advantage and ask all candidates [for gifts]. The parties that arise at the last moment teach people badly ... If a party gives away tuna cans with their party label, people receive them but do not commit. They receive but don't necessarily vote for that party; they off the labels."[86] In other words, partisan competition and the high levels of electoral fragmentation give voters greater room for maneuver with which to play off different candidates.

---

[82] Joel Pulache, secretary of APRA's Antonio Raymondi's neighborhood, Southern Piura, October 2, 2010.

[83] Jaime Bejarano, APRA secretary for the La Florida settlement (November 23, 2010) Kelly Coronado, APRA secretary for the Los Olivos settlement (September 28, 2010), and Joel Pulache, APRA secretary in the Antonio Raymondi neighborhood (October 2, 2010).

[84] Kelly Coronado, APRA secretary for the Los Olivos settlement and candidate to Council (September 28, 2010).

[85] Jaime Bejarano, APRA Secretary for the La Florida settlement (November 23, 2010).

[86] Kelly Coronado (September 28, 2010).

Thus, even within the context of domination by a well-established machine, the opposition had a big chance to vote out APRA. After their second term in office, APRA's support had weakened, even among partisans. Allegations of corruption against regional authorities had become more and more frequent. Yet despite these allegations, the sitting authorities managed to control the party elections to elect their core faction as candidates to regional and local offices, and Trelles ran for regional president for the third time.

On the other hand, the electoral alliance between Atkins and Ruiz worked well in the eyes of opposition voters. UC activists campaigned intensively in poor neighborhoods from the beginning of the race.[87] During the candidates' visits, according to one operator, they offered lunches and breakfasts "but involving people ... We do not buy consciences. In contrast, APRA uses state resources and gives away things like roof tiles."[88] If they were required to give social aid to people in need, "the money did not go through my hands" and donations were sent directly to the population.[89] Even if the party truly did not agree with this practice of distributing food or gifts while campaigning, in practice they did so because they knew that it is an established way of approaching poor voters. For instance, in urban low-income sectors of Piura, the organization of bingo games has become a common practice during campaigns, as a way to attract voters to candidates' events in the hope of winning a prize. "In the absence of decent operators and a party, you use these tactics because if you do not, the other [party] does."[90] Indeed, Ruiz adds that APRA delivered gifts "by the truckload."[91] He explains that once they counted sixteen trucks heading to rural areas in the Morropón and Ayabaca provinces with machetes, sickles, and shovels.

Active electioneering in low-income sectors through campaign clientelism helped UC convey the electoral viability of their joint ticket to the public and donors. Convincing voters and donors to both support Atkins and campaign for him was not easy at the beginning.[92] But the ease with

---

[87] Gregoria Muro, political operator in charge of UC's campaign (July 23, 2010).

[88] Gregoria Muro (July 23, 2010).

[89] Gregoria Muro, political operator in charge of UC's campaign (July 23, 2010).

[90] Maximiliano Ruiz, UC candidate for regional vice-presidency (July 20, 2010).

[91] Maximiliano Ruiz (November 17, 2010).

[92] Roberto García, Campaign Coordinator for northwest Piura city, UC (October 2, 2010).

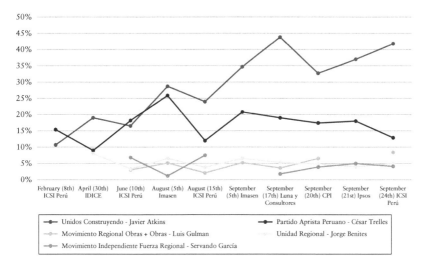

FIGURE 6.3. *2010 regional election in Piura: voting intention polls*
Sources: ICSI Perú, February 8, 2010; IDICE, April 30, 2010; ICSI Perú,
June 10, 2010; Imasen, August 5, 2010; ICSI Perú, August 15, 2010; Imasen,
September 5, 2010; Luna y Consultores, September 17, 2010; CPI, September 20,
2010; Ipsos, September 21, 2010; ICSI Perú, September 24, 2010; ICSI Perú,
October 3, 2010

which they attracted voters to their campaign events proved important
in projecting an image of electoral viability, and helped them raise more
funds for further campaign events. By August, the polls were clearly plac-
ing UC out on front (Figure 6.3). Once the polls confirmed Atkins as the
frontrunner, local UC committees began to gain more and more supporters[93] as well as more donations.[94]

UC operators attributed their electoral surge to being a credible option
that represented change. For Ruiz, candidate for vice-president, his (leftist) party expressed detachment to voters by accepting Atkins' leadership
as lead candidate, giving the alliance an image of unity that helped the
campaign.[95] The party symbol they selected (a pair of crossed hands)
represented this union of outwardly dissimilar options joining together
to defeat Trelles. Ruiz further believes that their joint visits (Atkins and

[93] Flor García, General Secretary of Los Sauces Neighborhood Council and local activist
for UC's campaign (October 2, 2010).
[94] Maximiliano Ruiz (November 17, 2010).
[95] Maximiliano Ruiz, UC candidate for the regional vice-presidency (November 17, 2010).

him) to low-income sectors was crucial in ratifying this mutual commitment to change. Thus, electioneering in poorer areas [campaign clientelism included] was, in his view, an important component of this initial
surge.

A second factor that ultimately proved important for UC's victory
was Atkin's candidacy. As political operators from the alliance highlight,
Atkins turned out to be an excellent candidate on the trail. On the one
hand, his professional trajectory was a valuable credential. His mana-
gerial experience was something many believed would help him while
governing. As Gamaniel Ventura pointed out, Atkins a former bank manager with a master's degree, was seen as a capable figure.[96] On the other
hand, the candidate also showed good character while interacting with
people at campaign events. In particular, his openness contrasted with the
incumbent's distant character and manner:

They call Atkins' wife Sandra and him, Javier. He is seen as someone close, familiar. Trelles has no such characteristics. He is a *caudillo* with organization and discipline. His cadres go and sell their product, but he does not sell himself. He does
not participate [in campaign activities] and when he does, he is not sympathetic.
To win an election in Peru it is not enough to have good organization; you need
to have a good candidate. (Abraham Parrilla, political operator working for UC,
July 26, 2010)

As Parrilla also noticed, Atkins seemed more willing to get in touch
with people and their concerns, actively campaigning in disadvantaged
areas. Indeed, Atkins managed to bridge the social distance and present
a political persona of someone who, despite not being from a working-
class background, genuinely cared for people's problems and wanted to
get closer to them. He did not come across as fake. As another political
operator explained:

[Atkins] is an employee [manager], not a businessman. He is from the middle
class. He is well-prepared but is also charismatic; he is a very simple guy. He is
a modern *pituco*,[97] not one from the Middle Ages. (Gamaniel Ventura, political
operator working for Unidos Construyendo, July 26, 2010)

Thus, a negative campaign that aimed to hurt him by labeling him the
"representative of the rich" did not work out.

---

[96] Gamaniel Ventura, political operator working for UC (July 26, 2010).
[97] Term used in Peru to denote a member of the upper classes.

Another local operator also points to the personal charisma of Atkins' wife as a factor that helped the candidate while campaigning:

The involvement of Mrs Sandra in the campaign did much to build more bases. What took us eight months she did in one with social work and her charisma. She has great social sensitivity and sympathy. (Roberto García, November 23, 2010)

In other words, through campaign clientelism Atkins' candidacy proved not only viable but also a desirable. People voted for change because they wanted to get rid of APRA and Trelles. But of all opposition lists it was the UC one they strategically supported as a credible and viable proposal for change, and, additionally, because the candidate was likable, established an emotional link with poor voters, and showed he cared about local needs while campaigning.

Toward the end of the race, the opposition strategically converged and supported UC for the regional presidency. Thus, for instance, many candidates publicly endorsed UC and presented a vote for them as a vote against corruption and fraud.[98] Even some APRA activists stopped supporting Trelles, and local UC operatives detected a spurt of "leader switching." They found that many APRA base-level *dirigentes* who already suspected Trelles was not going to win began electioneering for them.[99]

Something similar happened with APRA's turnout clients, who kept receiving APRA's gifts and participating in their campaign events but supported UC at the ballots. "There was a rather subjective problem of rejection. People said 'Trelles no more, he has robbed.' Even when Trelles arrived with small gifts, his candidacy turned out unlikable."[100] In particular, campaign clients from urban areas did not believe Trelles and, as a punishment, they received APRA's gifts but voted for the alliance.[101]

But APRA militants did not suspect at the time that so many voters were going to turn away from them. In fact, they did not see the result coming at all, and still hoped to make it to the run-off: UC not only won the election, but they did so by a landslide. Consequently, the result was

---

[98] *El Tiempo*, September 25, 2010.

[99] Flor García (October 2, 2010).

[100] Abraham Parrilla, political operator working for UC (July 26, 2010).

[101] Maximiliano Ruiz, UC's candidate for vice-president (November 17, 2010).

TABLE 6.8. *Piura: 2010 regional elections results*

Political organization	Last name	Names	Valid votes	Percentage
Unidos Construyendo	Atkins	Javier	319,790	46.00
APRA	Trelles	César	104,870	15.25
Movimiento Regional Obras + Obras	Gulman	Luis	67,115	9.76
Unidad Regional	Benites	Jorge	47,876	6.96
Movimiento Independiente Fuerza Regional	García	Servando	47,231	6.87
Others			100,991	14.68

Source: INFOgob – JNE

a death blow to APRA.[102] The result also surprised UC's campaign team; they were expecting to get just 37 percent of the vote. Therefore, everybody was surprised when the Electoral Tribunal declared UC the winner with 46 percent, more than 30 percentage points ahead of APRA, who only attained 15.25 percent of the vote (Table 6.8).

The Limits of Non-Clientelistic Strategies

Lastly, as with Cusco, the municipal race in the province of Piura followed its own dynamic of competition. Again, the candidates who received most attention from the public and media as front-runners did not run for the same tickets that led the regional race. But, as we will see, the municipal contest was unexpectedly influenced by coattail effects.

In 2006, José Aguilar from O + O, an independent politician and former mayor, well-known for his clientelistic tactics and support of the poor while governing, won the 2006 municipal election. He was loved by the needy because he proselytized on a daily basis, listening to people and helping them solve their problems.[103] For instance, if somebody died, Aguilar would receive the bereaved, comfort them, and buy the coffin and a plot in the cemetery.[104] He was also well known for drinking and eating out with the poor. From the 1990s, O + O focused on this type of

---

[102] Alberto Chumacero, APRA's secretary of organization in Piura (November 23, 2010).
[103] Luis Loja, political operator (September 27, 2010).
[104] Rolando Gutiérrez, activist from O + O (November 23, 2010).

"social work," translating into gestures that stayed in people's mind and helped O + O build their organization.[105]

However, after Aguilar's death in 2008, O + O was unable to retain power in the municipality. The deputy mayor, Mónica Zapata, an independent invited to participate on their list, ended up excluding O + O councilors from decision-making after taking over as mayor. Zapata's administration was widely criticized by the media and the citizenry for its perceived failure to deal with pressing problems and needs in the city, such as the reorganization of the municipal market, a hotspot for crime and general chaos. Nevertheless, Zapata ran for reelection in 2010, this time for Fuerza 2011, the *Fujimorista* ticket.

From the beginning of the municipal race, there was also a good deal of expectation and public discussion about the new O + O candidate, Ruby Rodríguez, the widow of Aguilar. As discussed earlier, O + O may have been a relatively well-established and organized local movement, but it was highly personalistic. Many interviewees believed that Rodríguez's candidacy would be able to exploit Aguilar's memory and retain the votes of the poor, but others were skeptical. Those who felt that Rodríguez's candidacy had potential cited her political trajectory, in which she had shown herself to be aware of local needs and in touch with poor people. Her supporters stressed she had a "humanitarian" character just as her husband did. Moreover, they pointed out that she had maintained a close relationship with certain social organizations, such as *Comedor Popular* and *Vaso de Leche* committees. Some political rivals shared this view, including a political operator working for UC:

Rubi [Rodríguez] has done good political work. She has her followers. They are loyal to her because she delivered for them in the past and many of these women are her *comadres*. She helps residents, connecting them with businessmen who can support them. She gives them gifts for their birthdays. That's her business; those details cement a sentimental bond. And others [politicians] are not interested in doing that work; they are doing something else. This *asistencialismo* implies an emotional bond; she does it well. The way she gives away things matters: she gives tenderly saying "sister this is little but it is what it is. When we are in charge it will be different." (Abraham Parrilla, September 23, 2010)

However, Rodríguez's detractors stressed she was not as likable as her husband because her personality was rather dry, and she was not a good speaker. In addition, they felt that Rodríguez was not prepared to govern.

[105] Rolando Gutiérrez (November 23, 2010).

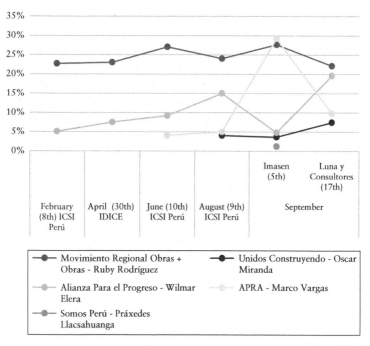

FIGURE 6.4. *Piura's City 2010 municipal election: voting intention polls*
Sources: ICSI Perú, February 8, 2010; IDICE, April 30, 2010; ICSI Perú, June 10, 2010;
ICSI Perú, August 9, 2010; Imasen, September 5, 2010; Luna y Consultores,
September 17, 2010

Unlike other candidates with professional backgrounds – such as Oscar
Miranda (UC), who was a physician, and Wilmar Elera (*Alianza Para el
Progreso* (APP)), who was an engineer – she had not even completed high
school. Her critics argued that the city's pressing problems needed a professional who would be better equipped to address them; in other words,
that Rodriguez did not have the professional expertise they thought necessary for an elected mayor.

O + O had an advantage over other tickets in that it was a known
brand among *Piuranos*. Moreover, Rodríguez herself had name recognition. Indeed, from February, Rodríguez led the voting intention polls
by a fair margin (Figure 6.4). From the beginning of the race, O + O
campaigned vigorously among the low-income sector, engaging in campaign clientelism.[106] Ruby, as she was widely known, actively visited the

[106] Gregoria Muro, political operator working for UC (July 23, 2010).

shantytowns and rural villages around the province as her husband had done before her.

However, O + O was not the only political organization that actively invested in campaign clientelism during the Piura city race. Press reports and interviewees pointed out that this tactic was also heavily used by the incumbent, with municipality funds, staff and logistics. For instance, *El Tiempo* reported in early July that Fuerza 2011 registered Mónica Zapata's candidacy in front of a crowd made up of municipal officials, women, and children.[107] The media also reported that Zapata distributed orange (her party's color) home supplies, such as pails and jugs, to *Comedor Popular* and *Vaso de Leche* committees during events organized by the local government.[108] Moreover, local O + O activists also reported that Zapata's people threatened beneficiaries of the municipality-run *Vaso de Leche* program with cutting back their benefits if they did not support her candidacy and participate in her rallies.[109] Similarly, Zapata was also accused of implementing a temporary work-for-food program in order to pay people to skip work and attend her final rally.[110]

Ultimately, however, having people turn up in numbers to her campaign events was not enough for Zapata to establish electoral viability. The press actively exposed and criticized her for using municipal resources to engage in campaign clientelism. Moreover, many criticized her tenure as being inefficient and responsible for the severe problems the city was facing, such as increased traffic, disorder, and crime. Thus, she had not shown that she could deliver what she promised. Finally, she was not able to persuade enough campaign clients that she had good character either. For instance, beneficiaries of municipal social programs such as *Vaso de Leche* pointed out that they attended her campaign activities because they feared the consequences of not doing so, but ended up voting for another candidate regardless.[111]

In contrast, Rodríguez did capitalize on her bought audiences and managed to persuade numerous campaign clients of her desirability. At her events, she talked with these clients about their problems, showing them that "she is a very good person, very humble."[112] And although

---

[107] *El Tiempo* (July 4, 2010).

[108] Rocío Farfán, reporter, *Cutivalú* Radio station (July 22, 2010).

[109] Nancy Tinoco, local O + O activist (November 23, 2011).

[110] Kelly Coronado, local APRA activist and candidate (September 28, 2010).

[111] Nancy Tinoco, local O + O activist (November 23, 2011); Francisco Fuentes, broker and political operator, San Sebastián (November 23, 2010).

[112] Nancy Tinoco, local O + O activist, northwest Piura (November 23, 2010).

some of the poor voters who witnessed Rodríguez's clientelism-based electioneering in their shantytowns echoed her rival's claims that she was neither a good speaker nor charismatic,[113] Rodríguez nevertheless proved able to convince many clients that she shared her husband's deep knowledge of local needs and interest in solving poor people's problems.

Another candidate who made gains in voting intention during the campaign was Wilmar Elera from the APP party. Elera had been candidate for mayor of Piura in the 2002 elections, when he finished second with 18.56 percent of the vote, and he still had some name recognition at the beginning of the 2010 race. An engineer by profession who was previously dean of Piura's *Colegio de Ingenieros*, Elera's public image was one of a professional committed to public affairs, and he constantly reinforced this through his interviews in the media. During the 2010 municipal contest, Elera actively participated in public debates organized by civil society organizations. In so doing, he was soon able to persuade many voters that he possessed the technical skills needed to solve the city's most urgent problems. His media appearances confirmed this. Furthermore, his campaign targeted the limitations of Rodríguez, his main rival, stressing that she was not a professional and would, thus, be unable to govern a complex city with pressing problems such as Piura.

This message was particularly influential to Piura's middle- and upper-class voters who used to dislike Aguilar's clientelistic approach to politics, which they regarded as "populist." But, Elera's message struck a chord with some poorer sectors as well. One experienced shantytown broker and political operator explained to me that to locals base their voting decision on the candidates' proposals, as well as their trajectory and profession. During the campaign, he continues, a group of residents, including himself, concluded that Rodríguez may have been good at managing social programs, but actually governing the city was another thing. "She is not a professional. She is going to be manipulated by politicians and advisors. In contrast, Elera is a professional and he is going to put this chaos in order."[114] Based on this reasoning, the shantytown's council decided to support Elera. In addition to this campaign messaging, Elera allied himself with interest groups who supported his candidacy, such as construction unions – powerful in Piura city because they regulate access to temporary construction work.[115]

---

[113] Focus group with women from the Los Polvorines settlement (July 9, 2011).
[114] Francisco Fuentes, *dirigente*, San Sebastián settlement (November 23, 2010).
[115] Óscar Peña, O + O activist, La Molina (November 23, 2010).

As election day approached, Elera's share of voting intention rose in the polls, coming very close to that of Rodríguez (see Figure 6.4) despite the former's lack of active engagement in campaign clientelism. Thus, by September 17, 19.6 percent of voters said they would vote for Elera, while 21.1 percent were minded to cast their ballot in favor of Rodríguez.[116] However, it should be noted that polling firms did not give consistent results about voting intention for municipal office. For instance, *Imasen*, a nationwide and supposedly reputable polling firm, published results that appeared to inflate APRA's share of voting intention for the regional and municipal elections.[117] With regard to Piura's municipal race, the poll penalized Elera's position in particular, thus, adding noise to the contest. Indeed, the municipal outcome was completely unexpected, and surprised everybody. Given their electoral history, the poll results, and their campaign, O + O activists expected to retain the support of the poor, which accounted for the majority of the electorate in Piura province. Consequently, they were very surprised when the first official counts pointed to Elera as the potential winner.[118]

After listening to these preliminary results, Elera celebrated with his team and declared to the press that the results showed Piura's voters wanted to have a professional as a mayor.[119] However, Elera was followed closely in the count by Rodríguez *and* Miranda, UC's candidate for mayor. Miranda had received very little attention during the race, but he was swept along by the electoral tide of Atkins: many people voted for UC's message for change in both Piura's regional and municipal elections. Thus, campaigning alongside Atkins meant that Miranda benefitted from the momentum for change and recognition of the UC symbol of the crossed hands. Moreover, Miranda was also a professional with good reputation, what could have helped him get votes from middle- and upper-class voters.

More than two days after election day, the electoral authorities finished counting the votes. After the votes from peripheral rural districts in Piura province came in, Rodríguez was declared mayor of Piura by 2,230 votes, followed by Miranda and Elera in third. As can be seen in Table 6.9, the electoral geography mattered in the end. The election was

---

[116] *Luna y Consultores* (September 17, 2010).

[117] See *Diario Correo*, "*Imasen* sobrevalora al APRA" (September 7, 2010). Available at: https://diariocorreo.pe/politica-y-economia/encuesta-de-imasen-sobrevalora-al-apra-195204/

[118] Segundo Mulatillo, O + O political operator (November 25, 2010); Nancy Tinoco, local O + O activist (November 23, 2011); Rolando Gutiérrez, O + O militant (November 23, 2010).

[119] *El Tiempo* (October 5, 2010).

TABLE 6.9. *Piura: 2010 municipal election results*

Political organization	Last name	Name	Valid votes	Percentage
Movimiento Regional Obras + Obras	Rodríguez	Ruby	61,128	20.97
Unidos Construyendo	Miranda	Oscar	58,898	20.20
Alianza para el Progreso	Elera	Wilmar	58,698	20.13
APRA	Vargas	Marco	31,936	10.95
Partido Democrático Somos Perú	Llacsahuanga	Práxedes	18,735	6.43
Fuerza 2011	Zapata	Mónica	1,606	3.98
Others			50,576	17.35

close to being a three-way tie in the capital district (Piura) and its contiguous urban district (Castilla). Elera received greater support in Piura district, where most of the middle and high class of Piura lives. What helped Rodríguez get elected, though, was the support she achieved in the most populous peripheral districts with higher pockets of rural poverty, where she actively canvassed through campaign clientelism.

In a nutshell, the two candidates who distinguished themselves as viable contenders during the race targeted their electoral appeal to different sociodemographic constituencies. While Elera was able to persuade mostly middle-class urban voters of his desirability through media appearances and policy debates, Rodríguez persuaded poorer and rural voters by actively using campaign clientelism tactics. Another sector of the electorate decided to support UC for the municipality too, despite their mayoral candidate not having publicly positioned himself as a viable or desirable contender on the trail. In the end, the election was decided by 2,230 votes, which largely came from districts in the province's hinterland.

CONCLUSION

In this chapter I provided empirical evidence that illustrates the ways in which the informational theory helps us understand the changing dynamics of the race in uncertain political contexts. Electoral campaigns in Peru, particularly subnational ones, are characterized by their high levels of improvisation and uncertainty. Within this context, donors and voters have little reliable electoral information with which make their choices.

TABLE 6.10. *Electoral results by district, poverty, and rurality*

Distrito	Population	% of poverty	% of rural population	Rodríguez (O + O)	Miranda (UC)	Elera (APP)	Others	Winner of district election
Piura	275,707	16.90	2.11	20.70	21.89	29.03	28.38	–
Castilla	130,996	20.70	0.87	19.86	20.06	17.89	42.19	Unidos Construyendo
Catacaos	69,414	54.90	3.07	14.96	26.18	7.69	51.17	Somos Peru
Cura Mori	17,732	62.30	13.30	9.71	4.44	1.12	84.73	Unidad Regional
El Tallán	4,936	79.90	22.25	5.33	27.48	0.88	66.31	Fuerza 2011
La Arena	36,135	58.00	8.93	21.50	12.30	2.57	63.64	Alternativa de Renovación Arenense
La Unión	37,914	45.70	1.64	12.91	16.68	29.32	41.09	Alianza Para el Progreso
Las Lomas	27,569	49.60	59.34	22.56	14.56	0.84	62.04	PPC-Unidad Nacional
Tambo Grande	103,651	43.80	63.56	43.88	15.85	2.33	37.94	Agro Sí

I analyzed two municipal and two regional campaigns in two very different departments of Peru: Cusco and Piura. Despite their differences, in both departments candidates compete *through* campaign clientelism.

First, to establish themselves as leading contenders in the race and attract the attention of strategic actors, candidates are forced by competition to actively engage in campaign clientelism. Signaling viability though campaign clientelism works as a first-stage or *selection* mechanism. This competitive dynamic reduces the viable number of contenders (up to a point) and allows strategic actors (donors and voters) to concentrate their information-gathering efforts on a few candidates who are expected to fare well. Strategic actors receive and contrast different sources of electoral information, including past electoral results, polls, and media coverage. As such, media coverage and poll results certainly matter and influence races. Nonetheless, turnout figures remain a very important piece of information within a context of great uncertainty.

Second, the analyses also show that establishing electoral viability through campaign clientelism is an important goal, but does not assure electoral victory in itself. In other words, my informational theory does not just imply a simple bidding process in which the candidate who offers more private benefits gets more electoral support. Thus, the *quantity* of gifts distributed is not decisive. Gifts are not used to drive voting choice, but to force interactions with poor voters; in the process of such interactions at campaign events, politicians need to create a link that may not outlast the campaign, but will at least endure through to election day. Therefore, candidates take advantage of bought audiences to convince voters through non-clientelistic appeals to support them at the polls.

But how do candidates persuade clients to support them? The cases studied here show that poor voters evaluate candidates' personal traits and mannerisms on the trail. Since most candidates particularize their promises to constituencies during their visits, voters look at questions of local knowledge, charisma/likability, signs of past fulfillment of campaign promises, or professionalism to decide their vote. These issues help candidates gain credibility within a context of high distrust in politics and politicians. Of all these dimensions, poor voters give particular weight to a candidate's personal traits (charisma) and their authenticity, as well as their local knowledge and willingness to address local needs.

In summary, the races analyzed in Cusco and Piura show that an examination of the strategies candidates use and how viability and desirability combine helps us make sense of electoral trajectories within uncertain electoral contexts, and, thus, aids in (indirectly) explaining vote choices.

Both electoral viability and desirability are necessary for a successful electoral strategy.

Moreover, the two cases analyzed also shed some light on issues concerning the implications and scope conditions of my theory. First, the case of Piura shows that my informational theory can extend to more organized political contexts. It shows us that having a machine party in power does not undermine campaign clientelism or alter the way it works. Both the incumbent machine and opposition candidates are pushed by strategic competition to engage in campaign clientelism to signal electoral viability to strategic actors and create interaction fields with poor voters who otherwise might not inform themselves about the electoral options available. Moreover, campaign clients do not sell out their votes, but evaluate candidates' personal performance on the trail based on questions of character, local knowledge, and professionalism. Yet having a party machine still matters in the sense that it creates an uneven playing field given the incumbent's resource and organizational advantages, modifying slightly the dynamic of the race. On the one hand, opposition candidates learn that they need to unite to defeat the machine. Hence, in one of the races analyzed, two former and ideologically dissimilar rivals joined together in an electoral alliance, and later on in the same race, other opposition groups publicly endorsed this joint ticket to assure its electoral victory amidst fears of fraud. On the other hand, this race also showed that voters can in fact unite around a message of change. But strategic coordination to vote out the machine was only possible because the message for change was credible. And it was credible because UC established electoral viability and, also very important, its candidate demonstrated desirability, particularly when contrasted with the incumbent.

Second, the analysis of the municipal race in Piura poses a question about the scope of my informational theory: what should we make of the fact that this contest involved a candidate appealing to the middle class and the explicit rejection of clientelistic mechanisms? How could Elera establish electoral viability without engaging actively in campaign clientelism? As the literature on clientelism suggests, poverty is an important pre-condition for clientelism to work well electorally. But, as Weitz-Shapiro contends, the use of clientelism creates an electoral trade-off that is especially relevant when competition is high: clientelism may gain votes from the poor but it is likely to cost a politician support from the middle class (Weitz-Shapiro 2012, 2014).

Piura is a department that has historically hosted a relatively sizeable pocket of Peru's landed elite and urban middle class. And the city remains somewhat large by Peruvian standards, save for Lima. But the city is also a highly unequal one in which a relatively small middle/upper class coexists (and is physically surrounded by) a large low-income sector. In the municipal election, Elera privileged strategies commonly used in urban districts that are more homogeneous in their sociodemographic composition: displays of print propaganda, participation in public debates, and media exposure. Through these means he stressed his professional expertise as the card that made his personal candidacy more appealing. Simultaneously, he tried to appeal to the middle class by openly rejecting the kind of clientelistic mechanisms commonly used to campaign in Piura. On its own terms, his strategy worked: Elera managed to signal himself as a viable contender and the best equipped candidate to address Piura's most pressing problems. However, the strength of his campaign was also its main limitation, and it did not prove enough to win the election. Elera did not cover enough ground in the province to visit and persuade poorer sectors, unlike the victor, Rodríguez (and, indeed, the UC candidate).

In the next, concluding chapter, I will further evaluate and discuss the implications of my theory for more organized political contexts, as well as considering its scope.

7

Conclusions

This book's main contribution is a new theory of electoral clientelism that explains why politicians use clientelistic inducements during campaigns when they lack solid political organizations. I propose an informational approach that stresses the *indirect* effects that investments in electoral clientelism have on voting intentions. I demonstrate that campaign clientelism, an important yet often overlooked form of electoral clientelism, takes place in Peru despite the absence of established political organizations. Politicians commonly distribute material goods during electoral contests in order to buy turnout at campaign events and rallies. I contend that campaign clientelism generates valuable information that is later utilized by strategic political actors to make electoral decisions. By influencing the dynamics of the race, campaign clientelism affects electoral preferences and, thus, the outcome of elections. In contrast, the particular subtypes of electoral clientelism that are normally studied, such as vote buying and turnout buying at the polls, rarely take place in Peru because they are not viable electoral strategies for winning elections.

Campaign clientelism affects election outcomes through two types of informational mechanisms, as I show in Chapter 2. First, campaign clientelism establishes candidates' electoral *viability*. By turning out large numbers of people at campaign events, candidates demonstrate their electoral prospects to the media, donors, benefit-seeking activists, and the general public. Candidates who mobilize more people increase their chances of winning elections. Campaign turnout serves as an especially important signal of electoral viability to donors and voters because the dearth of party organization means that there are few alternative sources of electoral information on the strength of candidates.

Second, campaign clientelism is important for persuading voters of the candidates' electoral *desirability*. Clients receive valuable electoral information while participating in campaign events. Voters are informed about the candidates' proposals, which are targeted to respective constituencies. At the same time, clients are directly exposed to candidates' public performances. This exposure is the best way of evaluating candidates' personal traits. Finally, attendees at rallies also observe their peers' reactions to the candidate, and such reactions often lead to "buzz" or positive word-of-mouth. The impact is twofold: whereas the size of campaign rallies can affect strategic donation and strategic voting considerations of all citizens through news coverage of the events, the content of rallies can influence voters who show up and members of their social networks who hear about the content post-hoc.

Campaign clientelism can be effective given its influence on how voters perceive both candidate viability and desirability. Demonstrating electoral viability is the first hurdle to pass for any candidate. Because donors and voters lack standard cognitive shortcuts with which to predict electoral strength in a race, such as partisanship, they will concentrate their information-gathering efforts on the candidates who are expected to fare well. But although demonstrating capability to mobilize large numbers of voters is a way of indicating electoral viability and, thus, helping raise campaign contributions, it does not mean that voters will simply offer blind support at the polls: electorally viable candidates also need to make sure they persuade voters of their electoral desirability. As I have argued, this persuasion is more easily achieved when candidates personally interact with poor voters at campaign events. Candidates' personal appeal can make the difference in electoral results, especially in tight races. In other words, viable *and* desirable candidates have better chances of actually winning office.

Why is Peru a good case for examining whether this theory is borne out? As I show in Chapter 3, Peru lacks both organized political parties and enduring clientelistic machines capable of structuring voting intentions long before the campaign season begins. Electoral politics is instead mostly structured around individual candidates, who put together their own personalistic vehicles at the start of their campaigns. Because they are short-sighted and other, less-expensive strategies are available to them, such as investing in pork-barrel politics and extracting resources through corruption, most politicians are not interested in building lasting machines. Furthermore, the central state apparatus is no longer used as a substitute for a machine, as was the case during Fujimori's authoritarian regime.

Despite the lack of stable political networks on the ground, politicians distribute material goods intensively while campaigning. The empirical distribution of material benefits, however, does not match the expectations of conventional approaches. First, since there are very few established machines, regular distribution of goods and favors to the needy is uncommon. Second, the distribution of goods starts early in the campaign, sometimes even several months prior to it; distribution of gifts increases as election day approaches but the practice is by no means limited to this day, or soon before it. In fact, distribution usually takes place at various campaign events. Candidates, thus, do not begin campaigning backed up by a base of voters, routinely serviced by ongoing political machines; rather, nearly all candidates start their campaigns without pre-existing support and hence a strong incentive to quickly increase their perceived viability beyond that of their competitors.

Campaign clientelism even overshadows standard vote-buying and turnout-buying practices. Turnout buying is not widespread, because mandatory voting laws are enforced and because the low levels of party identification mean that candidates rarely know for sure if they are buying the turnout of their own supporters. Vote buying is not a viable strategy in Peru either. As I showed in Chapter 3, monitoring vote choices in Peru, whether at the individual or group level, is virtually impossible. On the one hand, the absence of traditional machines means that candidates lack loyal local brokers and, thus, cannot effectively monitor choices in the voting booth or even attendance at campaign events. On the other hand, voters' belief in ballot secrecy is robust, meaning that they are invulnerable to the standard politician's threat to withhold valuable selective benefits if they do not support the candidacy in question at the polls. Thus, even when incumbents use threats as a means of mobilizing beneficiaries of social aid programs to their rallies, these campaign clients still decide their vote freely.

But why do politicians distribute material benefits even though they lack the organizational structure to guarantee the direct electoral pay-off of these investments? As demonstrated in Chapter 4, politicians actively invest in campaign clientelism in Peru precisely *because* they lack stable political organizations. In that chapter, I show that candidates distribute material incentives in order to attract poor voters to campaign events and to access crucial constituencies. By turning out large numbers of voters, politicians intend to demonstrate that they are strong candidates and should, therefore, be seen as serious contenders for election. Interviewed candidates and political operators alike acknowledged this key point. During focus group discussions, poor voters also said that politicians distribute goods as a "hook," to attract large numbers of people "for the picture." In addition, experimental evidence confirms that all else being equal, Peruvian voters do take mobilization at campaign events into account when deciding their vote choices. But the same cannot be said of information about gift distribution.

Second, as I argued in Chapter 5, campaign clientelism also provides politicians with captive audiences at whom they can target their persuasion strategies. While attending campaign events, poor voters gather several types of relevant information. They learn about specific proposals that may benefit them, especially the candidate's promises to provide local public goods for their communities. They also get to know the candidates' personal traits and witness their peers' reactions to the candidacies. To make their electoral choices, voters compare and contrast these types of information. Some voters even get together, debate, and collectively decide which candidate is the best electoral option for their communities. Thus, campaign clients use rallies and similar events to learn about candidates' proposals and traits and rank viable options according to their preferences. In addition, personal interactions with candidates allow poor voters to devise mechanisms to assess candidate credibility and help ensure they deliver on their promises.

In summary, in this book I demonstrate the importance of early investments in electoral clientelism during campaigns. Politicians devote time and resources to campaign clientelism in spite of a lack of established political organizations because it is a strategy that *indirectly* affects electoral choices. From this new perspective, electoral clientelism is more than just a marginal vote-getting strategy: it is a *campaigning* tool. But does this theory travel well to other countries with low political organization? As I discussed in the introduction, electoral clientelism remains a widespread phenomenon across the region, encompassing countries with more and those with less organized political parties. Unfortunately, we still do not have a precise indicator to measure the extent of campaign clientelism. The available survey measures show a general phrasing, and responses might be counting the prevalence of different types of electoral clientelism. Moreover, given the expectations of conventional theories, most research on electoral clientelism has been conducted in countries with more-organized partisan machines. Thus, the evidence available to fully empirically assess this question remains scarce.

Although more systematic enquiry is needed, the qualitative research that has been conducted suggests that campaign clientelism does take place in other countries with weakly organized party systems. Studies carried out in Bolivia (Lazar 2004, 2006, 2007) and Ecuador (De la Torre 2006; De la Torre and Conaghan 2009; Freidenberg 2010) confirm that politicians actively offer gifts, such as T-shirts, toys, food stamps, drinks, and so on, to attract voters to their campaign events. Moreover, the narrative explaining the process by which electoral clientelism takes place in these countries also provides preliminary evidence to suggest that my informational theory can travel to explain these practices.

To begin with, Lazar's illuminating work on El Alto (Bolivia) (Lazar 2004, 2006, 2007) provides us with several insights into how electoral clientelism might work in terms of indirect effects on vote choices. In El Alto, local politics stand out for its relatively high level of social organization and the preeminence of collective identities (Lazar 2006). Unions and community groupings, such as associations of *campesinos*, street traders and residents, develop well-established patterns of political behavior in their relationships with governments, including demonstrations and social mobilization. Moreover, they induce high rates of participation from their members through a combination of authoritarian measures (taking records of attendance and fining those who do not show up) and promotion of a sense of belonging and egalitarianism.

Despite the relevance of these collective identities and groups, the distribution of private inducements takes place regularly during campaigns in El Alto. How does this distribution take place? Does it conform to the expectations of existing vote-buying theories? Do community leaders serve as "local machine brokers" who enforce vote buying deals? This does not seem to be the case. Lazar argues that in El Alto, voters are not passive and acritical clients subject to control but citizens who "actively shape and take advantage of opportunities which arise during election time to bring the political process closer to home" (Lazar 2004: 229).[1] The campaign is "the one time" in which poor citizens find that they "count" and their support is sought, so they can "play parties off against each other" (Lazar 2004: 233). Poor voters feel able to do so because they trust in the secrecy of their vote. Consequently, they actively engage in what I have called campaign clientelism with several parties, attending several campaign events in exchange for gifts (Lazar 2004: 231–2).

---

[1] Similarly, Hummel finds that vote buying attempts are not effective in the city of La Paz either and vendors scoffed in private at parties clientelistic attempts (Hummel 2017: 1529).

In addition, politicians also buy access to campaign during meetings of community organizations. For example, Lazar notes that the parents' association of the local school held several political events during the campaign, at which parties donated materials for the school. While negotiating such deals, community leaders are aware that campaign clientelism will not compromise their members' votes given the secrecy of the ballot (Lazar 2004: 233). Thus, local leaders in El Palo are not so much loyal partisan agents as local intermediaries looking to maximize their collective returns (Holland and Palmer-Rubin 2015).

Why do parties distribute handouts if they cannot be sure that clients will vote for them? In keeping with my informational theory, Lazar explains that parties engage in these clientelistic exchanges, distributing handouts in exchange for participation at campaign events, because displaying large turnout at street rallies is the best way for voters to assess the viability of particular parties winning the local election (Lazar 2004: 234–5). Politicians behave in this way because they know that "the party with most 'people' is the one that voters expect to win and therefore are most likely to vote for" (Lazar 2004: 31).

However, in El Alto as in Peru, mobilizing large crowds is only part of the story. The personal characteristics of the candidates are also central to deciding vote choices in mayoral elections. Campaign clientelism is important for Lazar because it also allows more face-to-face interaction between poor voters and candidates and, thus, allows the development of personal connections. And politicians know that "elections are primarily a character assessment exercise" (Lazar 2004: 236). Voters will identity and reward perceived personal qualities in candidates, such as approachability, honesty, and generosity (Lazar 2004: 240).

In summary, Lazar's research on local politics in El Alto provide us with preliminary evidence that my informational theory can explain the dynamics of electoral clientelism in Bolivia. When politicians distribute handouts during election time, they are not buying votes directly but participation at campaign events. They do so because, first, visual displays of turnout at rallies sends out important signals of a candidate's electoral prospects. And second, rallies allow candidates to personally interact with voters, and persuade them that they are desirable contenders.

In turn, available research on the Ecuadorian finds evidence to suggest that politicians also engage in campaign clientelism there. Before discussing this evidence, it is important to recall that clientelism has long been a dominant practice in Ecuador (Pachano 2001), and that the country's party system is weakly institutionalized and fragmented (Mainwaring and

Scully 1995; Payne *et al.* 2007). Relational clientelism through problem-solving still exists at the local level (De la Torre 2006; Freidenberg 2010). However, since the 1990s, clientelism has lost its traditional efficacy and is in crisis, destabilizing the political system (Ospina 2006).

The articles on the Ecuadorian case suggest that campaign clientelism might be a common tactic within this competitive context. Politicians actively offer gifts to attract voters to their campaign events (De la Torre 2006; De la Torre and Conaghan 2009; Freidenberg 2010). With these inducements, candidates mobilize the so-called *acarreados* to rallies,[2] including voters from established clientelistic networks as well as poor voters who are not part of existing problem-solving networks (De la Torre 2006).

Why do politicians in Ecuador care about ensuring packed rallies in an era of mass media? First, local politicians take advantage of rallies to draw crowds and, thus, demonstrate their mobilization capability to the presidential candidate (De la Torre 2006: 38; De la Torre and Conaghan 2009: 345). Second, like in Peru, a hybridization of campaigns can be observed in which traditional and modern modes of electioneering are combined (De la Torre and Conaghan 2009). "The video and photos of a candidate surrounded by hundreds or thousands of ordinary citizens send a powerful message about the support that he or she enjoys" (De la Torre and Conaghan 2009: 345). In other words, campaign clientelism appears to be a convenient campaign tool because it produces information.

Moreover, and again like in Peru, there is evidence that business interests in Ecuador make aggressive use of private resources to invest in campaign clientelism. For instance, the distribution of gifts and even cash as part of Álvaro Noboa's presidential campaigns in 2002 and 2006 became widely known throughout the region (De la Torre and Conaghan 2009: 349). During the 2006 election, his rallies followed a script: in addition to putting on entertainment for the crowd, he regularly delivered computers, wheelchairs, and micro-loans to poor voters (De la Torre 2006: 39). On many occasions, these rallies were preceded by the deployment of medical teams that offered free services and medication to attract participants. In addition, while people lined up for these services, Noboa's activists collected their signatures to register them for a housing plan that the candidate promised to implement after gaining office.

But this distribution of material incentives during campaign events does not assure clients' loyalty at the ballot box (De la Torre 2006). In

---

[2] People mobilized to campaign events through material inducements.

Ecuador's fluid and competitive political context, the negotiation power of clients has increased considerably (Ospina 2006). Voters who did not enjoy ongoing clientelistic relations with Noboa's private foundation and only sporadically received the likes of free medication and services from his party were quite free to do so while still voting for other candidate (De la Torre 2006: 40). Although the author makes no explicit mention of trust in the secret ballot, his interpretation may mean that most voters believe in its efficacy.

There is another element that De la Torre and Conaghan stress in their analysis of the 2006 Ecuadorian presidential campaign that is relevant to assessing the value of my informational theory. Besides generating information about candidates' electoral viability, campaign clientelism also helps candidates to personalize their message. But how? During campaign events, candidates try to persuade clients of their personal appeal and build personal credibility. Campaign clientelism allows candidates to amass a captive audience to whom they can direct their public performance. In a crowded field of contenders – as is typical in Ecuador's elections – candidates work hard to "showcase" their individual attributes while campaigning (De la Torre and Conaghan 2009). In addition, De la Torre also briefly refers to something akin to what I call positive buzz, and its importance for persuading attendants at rallies to support a candidate at the polls. He mentions how Correa's personal performance in these public appearances was not only effective in personally connecting with voters, but also in generating collective enthusiasm for his candidacy, even among "hauled" voters (De la Torre 2006: 46). In other words, through campaign clientelism, candidates summon an audience to whom they direct personalized messages. If capable enough, some of these candidates will be convincing enough to create a buzz among attendees, and this will reinforce their image as a desirable contender.

In summary, preliminary evidence suggests that my informational theory might be usefully applied to understand the logic of electoral clientelism in other Latin American countries with weakened party structures. Although more research would certainly be needed to confirm these intuitions, current evidence suggests that campaign clientelism is a widely used campaign tactic in Bolivia and Ecuador, as I have pointed out.

Besides illuminating the logic of electoral clientelism in weakly organized political contexts, my informational theory could also have important implications for understanding clientelism in more organized settings. Do the informational effects of electoral clientelism operate only in unorganized contexts? And if these effects also operate in organized settings, how do politicians' strategies differ? In the following section I address this issue.

THE INDIRECT EFFECTS OF ELECTORAL CLIENTELISM IN CONTEXT WITH CONSOLIDATED CLIENTELISTIC MACHINES

What would this new approach expect to observe in an organized political context? While the way in which campaign clientelism is conducted surely differs in organized contexts, this strategy should also produce indirect effects on electoral choices in such settings. Turnout at rallies and other public events during campaigns should still serve to inform strategic actors about the potential electoral strength of candidates *and* local brokers, thus, helping them make their electoral choices. Indeed, in organized settings, there may be more unorganized interstices in politics than prevailing approaches allow. If this is in fact the case, politicians should have incentives to try to influence unattached poor voters while campaigning.

What nuances should we expect to find in organized political contexts? First, buying the participation of unaffiliated voters with goods should occur *less* frequently overall than in contexts with low political organization, where campaign clientelism helps politicians improvise organizational structures on the trail. In contrast to contexts where politicians lack stable links at the local level, most (but not all) campaign clients in organized contexts should be stable machine members. Moreover, in these settings, campaign clientelism organizers will typically be local brokers who are able to monitor clients' attendance at rallies and may do so if it is thought necessary.

Second, in organized contexts campaign clientelism should be essential for signaling candidate viability (but not for persuasion) during primaries and other sorts of party elections. In these types of elections, partisan preferences are held constant, and stable clients have incentives to support their brokers in order to continue receiving benefits. Therefore, sheer weight of numbers should matter more as an indicator of candidates' and brokers' power *within* a party. During general elections, on the other hand, candidates' partisanship informs voters about their electoral viability.

Third, campaign clientelism should be crucial for persuading voters during general elections in organized settings, but not necessarily for signaling candidate viability. In these campaigns, politicians and brokers have greater incentives to mobilize and influence poor, non-machine voters. Given that parties need to appeal to a wider constituency in order to win, it makes more sense to buy non-machine voters' participation at campaign events and expect that the candidate will be able to persuade them of his desirability *in situ*. During general elections, opposition candidates may also have the chance to use campaign clientelism and try to persuade voters of their electoral desirability.

Finally, in contexts with organized machines and political parties, electoral volatility and government turnover is lower than in unorganized settings. Politicians will be more likely to follow a partisan political career, and political parties should have better chances of staying in power. Therefore, in organized settings, clientelistic resources should be obtained mostly from the state – unlike unorganized contexts, where campaign clientelism resources come principally from private donors.

In the next section, I provide preliminary evidence to support these theoretical expectations. I focus on Argentina, a case that greatly contrasts with Peru given the strength of Argentine partisan machines. This case is, thus, well-suited to exploring the generalizability of my theory to organized settings. Fortunately, clientelism in Argentina has been studied intensively. The body of research (Auyero 2000, 2001; Levitsky 2003; Calvo and Murillo 2004, 2008, 2013; Brusco *et al.* 2004; Stokes 2005; Kemahlioglu 2006; Weitz-Shapiro 2008, 2012, 2014; Szwarcberg 2009, 2012a, 2015; Scherlis 2010; Zarazaga 2011, 2014; Oliveros 2013, 2016) focuses principally, but not exclusively, on different subnational branches of the *Partido Justicialista* (PJ), also known as Peronist Party. The PJ is a well-established machine organization that has increased its subnational electoral dominance in Argentina over the last few decades. Although I draw mostly on evidence from the Argentine case, I will also present some results from studies of clientelism in other countries.

Empirical Analysis

The level of consolidation of clientelistic machines in Argentina, is not its only difference from Peru. Historically, Argentina has also been more economically developed than Peru, giving rise to a considerably larger middle class and a bigger and stronger labor force. Although Argentina is plagued by institutional weakness (Levitsky and Murillo 2005), in political terms this weakness certainly pales when compared to Peru (Levitsky 2013). In the 2000s, Argentina's oldest mass political party, the *Unión Cívica Radical* (UCR), collapsed and became electorally irrelevant – along with other small political parties, as well as newer ones (Lupu 2016). However, unlike in Peru, Argentina's entire party system did not collapse. The PJ, a populist party once comparable to *Partido Aprista Peruano* (APRA) in terms of its historical trajectory (Collier and Collier 1991), was able to transform and successfully adapt to the neo-liberal challenges of the 1980s and 1990s (Levitsky 2003; Burgess and Levitsky 2003). APRA, by contrast, was less successful in achieving this transformation and was, thus, unable to stop the collapse of the party system at the beginning of the 1990s. Moreover, the PJ has become a hegemonic actor in Argentine politics, with increasingly strong subnational strongholds (Levitsky 2003; Calvo and Murillo 2004; Levitsky and Murillo 2008), whereas APRA has enjoyed only sporadic electoral success and has declined its support at the subnational level over time (Vergara 2012). Argentina's confederation of strong Peronist provincial factions stands in sharp contrast to Peru's "democracy without parties." Finally, while the neoliberal status quo has taken root in Peru in spite of the recent Latin American turn to the left (Meléndez and León 2009; Muñoz and Dargent 2012; Vergara and Encinas 2016), the Kirchner governments in Argentina moved the country back toward a more regulated economy. The extent to which these reforms might be reversed by the current administration remains to be seen.

Despite important differences between Peru and Argentina, the informational logic of campaign clientelism is nevertheless strongly present in Argentina's organized setting. While much of the literature on electoral clientelism has focused almost exclusively on Argentine machines as vote buyers, the activities and strategies of local brokers actually go beyond direct vote-getting practices. As Zarazaga points out, "scholars and the media have underestimated the most common way brokers have of winning votes: by campaigning. One of the main goals of all brokers is to promote their political bosses" (Zarazaga 2014: 30). Moreover, they campaign through non-clientelistic means, behaving as propaganda agents. They also act as rally mobilizers. Indeed, mobilizing clients is part of Argentine local brokers' "business as usual." As Auyero (2001) and Szwarcberg (2015) show, besides helping solve their clients' daily problems, brokers devote a considerable part of their full-time political jobs to mobilizing their clients to attend political rallies. In the words of Oliveros,

Many low and mid-level positions in the bureaucracy are distributed with the goal of maintaining a network of activists on the ground that performs a number of different political activities, such as helping with electoral campaigns or attending rallies, that are key for getting or keeping electoral support. (Oliveros 2012: 2)

Surprisingly, with the exception of Szwarcberg, scholars do not theorize about the informational effects of attending rallies. Szwarcberg has shown, persuasively, that turnout at rallies in Argentina does in fact provide information to strategic actors, both within and outside political machines (Szwarcberg 2009, 2012, 2015). First, turnout buying at rallies offers information about political competition within partisan machines. Rallies give party brokers and bosses an opportunity to make the number of their followers visible and quantifiable. For instance, party bosses can monitor their brokers' reliability by comparing turnout at rallies and at the polls. These numbers are subsequently used by party members to advance their political careers, negotiating positions, offices, and clientelistic resources.

Second, turnout at rallies also provides information for nonpartisans about the incumbent's strength. As Szwarcberg explains:

By publicly displaying the party's support, rallies encourage or discourage opposition coordination by signaling potential or existing rivals within and outside the party the strength or weakness of the machine. Overcrowded rallies send the opposition a powerful signal that there is not much space for political alternatives, and increase the costs and potential benefits of building a parallel political organization for party members who might be considering leaving the party. (Szwarcberg 2012: 6)

Turnout figures can help incumbents send out an image of invincibility that will encourage voters, activists, and funders to abandon hopeless opposition candidates (Magaloni 2006: 9; Szwarcberg 2012b, 2015). However, they can also help the opposition to coordinate and vote out incumbents, even when these incumbents are backed by a consolidated clientelistic machine – just like what occurred in Piura during the 2010 regional election.[3] According to Szwarcberg:

The rallies organized by the Alianza contributed to coordinating the opposition and assuring voters that it was possible to defeat the PJ in its electoral stronghold: the province of Buenos Aires. Overcrowded rallies provided the Alianza's candidate, Graciela Fernández Meijide, the confidence necessary to call voters "to receive with one hand [welfare programs and goods delivered by the government] and to vote with the other." (Szwarcberg 2012b: 14)[4]

---

[3] See Chapter 6.
[4] *Alianza por el Trabajo, la Justicia y la Educación* was a political coalition formed in 1997 by the UCR and the *Frente País Solidario* (FREPASO). The Alianza won national office in 1999 but was dissolved after president Fernando De la Rúa resigned amidst a severe economic crisis in 2001.

In addition, the structure of political networks in Argentina, which are vertically organized around political parties to foster intra-party competition, confirms that networks are important for electoral coordination (Calvo and Murillo 2013: 864). Thus, based on this evidence, I can confidently conclude that bought turnout provides strategic actors with information about electoral viability even in contexts with organized machines and parties.

What differences do we find in how electoral clientelism is practiced in Argentina compared with Peru? First, many of these rallies are organized during nonelectoral times to demonstrate support for the local incumbent or receive a party authority in the district. For instance, Auyero (2001) opens his book with a very detailed account of how PJ brokers mobilized their clients to a rally commemorating the birthday of the leader of the Peronist movement in the city of Cóspito (Buenos Aires). This rally, however, was also intended as a public show of support for Cóspito's mayor, who had recently been accused of corruption.

Although Argentine brokers mobilize their own clients, they *buy* the attendance of these clients at each rally, distributing minor consumer goods and small amounts of cash to convince voters to come to these rallies (Auyero 2001; Szwarcberg 2009). Goods serve as selective incentives to assure clients' participation. Brokers buy the participation of individuals by distributing, for example, boxes of food, mattresses, construction materials, school supplies, and T-shirts. As Szwarcberg explains, the exchange of small goods for participation is a common practice in political mobilization in Argentina:

Anyone who stops by at a broker's house or political association (when these two do not overlap) the day of a rally will observe the distribution of free food, construction materials, cleaning products, alcohol, and in some cases even marijuana, to voters in exchange for participation. In addition, one will observe one or more buses, parked in the street ready to pick up and drive voters to attend rallies. (Szwarcberg 2009: 182)

In turn, a client from La Matanza (Gran Buenos Aires) describes this practice as follows:

They come to pick us up at home with the bus. The first stop is in San Justo. They make you go to the local political association that belongs to the broker who brought you in, and after taking attendance they give you a pack of cigarettes, a sandwich, and wine. When we get back from the rally, they give you the merchandise [generally a box with cooking and cleaning products]. (Otero 1997: 36; quoted by Szwarcberg 2009: 158)

In contrast to Peru, rallies in Argentina are organized on such a regular basis that brokers must take some sort of action to assure their clients' participation. Thus, they provide machine clients, who already receive assistance and sometimes permanent benefits, with additional selective incentives to participate at rallies. Besides distributing minor consumption goods, some brokers alternate the invitations among different clients so as not to overwhelm them with requests or tire them out through continual participation (Vommaro and Quirós 2011: 76). Brokers also combine persuasive and coercive tactics to mobilize clients to rallies (Szwarcberg 2015). As already noted, the goal of all these different tactics is to assure a large turnout at public events.

Undoubtedly, Argentine clients and local brokers are not as "free" as Peruvian ones. Argentine clients depend on brokers for their *daily survival*, so they cannot unilaterally decide to sell their participation at any political event that happens to be taking place in the area. There is a tacit rule that guides the broker–client relationship: "when you follow a *referente*, you follow one and not another; and if, eventually, you want to follow another [to a rally], you have to first rule out the possibility that your broker needs you" (Vommaro and Quirós 2011: 78).[5] "Whereas voter actions inside the ballot box are invisible to brokers, their participation in rallies is not" (Szwarcberg 2009: 125). Local brokers *can* monitor clients' participation by taking attendance at rallies and, thus, credibly threaten them with punishment if they do not show up when expected (Szwarcberg 2009). If a client decides, individually, to participate in another broker's rally, they risk being punished by their patron.

Moreover, while Argentine local brokers and their networks can certainly change their political allegiances, serving different candidates in different campaigns, they have to be more careful than their Peruvian counterparts, most of whom do not have a stable network of regular followers. This is because Argentine brokers, to be able to sustain their networks, depend on transfers from their political patrons. Indeed, it is more common for brokers to move between bosses belonging to the same partisan "family of origin" (Scherlis 2010: 252) than it is for them to switch between parties, as in Peru. Indeed, subnational clientelistic networks in Argentina tend to be more stable than political networks organized at higher echelons of the state; as long as they continue receiving resources, the brokers' clientelistic networks can easily survive a change of governor or mayor (Scherlis 2010: 230). That said, we should not underestimate

---

5 Brokers are called "referents" or "punteros" in Argentina.

the extent of "double dipping" among brokers in more organized contexts since existing research, such as Luna (2014) and Calvo and Murillo' (forthcoming), has pointed to the prevalence of this practice.

Finally, the evidence also shows that Argentine politicians rely much more on state resources to engage in clientelism than Peruvian politicians do. Clientelistic machines in Argentina are usually organized based on the distribution of two types of valuable resources that are provided mostly from subnational state offices: temporary public jobs and social benefits (Auyero 2001; Scherlis 2010; Oliveros 2013, 2016; Zarazaga 2014; Weitz-Shapiro 2014; Szwarcberg 2015). Public jobs are particularly important for recruiting local brokers and assuring a stable income for them and their close collaborators. Most local brokers live in the neighborhood they organize and represent. Therefore, they are well informed about people's needs and can help them solve their everyday problems. Machine clients, in turn, receive social benefits, such as food aid, unemployment benefits, handouts, medication, and services on a regular basis. As already explained, in addition to these regular benefits, brokers distribute minor consumer goods and small amounts of cash to convince poor voters to attend their rallies. Politicians use mostly public resources to finance these handouts. In particular, access to municipal resources seems to be crucial in Argentina (Auyero 2001; Oliveros 2013; Weitz-Shapiro 2014; Szwarcberg 2015).

Besides these differences, what similarities can be found in how campaign clientelism is carried out in organized and unorganized contexts? First, rallies and other public events are particularly important during campaigns. During general elections, brokers actively engage in campaigning, for the most part mobilizing their clients to rallies and other campaign events. For example, 73 percent of the PJ brokers interviewed by Zarazaga said they visited voters' homes during the 2009 legislative election, and 64 percent answered that they organized neighborhood meetings so that voters could meet the candidates (Zarazaga 2014: 30). In turn, Szwarcberg, who studied turnout buying at rallies during the 2005 mid-term election, the 2006 radical primary, and the 2009 legislative election, was struck by the amount of electoral activities that took place in San Luis province during the 2009 election (Szwarcberg 2012b: 102). Activities "took place not only daily, but also two or three times during the same day. This is yet another indicator of Peronists' incessant and intense campaigning to diffuse their image of invincibility" (Szwarcberg 2012b: 102).

Moreover, and as expected, mobilizing clientelistic machines is particularly important *during primary elections* in Argentina (Scherlis 2010:

249; Zarazaga 2014). This is important because there is greater electoral uncertainty in primaries than in general elections (Bartels 1988). In general elections, partisanship plays a bigger role in determining vote choices. During primaries, however, candidates do not distinguish themselves along partisan or ideological lines (Zarazaga 2012: 25). Brokers buy the votes of their followers and also transport them to vote to assure their participation (Zarzaga 2014: 34). In addition, the broker plays the role of party polling official at each station, trying both to commit fraud themselves and prevent fraud by competitors (Zarazaga 2014: 35). They are motivated to do so because their political career (and survival) depends on it, as they are evaluated based on the number of people they turn out (Szwarcberg 2015).

Buying poor voters' participation at campaign events is also common in other Latin American countries with consolidated party machines, such as Mexico (Schedler and Manríquez 2004). In this country, partisan machines likewise buy turnout at campaign events by distributing gifts. In the Mexican vernacular, *los acarreados* ("the hauled ones") is the equivalent of the Peruvian term, *portátil*. During the 2012 presidential elections, several websites discussed and condemned the practice by Peña Nieto's party, the *Partido Revolucionario Institucional* (PRI) of taking *los acarreados* to campaign events.[6]

Returning to the Argentine case, another similarity between organized and unorganized contexts is that Argentine brokers also buy the participation of out-of-network citizens at rallies – that is, poor voters who do not depend on brokers' benefits as a matter of routine – even if most campaign mobilization uses machine clients. In addition, candidates commonly buy participation from organizations that are not affiliated with the machine, such as soccer hooligans and gangs (Auyero 2001; Szwarcberg 2015, 2012b: 94–5). Some of the voters mobilized at rallies are on the fringes of the network, waiting their turn to become clients (Auyero 2001; Quirós 2006; Szwarcberg 2009), but they are not (yet) regular machine beneficiaries. Thus, even in contexts where dominant machines govern, in reality there are more unorganized margins in poor neighborhoods than is usually recognized by most scholars of clientelism.

Brokers in Argentina buy non-machine voters' participation at rallies both during electoral and nonelectoral times. Nevertheless, this practice

---

[6] See, for instance, the following posts: http://thinkmexican.tumblr.com/post/24736013907/
pri-azteca-stadium-confront-anti-pena-nieto-protest, http://vivirmexico.com/2012/04/
acarreados-la-rudimentaria-estrategia-politica-para-buscar-votos, www.taringa.net/posts/
videos/14996864/Infraganti-PRIistas-Pagando-a-acarreados-Mexico.html

is more common and attractive during general elections, when brokers are expected to prove their efficacy as propaganda agents as well (Zarazaga 2014). Brokers are especially likely to mobilize unaffiliated voters when they are not able to fulfill their expected turnout quota of buses with regular clients. A broker from La Matanza provides this account:

For the last time that the president came I gave US $12 or a food handout to each person. They got to pick which one they preferred. I even got some members of the Radical Party in my bus. I just needed to show I could fill a bus. (Zarazaga 2012: 23)

Thus, turnout figures are important even in organized contexts.

Preliminary evidence also indicates that, as expected, buying the participation of nonaffiliated voters at rallies in Argentina is more common during general elections. As recent studies have shown, much of brokers' activities during general elections includes campaigning and organizing rallies (Szwarcberg 2012b, 2015; Oliveros 2013; Zarazaga 2012, 2014). Indeed, 86 percent of the brokers whom Zarazaga interviewed "declared that their bosses gave them far more resources during the general election, and all of them said that brokers in general use material incentives to get votes" (Zarazaga 2012: 28). Moreover, it is important to point out that the survey used by scholars as a quantitative indicator to study vote buying in Argentina (Brusco *et al.* 2004; Stokes 2005) asks respondents only if they received something from a candidate or party during the campaign. Thus, what scholars have interpreted as direct vote-getting strategies (vote buying or turnout buying at the polls) may actually include campaign clientelism practices as well. Of course, more data would be needed to verify this point.

Intuitively, it makes sense for machines to buy the turnout of nonmachine members more frequently during general elections. In these elections, both party bosses and brokers have incentives to reach as many unaffiliated or undecided voters as possible. Given that brokers organize rallies in which voters can get to know the candidate (Oliveros 2012; Zarazaga 2014; Szwarcberg 2015), politicians will have chances to influence nonaffiliated voters *in situ*. During primary elections, by contrast, brokers must make sure that activists affiliated with the party turn out and vote for their nominee.

In addition, as explained by Szwarcberg, opposition candidates also engage in campaign clientelism during general elections, and sometimes they are even able to coordinate and vote out consolidated machines (Szwarcberg 2012a: 14). This is similar to what was observed in Piura, where the presence of a very organized party and a regional machine altered the dynamics of the regional race, but not the way in which campaign clientelism works. There, both the incumbent machine and opposition candidates were pushed by strategic competition to engage in campaign clientelism to signal electoral viability to strategic actors and create fields of interaction with poor voters who otherwise might not inform themselves about the electoral options available. Yet having a party machine still matters in the sense that it creates an uneven playing field given the incumbent's resource and organizational advantages. This imbalance made opposition candidates learn that they needed to unite to defeat the machine, helping voters to unite around a message of change. And it was credible because UC established electoral viability and, just as importantly, its candidate projected electoral desirability on the trail, particularly when contrasted with the incumbent.

Obviously, opposition candidates will be more effective at buying the participation of non-machine members at campaign events than that of machine members. Recent field experimental studies conducted in São Tomé and Principe (Africa) also confirm that *both* incumbents and political challengers distribute cash and gifts during campaigns. Moreover, these studies also find that in contexts of incumbent dominance, the challengers benefit electorally *more* from this type of campaign investment, as they are able to counteract the incumbency advantage (Vicente 2014). This finding provides additional evidence to indicate that competition increases the overall frequency of turnout buying of unaffiliated poor voters.

Up to this point, I have shown that campaign clientelism takes place in Argentina, a setting with organized parties, and that brokers mobilize mostly (but not exclusively) established machine clients to attend these public events. They do so because politicians take turnout size into account in evaluating the effectiveness of brokers and because voters use this information to update the perceived viability of candidates during elections. But, how do clients decide their vote intentions in organized contexts? Several authors stress that machine and patronage clients generally have *established* political loyalties in Argentina. According to Auyero, "attendance at rallies provides information about individuals' commitments to brokers (and brokers' commitments to their followers)" (Auyero 2001: 99). These commitments are not forged during the campaign but are the result of long-term interactions in which brokers prove to be useful for solving their clients' everyday problems. Turnout buying is, therefore, a practice that reinforces a (meaningful and/or convenient) ongoing patron–client relationship. From this perspective, clients' political loyalties are decided long before the campaign season begins.

It should be noted, however, that these electoral loyalties are *conditional* on the brokers' continuing transfers (Zarazaga 2014; Díaz-Cayeros *et al.* 2016; Oliveros 2016). To assure voters' loyalty at the polls, Argentine brokers must demonstrate that they are credible and reliable; they have to build and sustain a *reputation* by showing that they deliver on a regular basis and fulfill their promises (Zarazaga 2014).

In fact, every broker interviewed by Zarazaga admitted to practicing vote buying but added that "without resources they would sooner or later lose their followers" (Zarazaga 2014: 32). Similarly, in the specific case of patronage contracts, public sector employees vote for the machine because they understand that their jobs are tied to the political success of the incumbent; thus, the interests of clients and political bosses are aligned (Oliveros 2016).

So, does persuasion of voters at campaign rallies take place in Argentina? Despite these ongoing and apparently self-enforced commitments, candidates and brokers still employ "persuasive strategies" at rallies attended by voters in Argentina. For example, party nominees use pronouncements and charisma to woo participants (Szwarcberg 2009: 126). Auyero, for example, has emphasized the dramaturgical content of rallies, in which candidates and brokers publicly perform as Eva Perón and, therefore, appeal to and reproduce Peronist identities (Auyero 2001: Chapter 4). The efficacy of these persuasive strategies, Szwarcberg clarifies, relies on the ability of brokers and candidates to *convince* clients: "charismatic leaders are able to persuade voters to support them [at the polls] without the need to turn to coercive strategies" (Szwarcberg 2009: 145). According to this author, brokers turn to coercive strategies (monitoring attendance at rallies and threatening clients with punishment) primarily when they have chosen an unpopular nominee for the election:

Attendance can be taken before, during, and after the rally. Fieldwork notes suggest that brokers who take attendance in all the instances support an unpopular candidate. In taking attendance throughout the rally, brokers might be trying to avoid clients sneaking out. This observation supports the hypothesis that coercive strategies are intensified in cases where there is a mismatch between broker and client preferences. (Szwarcberg 2009: 150)[7]

---

[7] As Szwarcberg notes, formal models of vote buying applied to Argentina (Brusco *et al.* 2004; Stokes 2005) assume that clients' preferences will always be *different* than those of their brokers. However, this is not always the case empirically.

In addition, it should be recalled that brokers also mobilize non-machine voters to attend rallies. Politicians' performances at these public gatherings is directed at these constituencies as well, since they hope to convince some of these nonaffiliated poor voters to support their candidate.

Furthermore, research conducted in Argentina also indicates that poor voters' perceptions about the reliability of brokers vary according to their *position* in the clientelistic network (Auyero 2001; Calvo and Murillo 2008, 2013). One quantitative study demonstrates that voters' proximity to partisan networks of activists increases their perceived likelihood of receiving handouts and a public job from the PJ and the UCR (Calvo and Murillo 2008: 33–4, 2013: 865–6). In addition, ethnographic studies show that collective representations about clientelism vary according to voters' level of familiarity with the brokers (Auyero 2001). Auyero distinguishes between the brokers' "inner" and "outer" circles (Auyero 2001: 93–4). The broker's inner circle is composed of family members, friends, and close collaborators; in other words, clients in this inner circle have close, personalized relations with the broker. In contrast, the outer circle is constructed through "weak ties" (Granovetter 1983). The broker helps the clients in the outer circle but their contacts are intermittent; clients do not really develop ties of friendship or fictive kinship with the broker. Consequently:

> Those with less intimate relationships with brokers are able to obtain goods and services when they need them, but they do not always offer loyalty in return. Nevertheless, this outer circle is an important part of the network surrounding the broker. And the distinction between the inner and outer circle is a fluid one, more a product of analysis than of reality. Status (inner vs. outer circle) depends on such factors as amount of resources available, number of brokers competing for electoral posts, and the opportunity structure in local politics. (Auyero 2001: 179)

This variation in the *intensity* of patron-client ties may make a difference for influence. Clients who are closer to brokers will be a great deal more loyal on election day. They do not need to be influenced at campaign events: they show up there to demonstrate their support and gratitude toward their broker. In contrast, clients located in the broker's outer circle may need to be persuaded of the candidate's desirability, as Peruvian campaign clients are. Thus, although more data would be needed to confirm the effectiveness of the persuasion mechanism in organized settings, the existing evidence suggests that politicians *do* try to influence attendees at rallies, particularly clients in the outer network and nonaffiliated participants.

In summary, this comparative section has shown that my informational theory can also inform our understanding of electoral clientelism in contexts with organized parties and machines. Both signaling turnout and persuasion at campaign events seem to be relevant in Argentina, as was the case in Piura. As the evidence from Argentina shows, machine brokers buy participation at rallies and other campaign events because turnout provides visible information about the politicians' power and electoral viability. Moreover, local brokers mobilize and work permanently to try to ensure that established machine clients continue supporting them at the polls. However, politicians' skills at influencing may be crucial to convince clients in brokers' outer circles to keep supporting their boss's candidacy at the polls. Moreover, brokers also mobilize non-machine voters to attend the rallies, where they seek to persuade them to support their candidates. Signaling electoral viability is more important during primaries, and persuading clients at rallies seem to be more relevant during general elections. While more research is needed to confirm these preliminary findings, all of this does suggest that my informational approach can shed light on clientelistic behavior in organized political contexts. Having shown that my theory can travel to other contexts with weakly organized parties and that it also has implications for more organized political contexts, in the next section I briefly discuss more about other scope conditions that might be relevant for further consideration and empirical assessment in future research.

SCOPE CONDITIONS

The organizational weakness of political parties is the main scope condition that distinguishes my informational theory of clientelism from existing ones. My approach can explain how electoral clientelism works within an extreme case of political party weakness, such as Peru. Campaign clientelism is a campaigning tool that allows Peruvian politicians to develop mixed electoral strategies on the trail. In this chapter, I have also provided preliminary evidence to show that my theory also has transferable potential to explain the logic of clientelistic investments during campaigns in other Latin American countries with weakly organized parties. This lead is not trivial. Many elements show us that campaigns in many countries in the region, and perhaps even around the world, stand to become more like those in Peru. The weakening of traditional partisan structures on an international level has long since been noted by scholars (Katz and Mair 1995; Dalton and Wattenberg 2002; Wattenberg 2009). At the same time, personalistic appeals are becoming increasingly important as an electoral strategy of mobilization (McAllister 2007; Kriesi 2012; Cross and Young 2015). Meanwhile, campaigns are becoming more and more expensive and highly dependent on financial contributions (Bartels 2008; Gillens 2014).

Within Latin America in particular, political parties as collective entities have weakened in several countries besides Peru (Mainwaring 2006; Gutiérez 2007; Morgan 2011; Dargent and Muñoz 2011; Seawright 2012; Luna and Rosenblatt 2012; Luna 2014; Rosenblatt forthcoming), while few new parties have been successfully built (Levitsky *et al.* 2016). Campaign spending is also on the rise, while not all countries have been successful in regulating political financing to prevent overreliance on private funds, the entry of illegal funds, the undue influence of interest groups, corruption, serious electoral inequalities, and so forth (Casas-Zamora and Zovatto 2015). Moreover, it must be noted that the ready availability of illegal money to influence electoral campaigns is particularly prominent at the subnational level in several countries, where state institutions also tend to be weaker. Thus, there is in fact a propitious terrain in which mixed electoral strategies based on campaign clientelism may become an attractive strategy worldwide.

Furthermore, I have also provided evidence to show that my informational theory has implications for the way in which electoral clientelism works in contexts with organized parties and machines. Although the weight and form that the causal mechanisms take is certainly different than in less organized contexts, both turnout signaling and persuasion at campaign events seem to be influential in Argentina, one of the most studied cases in the clientelism literature. Thus, although conceived primarily for contexts with low political organization, my theory could be extended to explain how informational effects also take place in more organized political settings.

Besides political organization, what other contextual factors may be important for defining scope conditions for my argument? Poverty, either directly or when manifested through income inequality, has been highlighted by scholars as an important pre-condition for clientelism to work electorally. This includes both traditional studies on the political effects of the modernization process (Hungtinton 1968; Scott 1969, 1972; Powell 1970; Lemarchand and Legg 1972; Graziano 1973), as well newer works on clientelism (Kitschelt 2000; Wantchekon 2003; Robinson and Verdier 2003; Brusco *et al.* 2004; Calvo and Murillo 2004; Desposato 2007; Hicken 2007; Stokes 2007a; Kitschelt and Wilkinson 2007; Weitz-Shapiro 2012, 2014; Stokes *et al.* 2013).

Poverty is indeed another factor that influences the scope of my argument. For campaign clientelism to work as I expect it to, it is important for a sizable proportion of those living within the electoral district to be subject to poverty. Given that the gifts boost the utility of income of poor people (Stokes 2007; Stokes *et al.* 2013), poorer voters will be more likely to sell their participation at campaign events for a gift. Indeed, in previous chapters I have provided extensive documentation, including both survey and qualitative data, to show that poor voters are more likely to attend campaign events in order to receive a gift. However, given that much of the qualitative material was collected in two departments that are not among the poorest in the country – Cusco and Piura are in the second group of poverty severity across Peruvian departments – it might be useful to provide out-of-sample empirical evidence to support the expected relationship between socioeconomic need and campaign clientelism in Peru.

An unpublished manuscript by González-Ocantos, Kiwied, Meléndez, Osorio, and Nickerson presents the results of a survey list experiment intended to measure the extent of electoral clientelism across departments in Peru, extending beyond the 2010 subnational elections (González Ocantos *et al.* 2013). The list experiment asked voters to indicate the number of campaign activities they took part in during the last electoral campaign. The treated group included as an additional item that the respondent was given a gift or a favor. The list experiment results show that the distribution of gifts or favors during electoral campaigns was, as expected, negatively correlated ($r = -0.41$) with GDP per capita at the department level. Although the relationship leaves some cases of low and high clientelistic offers unexplained, as in other aggregate-level analyses (Stokes *et al.* 2013: 155) it confirms an existing association between socioeconomic welfare and clientelistic effort. As an additional test, using the same data, I plotted the percentage of population living in poverty on the percentage of the population that was targeted with gifts (Figure 7.1). Here, I found that the correlation between clientelistic offers and poverty is positive but not substantive ($r = 0.33$) as well.

Overall, these findings should be interpreted with caution given the inefficiency of this list experiment, which gave implausible estimates (e.g., some negative estimates and one estimate greater than 100 percent) due to small N at the department level (González Ocantos *et al.* 2013). Thus, for example, it might be the case that the estimates of clientelistic offers in Huancavelica and Amazonas, both very poor departments, underestimate the true level of clientelistic effort. That caveat aside, this data can

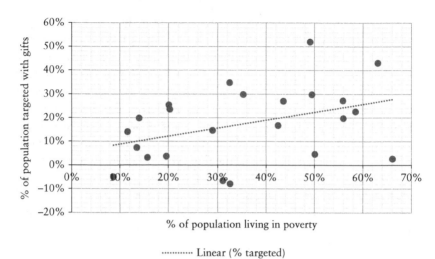

FIGURE 7.1. *Percentage of population targeted with gifts, by poverty rate in Peruvian departments*
Source: González-Ocantos *et al.* (2013). Authors' own survey conducted by *Imasen* in 2010

still be taken as complementary evidence to confirm that campaign clientelism is at least partially associated with the extent of poverty in Peru.

However, a correlation between poverty and prevalence of clientelism of a similar magnitude ($r = 0.37$) to that found in Peru can be observed across Latin American countries as a whole (Figure 7.2). Thus, it seems that although an important and necessary scope condition, poverty alone does not explain the prevalence of clientelistic inducements.

Moreover, poverty need not to be that high for campaign clientelism to work – a sizable but still minority proportion of around 30 percent of people living in poverty seems to be enough. This was the case, for example, in the mayoral races studied. In the provinces of Cusco and Piura, the poverty rates are 24.7 percent and 32 percent, respectively (INEI/UNFPA 2010).

Indeed – as other scholars have suggested (Weitz-Shapiro 2014; Luna 2014; Holland 2017) – more than looking for the prevalence of poverty itself, it might be more important for future research to study the interaction of poverty and other institutional factors, as well as to assess the type of territorial electoral structure in question and how this structure affects the electoral costs of engaging in campaign clientelism. Most cities in Peru are, like other Latin American cities, sociodemographically fragmented;

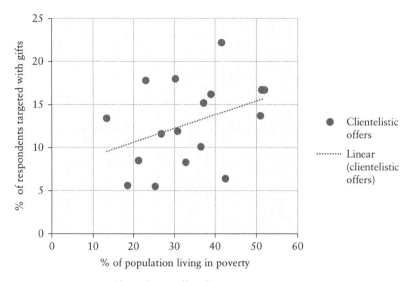

FIGURE 7.2. *Clientelistic offers by poverty rate in Latin America*
Sources: LAPOP (2010); World Bank Database: World Development Indicators

that is, they have people of comparable socioeconomic backgrounds living close together and segregated from those of different backgrounds (Luna 2014: 273). Consequently, when district boundaries cut across the territorial distribution of socioeconomic groups, a bigger middle class in an electoral district will mean clientelism "creates an electoral trade off in terms of support from different groups of constituents" (Weitz-Shapiro 2014: 4). This is because the nonpoor might object to clientelism either on grounds of self-interest or moral concern about this practice (see also Banfield and Wilson 1963; Shefter 1977; Bratton 2008; Hicken 2011; Gonzalez Ocantos *et al.* 2014). Hence, in such contexts, and particularly when competition is high, politicians will have incentives to denounce clientelistic strategies in the hope of damaging the reputation of their rivals (Weitz-Shapiro 2012, 2014). However, in larger districts campaign clientelism may be easier to hide easier from nonpoor constituencies, making it a feasible campaign strategy within sociodemographically heterogeneous districts. Where district boundaries reinforce territorial segregation, campaign clientelism will become a feasible strategy only in those districts with a predominantly poor population. In predominantly nonpoor districts, small gifts will simply not work as an effective inducement to buy enough participation at campaign events.

One of the races analyzed in Chapter 5 can, in fact, be explained by taking into consideration the sociodemographic composition of electoral districts, a factor not included in my original research design. Indeed, the case of Piura's municipal election illustrates the electoral potential, but also the limits, of an electoral strategy that involves openly criticizing the use of campaign clientelism as an electioneering method in an electoral district where a sizeable minority of voters are middle class. Toward the end of the race, one candidate positioned himself as an electorally competitive option. By privileging media appearances and policy-oriented debates, he convinced a sector of the electorate that he had the professional trajectory and technical knowledge needed to solve Piura's most urgent problems. Simultaneously, he actively criticized his main contender for engaging in clientelism while campaigning and highlighted her low levels of education and lack of technical expertise. Although he was able to sway voters in the two urban districts with a higher presence of middle class voters and fought vote by vote to the finale, he was ultimately defeated by a very small margin (less than 2,500 votes) by the clientelistic candidate. Thus, in this election clientelism created an electoral trade-off in terms of support from different groups of constituents. But as well as being sociodemographically fragmented, Piura is also a large electoral district. In a fragmented electoral context typical of Peruvian politics where a municipal election can be won with barely 20 percent (and even less) of the vote, displaying mixed electoral strategies based on campaign clientelism helped the winning, clientelistic candidate to persuade enough poor voters of both her electoral viability and desirability. This candidate personally visited and campaign intensively in both poor and rural constituencies. While her support was very competitive in urban areas as well (Table 6.9), her strong electoral support in poor-rural constituencies, where media-based campaigning is not that effective, helped her attain victory. Hence, in a heterogeneous but large district such as Piura, campaign clientelism still is an appealing strategy for electoral mobilization since it allows candidates to reach and persuade voters in peripheral constituencies that may make the difference electorally.

Finally, it is worth discussing a third scope condition that is usually attributed to clientelism in general: the weakness of state institutions. Low state capacity – understood as the lack of a professional civil service – has been a factor associated in the literature with organized partisan clientelism that is sustained with public resources (Shefter 1994; Geddes 1994; Kitschelt 2000; Grindle 2012). In this case, easy, non-supervised access to public resources that can be used to engage in patronage and other forms of clientelism gives political machines a comparative advantage over competitors and, ultimately, allows them to entrench themselves in power.

Having weak state institutions seems to be a relevant scope condition for the way campaign clientelism works as well. On the one hand, although the main financial source in campaign clientelism is private resources, subnational incumbents also use public funds to distribute gifts while campaigning. On the other hand, the central state's limited capacity to enforce the law and sanction abuses of power by public officials is crucial for understanding the high levels of corruption that habitually follow heavy investment in campaign clientelism.

However, although low state capacity may in fact be a necessary condition for clientelism to take place, this factor alone does not distinguish my theory from other theories of clientelism. More than a weak state, what seems to make the difference between the Peruvian case and others such as Argentina with more organized clientelism is the presence (or absence) of relatively strong or weak parties that can take advantage (or not) of this low state capacity to extract resources for political gain. While in traditional studies of clientelism the main beneficiaries of state weakness are entrenched political parties, in the Peruvian case it is business interests and individual politicians that benefit the most from the extraction of state resources – in the form of corruption associated with public projects. Given the scarcity of organized political parties, business/private actors are able to take advantage and "colonize" this weak state. This has been particularly true ever since state institutions started receiving immense amounts of resources given the economic boom and existing fiscal decentralization rules (Muñoz *et al.* 2016). Thus, I argue that, more than state capacity, the relevant scope condition for my theory is the strength of political organizations.

In summary, while moderate poverty rates and low state capacity are important scope conditions for my argument to travel to other contexts, what really distinguishes my theory's implications and applicability is the strength of partisan organizations. Simultaneously, the sociodemographic electoral structure might become an important additional factor to understand the logic as well as limits of campaign clientelism as a mixed strategy of electoral mobilization.

I have already shown the potential of my theory for explaining how mixed electoral strategies that combine campaign clientelism, particularistic promises, and personalistic appeals work in contexts of weakly organized parties. But what are the broader implications of these findings for comparative politics? How do they inform our understanding of the relations between politicians and the poor? What do they add to existing debates in the literature on parties? How does this subtype of electoral clientelism affect the quality of democracy? My theory informs broader theoretical debates in comparative politics. In the following subsections, I discuss the implications of my theory for the general literature on electoral clientelism, as well as for debates about political parties, the relation between the media and campaigns, and the effects of clientelism on the quality of democracy.

THEORETICAL IMPLICATIONS

Contributions to the Literature on Clientelism and Political Parties

In this book I pinpoint several limitations in prevailing theories of electoral clientelism and go on to address many of those issues. First, existing approaches have exaggerated the importance of monitoring and of the logistical contributions of established networks. For the informational theory, however, political organization is not a necessary condition for electoral clientelism, or a prerequisite for politicians to make efficient electoral investments. Certainly, established networks are important for sustaining relational clientelism (long-term clientelistic relations) and other forms of electoral clientelism besides campaign clientelism. But they need not be present for more sporadic political exchanges to take place. This theoretical revision is an important one and involves changing the focus of the causal effect of interest. Rather than assuming that the effect of distributing material benefits on electoral choices is principally a direct one, as conventional approaches do, my informational theory stresses, instead, the powerful *indirect* effects that material investments create during campaigns. Once indirect causal effects are taken into account, the puzzle of clientelistic distribution without political organization vanishes.

The recent wave of literature on political clientelism in comparative politics focuses so singularly on the mechanics of voter targeting and compliance that theories sometimes isolate clientelistic exchanges from the broader context of political competition for office. For instance, many leading studies assume that a single dominant incumbent buys votes or turnout at the polls (Stokes 2005, 2007a; Dunning and Stokes 2007; Nichter 2008, 2010; Gans-Morse *et al.* 2014; Stokes *et al.* 2013).[8]

---

[8] Finan and Schechter (2012) and Zarazaga (2011) are important exceptions.

I depart from this orthodoxy by showing that candidates compete, partly, through campaign clientelism. They use it to convey several types of information, both to the general public (donors and voters) and to campaign clients themselves. Competition under uncertainty is, to be sure, at the core of my informational theory. Moreover, as my empirical research demonstrates, campaign clientelism is a strategy of mobilization that is accessible to most candidates as long as they are able to gather the necessary financial resources. By explicitly theorizing political competition, my theory explains why electoral clientelism can be associated with volatile and competitive political contexts. While dominant machines immune to competition do exist, they are far from being the modal case of clientelistic relations in democratic systems. Indeed, researchers have documented the coexistence of widespread distribution of material benefits during campaigns in various non-Latin American countries that lack institutionalized party systems, such as Kenya, Malawi, and Zambia (Van de Walle 2007; Banégas 2011; Kramon 2016, 2017).

Moreover, I put campaigns at the center of my theory of clientelism and electoral competition. My approach theorizes electoral clientelism as a complex game that takes place *throughout* the campaign and affects not just vote choices but the dynamics of the race itself. Campaigns in contexts without organized parties are more volatile and uncertain than in more institutionalized political contexts. Voters are faced with a greater number of candidates and have less prior information about them than do voters in institutionalized party systems. The fortunes of candidates can, thus, fluctuate considerably during campaigns, and politicians know it. Campaign clientelism strategies are devised precisely to manipulate public perceptions and, thus, be able to influence the campaign's dynamics.

As well as focusing on the tactics of elites, including politicians and campaign donors, my informational approach also emphasizes the strategic logic of voters during campaigns. In making their electoral choices, clients not only compare the benefits they receive relative to their political preferences, but as we know from Duverger (1954) and Cox (1997), they also weigh up the changing electoral prospects of contending candidates. In contrast, most formal models of political clientelism assume that voters vote sincerely – that is, they do not weigh their utilities by the probability that the parties will win.[9] As Nichter points out, most contemporary studies of vote buying in the discipline, including his own previous work, stress the strategic nature of voters but model *only* the tactics

---

[9] See, for instance, Gans-Morse et al. (2014), Nichter (2008, 2010), Zarazaga (2011).

of politicians (Nichter 2009; Nichter and Peress 2017). My informational theory, by contrast, takes into account strategic voting.

A third issue I address in this book is how politicians assure loyalty at the polls. Existing approaches of electoral clientelism differ in the micro-level mechanisms they propose: fear of punishment (Brusco *et al.* 2004; Stokes 2005; Chandra 2007; Kitschelt and Wilkinson 2007; Dunning and Stokes 2007; Nichter 2008, 2010), reciprocity (Gouldner 1960; Lemarchand and Legg 1972; Scott 1972; Auyero 2001; Schaffer 2007a; Wang and Kurzman 2007; Finan and Schechter 2012; Lawson and Greene 2014), and alignment of interests (Magaloni *et al.* 2007; Oliveros 2012; Zarazaga 2012; Díaz-Cayeros *et al.* 2016). However, all of these theories assume that, in one way or another, consolidated organizational networks or long-term clientelistic relations are important in assuring that clients fulfill their commitments at the polls.

But how do politicians influence vote choices with electoral invest-ments if they do not have established machines? This is the forth issue addressed. Prevailing theories fall short of providing a convincing answer to this question. My informational theory, on the other hand, explicitly addresses it: by focusing on the indirect effects of campaign clientelism, I highlight the importance of persuading voters while also campaigning *through non-clientelistic means.* Voters are opportunistic, and politicians are fully aware of this opportunism. Therefore, after buying participa-tion at campaign events, they need to convince turnout clients to support them at the polls. To persuade voters that they are desirable candidates while campaigning, they combine campaign clientelism, particularistic promises, and personalistic appeals. In fact, candidates' personal charac-teristics and their interaction with voters at campaign events – and not just information about candidates distributing gifts while campaigning (Kramon 2017) – is what helps them build credibility and influence indif-ferent voters. Hence, from this perspective, persuasion is not just a func-tion of the material benefits received, and nor is it primarily a prospective assessment of the goods to be received in the future.

Fifth, my theory also differs from existing approaches to clientelism in that it stresses the increasing importance of private campaign financing, which has, thus, far been downplayed by the literature (Luna 2016: 31). Although public resources are frequently used to finance the distribu-tion of handouts during campaigns, private donations finance a sizable share of this distribution in several contexts. However, the existent litera-ture focuses solely on public resources and the clientelistic ends to which they are assigned (Auyero 2001; Calvo and Murillo 2004; Weitz-Shapiro

2014; Szwarberg 2015; Díaz-Cayeros *et al.* 2016). Therefore, they are missing part of the picture.

Finally, why do politicians in some contexts, such as Peru, not invest more in building longer-standing political organizations? Why have new parties (or machines) not been able to consolidate themselves two decades after the traditional party system collapsed? My book provides some clues regarding why parties have not been *re-built* in competitive regimes where parties are weak. The overlooked clientelistic tactic of campaign clientelism requires little organizational capacity but can profoundly influence the electoral behavior of political actors (donors, benefit-seeking activists, and voters). It is very easy for amateur politicians to improvise electioneering structures that deal with the kind of problems that partisan organizational structures used to solve during campaigns. The availability of these organizational substitutes may explain the delay in the construction or reconstruction of organized parties (Hale 2006; Zavaleta 2014; Levitsky and Zavaleta 2016). Such organizational substitutes might be particularly attractive in other countries with widespread poverty and inchoate parties, such as Kenya, Malawi, or Zambia, since candidates may benefit more from investing in campaign clientelism than engaging in party building.[10]

Besides engaging with the party literature, my theory also informs the contemporary debate about media and campaigns. In the following section I examine this debate and show how my theory highlights the complementarity of traditional and media-based campaigning.

MEDIA AND CAMPAIGNS

Ever since the advent of mass-media usage in elections, some political scientists have been predicting the decline of traditional campaigning. Door-to-door canvassing, rallies, and other forms of interpersonal contact during campaigns were expected to be progressively replaced by communication through mass media (Norris 2000: 179). Moreover, certain scholars have argued that the media also threatens mass political parties. They point out that given their increasing dependence on the media, Western countries have experienced the rise of "parties without partisans"; that is, of institutions with ever-diminishing organizational capacity to reach people on the ground during campaigns (Dalton and

---

[10] See, for example, Kramon's (2017) analysis of electoral clientelism in Kenya, and Banégas's (2011) study of Benin.

Wattenberg 2002). This process by which political institutions were seen to be increasingly dependent on the media was called the "mediatization" of politics (Mazzoleni and Schulz 1999).

Meanwhile, other scholars continued to recognize the importance of on-the-ground electioneering. As early as the 1970s, Wolfinger demonstrated that political machines had not withered away in the United States. The precinct work of machine politics was still widespread and visible, particularly in low-salience elections such as state and local contests or party primaries (Wolfinger 1972). Academics studying campaign modernization around the world also recognized that new technologies and techniques are blended together with preexisting modes of campaigning, producing hybridization (Swanson and Mancini 1996: 268–9; Plasser and Plasser 2002: 19). Moreover, recent research reaffirms the importance of social communications and close contact, even in environments sometimes characterized as highly penetrated by the mass media. For instance, experimental studies have shown that partisan mobilization efforts ("Get out the Vote" operations), including door-to-door canvassing, are still important in American campaigns. These studies find that GOTV efforts affect turnout levels at the polls (Shaw 2006; Green and Gerber 2008). In addition, Nielsen's study of congressional campaigns has confirmed that personalized interaction (face-to-face communication about politics) during campaigns is very important in the United States today (Nielsen 2012). In his own words, the mass media:

have not crowded out everything else nor put an end to the development of older practices of communication. Campaigns need to spread the word, and they cannot rely on 'the media' alone to do it, no matter how much they massage reporters or how many thirty-second television spots they buy. There is simply too much content out there, too little attention being paid. Hence, campaigns develop what political operatives called a 'layered' approach. They rely not only on advertisements and news coverage but also on direct mail, digital marketing, and field operations. (Nielsen 2012: 17)

While scholars have emphasized the increasing importance of televised presidential campaigns in contemporary Latin America (Weyland 2001; Mazzoleni *et al.* 2003; Boas 2005, 2010, 2016), the simultaneous persistence and prominence of rallies and campaign events has also been stressed (De la Torre 2006; Szwarcberg 2009, 2012, 2015). Indeed, by actively studying clientelistic politics in organized settings, Latin American specialists have implicitly recognized the persistence of field operations during campaigns.

In addition to confirming the continuing importance of electioneering despite the rise of media politics and polling, my informational theory provides an explanation as to *why* street campaigning has not faded away in contexts without consolidated political organizations. Just like in the Latin America of the past, when candidates had to mobilize partisans and sympathizers to the plazas to demonstrate electoral strength, my research confirms that *visual* demonstrations of strength still matter in the region. Particularly in subnational elections in low-organization settings, characterized by electoral volatility and scarce polling information, head counting is still a powerful cue for assessing appeal and electoral viability. Moreover, my theory contends that street politics and media politics complement each other, as the media can *amplify* the effects of campaign clientelism. Indeed, political marketing and traditional campaigning have more intersections than commonly thought. For instance, Cánepa and Málaga (2011) examine the cultural content of spots and propaganda during the last election in Cusco (Peru), held in 2010. They find that many of the spots and videos they analyze actually use the candidates' performance at campaign activities to produce a culturally and politically appealing message. Through campaign clientelism, therefore, political marketing meets street politics.

In summary, traditional campaigning is still an important part of present-day electoral contests. Street mobilization is a particularly effective way of persuading voters of a candidate's electoral viability and desirability, especially in contexts lacking stable political organizations as well as in low-salience elections. Indeed, street mobilization may be even more relevant in Latin America today, given the increasing number of authorities that have been elected since decentralization processes took place.

In addition to its theoretical relevance, my informational theory also has normative implications. In the next section I discuss the implications of my theory for democracy.

QUALITY OF DEMOCRACY

They [politicians] have money but no organization (Víctor Villa, political operator, Cusco, May 25, 2010).

If electoral clientelism works as my informational theory contends, it may be less problematic for democratic accountability than scholars have suggested for more organized political contexts. Indeed, some have pointed out that clientelism should not necessarily be seen as a diminished form of political linkage: relational clientelism implies bonds of accountability and responsiveness between patrons and clients. Clientelism can, in fact, be a mechanism that the underprivileged use for securing regular access to state benefits in the absence of welfare states (Weingrod 1968; Powell 1970b; Archer 1990; Kitschelt 2000; Kitschelt and Wilkinson 2007; Zarazaga 2012). Nonetheless, the consensus in the existing literature of electoral clientelism is that it has profoundly negative implications for the way democracy works (Hicken 2011: 302). From this conventional perspective, clientelism is viewed as a relationship based on political *subordination* in which a voter exchanges part of his or her political rights for material benefits (Weingrod 1968; Scott 1969; Powell 1970b; Scott 1972; Graziano 1973).[11] Even if clientelistic relations are viewed as legitimate and normal by a broker's followers, clientelistic networks reproduce domination and inequality (Auyero 2000: 75, 2001).

In vote-buying models, it is assumed that the political right being exchanged is the vote (Stokes 2005, 2007b).[12] The machine induces voter compliance by monitoring clients and threatening them with punishment. In other words, clients abide by the agreement because they fear losing particularistic benefits. Alternative models stress that clients vote for the machine out of gratitude. In either case, however, "a person whose vote is purchased for an individualized payment is, for all practical purposes, lost to the process of collective deliberation, mandate making, and retrospective evaluations of governments" (Stokes 2007b: 90).[13]

This book has demonstrated, however, that the model of clientelism Stokes refers to does not work in contexts lacking solid political organizations. In such settings citizens do sell their participation in campaign events but decide whether to support the buyers with their votes according to their assessment of candidates' personal traits and particularistic promises. Indeed, as I have shown, poor voters portray themselves as pragmatic citizens and not frightened and submissive clients. Thus, although campaign clientelism still raises some normative concerns – voters *can* be misled when public perceptions of electoral prospects are manipulated by turnout buyers – clients are not passive citizens subject to perverse accountability.

---

[11] See also Fox (1994: 153).

[12] Other theories identify other political rights that are potentially restricted by clientelistic conditionality, such as the right to associational autonomy (Fox 1994).

[13] As Nichter points out, Stokes's (2005) influential model assumes that the machine rewards citizens for voting *against* their electoral preferences (Nichter 2014: 316).

Thus, campaign clients are not diminished citizens – they do evaluate and express their electoral preferences and they do engage in public deliberation. In my informational model, politicians still need to persuade clients to support them at the polls while personally interacting with them on the trail. Clients get informed by participating in campaign events, and this information helps them form their electoral preferences. They do so, taking into consideration other participants' reactions and preferences. Many clients, in fact, explicitly discuss the desirability of different candidates with their peers before deciding their vote choices. Moreover, as my research shows, campaign clients can retrospectively evaluate their governments and, thus, hold unresponsive authorities accountable at the polls. In fact, information generated through campaign clientelism can help strategic voters coordinate their electoral choices and vote out unpopular incumbents.

In a context without stable and organized political affiliations, however, campaign clientelism cannot prevent other negative outcomes for the quality of democracy. First, while retrospective evaluations are plausible and commonly employed, most campaign clients do not enter stable clientelistic relations after campaigns are over. Consequently, most poor voters do not get access to the regular clientelistic goods and services or the levels of government responsiveness that voters sometimes enjoy in long-term clientelistic relationships (Scott 1976; Kitschelt 2000; Auyero 2001; Zarazaga 2014).

Second, in the absence of organizational infrastructure, campaign clientelism may skew electoral politics toward the wealthier even more than where long-lasting clientelistic relations exist. Organizations have historically allowed for the rise of the less independently wealthy into elected positions, as in the case of communist and social democratic parties in Europe (Lipset and Rokkan 1967), labor-mobilizing parties in Latin America (Roberts 2002; Burgess and Levitsky 2003), as well as the left-wing parties that organized and mobilized the poor during the late 1970s and 1980s in Peru (Cameron 1994; Stokes 1995; Dietz 1998; Tanaka 1998). In fact, the lack of organized parties with the capacity to cover campaign expenses for either media ads or clientelistic rallies makes it difficult for poorer people to get elected, unless they "sell their soul" to better-off donors. Several interviewees who were politically active in the 1980s complain about this fact. The increasing participation of businesspeople in politics during the last decade (Muñoz 2010; Muñoz and García 2011; Levitsky 2013; Zavaleta 2014) is not coincidental. The main difficulty that *dirigentes* from poor neighborhoods confront when competing for office is the lack of resources.[14] As Washington Román, union leader and former candidate for Cusco's regional president comments, the last elections have been won principally by "businessmen with money who utilize *dirigentes*."[15] Without political parties, the monetization of politics reaches its peak.

Effectively, a third and serious problem for Peru's democracy with weak parties is that campaign clientelism makes politics more dependent on money by raising the financial barriers to running a successful campaign. To be able to invest in campaign clientelism from the initial stages of the race onward, candidates need to be well-off or have close connections to wealthy people. Campaign donations, thus, become an increasingly important form of political participation in which the wealthy have, obviously, unfair advantages (Bartels 2008). The increasing number of businesspeople running their own campaigns confirms this is the case. Moreover, given that ever-increasing financial resources are now needed to run successful campaigns, illegal business and organized crime are becoming more and more involved in politics.

This trend is worrisome: when money and contributors grow in importance, pleasing the donors also becomes imperative (Gilens 2014). Pleasing donors, in turn, gives rise to three additional problems for the quality of democracy. First, the rising costs of electoral campaigns risks political equality and distorts political representation. Research conducted in the United States (Bartels 2008; Hacker and Pierson 2011; Gilens 2014) and Latin America (Fairfield 2015) provides empirical evidence to show how excessive reliance on private campaign contributions actually biases political representation and government responsiveness: policymakers take the interests of the wealthy into account more often and more extensively than they do median voter preferences. Socioeconomic inequality is, thus, reinforced by electoral politics, making effective political equality, promised by democracy, unlikely.

Second, particularly within a context of weak state institutions, widespread corruption also becomes a likely phenomenon. While citizens are still able to vote out unresponsive incumbents, they cannot prevent the entrenchment of widespread corruption at multiple levels of government (Tanaka 2005b). As I showed in Chapter 3, strategic donations often translate into corruption. Without stable political organizations to

---

[14] Personal interview with political operator Víctor Raúl Tomaylla (Cusco, May 23, 2010); union leader and former candidate Washington Román (Cusco, May 17, 2010); former candidate Sergio Sullca (Cusco, December 15, 2010).

[15] Personal interview (Cusco, May 17, 2010).

lengthen politicians' time horizons, corruption proliferates. After gaining office, most politicians do not build long-term clientelistic linkages, preferring to extract resources for personal or small-group gain while they can. To do so, they engage in pork-barrel spending, which also allows them to pay back campaign contributions by perverting public procurement procedures. Businesses are well aware of this. Consequently, during campaigns they try to position themselves better for future negotiations by generously supporting the most viable candidates.

Finally, democracy suffers when the monetization of campaigns incentivizes the entry of illegal funds into the political process. By running their own candidates to gain office directly or by making campaign contributions and indirectly influencing policy-making, illegal private actors affect the quality of democracy by reinforcing the un-rule of law (O'Donnell 2002). When illegal economic activities expand, so too does violence as a means of solving disputes, doing business, or just exercising power, thus, increasing civil rights violations. Moreover, the expansion of illegal activities may also reinforce or even decrease state capacity. With the goal of assuring the nonenforcement of existing regulation or impunity, illegal business is usually willing not only to buy off politicians but also nonelected public officials as well. Thus, the autonomy and quality of state bureaucracies are also likely to suffer, indirectly affecting government responsiveness.

In short, when campaign clientelism becomes the modal electoral clientelistic strategy, elected officials end up being more accountable to campaign donors than to clients. Thus, although voters are not submissive subordinates accountable to patrons in Peru in its absence of political organizations, most voters are not the principals in these political relationships either.

CONCLUSION

Overall, my informational theory provides a rationale for why politicians buy turnout at campaign events even in contexts with low political organization. Furthermore, this theory informs important debates in comparative politics, and can be productively applied to organized political contexts as well. Mobilizing large numbers of people to attend rallies during campaigns will remain important wherever strategic actors (donors and voters) lack complete electoral information, regardless of the degree of organization in the political system. Therefore, the overall lesson from this investigation is that a proper understanding of electoral clientelism requires assessment of informational dynamics as well as direct vote-getting ones. My research shows that – as in the past, when candidates had to mobilize sympathizers to the streets to demonstrate electoral strength – head counting is still a powerful cue for assessing power and electoral viability. In addition, my research also opens a fruitful avenue of research by showing how, while trying to persuade voters of their desirability as candidates, politicians mix electoral strategies in the field. From this perspective, then, campaign clientelism is not inimical but functional for the personalization of politics, at least within weakly organized political contexts. Campaign clientelism is, thus, a tactic that is deployed in order to buy audiences for persuasion through non-clientelistic appeals.

Appendices

APPENDIX I: CALVO AND MURILLO'S METHOD

Calvo and Murillo's method relies on developments in network analysis to estimate hard-to-count populations and uncover network structures from individual-level data (McCarty *et al.* 2001; Zhen *et al.* 2006). This survey methodology relies on interviews consisting of a series of count questions of the general "How many X's do you know?" type. Using these count questions as input, Calvo and Murillo's method allows for the indirect measurement of political networks through the simultaneous estimation of each respondent's personal network, and their predisposition to establish ties with particular political groups. The advantage of this survey strategy is its ability to retrieve valid samples from populations that are poorly represented among adult voters (in this case, political networks of local intermediaries).

Following Zhen *et al.* (2006), Calvo and Murillo (2008) use an over-dispersed Poisson model to estimate three sets of parameters of interest: (i) parameters measuring the relative size of the respondent's personal network; (ii) parameters measuring the prevalence of different political networks in the population; and (iii) parameters that explore individual-level deviations from the estimated personal network and group prevalence. To this end, the instrument asks respondents to provide counts of groups whose frequency in the population is known through the electoral registry (i.e., "How many individuals do you know whose name is *Rosa*?") and counts of groups whose frequencies in the population we seek to estimate (i.e., "How many activists from the *Partido Aprista Peruano* do you know?").

The information about the known groups (i.e., frequency of people named Rosa in the population) is used as an *offset* to estimate a model that measures the size of the respondents' personal networks. Then, in a second stage, these first estimates are used for estimating the prevalence of political networks in the population. The vector of over-dispersed parameters provides us with information about individual-level deviations from the overall group prevalence; that is, the degree to which a respondent knows more individuals (e.g., of party X) than would be expected given her personal network size and group prevalence. In other words, this last set of parameters allows us to measure the relative proximity of respondents to different political groupings.[1]

The Peruvian survey included questions about the following known parameters: the nine most common first names of Peruvian voters in the 2010 electoral registry, and people who were born, married, and passed away during the previous year.[2] The items for estimating the networks of interest included questions about the number of activists and candidates of different political organizations, as well as questions about the number of public employees of different sorts that each survey respondent knows personally. To maximize the chances of obtaining reliable estimates, the survey included only questions about political organizations that, as of 2010, were represented in Congress and had won the national executive office after 1980. This condition left the following political groups: *Acción Popular*, APRA, *Fujimorismo*, and *Perú Posible*. In addition, the survey included a generic question about the number of candidates and collaborators from regional or local movements that the respondent knows personally. This was intended to provide a rough estimate to capture the countless number of regional and local "movements" that compete in elections since the collapse of Peru's party system. The estimation was conducted using the statistical program R.

---

[1] For technical details about the estimation procedure, see Calvo and Murillo (2008).

[2] Before asking the questions, the interviewer reads a text that explaining that "knowing someone" means that the respondent knows someone *personally*, meaning that: that person knows the respondent as well (her name or at least who they are), that the respondent has been in contact with this person for the last two years, and that she can contact the person via telephone, email, or in any other way.

APPENDIX 2: BALANCE TEST OF SURVEY
EXPERIMENT INCLUDED IN IPSOS 2012

	Mean in treated A (100)	Mean in control	p-Value for diff
Female	0.49	0.49	0.944
Age	2.02	2	0.767
Lima	0.37	0.37	0.884
Rural	0.21	0.18	0.33
SES	3.33	3.4	0.344
Indigenous	0.19	0.18	0.856
Education	5.42	5.42	1

	Mean in treated B (1000)	Mean in control	p-Value for diff
Female	0.54	0.49	0.179
Age	1.97	2	0.603
Lima	0.38	0.37	0.827
Rural	0.2	0.18	0.532
SES	3.37	3.4	0.734
Indigenous	0.15	0.18	0.22
Education	5.42	5.42	0.987

	Mean in treated A (100)	Mean in treated B (1000)	p-Value for diff
Female	0.49	0.54	0.158
Age	2.02	1.97	0.415
Lima	0.37	0.38	0.715
Rural	0.21	0.2	0.728
SES	3.33	3.37	0.528
Indigenous	0.19	0.15	0.159
Education	5.42	5.42	0.986

*Since performing a balance test between three groups was not possible with Stata 14, I choose to perform three balance tests, comparing both treatment groups to the control and comparing both treatments between them. As the results show, there is balance across all the covariates considered.

APPENDIX 3: FIGURE 4.1 DATA TABLE AND RESULTS

		Proportion	95% conf. interval	
Improbable	Low turnout	49.74%	44.76%	54.73%
	High turnout	39.59%	34.83%	44.55%
	Control	43.46%	38.55%	48.49%
Probable	Low turnout	50.26%	45.27%	55.24%
	High turnout	60.41%	55.45%	65.17%
	Control	56.54%	51.51%	61.45%

APPENDIX 4: FIGURE 4.2 DATA TABLE AND RESULTS

How likely are you to vote for a candidate like Jose?
[7 = highly likely, 1 = highly unlikely]

	Linearized			
	Mean	Std. error	[95% conf. interval]	
Control	3.785434	0.1006731	3.585924	3.984945
Treatment	3.162827	0.0858085	2.992774	3.332879

Test [t1] Control = [t1] Treatment.
Adjusted Wald test.
(1) [t1] Control−[t1] Treatment = 0.
$F(1, 110) = 25.29$.
Prob. > F = 0.0000.

APPENDIX 5: FIGURE 4.3 DATA TABLE AND RESULTS

ATE comparison: How likely are you to vote for a candidate like Jose? [7 = highly likely, 1 = highly unlikely]

	Coef.	Std. err.	t	P>t	[95% conf. interval]		Conf. inter. (+/−)
AB	−0.977956	0.2302702	−4.25	0	−1.436389	−0.519523	0.46
C	−0.537951	0.1766346	−3.05	0.003	−0.888433	−0.18747	0.35
DE	−0.525299	0.2126223	−2.47	0.016	−0.948684	−0.101914	0.42

APPENDIX 6: FIGURE 4.4 DATA TABLE AND RESULTS

How likely is a candidate like Jose to win? [7 = highly likely, 1 = highly unlikely]

	Linearized		
	Mean	Std. error	[95% conf. interval]
Control	4.074709	0.0900132	3.896342	4.253076
Treatment	4.106542	0.0921368	3.923966	4.289117

Test [t1] Control = [t1] Treatment.
Adjusted Wald test.
(1) [t1] Control–[t1] Treatment = 0.
$F(1, 111) = 0.06$.
Prob. $> F = 0.8125$.

APPENDIX 7: FIGURE 4.5 DATA TABLE AND RESULTS

How likely is that a candidate like Jose will help people living in poverty? [7 = highly likely, 1 = highly unlikely]

	Linearized		
	Mean	Std. error	[95% conf. interval]
Control	3.778052	0.1099553	3.560168	3.995936
Treatment	3.411323	0.0787738	3.255228	3.567419

Test [t1] Control = [t1] Treatment.
Adjusted Wald test.
(1) [t1] Control – [t1] Treatment = 0.
$F(1, 111) = 7.87$.
Prob. $> F = 0.0059$.

APPENDIX 8: FIGURE 4.6 DATA TABLE AND RESULTS

ATE comparison by SES: How likely is that a candidate like Jose will help people living in poverty? [7 = highly likely, 1 = highly unlikely]

	Coef.	Std. err.	t	$P > t$	[95% conf. interval]		Conf. inter. (+/−)
AB	−0.37524	0.2342123	−1.6	0.113	−0.841521	0.0910408	0.47
C	−0.540099	0.1803304	−3	0.003	−0.897914	−0.1822846	0.36
DE	−0.215101	0.2387247	−0.9	0.37	−0.690365	0.2601635	0.48

APPENDIX 9: FIGURE 4.7 DATA TABLE AND RESULTS

ATE comparison by SES: How likely is that a candidate like Jose will do the public works that the district needs? [7 = highly likely, 1 = highly unlikely]

	Coef.	Std. err.	t	$P > t$	[95% conf. interval]		Conf. inter. (+/−)
AB	−0.577551	0.2354682	−2.45	0.016	−1.046428	−0.1086741	0.47
C	−0.489071	0.1507902	−3.24	0.002	−0.7882711	−0.1898702	0.30
DE	−0.123328	0.2259711	−0.55	0.587	−0.5732014	0.3265463	0.45

APPENDIX 10: FIGURE 4.8 DATA TABLE AND RESULTS

How likely is that a candidate like Jose will fulfil his campaign promises? [7 = highly likely, 1 = highly unlikely]

	Linearized Mean	Std. error	[95% conf. interval]	
Control	3.686326	0.0928087	3.502419	3.870232
Treatment	3.311406	0.0875576	3.137905	3.484907

Test [t1] Control = [t1] Treatment.
Adjusted Wald test.
(1) [t1] Control−[t1] Treatment = 0.
$F(1, 111) = 9.37$.
Prob. $> F = 0.0028$.

APPENDIX 11: FOCUS GROUP GUIDE (SPANISH)

Presentación

FACILITADOR(A): Buenos días/tardes. Mi nombre es _____ _____. Los hemos citado aquí porque nos encontramos realizando un estudio para conocer más acerca de su opinión sobre las campañas electorales en Perú, con el objetivo de entender cómo los políticos y los votantes toman decisiones y resuelven problemas. Este es un estudio académico independiente para la Universidad de Texas en Austin; no estamos vinculados a ningún partido político o agencia gubernamental. Las opiniones y comentarios que nos brinden serán tratados de forma confidencial, por lo que trabajaremos anónimamente. Recuerden que no hay opiniones buenas o malas, y que como investigador/a, yo no me sentiré afectado/a por lo que digan. Siéntanse en plena libertad para expresar su punto de vista. Esta reunión no tomara más de 1 hora y media de su tiempo. Muchas gracias por su atención.

Perfil De Los Entrevistados (Indicar Que Se Empezará A Grabar Luego De La Presentación)

a. Para empezar, quisiera que me digan sus nombres (sin apellido), edad, y a qué se dedican, también si están casados o si tienen hijos. *(ANOTAR NOMBRES EN ETIQUETAS Y ENTREGÁRSELOS A CADA PARTICIPANTE).*

Tema 1: Experiencia En Campañas Electorales

1. ¿Podrían contarme un poco cómo son las campañas políticas en _____?
   1.1 ¿Qué actividades de campaña organizan los políticos?
   1.2 ¿Cómo participa la población de _____ en las campañas? ¿Forman comités para apoyar a algún candidato?
2. PREGUNTAR SI NO SALE ESPONTÁNEAMENTE A PARTIR DE LA PREGUNTA ANTERIOR: En su experiencia, ¿cómo tratan de convencer los candidatos a los electores de _____ que para que voten por ellos?
   1.3 ¿Qué les ofrecen los candidatos?
   1.4 ¿Qué tipo de cosas les prometen?
3. Díganme, por lo que saben y han escuchado, ¿cómo creen que la gente decide su voto? ¿Qué es lo que más pesa en su decisión? (SÓLO COMO AYUDA SI LA RESPUESTA NO ES ESPONTÁNEA):
   1.5 ¿La trayectoria y/o características del candidato?
   1.6 ¿Las propuestas o plan de gobierno?
   1.7 ¿Las promesas de obras que construirán?
   1.8 ¿La opinión de familiares y/o amigos?
   1.9 ¿La información y opinión de los medios?
   1.10 ¿Otros?

Tema 2: Reparto De Presentes En Campaña: Frecuencia Y Modalidades

1. Por lo que saben y han escuchado, durante las campañas electorales del 2010 (municipales/regionales) y del de este año (congresales y

presidenciales), ¿con qué frecuencia los candidatos/movimientos políticos repartieron presentes, como víveres, materiales de construcción, utensilios, artefactos, como parte de sus actividades de campaña política en _____?

2. Cuando vienen y les ofrecen los presentes, ¿cómo se organiza el reparto de víveres o presentes? ¿Qué modalidades se dan?

   a. ¿En qué tipo de actividades por ejemplo?

   b. ¿A quiénes distribuyen (a todos los presentes en una actividad, por sorteo, o es selectivo, solo a seguidores conocidos del candidato)?

   c. ¿Hay sectores de la población a los que los candidatos les reparten más víveres/regalos?

   d. ¿Alguna vez algún candidato ha repartido dinero? ¿Cómo?

3. En su opinión, ¿quiénes repartieron y/o sortearon más presentes durante las últimas campañas: los candidatos a la alcaldía, a la región, al congreso o a la presidencia?

4. En su opinión, ¿el reparto de regalos en campaña ha aumentado en estos últimos procesos electorales o siempre ha sido así de frecuente?

Razones De Voto Y Regalos

5. ¿Por qué creen que los políticos reparten regalos? ¿Qué esperan conseguir con eso?

6. De lo que ha visto y escuchado, ¿qué opina la gente de _____ sobre esta costumbre de repartir regalos o víveres en la campaña? ¿Les parece bien, mal, que los candidatos lo hagan o les es indiferente?

   6.1 ¿Qué dice la gente del/los candidato(s) que lo hace?

   6.2 ¿Y qué dice la gente del (los) candidato(s) que no lo hacen?

   6.3 ¿Y ustedes qué opinan?

7. En su experiencia, ¿la gente cambia o decide su voto en función del regalo que recibe?

8. ¿Qué tipo de personas se dejan convencer más rápido con los famosos regalos de los candidatos?

   8.1 ¿Por qué cree que votan por recibir el regalo?

Gratitud Y Solución De Problemas

9. Voy a leerles una frase. "Cuando alguien me hace un favor, me siento obligado a devolver ese favor." Hay gente que piensa así.

¿Cree que la gente que recibe un presente de un candidato debería sentirse obligado a votar por él o ella como si estuviera devolviendo un favor? ¿Por qué? ¿En qué tipo de situaciones?

10. Por lo que saben, los políticos que reparten regalos en campaña, ¿se acuerdan de la gente una vez electos (siguen ayudándola a resolver sus necesidades cuando son autoridades) o estas son sólo actividades de campaña?

    10.1 ¿Cuándo ya son autoridades, quiénes se acuerdan más de la gente: alcaldes distritales, alcaldes provinciales, presidente regional, consejeros regionales, congresistas, presidente de la República?

11. ¿Cree que la gente debería sentir obligación de votar por los políticos que, una vez electos les continúan repartiendo ayuda y les ayudan a solucionar sus problemas?

    11.1 ¿Cree que la gente lo hace? ¿En qué casos?

12. Si normalmente las autoridades electas ya no ayudan a la gente a solucionar sus necesidades más urgentes, ¿cómo hace la gente normalmente en su barrio/caserío para solucionar sus problemas? ¿a quiénes recurren, por ejemplo, las personas más necesitadas cuando les faltan los alimentos o necesitan comprar medicinas en caso de enfermedad?

Muchas gracias por su atención...

APPENDIX 12: LIST OF INTERVIEWS AND FOCUS GROUPS

Interviews

Lima

Abugatas, Javier. Professor, PUCP. Former vice minister of finance. September 18, 2009.

Acurio Velarde, Gastón. Former senator, AP. Lima, April 20, 2010.

Alcazar, Lorena. Expert in public policy; senior researcher, GRADE. Lima, June 9, 2010.

Alva Orlandini, Luis. Former deputy, senator, congressman, minister, AP. Lima, April 7, 2010.

Anonymous political operator, *Fujimorismo*. February 17, 2010.

Arizabal, Hernando. Member of the National Intelligence Service during the transition government (2000–1). Lima, August 3, 2010.

Armas Vela, Carlos. Former congressman, APRA. Lima, March 8, 2010.

Ballón, Eduardo. Expert in regional politics, DESCO. Party member of *Vanguardia Revolucionaria* in Piura during the 1980s. Lima, July 6, 2010.

Barreda, Javier. Member of the political committee, APRA. Lima, September 6, 2012.

Barreda, Santiago. Party member, APRA. Lima, June 9, 2009.

Blondet, Cecilia. Former minister of women and development; Executive Director of Proética. Lima, November 6, 2010.

Caballero, Victor. Head of PRONAA during the Toledo administration. October 23, 2009.

Caceres Velazquez, Roger. Former deputy, senator, and congressman, *Frente Nacional de Trabajadores y Campesinos* (FRENATRACA). March 23, 2010.

Chavez, Martha. Congresswoman, *Fujimorismo*. Lima, April 16, 2010.

Contreras, Carlos. Professor, Pontifica Universidad Católica del Perú (PUCP).

Du Bois, Fritz. Editor of *Perú21*, daily newspaper. Lima, August 13, 2009.

Fort, Ricardo. Development expert; associate researcher, GRADE. Lima, April 14, 2010.

Francke, Pedro. Social policy expert. Head of FONCODES during the Toledo administration. Lima, April 6, 2010.

Gómez, Jorge. San Martín de Porras (Lima) councilor. Lima, June 16, 2011.

Gonzales de Olarte, Efrain. professor, PUCP; regional economic specialist. Lima, July 14, 2009.

Grandez, Felix. technical secretary, *Mesa de Concertación Para la Lucha Contra la Pobreza*. Lima, April 27, 2010.

Guerra García, Francisco. Former member of the *Democracia Cristiana* party. March 12, 2010.

Hinojosa, Iván. Professor, PUCP. Worked in the *Centro Bartolomé de las Casas* (CBC) in Cusco during the 1980s. Lima, November 6, 2009.

Huber, Ludwig. Researcher, IEP. Lima, October 15, 2009.

Hume, María Jesús. Vice minister of commerce in the 1980s. October 30, 2009.

Illescas, Javier. World Bank – Peru. July 22, 2009.

Kouri, Alex. Former governor of Callao, *Chim Pum Callao* regional movement. Lima, January 10, 2010.

Lombardi, Guido. Journalist and former congressman. August 5, 2012.

Losada, Carmen. Former congresswoman, *Fujimorismo*. Lima, April 8, 2010.

Lucioni, Guido. Candidate for congressman, *Fujimorismo*. Lima February 5, 2010.

Matta, Walter. Teacher, former reform committee member at the Ministry of Education. Lima, April 20, 2010.

Medina, Percy. Technical secretary, *Asociación Civil Transparencia*. Lima, April 13 and April 30, 2010.

Monge, Carlos. Expert in decentralization and regional politics. October 12, 2009.

Monteagudo, Manuel. Official, *Banco Central de Reserva*. July 3, 2009.

Pajuelo, Ramón. Researcher, IEP; former associate researcher at the CBC, Cusco. Lima, April 9, 2010.

Pedraza, Magno. Former political operator in Northern Lima. Lima, June 13, 2010.

Pollarolo, Pierina. Specialist in public employment. September 30, 2009.

Prieto, Janette. Former Oxapampa (Junín) mayor, *Somos Perú* party. Lima, October 10, 2009.

Quiñones, Nilton. Budget specialist, *Mesa de Concertación Para la Lucha Contra la Pobreza*. Lima, April 30, 2010.

Remy, Marisa. Researcher, IEP; expert in local politics; worked at the *Centro de Investigación y Promocion del Campesinado* (CIPCA) in Piura during the 1990s. Lima, October 30, 2009.

Roca, Carlos. Former deputy and mayoral candidate for Lima, APRA. April, 6, 2010.

Rocha, Blanca. Former deputy, AP. Lima, March 23, 2010.

Romero, Jhon. Politician, APRA. Lima, June 10, 2009.

Roncagliolo, Rafael. Executive director, International Idea – Peru. October 14, 2009.

Sanborn, Cynthia. Professor, *Universidad del Pacífico*. October, 14, 2009.

Tanaka, Martín. Professor PUCP; researcher IEP. Lima, September 29, 2009.

Távara, Jose. Former mayor of Carabayllo district (Lima), Izquierda Unida. March 2, 2010.

Tejada, David. Politician, *Partido Nacionalista del Peruano* (PNP). Lima, October 7, 2009.

Torres, Javier. Director, *Asociación Servicios Educativos Rurales* (SER); specialist in electoral education. October 22, 2009.

Torres, Marcos. Political operator and congressional adviser, *Fujimorismo*. Lima, February 5, 2010.

Trivelli, Carolina. Researcher, IEP. October 16, 2009.

Ugarte, Mayen. Professor PUCP; public administration specialist. July 15, 2009.

Vásquez, Absalón. Political operator and former minister of agriculture, *Fujimorismo*. Lima, December 12, 2012.

Vasquez, Enrique. Professor, *Universidad del Pacífico*. Head of PRONAA during Fujimori's first term. October 19, 2009.

Velorio, Gloria. Former district Coordinator, PRONAA. Lima, August 10, 2010.

Webb, Richard. Researcher, Instituto del Perú, *Universidad San Martín de Porres*. June 8, 2009.

Cusco

Alatriste, Germán. Party member, APRA. May 23, 2010.

Aldazábal, José. Political operator and councilman of Santiago district. Cusco, September 6, 2010.

Anonymous political operator; former member of *Puka Llacta Party* who worked for Fujimori. Cusco, August 2 and September 1, 2010.

Ayala, Fernando. Official, *Oficina Nacional de Procesos Electorales* (ONPE) – Cusco. Cusco, May 21, 2010.

Azpur, Javier. Expert in regional politics, *Grupo Propuesta Ciudadana*. Worked in Arariwa in Cusco during the 1990s. November 10, 2009.

Berríos, Marleni. Officer, *World Vision* – Pachacutec Office. Cusco, December 17, 2010.

Bornza, Sarina. *Transparencia* coordinator – Cusco. Cusco, May 12, 2010.

Campana, Silvio. Ombudsman Representative. Cusco, May 24, 2010.

Carrillo, Carlos. Journalist, *Radio Programas del Perú* (RPP) correspondent. Cusco, September 6, 2010.

Carrión Astete, Mario. Journalist; anchor of *La Jornada Informativa* TV show, Channel 35. Cusco, August 27, 2010.

Chacón, Carlos. Former mayor of Cusco (1986–9); independent who ran for APRA. Lima, April 16, 2010.

Chávez, Rubén. Official, *World Vision* – Huancaro. Cusco, December 20, 2010.

Chevarría, Franz. Candidate for mayor, APRA. Cusco, August 27, 2010.

Choque, Miguel. Legal representative, PNP. Councilor of San Sebastián municipality. Cusco, May 19 and 20, 2010.

Coa, Gabriela. School of Governability, Centro Guamán Poma y Ayala. Cusco, December 22, 2010.

Coa, Rubén. General secretary and candidate for Congress, PNP. Former councilman of Espinar province. Cusco, May 25, September 4, December 18, 2010.

Del Carpio, Anibal. Politician, *Fuerza 2011*. Former congressman and president of CTAR Cusco. May 25, 2010.

Delgado, Alberto. Former coordinator, *Mesa de Lucha Contra la Pobreza* – Cusco. Cusco, May 13, 2010.

Delgado, Oliver. Journalist and media political operator; advised William Cuzmar, Qosqollay's mayoral candidate for Cusco. Cusco, September 1, 2010.

Eliorreta, Igor. Expert in local government, Centro Guamán Poma y Ayala. Cusco, September 7, 2010.

Estrada, Aldo. Legal representative, *Pan* regional movement. Cusco, December 20, 2010.

Fernández Baca, Inés. Director of COINCIDE. Former coordinator, *Mesa de Concertación Para la Lucha Contra la Pobreza*. Cusco, May 19, 2010.

Figuero, Serly. Councilor of Cusco. Candidate for reelection, *Patria Arriba Perú Adelante* (PAPA). Cusco, December 21, 2010.

Florez Ochoca, Jorge. Anthropologist, *Universidad San Cristóbal Abad del Cusco*. May 14, 2010.

Fuentes, Juan. Political operator and adviser to Wanchaq mayor (*Qosqollay* movement). Former adviser of mayor Daniel Estrada of Cusco. Cusco, September 6, 2010.

García, Alexander. Former coordinator of the *Vaso de Leche* Program (Cusco Municipality). Cusco, December 21, 2010.

Gatica, Edmundo. Political operator, *Fujimorismo*. Cusco, September 6, 2010.

Gutiérrez Samanez, Julio. Former councilor of Santiago district, IU. Cusco, May 24, 2010.

Hancco, Ricardo. Candidate for councilor of Santiago, *Tierra y Libertad*. Former councilor of Santiago (IU). Cusco, September 7, 2010.

Huamán, Marco Antonio. Candidate for councilman of Cusco, *Tierra y Libertad*; president of the Northeast Defense Front. Cusco, September 7, 2010.

Huañac, María Luisa. Political operator, Norwest Cusco, APRA. Cusco, August 27, 2010.

Huilca, Flor. Former journalist, *La República – Gran Sur*. Lima, April 29, 2010.

Huillca, Carlos. Candidate for councilor of Santiago, *Tierra y Libertad*. Cusco, May 13, 2010.

Mamani, Adolfo. Political operator working for *Tierra y Libertad*. Cusco, August 31, 2010.

Mamani, Efraín. Member of *Autogobierno Ayllu* regional movement. Cusco, December 16, 2010.

Marín, Henry. Journalist and media political operator. Cusco, September 2, 2010.

Martorell, Mario. Adviser to Cusco's mayor. Former *Aprista*; former congressional and mayoral candidate. Cusco, May 17, 2010.

Members of the *Pata Pata* producers association, San Jerónimo. Cusco, May 17, 2010.

Mendoza, Juan. Former member of *Vanguardia Revolucionaria* in Cusco. November 9, 2009.

Molero, Rubén. Councilman of Cusco; candidate for reelection, PAPA. Cusco, September 1, 2010.

Monzón, Dora. State attorney for corruption cases. Cusco, September 6, 2010.

Moscoso, Carlos. Candidate for mayor of Cusco, *Fuerza Cusco* local movement. Cusco, December 18, 2010.

Nieto Degregori, Luis. *Centro Guamán Poma y Ayala*. Cusco, May 22, 2010.

Noa, Víctor Raúl. President of the Agrarian League of Santiago. Cusco, December 22, 2010.

Oporto, Delia. Organization Coordinator, *Fuerza 2011 (Fujimorismo)*. Cusco, May 19, 2010.

Paredes, Carlos. Former member of *Vanguardia Revolucionaria* (later *Partido Unificado Mariateguista* – PUM) in Cusco. Lima, November 7, 2009 and August 13, 2010.

Pasapera, Marco. Regional coordinator, ONPE – Cusco. Cusco, May 24, 2010.

Peralta, Rosario. Women's affairs secretary, *Partido Humanista*. Cusco, May 17, 2010.

Pezo, Ricardo. Candidate for councilor of Santiago, PAPA regional movement. Cusco, September 2, 2010.

Pino, Vidal. Former member of IU and adviser to Cusco's mayor Daniel Estrada. Cusco, December 21, 2010.

Polo y La Borda, Jorge. Historian, *Universidad San Cristóbal Abad del Cusco*. May 14, 2010.

Quispe, Felipe. Member of the Agrarian League of Santiago. Cusco, December 22, 2010.

Román, Washington. Journalist and union leader. Former candidate for regional president. Cusco, May 17, 2010.

Romero, Roberto. Adviser to Cusco's mayor. Former party member of *Partido Comunista del Perú Patria Roja*. Cusco, August 27 and December 17, 2010.

Rozas, Rolando. Political operator, PNP. Cusco, September 3, 2010.

Rozas, Wilber. Candidate for regional president, *Tierra y Libertad* regional movement. Former mayor of Anta province. Cusco, May 24, 2010.

Salcedo, Víctor. Journalist, *La República - Gran Sur* newspaper. Cusco, September 1, 2010.

Saloma, Adolfo. Politician, *Movimiento Nueva de Izquierda (Patria Roja)*. Former President of Cusco's Regional Assembly (1990–2). Cusco, May 20, 2010.

Saucedo, Elena. Community advisor for Huancaro; member of the *Central de Organizaciones de Mujeres del Distrito de Santiago* (CODEMUSA). Cusco, May 17, 2010.

Sicus, Julia. *Campesino* communities' representative to Cusco's Community Council. Cusco, December 20, 2010.

Sullca, Sergio. Candidate for mayor of Santiago, *Tierra y Libertad* regional movement. Cusco, May 25, August 25, and December 12, 2010.

Tomaylla, Víctor Raúl. Secretary of organization, Cusco and candidate for mayor of Wanchaq, APRA. May 23, 2010.

Valcárcel Villegas, Alberto. Candidate for mayor of Urubamba province, AP. Urubamba, August 30, 2010.

Valcárcel, Jorge. Political operator. Political adviser to candidate Máximo San Román, *Pan* regional movement. Cusco, December 19, 2010.

Valencia Miranda, Carlos. Candidate for regional president, *Fuerza 2011*. Former mayor of Cusco, Vamos Vecino. Cusco, May 20, 2010.

Vargas, Robert. Coordinator of the *Voto Informado* program in Cusco, *Jurado Nacional de Elecciones*. Cusco, May 13, 2010.

Verano, Wilfredo. Political operator in Santiago district, working for Qosqollay. Cusco, September 7, 2010.

Vilca Ochoa, Danilo. Provincial secretary, *Unión Por el Perú*. Cusco, May 20, 2010.

Villa, Pablo. Secretary, *Pata Pata* producers association, San Jerónimo. Cusco, May 24 and December 17, 2010.

Villa, Víctor. Political operator. Founder of *Maíz* movement, former *Aprista*. Cusco, August 31, 2010.

Villanueva, Armando. Former candidate to Congress and regional president, AP. May 14, 2010.

Wilfredo, Teresa. Local Governments Program, CBC. Cusco, May 18, 2010.

Zeisser, Marco. Director of CBC. Cusco, May 18, 2010.

Piura

Aguilar Hidalgo, Juan. Former coordinator of *Transparencia* – Piura; Rural coordinator. July 19, 2010.

Albirena, Luis. Governability Program, CIPCA. Piura, July 20, 2010.

Albuquerque, Manuel. Local Governments Program, CIPCA. Piura, July 21, 2010.

Atkins, Javier. Candidate for regional president, *Unidos Construyendo*. Piura, July 7, 2011.

Bayona, Robespierre. Deputy for Piura (1985–90), IU-PUM. Piura, July, 23, 2010.

Bejarano, Jaime. APRA activist. General Secretary of La Florida Neighborhood Council. Piura, November 23, 2010.

Bustamente, Cecilia. Coordinator, *Mesa de Lucha Contra la Pobreza* – Piura. July 22, 2010.

Calle, Alex. Political operator, APRA. Assistant of congressman Jhony Peralta in Piura. November, 15, 2010.

Castillo Navarrete, Juan. Former mayor of Canchaque (Huancabamba), APRA. September 26, 2010.

Castillo, Juan. Political operator and adviser to congressman for Piura, Jhony Peralta (APRA). Lima, July 9, 2010.

Chasquero, Francisca. APRA, General Secretary of *Ciudad del Niño* local committee. Piura, November 25, 2010.

Chávez, Flor de María. Expert in gender and social policy. Piura, November 17, 2010.

Chumacero, Alberto. Secretary of Organization in Piura, APRA. November 23 and 24, 2010.

Coronado, Kelly. Candidate for councilwoman of Piura, APRA. General secretary of Los Olivos local committee. Piura, September 28, 2010.

Correa, Humberto. Economist; adviser of Piura's Regional Government. Piura, July 22, 2010.

de Jo, Maruja. Former coordinator, *Mesa de Lucha Contra la Pobreza* – Piura. July 20, 2010.

Diez, Alejandro. Anthropologist; specialist in Piura. Professor, PUCP. Lima, June 15, 2010.

Farfán, Rocío. Reporter *Cutivalú Radio*. Piura, July 22, 2010.

Fernández, Jhon. Reporter, *Cutivalú Radio*. July 11, 2011.

Fuentes, Francisco. General secretary of San Sebastián Neighborhood Council. Piura, November 23, 2010.

Galecio, Miguel. Regional councilman, *Obras+Obras*. Piura, November 23, 2010.

García Santillán, Roberto. Campaign coordinator for the northwest of Piura city, *Unidos Construyendo*. October 2 and November 23, 2010.

García, Flor. Activist, *Unidos Construyendo*. General secretary of Los Sauces Neighborhood Council. Piura, October, 2, 2010.

Guevara, Lili. Journalist, *El Tiempo* newspaper. Piura, November 20, 2010 and July 7, 2011.

Gulman Checa, Luis. Candidate for regional president of Piura, *Obras + Obras* regional movement. July 20, 2010.

Gutiérrez, Rolando. Councilor of Piura, *Obras + Obras*. Piura, November 23, 2010.

Helguero, Luz María. Editor of *El Tiempo* newspaper and former candidate to Congress for Piura. July 22, 2010.

Huamanchumo, Mariano. Political operator. July 21, 2010.

Loja, Luis. Political operator. Assistant of congress woman Marisol Espinoza (PNP) in Piura. Piura, July 19 and September 27, 2010.

Luna Vargas, Andrés. Candidate to congress for Piura, PNP. Senator (1985–90) for IU – PUM. Piura, September 22, 2010.

Miñán, Daniel. *Obras + Obras* activist, El Rosal settlement. Piura, November 23, 2010.

Miranda, Karina. Journalist, *La Hora* newspaper. Piura, July 22, 2010.

Mora, Inuñán. General Secretary of El Rosal Neighborhood Council. Piura, November 23, 2010.

More, José. Mayor of Catacaos and candidate for councilman of Piura, *Obras + Obras*. Piura, September 18, 2010.

Mulatillo, Segundo. Political operator, *Obras + Obras*. Piura, November 25, 2010.

Muro, Gregoria. Political operator, *Unidos Construyendo*. Piura, July 23, 2010.

Nakasaki, Carlos. Councilman for Piura, *Obras + Obras*. Piura, November 16, 2010.

Ortiz Granda, Luis Alberto. Candidate for regional vice president of Piura, APRA. Piura, July 26, 2010.

Parrilla, Abraham. Political operator working for *Unidos Construyendo* in the 2010 regional election. July 26, September 23 and November 17, 2010.

Patiño, Ramiro. Former coordinator of *Transparencia* - Piura. Piura, July 23, 2010.

Paz, Telmo. Adviser to congresswoman for Piura Fabiola Morales (*Unidad Nacional*). Lima, July 2, 2010.

Peña, Óscar. *Obras + Obras* activist, La Molina. Piura, November 23, 2010.

Pinday, Mari. Political operator. Piura, November 26, 2010.

Pulache, Joel. General Secretary of Antonio Raymondi local committee, APRA. October 2, 2010.

Revesz, Bruno. Expert in rural development in Piura, CIPCA. Lima, July 16, 2010.

Rodríguez, Elizabeth. Political operator. Piura, July 24, 2010 and June 7, 2011.

Ruíz, Maximiliano. Candidate for regional vice president of Piura, *Unidos Construyendo*. Former mayor of Morropón. Piura, July 20 and November 17, 2010; July 7, 2011.

Saavedra, María. Resident of La Florida settlement, Northwest Piura. Piura, November 20, 2010.

Saldarriaga, José. *Unidos Construyendo* activist, Northwest Piura. Piura, November 23, 2010.

Sueiro, Ernesto. Expert in rural development. Member of *Vanguardia Revolucionaria* during the 1980s in Piura. Lima, July 12, 2010.

Talledo, Miguel. Legal representative, APRA. July 23 and November 17, 2010.

Tinoco, Nancy. *Obras + Obras* activist, Los Algarrobos settlement. Piura, November 23, 2010.

Toro, Humberto. Politician. Former candidate to congress. Member of PUM. Piura, September 23, 2010.

Tume Ruesta, César. Political operator, APRA. Piura, November 26, 2010.

Urbina, Rodrigo. Political operator. Former member of the *Movimiento Institucional Revolucionario* (MIR). Piura, July 23 and November 15, 2010.

Ventura, Gamaniel. Political operator working for *Unidos Construyendo* in the 2010 regional election. July 26, 2010.

Vílchez, José Guillermo. President of the Cura Mori producers' association. Piura, November 17, 2010.

Vilela, Ana Lilian. Adviser to congresswoman for Piura Marisol Espinoza (PNP). Lima, July, 2, 2010.

Zapata, Nardi. APRA, General secretary of López Albújar local committee. November 25, 2010.

Zapata, Vicente. Member of the civic committee, bank employees' federation. Piura, July 25, 2010.

Zárate, Gloria. Member of *Transparencia* – Piura. Piura, September 22, 2010.

Zegarra, Miguel. Coordinator of *Transparencia* – Piura; Program coordinator, CIPCA. Piura, July 19, 2010.

Puno

Flores, Gustavo. *Fujimorismo* candidate and former congressman. Puno, June 10, 2010.

Herquinio, Luz. Ombudsman representative. Puno, June 12, 2010.

Nuñez, Jorge. Political operator working for *Reforma Regional Andina, Integración, Participación Económica y Social Puno* (RAICES–PUN) regional movement in the 2010 subnational election. Puno, June 12, 2010b.

Valdivia, Miguel. Political operator, *Partido Democrático Regional* (PDR) regional movement. Former activist of the *Partido Unificado Mariateguista* (PUM). Puno, June 10, 2010.

Focus groups

Cusco

1. Female voters. Pueblo Nuevo settlement – Huancaro, Santiago. Cusco, July 23, 2011.
2. Male voters. Villa Primavera settlement – Huancaro, Santiago. Usco, July 23, 2011.

3. Female voters. Rural Cusco. Cusco, Centro Bartolomé de las Casas, August 15, 2011.
4. Male voters. Rural Cusco. Cusco, Centro Bartolomé de las Casas, August 18, 2011.
5. Female voters. Vaso de Leche committee, Picol community, San Jerónimo. Cusco, September 3, 2011.
6. Female voters. Sucso Auccaylle community, San Jerónimo. Cusco, September 4, 2011.
7. Male voters. Ocoruro community, Province of Anta. Cusco, September 8, 2011.
8. Voters. Compone community, Province of Anta. Cusco, September 8, 2011.
9. Female voters. Ocollompampa community, San Jerónimo. Cusco, September 11, 2011.

Piura

1. Female voters. Los Polvorines settlement. Piura, July 9, 2011.
2. Female voters. El Indio settlement, Castilla. Piura, July 10, 2011.
3. Male voters. Los Polvorines settlement. Piura, July 11, 2011.
4. Male voters. El Indio settlement, Castilla. Piura, July 11, 2011.
5. Female voters. Bellavista, Sullana. Piura, August 7, 2011.
6. Female voters. Alamor village, Lancones, Sullana. Piura, August 1, 2011.
7. Young voters. Jibito village, Sullana. Piura, August 5, 2011.
8. Male voters. Jibito village, Miguel Checa, Sullana. Piura, August 6, 2011.
9. Female voters. Jibito village, Miguel Checa, Sullana. Piura, August 6, 2011.

References

Abramson, Paul R., John H. Aldrich, André Blais, Matthew Diamond, Abraham Diskin, Indridi H. Indridason, Daniel J. Lee, and Renan Levine. 2010. "Comparing Strategic Voting Under FPTP and PR." *Comparative Political Studies* 43 (1): 61–90. doi:10.1177/0010414009341717.

Alberti, Giorgio, and Fernando Fuenzalida. 1969. "Pluralismo, Dominación y Personalidad." In *Dominación y Cambios En El Perú Rural*, José Matos Mar et al., eds. Lima, Perú: Instituto de Estudios Peruanos, IEP, pp. 285–324. Available at: http://archivo.iep.pe/textos/DDT/dominacioycambiosenel perurural.pdf.

Alcázar, Lorena. 2007. "¿Por Qué No Funcionan Los Programas Alimentarios y Nutricionales En El Perú? Riesgos y Oportunidades Para Su Reforma." In *Investigación, Políticas y Desarrollo En El Perú*, edited by Grupo de Análisis para el Desarrollo. Lima: GRADE, pp. 185–234. Available at: www.grade .org.pe/upload/publicaciones/archivo/download/pubs/Libros/InvPolitDesarr .pdf#page=180.

Alcázar, Lorena, José Roberto López, and Erik Wachtenheim. 2003. "*Las Pérdidas En El Camino. Fugas En El Gasto Público: Transferencias Municipales, Vaso De Leche y Sector Educación*." Lima: GRADE. Available at : www.grade .org.pe/upload/publicaciones/archivo/download/pubs/LA-perdidas%20 en%20el%20camino.pdf.

Ames, Barry. 1987. *Political Survival: Politicians and Public Policy in Latin America*. Berkeley: University of California Press.

2001. *The Deadlock of Democracy in Brazil*. Ann Arbor: University of Michigan Press.

Angell, Alan, Maria D'Alva Kinzo, and Diego Urbaneja. 1992. "Latin America." In *Electioneering: A Comparative Study of Continuity and Change*, David Butler and Austin Ranney, eds. Oxford: Clarendon Press, 43–68.

Ansión, Juan, Alejandro Dierz, and Luis Mujica, eds. 2000. *Autoridad En Espacios Locales. Una Mirada Desde La Antropología*. Lima: Fondo Editorial PUCP.

Aragón, Jorge and José Luis Incio. 2014. "La reelección de autoridades regionales y municipales em el Perú, 2006–2014." *Revista Argumentos* 5: 16–30

Archer, Ronald P. 1990. *The Transition from Traditional to Broker Clientelism in Colombia: Political Stability and Social Unrest*. Notre Dame, Ind: University of Notre Dame, Helen Kellogg Institute for International Studies.

Arellano, Javier. 2008. "Resurgimiento Minero En Perú: ¿una Versión Moderna De Una Vieja Maldición?" *Colombia Internacional* 67: 60–83.

Asamblea Nacional de Gobiernos Regionales. 2012. "*Informe Anual Del Proceso De Descentralización 2011. Informe Presentado a La Comisión De Descentralización, Regionalización, Gobiernos Locales y Modernización De La Gestión Del Estado Del Congreso De La República*." Lima: ANGR.

Auyero, Javier. 2000. "The Logic of Clientelism in Argentina: An Ethnographic Account." *Latin American Research Review* 35 (3): 55–81.

2001. *Poor People's Politics: Peronist Survival Networks and the Legacy of Evita*. Durham, NC: Duke University Press.

Baker, Andy; Barry Ames and Lucio Renno. 2006. "Social Context and Campaign Volatility in New Democracies: Networks and Neighborhoods in Brazil's 2022 Elections." *American Journal of Political Science* 50(2): 282–399

Baldwin, Kate. 2010. "Big Men and Ballots. The Effects of Traditional Leaders on Elections and Distributive Politics in Zambia." PhD Dissertation. New York, NY: Columbia University.

2015. *The Paradox of Traditional Chiefs in Democratic Africa*. New York: Cambridge University Press.

Banégas, Richard. 2011. "Clientelismo Electoral Y Subjetivación Política En África. Reflexiones a Partir Del Caso de Benín." *Desacatos. Revista de Antropología Social* 36: 33–48.

Banfield, Edward, and James Wilson. 1963. *City Politics*. Cambridge, MA: Harvard University Press and MIT Press.

Baraybar, Viviana. 2016. Oro y violencia en Perú y Colombia: estructuras sociales y efecto diferenciado del boom de recursos. BA Thesis in Political Science. Lima: Pontificia Universidad Católica del Perú.

Barrenechea, Rodrigo. 2014. *Becas, Bases y Votos. Alianza Para el Progreso y la Política Subnacional en el Perú*. Lima: IEP.

Bartels, Larry. 1988. *Presidential Primaries and the Dynamics of Public Choice*. Princeton, N.J: Princeton University Press.

2008. *Unequal Democracy: The Political Economy of the New Gilded Age*. New York: Princeton University Press

Battle, Margarita, and Jennifer Cyr. 2014. "El Sistema de Partidos Multinivel: El Cambio Hacia La Incongruencia Y El Predominio de Nuevos Partidos En El Perú (1980-2011)." In *Territorio Y Poder: Nuevos Actores Y Competencia Política En Los Sistemas de Partidos Multinivel En América Latina*, Flavia Freidenberg and Julieta Suárez-Cao, eds. Biblioteca de América 50. Salamanca, España: Ediciones Universidad de Salamanca, 223–59.

Bellatín, Paloma. 2014. *De La Comunidad Al Partido: El Estudio de Caso Del Movimiento Político Regional Autogobierno Ayllu*. Lima: Pontificia Universidad Católica del Perú.

Benoit, Kenneth, Daniela Giannetti, and Michael Laver. 2006. "Voter strategies with restricted choice menus." *British Journal of Political Science*, 36 (03): 459–85.

Berelson, Bernard, Paul F. Lazarsfeld, and William N. McPhee. 1954. *Voting: A Study of Opinion Formation in a Presidential Campaign*. Chicago: University of Chicago Press.

Berger, Peter L., and Thomas Luckmann. 1967. *The Social Construction of Reality: a Treatise in the Sociology of Knowledge*, Anchor books, ed. Garden City, NY: Doubleday.

Boix, Carles. 1999. "Setting the Rules of the Game: The Choice of Electoral Systems in Advanced Democracies." *The American Political Science Review* 93 (3): 609–24

Blondet, Cecilia. 2004. "Los Comedores Populares: 25 Años De Historia." In *Cucharas En Alto. Del Asistencialismo Al Desarrollo Local: Fortaleciendo La Participación De Las Mujeres*, edited by Cecilia Blondet and Carolina Trivelli. Sociología y Política 39. Lima: IEP.

Boas, Taylor C. 2005. "Television and Neopopulism in Latin America: Media Effects in Brazil and Peru." *Latin American Research Review* 40 (2): 27–49. doi:10.1353/lar.2005.0019.

2010. "Varieties of Electioneering: Success Contagion and Presidential Campaigns in Latin America." *World Politics* 62 (4): 636–75.

2016. *Presidential Campaigns in Latin America. Electoral Strategies and Success Contagion*. New York: Cambridge University Press.

Boesten, Jelke. 2010. *Intersecting Inequalities: Women and Social Policy in Peru, 1990-2000*. University Park, Pa: Pennsylvania State University Press.

Bourricaud, Francois. 1966. "Structure and Function of the Peruvian Oligarchy." *Studies in Comparative International Development* 2 (2): 17–31.

Bratton, Michael. 2008. "Vote Buying and Violence in Nigerian Election Campaigns." *Electoral Studies* 27 (4): 621–32. doi:10.1016/j.electstud.2008.04.013.

Bratton, Michael, and Nicholas Van de Walle. 1997. *Democratic Experiments in Africa: Regime Transitions in Comparative Perspective*. Cambridge: Cambridge University Press.

Brusco, Valeria, Marcelo Nazareno, and Susan C. Stokes. 2004. "Vote Buying in Argentina." *Latin American Research Review* 39 (2): 66–88.

Burgess, Katrina, and Steven Levitsky. 2003. "Explaining Populist Party Adaptation in Latin America Environmental and Organizational Determinants of Party Change in Argentina, Mexico, Peru, and Venezuela." *Comparative Political Studies* 36 (8): 881–911. doi:10.1177/0010414003256112.

Burt, Jo-Marie. 2007. *Political Violence and the Authoritarian State in Peru: Silencing Civil Society*. 1st edn. New York: Palgrave Macmillan.

Calvo, Ernesto, and Maria Victoria Murillo. 2004. "Who Delivers? Partisan Clients in the Argentine Electoral Market." *American Journal of Political Science* 48 (4): 742–57.

2008. "When Parties Meet Voters: Partisan Networks and Distributive Expectations in Argentina and Chile." Paper presented at the 2008 Meeting of the American Political Science Association, August 28–31. Boston, Massachusetts.

2013. "When Parties Meet Voters Assessing Political Linkages Through Partisan Networks and Distributive Expectations in Argentina and Chile." *Comparative Political Studies* 46 (7): 851–82.

2019. *Non-Policy Politics: Richer Voters, Poorer Voters, and the Diversification of Electoral Strategies*. Cambridge: Cambridge University Press.

Cameron, Maxwell A. 1994. *Democracy and Authoritarianism in Peru: Political Coalitions and Social Change*. New York: St. Martin's Press.

Campbell, Angus, Philip Converse, Donald Stokes, and Warren Miller. 1960. *The American Voter*. University of Michigan, ed. New York: Wiley.

Cánepa, Gisela, and Ximena Málaga. 2011. "Marketing Electoral: El Uso De Viejos y Nuevos Repertorios Culturales En Busca De La Representatividad Política. El Caso Del Cusco En Las Elecciones De 2010." In *Perú Debate. El Nuevo Poder En Las Regiones. Análisis De Las Elecciones Regionales y Municipales 2010*. Lima: Departamento de Ciencias Sociales – PUCP, 29–39.

Canseco, Fiorella. 2016. Implementación de la ley forestal y de fauna silvestre 27308: el caso de Ucayali en el período 2011–2014. BA Thesis in Political Science. Lima: Pontificia Universidad Católica del Perú.

Carrión, Julio, ed. 2006. *The Fujimori Legacy: The Rise of Electoral Authoritarianism in Peru*. University Park, Pa: Pennsylvania State University Press.

Carrión, Julio, Patricia Zárate, and Elizabeth Zechmeister. 2015. *Cultura Poítica de la democracia en Perú y en las Américas, 2014: Gobernabilidad democráticas a través de 10 años del Barómetro de las Américas*. Lima: IEP, Vandberbilt University, LAPOP, USAID.

Casas-Zamora, Kevin and Daniel Zovatto. 2015. *El costo de la democracia: ensayos sobre el financiamiento político en América Latina*. Mexico DF: Universidad Autónoma de México.

Centeno, Miguel Ángel. 2009. "El Estado En América Latina." *Revista CIDOB D'afers Internacionals*, 11–31.

Chandra, Kanchan. 2004. *Why Ethnic Parties Succeed: Patronage and Ethnic Headcounts in India. Cambridge Studies in Comparative Politics*. Cambridge, UK; New York: Cambridge University Press.

    2007. "Counting Heads: A Theory of Voter and Elite Behavior in Patronage Democracies." In *Patrons, Clients, and Policies: Patterns of Democratic Accountability and Political Competition*, Herbert Kitschelt and Steven Wilkinson, eds. Cambridge, UK: Cambridge University Press, 84–109.

Chhibber, Pradeep, and Irfan Nooruddin. 2004. "Do Party Systems Count? The number of Parties and Government Performance in the Indian States." *Comparative Political Studies* 37 (2): 152–187. doi: https://doi.org/10.1177/0010414003260981

Chubb, Judith. 1981. "The Social Bases of an Urban Political Machine: The Case of Palermo." *Political Science Quarterly* 96 (1): 107–25. doi:10.2307/2149679.

Cicero, Quintus Tullius. 2012. "Campaign Tips from Cicero." *Foreign Affairs*, May 1. Available at: www.foreignaffairs.com/articles/137527/quintus-tullius-cicero-and-james-carville/campaign-tips-from-cicero?page=2.

Collier, Ruth Berins, and David Collier. 1991. *Shaping the Political Arena: Critical Junctures, the Labor Movement, and Regime Dynamics in Latin America*. Princeton, N.J: Princeton University Press.

Conaghan, Catherine M. 2005. *Fujimori's Peru: Deception in the Public Sphere. Pitt Latin American Series*. Pittsburgh, PA: University of Pittsburgh Press.

Congreso de la República. 2016. *Narcotráfico y política: Informe de la comisión multipartidaria encargada de investigar la influencia del narcotráfico en los partidos políticos, movimientos regionales y locales.* Lima: CIDDH y Congreso de la República.

Conniff, Michael. 1982. *Latin American populism in comparative perspective.* New Mexico: University of New Mexico Press.

Conroy-Krutz, Jeffrey, and Caroline Logan. 2013. "Museveni and the 2011 Ugandan Election: Did the Money Matter?" In *Voting and Democratic Citizenship in Africa*, Michael Bratton, eds. Boulder, Colo: Lynne Rienner Publishers, 139–56.

Contreras, Carlos. 2002. *El Centralismo Peruano En Su Perspectiva Histórica.* Lima: IEP.

Converse, Philip E. 1964. "The Nature of Belief Systems in Mass Publics." In *Ideology and Discontent*, David E. Apter, ed. New York, NY: Free Press.

Córdova, Beatriz Pilar, and Jose Luis Incio. 2013. "La ventaja del incumbente en el ámbito subnacional: un análisis de las dos últimas elecciones municipales en Perú." *Papel Político* 18 (2): 415–36.

Cornelius, Wayne. 2004. "Mobilized Voting in the 2000 Elections: The Changing Efficacy of Vote Buying and Coercion in Mexican Electoral Politics", in *Mexico's Pivotal Democratic Election: Candidates, Voters, and the Presidential Campaign of 2000*, Jorge I. Domnguez and Chappell Lawson, eds. Stanford, CA: Stanford University Press, 47–65.

Coronel, José, Carlos Iván Degregori, and Ponciano Del Pino. 1998. "Gobierno, Ciudadanía y Democracia: Una Perspectiva Regional." In *El Perú De Fujimori: 1990-1998*, John Crabtree and James J. Thomas, eds. Lima: Universidad del Pacífico/ Instituto de Estudios Peruanos, 437–65.

Cotler, Julio. 1967. "The Mechanics of Internal Domination and Social Change in Peru." *Studies in Comparative International Development* 3 (12): 229–46.

   1969. "Actuales Pautas De Cambio En La Sociedad Rural Del Perú." In *Dominación y Cambios En El Perú Rural*, José Matos Mar et al., eds. Lima: Instituto de Estudios Peruanos, 60–79.

   1978. *Clases, Estado Y Nación En El Perú. 1. ed. Perú Problema; 17.* Lima: Instituto de Estudios Peruanos.

Cotler, Julio, and Romeo Grompone. 2000. *El Fujimorismo: Ascenso y Caída De Un Régimen Autoritario.* 1st edn. Serie Ideología y Política15. Lima: Instituto de Estudios Peruanos.

Cox, Gary W. 1997. *Making Votes Count: Strategic Coordination in the World's Electoral Systems. Political Economy of Institutions and Decisions.* Cambridge; New York: Cambridge University Press.

   2007. "Swing Voters, Core Voters and Distributive Politics." Available at: www .isn.ethz.ch/isn/Digital-Library/Publications/Detail/?ots591=0c54e3b3-1e9c- be1e-2c24-a6a8c7060233&lng=en&id=45865.

   2009. "Authoritarian Elections and Leadership Succession, 1975-2004". American Political Science Association 2009 Annual Meeting. Toronto, Canada. Available at: http://papers.ssrn.com/sol3/papers.cfm?abstract_id=1449034.

Cox, Gary W., and Morgan Kousser. 1981. "Turnout and Rural Corruption: New York as a Test Case." *American Journal of Political Science* 25 (4): 646.

Cox, Gary W., and Mathew D. McCubbins. 1986. "Electoral Politics as a Redistributive Game." *The Journal of Politics* 48 (2): 370–389. doi:10.2307/2131098.

Cyr, Jennifer. 2012. "Collapse to Comeback? Explaining the Fates of Political Parties in Latin America." PhD Dissertation. Chicago: Northwestern University, Department of Political Science.

2016. "The Unique Utility of Focus Groups for Mixed-Methods Research." *Political Science & Politics* 50(4): 1038–42

2017. *The Fates of Political Parties. Institutional Crisis, Continuity, and Change in Latin America.* Cambridge: Cambridge University Press.

Dalton, Russell J., and Martin P. Wattenberg, eds. 2002. *Parties without Partisans: Political Change in Advanced Industrial Democracies. Comparative Politics.* New York: Oxford University Press.

Dargent, Eduardo. 2012. *El Estado En El Perú. Una Agenda de Investigación.* Lima: Escuela de Gobierno y Políticas Públcias – PUCP.

2014. *Technocracy and Democracy in Latin America: The Experts Running Government.* New York: Cambridge University Press.

Dargent, Eduardo, and Paula Muñoz. 2011. "Democracy Against Parties? Party System Deinstitutionalization in Colombia." *Journal of Politics in Latin America* 3 (2): 43–71.

2012. "Perú 2011: Continuidades y Cambios En La Política Sin Partidos." *Revista De Ciencia Política* 32 (1): 245–68.

2016. "Peru: A Close Win for Continuity." *Journal of Democracy* 47 (4): 145–58.

De Gramont, Diane. 2010. "*Leaving Lima Behind? The Victory and Evolution of Regional Parties in Peru*". Thesis, Harvard College. Massachusetts: Harvard.

De la Torre, Carlos. 2000. *Populist Seduction in Latin America: The Ecuadorian Experience. Ohio University Research in International Studies.* Athens: Ohio University Press.

2006. "Escenificaciones, Redes Y Discursos En La Segunda Vuelta Electoral." *Ecuador Debate* 69: 37–50.

De la Torre, Carlos, and Catherine Conaghan. 2009. "The Hybrid Campaign Tradition and Modernity in Ecuador's 2006 Presidential Election." *The International Journal of Press/Politics* 14 (3): 335–52.

Desposato, Scott. 2007. "Parties for Rent? Careerism, Ideology, and Party Switching in Brazil's Chamber of Deputies." *American Journal of Political Science*, 50(1):62–80.

Díaz-Cayeros, Alberto, Beatriz Magaloni, and Federico Estevez. 2007. "Strategies of Vote Buying: Social Transfers, Democracy and Welfare in Mexico." Manuscript.

2016. *The Political Logic of Poverty Relief. Electoral Strategies and Social Policy in Mexico.* New York: Cambridge University Press.

Dietz, Henry A. 1998. *Urban Poverty, Political Participation, and the State: Lima, 1970–1990. Pitt Latin American Series.* Pittsburgh: University of Pittsburgh Press.

Dixit, Avinash, and John Londregan. 1996. "The Determinants of Success of Special Interests in Redistributive Politics." *The Journal of Politics* 58 (4): 1132–55.

Dornbusch, Rudiger, and Sebastian Edwards, eds. 1991. *The Macroeconomics of Populism in Latin America.* Chicago: University of Chicago Press.

Downs, Anthony. 1957. *An Economic Theory of Democracy*. New York: Harper.
Dunning, Thad, and Susan Stokes. 2007. "Persuasion vs. Mobilization". Paper Prepared for the Conference on Elections and Distribution Held at Yale University, October 25–26, New Haven, Connecticut.
　2008. "Clientelism as Persuasion and as Mobilization." Paper presented at the annual meeting of the APSA 2008 Annual Meeting, Hynes Convention Center, Boston, Massachusetts, August 28.
Duverger, Maurice. 1954. *Political Parties, Their Organization and Activity in the Modern State*. London, New York: Methuen; Wiley.
　1986. "Duverger's Law: Forty Years Later". In *Electoral laws and their political consequences*, Bernand Grofman, and Arend Lijphart, eds. New York: Agathon Press, 68–84.
Eisenstadt, S. N., and Luis Roniger. 1984. *Patrons, Clients, and Friends: Interpersonal Relations and the Structure of Trust in Society*. Cambridge: Cambridge University Press.
Faughnan, Brian M., and Elizabeth J Zechmeister. 2011. Vote Buying in the Americas. Americas Barometer Insights: 2011.
Fenno, Richard F. 1996. "*Senators on the Campaign Trail: The Politics of Representation*." Julian J. Rothbaum Distinguished Lecture Series, vol. 6. Norman: University of Oklahoma Press.
Fernández-Vázquez, Pablo, Pablo Barberá, and Gonzalo Rivero. 2015. "Rooting Out Corruption or Rooting for Corruption? The Heterogeneous Electoral Consequences of Scandals." *Political Science Research and Methods* 4 (2): 379–97.
Finan, Federico, and Laura Schechter. 2012. "Vote-Buying and Reciprocity." *Econometrica* 80 (2): 863–81
Fox, Jonathan. 1994. "The Difficult Transition from Clientelism to Citizenship: Lessons from Mexico." *World Politics* 46 (2): 151–84. doi:10.2307/2950671.
Fuenzalida, Fernando. 1971. "Poder, Etnia y Estratificación Social En El Perú." In *Perú: Hoy*, Fernando Fuenzalida et al., eds. México D.F.: Siglo XXI, 86–174.
Freidenberg, Flavia. 2010. "La Política Se Fue de Fiesta." *Nueva Sociedad* 225: 120–38.
Freidenberg, Flavia, and Julieta Suárez Cao, eds. 2014. *Territorio y poder: nuevos actores y competencia política en los sistemas de partidos multinivel en América Latina*. 1st edn., Biblioteca de América 50. Salamanca: Ediciones de la Universidad de Salamanca.
Gans-Morse, Jordan, Sebastián Mazzuca, and Simeon Nichter. 2014. "Varieties of Clientelism: Machine Politics during Elections." *American Journal of Political Science* 58 (2): 415–32.
Gay, Robert. 1990. "Community Organization and Clientelistic Politics in Contemporary Brazil: A Case Study from Suburban Rio De Janeiro." *International Journal of Urban and Regional Research* 14 (4): 648–66.
Geddes, Barbara. 1994. *Politician's Dilemma: Building State Capacity in Latin America*. Berkeley: University of California Press.
Gerber, Alan S., James G. Gimpel, Donald P. Green, and Daron R. Shaw. 2011. "How Large and Long-Lasting Are the Persuasive Effects of Televised Campaign

Ads? Results from a Randomized Field Experiment." *American Political Science Review* 105 (01): 135–50. doi:10.1017/S000305541000047X.

Gilens, Martin. 2014. *Influence and Affluence, Economic Inequality and Political Power in America*. New York: Princeton University Press.

Gingerich, Daniel W. 2013. *Political Institutions and Party-Directed Corruption in South America: Stealing for the Team. Political Economy of Institutions and Decisions*. Cambridge: Cambridge University Press.

Goffman, Erving. 1959. *The Presentation of Self in Everyday Life*. Garden City, N.Y: Doubleday.

Gonzales de Olarte, Efraín. 1998. *El Neoliberalismo a La Peruana: Economía Política Del Ajuste Estructural, 1990-1997*. Lima: Instituto de Estudios Peruanos Y Consorcio de Investigación Económica.

González-Ocantos, Ezequiel, Kiewiet de Jonge, Chad, Meléndez, Carlos, Osorio, Javier, and David W Nickerson. 2013. "Vote Buying in the America." Manuscript. Prepared for Presentation at the 2013 Annual Conference Midwest Political Science Association, April 11–14, 2013, Chicago, IL.

2012. "Vote Buying and Social Desirability Bias: Experimental Evidence from Nicaragua." *American Journal of Political Science* 56 (1): 202–17.

Gonzáles-Ocantos, Ezequiel, Kiewiet, Chad, and David Nickerson. 2014. "The Conditionality of Vote Buying Norms: Experimental Evidence from Latin America." *American Journal of Political Science* 58 (1): 197–211.

González-Ocantos, Ezequiel, and Paula Muñoz. 2018. "Clientelism." In *The SAGE Handbook of Political Sociology*. Vol. 2. Sage Publications, 750–77

Gouldner, Alvin W. 1960. "The Norm of Reciprocity: A Preliminary Statement." *American Sociological Review* 25 (2): 161–78. doi:10.2307/2092623.

Graham, Carol. 1991. "The APRA Government and the Urban Poor: The PAIT Programme in Lima's Pueblos Jovenes." *Journal of Latin American Studies* 23 (1) (February): 91–130. doi:10.2307/157535.

1992. *Peru's APRA: Parties, Politics, and the Elusive Quest for Democracy*. Boulder: L. Rienner Publishers.

Graham, Carol, and Cheikh Kane. 1998. "Opportunistic Government or Sustaining Reform? Electoral Trends and Public-Expenditure Patterns in Peru, 1990–1995." *Latin American Research Review* 33 (1): 67–104.

Granovetter, Mark. 1983. "The Strength of Weak Ties: A Network Theory Revisited." *Sociological Theory* 1 (1): 201–33. doi:10.2307/202051.

Graziano, Luigi. 1973. "Patron-Client Relationships in Southern Italy." *European Journal of Political Research* 1 (1): 3–34. doi:10.1111/j.1475-6765.1973.tb01281.x.

1976. "A Conceptual Framework for the Study of Clientelistic Behavior." *European Journal of Political Research* 4 (2): 149–74. doi:10.1111/j.1475-6765.1976.tb00526.x.

Green, Donald P., and Alan S. Gerber. 2008. *Get Out the Vote: How to Increase Voter Turnout*. Washington, DC: Brookings Institution Press.

Grindle, Merilee. 2012. *Jobs for the Boys*. Cambridge, MA: Harvard University Press.

Grompone, Romeo. 2000. *"Al Día Siguiente: El Fujimorismo Como Proyecto Inconcluso De Transformación Política y Social."* In Serie Indeología y Política 15. Lima: IEP, 77–174.

Grupo Propuesta Ciudadana. 2007. *Vigilancia Del Proceso De Descentralización. Reporte Nacional No 11 – Balance 2003-2006.* Lima: GPC.

Grzymala-Busse, Anna. 2008. "Beyond Clientelism." *Comparative Political Studies* 41 (4–5): 638–73. doi:10.1177/0010414007313118.

Guasti, Laura. 1977. "Peru: Clientelism and Internal Control." In *Friends, Followers, and Factions: A Reader in Political Clientelism.* Berkeley, Los Angeles: University of California Press, 422–38.

Gutiérrez, Francisco. 2007. *¿Lo Que El Viento Se Llevó?: Los Partidos Políticos Y La Democracia En Colombia, 1958-2002.* Bogotá: Grupo Editorial Norma.

Gutiérrez, Julio. 1986. *Así Nació El Cuzco Rojo. Contribución a Su Historia Política: 1924–1934.* Cusco: Tarea.

Hacker, Jacob, and Paul Pierson. 2011. *Winner-Take- All Politics: How Washington Made the Rich Richer—and Turned its Back on the Middle Class.* New York: Simon & Schuster.

Hale, Henry E. 2006. *Why Not Parties in Russia? Democray, Federalism, and the State.* Cambridge; New York: Cambridge University Press.

Hansen, Ketil F. 2010. "Inside Electoral Democracy: Gift-Giving and Flaunting in Political Campaigning in Cameroon." *Journal of Asian and African Studies* 45 (4): 432–44.

Hawkins, Kirk A, and Guillermo Rosas. 2006. "Social Spending in Chávez's Venezuela." Paper Presented at the Annual Meeting of the Southern Political Science Association, Atlanta, GA, January.

Heckelman, Jac C. 1998. "Bribing Voters without Verification." *The Social Science Journal* 35 (3): 435–43. doi:16/S0362-3319(98)90010-6.

Hicken, Allen. 2007. "How Do Rules and Institutions Encourage Vote Buying?" In *Elections for Sale: The Causes and Consequences of Vote Buying,* Frederic Charles Schaffer, eds. Boulder, Colo: Lynne Rienner Publishers, 47–60.

2011. "Clientelism." *Annual Review of Political Science* 14 (1): 289–310.

Hilgers, Tina. 2008. "Causes and Consequences of Political Clientelism: Mexico's PRD in Comparative Perspective." *Latin American Politics and Society* 50 (4): 123–53.

2011. "Clientelism and Conceptual Stretching: Differentiating among Concepts and among Analytical Levels." *Theory and Society* 40 (5): 567–88.

Hirschman, Albert O. 1970. *Exit, Voice, and Loyalty Responses to Decline in Firms, Organizations, and States.* Cambridge, MA: Harvard University Press.

Holland, Alisha. 2017. *Forbearance as Redistribution. The Politics of Informal Welfare in Latin America.* New York: Cambridge University Press

Holland, Alisha, and Brian Palmer-Rubin. 2015. "Beyond the Machine Clientelist Brokers and Interest Organizations in Latin America." *Comparative Political Studies,* 49 (9): 1186–223. doi: https://doi.org/10.1177/0010414015574883

Huckfeldt, Robert, and John Sprague. 1987. "Networks in Context: The Social Flow of Political Information." *The American Political Science Review* 81 (4): 1197–216.

Hummel, Calla. 2017. "Disobedient Markets: Street Vendors, Enforcement, and State Intervention in Collective Action." *Comparative Political Studies* 50(11): 1524–55.

Huntington, Samuel. 1968. *Political Order in Changing Societies*. London: Yale University Press.

Jurado Nacional Electoral (JNE). 2010. *Perfil del Elector Peruano*. Lima: JNE/ PNUD. Available at: http://portal.andina.com.pe/EDPEspeciales/2011/ perfil_elector_JNE.pdf

Katz, Richard, and Peter Mair. 1995. "Changing Models of Party Organization and Party Democracy. The Emergence of the Cartel Party." *Party Politics* 1 (1): 5–28

Kaufman, Robert R. 1974. "The Patron-Client Concept and Macro-Politics: Prospects and Problems." *Comparative Studies in Society and History* 16 (3): 284–308.

Keefer, Philip. 2007. "Clientelism, Credibility, and the Policy Choices of Young Democracies." *American Journal of Political Science* 51 (4): 804–21.

Kemahlioglu, Ozge. 2006. *When the Agent Becomes the Boss: The Politics of Public Employment in Argentina and Turkey*. New York: Columbia University Press.

King, Gary, Robert Keohane, and Sidney Verba. 1994. *Designing Social Inquiry: Scientific Inference in Qualitative Research*. Princeton, N.J: Princeton University Press.

Kitschelt, Herbert. 2000. "Linkages between Citizens and Politicians in Democratic Polities." *Comparative Political Studies* 33 (6–7): 845–79.

2007. "The Demise of Clientelism in Affluent Capitalist Democracies." In *Patrons, Clients, and Policies: Patterns of Democratic Accountability and Political Competition*, Herbert Kitschelt and Steven Wilkinson, eds. Cambridge, UK: Cambridge University Press, 298–321.

Kitschelt, Herbert, and Daniel Kselman. 2011. "Organizational Extensiveness and Political Clientelism: The Formal and Informal 'Ties That Bind'". Paper prepared for presentation at the Workshop on Democratic Accountability Strategies, Duke University, May 18–19, Durham NC.

Kitschelt, Herbert, and Melina Altamarino. 2015. "Clientelism in Latin America: Effort and Effectiveness." In *The Latin American Voter: Pursuing Representation and Accountabilityin Callenging Contexts*, Ryan Carlin, Mathew Singer, and Elizabeth Zechmeister, eds. Ann Arbor: University of Michigan Press, 246–74.

Kitschelt, Herbert, and Steven Wilkinson. 2007. *Patrons, Clients, and Policies: Patterns of Democratic Accountability and Political Competition*. Cambridge, UK: Cambridge University Press.

Kitschelt, Herbert, Kirk Hawkins, Luna Juan Pablo, Guillermo Rosas, and Elizabeth Zechmeister. 2010. *Latin American party Systems*. Durham: Duke University Press.

Klaren, Peter F., and Víctor Raúl Haya de la Torre. 1976. *Formación de Las Haciendas Azucareras Y Orígenes Del APRA*. Vol. 5. Lima: IEP.

Knight, Alan. 1998. "Populism and Neo-populism in Latin America, Especially Mexico." *Journal of Latin American Studies* 30 (2): 223–48.

Kramon, Eric. 2011. "Vote Buying and the Credibility of Clientelistic Appeals Experimental Evidence from Kenya." Paper Prepared for Delivery at the 2011 Midwest Political Science Association Meeting.

2013. "Vote Buying and Electoral Turnout in Kenya." In *Voting and Democratic Citizenship in Africa*, Michael Bratton, ed. Boulder, Colo: Lynne Rienner Publishers, 101–19.

2016. "Electoral Handouts as Information: Explaining Unmonitored Vote Buying." *World Politics* 68 (3): 454–98.

2017. *Money for Votes. The Causes and Consequences of Electoral Clientelism in Africa*. New York: Cambridge University Press

Kriesi, Hanspeter. 2012. "Personalization of national election campaigns." *Party Politics*, 2012 18 (6): 825–44.

Krishna, Anirudh. 2007. "Politics in the Middle: Mediating Relationships between the Citizens and the State in Rural North India." In *Patrons, Clients, and Policies: Patterns of Democratic Accountability and Political Competition*, Herbert Kitschelt and Steven Wilkinson, eds. Cambridge, UK: Cambridge University Press, 141–58.

Kuenzi, Michelle, and Gina Lambright. 2001. "Party System Institutionalization in 30 African Countries." *Party Politics* 7 (4): 437–68.

Landé, Carl H. 1977. "The Dyadic Basis of Clientelism." In *Friends, Followers, and Factions. A Reader on Clientelism*, xiii–xxvii. Berkeley: University of California Press.

Lago, Ignacio. 2008. "Rational Expectations or Heuristics?" *Party Politics* 14 (1): 31–49.

Lavine, Howard, and Thomas Gschwend. 2007. "Issues, party and character: The moderating role of ideological thinking on candidate evaluation." *British Journal of Political Science* 37(1): 139–63.

Lawson, Chappell, and Kenneth F. Greene. 2011. "*Reciprocity and Self-Enforcing Clientelism.*" Massachusetts Institute of Technology, University of Texas at Austin

2014. "Making Clientelism Work: How Norms of Reciprocity Increase Voter Compliance." *Comparative Politics* 47 (1): 61–85.

Lawson, Chappell, and James A. McCann. 2005. "Television News, Mexico's 2000 Elections and Media Effects in Emerging Democracies." *British Journal of Political Science* 35 (1): 1–30.

Lazar, Sian. 2004. "Personalist Politics, Clientelism and Citizenship: Local Elections in El Alto, Bolivia." *Bulletin of Latin American Research* 23 (2): 228–43.

2006. "El Alto, Ciudad Rebelde: Organisational Bases for Revolt." *Bulletin of Latin American Research* 25 (2): 183–99.

2007. *El Alto, Rebel City: Self and Citizenship in Andean Bolivia*. Durham: Duke University Press.

LeBas, Adrienne. 2011. *From Protest to Parties: Party-Building and Democratization in Africa*. Oxford: Oxford University Press.

Lemarchand, René. 1972. "Political Clientelism and Ethnicity in Tropical Africa: Competing Solidarities in Nation-Building." *The American Political Science Review* 66 (1): 68–90. doi:10.2307/1959279.

Lemarchand, Rene, and Keith Legg. 1972. "Political Clientelism and Development: A Preliminary Analysis." *Comparative Politics* 4 (2): 149–78. doi:10.2307/421508.

León, Gianmarco. 2017. "Turnout, Political Preferences and Information: Experimental Evidence from Perú." *Journal of Development Economics* 127: 56–71.

Levitsky, Steven. 2003. *Transforming Labor-Based Parties in Latin America: Argentine Peronism in Comparative Perspective.* Cambridge, UK; New York: Cambridge University Press.

2013. "Peru: Challenges of a Democracy without Parties." In *Constructing Democratic Governance*, by Michael Shifter and Jorge Dominguez, eds., 4th edn. The Johns Hopkins University Press, 282–315.

Levitsky, Steven, James Loxton, Brandon Van Dyck, and Jorge I. Domínguez. 2016. *Challenges of Party-Building in Latin America.* New York: Cambridge University Press.

Levitsky, Steven, and Lucan Way. 2002. "The Rise of Competitive Authoritarianism." *Journal of Democracy* 13 (2): 51–65.

Levitsky, Steven, and Maria Victoria Murillo, eds. 2005. *Argentine Democracy: The Politics of Institutional Weakness.* University Park, Pa: Pennsylvania State University Press.

2008. "Argentina: From Kirchner to Kirchner." *Journal of Democracy* 19 (2): 16–30.

Levitsky, Steven, and Mauricio Zavaleta. 2016. "Why No Party Building in Peru?" In *Challenges of Party-Building in Latin America*, Steven Levitsky, James Loxton, Brandon Van Dyck, and Jorge Dominguez, eds. Cambridge: Cambridge University Press.

Levitsky, Steven, and Maxwell Cameron. 2003. "Democracy without Parties? Political Parties and Regime Change in Fujimori's Peru." *Latin American Politics and Society* 45 (3): 1–33.

Leys, Colin. 1959. "Models, Theories, and the Theory of Political Parties." *Political Studies* 7 (2): 127–46

Lindbeck, Assar, and Jörgen W. Weibull. 1987. "Balanced-Budget Redistribution as the Outcome of Political Competition." *Public Choice* 52 (3): 273–97.

Lindberg, Staffan I. 2003. "'It's Our Time to Chop': Do Elections in Africa Feed Neo-Patrimonialism rather than Counter-Act It?" *Democratization* 10 (2): 121–40.

2008. *Democracy and Elections in Africa.* Baltimore: Johns Hopkins University Press.

Lipset, Seymour Martin, and Stein Rokkan. 1967. *Party Systems and Voter Alignments: Cross-National Perspectives. International Yearbook of Political Behavior Research*, vol. 7. New York: Free Press.

Lohmann, Susanne. 1994. "The Dynamics of Informational Cascades: The Monday Demonstrations in. Leipzig, East Germany, 1989–91." *World Politics* 47 (1): 42–101

López, Sinesio. 1997. *Ciudadanos Reales e Imaginarios: Concepciones, Desarrollo y Mapas De La Ciudadanía En El Perú.* Lima, Perú: Instituto de Diálogo y Propuestas.

Lowenthal, Abraham F., ed. 1975. *The Peruvian Experiment: Continuity and Change Under Military Rule.* Princeton, N.J: Princeton University Press.

Luna, Juan Pablo. 2014. *Segmented Representation: Political Party Strategies in Unequal Democracies. Oxford Studies in Democratization.* Oxford, United Kingdom: Oxford University Press.

2016. "Chile's Crisis of Representation." *Journal of Democracy* 27 (3): 129–38.

Luna, Juan Pablo, and David Altman. 2011. "Uprooted but Stable: Chilean Parties and the Concept of Party System Institutionalization." *Latin American Politics and Society* 52 (2): 1–28. doi: 10.1111/j.1548-2456.2011.00115.x

Luna, Juan Pablo, and Fernando Rosenblatt. 2012. "¿Notas para una autopsia? Los partidos políticos en el Chile actual." In *Democracia con partidos*, F.J. Diaz, and L. Sierra, eds. CEP-CIEPLAN.

Lupia, Arthur, and Mathew D. McCubbins. 1998. *The Democratic Dilemma: Can Citizens Learn What They Need to Know? Political Economy of Institutions and Decisions*. Cambridge, UK; New York: Cambridge University Press.

Lupu, Noam. 2016. *Party Brands in Crisis: Partisanship, Brand Dilution, and the Breakdown of Political Parties in Latin America*. New York, NY: Cambridge University Press.

Luskin, Robert C. 1987. "Measuring Political Sophistication." *American Journal of Political Science* 31 (4): 856–899. doi:10.2307/2111227.

Lyne, Mona. 2007. "Rethinking economics and institutions: the voter's dilemma and democratic accountability." In *Patrons, Clients, and Policies: Patterns of Democratic Accountability and Political Competition*, Herbert Kitschelt and Steven Wilkinson, eds. Cambridge: Cambridge University Press, 159–81.

Magaloni, Beatriz, Alberto Díaz-Cayeros, and Federico Estévez. 2007. "Clientelism and Portafolio Diversification: A Model of Electoral Investment with Applications to Mexico." In *Patrons, Clients, and Policies: Patterns of Democratic Accountability and Political Competition*, Herbert Kitschelt and Steven Wilkinson, eds. Cambridge, UK: Cambridge University Press, 182–205.

Mahler, Matthew. 2011. "The Day Before Election Day." *Ethnography* 12 (2): 149–73.

Mainwaring, Scott. 2006. "The Crisis of Representation in the Andes." *Journal of Democracy* 17 (3): 13–27.

Mainwaring, Scott, and Timothy R. Scully. 1995. *Building Democratic Institutions: Party Systems in Latin America*. Cambridge: Cambridge University Press.

Manzetti, Luigi and Carole Wilson. 2007. "Why Do Corrupt Governments Maintain Public Support?" *Comparative Political Studies* 40 (8): 949–70.

Marcus-Delgado, Jane, and Martín Tanaka. 2001. *Lecciones Del Final Del Fujimorismo: La Legitimidad Presidencial y La Acción Política*. 1st edn. Colección Mínima47. Lima: IEP.

Martínez, Mar, and Margarita Corral. 2015. "Clientelismo En Guatemala Y El Salvador:?ʿ Condicionan Los Distritos El Comportamiento Clientelar?" *Revista Latinoamericana de Política Comparada* 1 (9): 35–52.

Mayobre, José Antonio. 1996. "Politics, Media, and Modern Democracy: The Case of Venezuela." In *Politics, Media, and Modern Democracy: An International Study of Innovations in Electoral Campaigning and Their Consequences*, edited by David L. Swanson and Paulo Mancini, eds. Westport, CT: Praeger, 227–45.

Mazzoleni, Gianpietro, Julianne Stewart, and Bruce Horsfield, eds. 2003. *The Media and Neo-Populism: A Contemporary Comparative Analysis*. Praeger Series in Political Communication. Westport, CT: Praeger.

Mazzoleni, Gianpietro, and Winfried Schulz. 1999. "'Mediatization' of Politics: A Challenge for Democracy?" *Political Communication* 16 (3): 247–61. doi:10.1080/105846099198613.

McAllister, Ian. 2007. "The Personalization of Politics," in *The Oxford Handbook of Political Behavior*, Dalton, Russell and Hans-Dieter Klingemann, eds. New York: Oxford University Press, 571–88.

McCarty, Christopher, Peter D. Killworth, H. Russell Bernard, Eugene C. Johnsen, and Gene A. Shelley. 2001. "Comparing Two Methods for Estimating Network Size." *Human Organization* 60 (1): 28–39.

McKelvey, Richard D, and Peter C Ordeshook. 1985. "Elections with Limited Information: A Fulfilled Expectations Model Using Contemporaneous Poll and Endorsement Data as Information Sources." *Journal of Economic Theory* 36 (1): 55–85.

Mead, George Herbert. 1947. *Mind, Self, and Society from the Stand-point of a Social Behaviorist*. Chicago: University of Chicago Press.

Meléndez, Carlos, and Carlos León. 2009. "Perú 2008: El Juego de Ajedrez de La Gobernabilidad En Partidas Simultaneas." *Revista de Ciencia Política* 29 (2): 591–609.

Meléndez, Carlos, and Sofía Vera. 2006. "Si 'todos Perdieron',?` Quién Ganó? Los Movimientos Regionales En Las Elecciones de Noviembre Del 2006." *Argumentos. Coyuntura Electoral* 1 (8).

Menéndez-Carrión, Amparo. 1985. *Clientelismo Electoral Y Barriadas: Perspectivas De Análisis*. Lima, Perú: IEP.

Morgan, Jana. 2011. *Bankrupt Representation and Party System Collapse*. University Park, Pa: Penn State University Press.

Moser, Robert G. 2001. *Unexpected Outcomes: Electoral Systems, Political Parties, and Representation in Russia. Pitt Series in Russian and East European Studies*. Pittsburgh: University of Pittsburgh Press.

Moser, Robert G., and Ethan Scheiner. 2009. "Strategic Voting in Established and New Democracies: Ticket Splitting in Mixed-member Electoral Systems." *Electoral Studies* 28 (1): 51–61.

Mülier, Wolfgang. 2007. "Political Institutions and Linkage Strategies." In *Patrons, Clients, and Policies: Patterns of Democratic Accountability and Political Competition*, Herbert Kitschelt and Steven Wilkinson, eds. Cambridge, UK: Cambridge University Press, 251–75.

Muñoz, Paula. 2005. *El diseño institucional municipal 1980-2004 y sus implicancias para las zonas rurales*. Lima: Asociación Servicios Educativos Rurales (SER).

　　2007. "*La Incertidumbre De La Política Regional. Estudio Sobre La Articulación Entre El Gobierno Regional y Los Gobiernos Locales De Puno (2003-2007)*." Puno: Asociación Servicios Educativos Rurales (SER). Available at: www .scribd.com/doc/93070447/La-Incertidumbre-de-La-Politica-Regional-Puno.

　　2010. "¿Consistencia Política Regional O Frágiles Alianzas Electorales?" *Argumentos* 3. Available at: http://revistargumentos.org.pe/index.php?fp_cont=950.

　　2014. "An informational theory of campaign clientelism: The case of Peru." *Comparative Politics* 47 (1): 79–98.

2016. "Clientelismo de Campaña, Obrismo Y Corrupción: Baja Accountability Democrática En Perú." In *Participación, Competencia Y Representación Política*, Jorge Aragón, ed. Lima: IEP/JNE, 159–78.

Muñoz, Paula, and Andrea García. 2011. "Balance de Las Elecciones Regionales 2010: Tendencias, Particularidades Y Perfil de Los Candidatos Más Exitosos." In *El Nuevo Poder En Las Regiones. Análisis de Las Elecciones Regionales Y Municipales 2010*. Lima: Departamento de Ciencias Sociales - PUCP, 8–17.

Muñoz, Paula and Eduardo Dargent. 2016. "Patronage, Subnational Linkages, and Party-Building: The cases of Colombia and Peru." In *Challenges of Party-Building in Latin America*, edited by Steven Levitsky et al. New York: Cambridge University Press, 187–216.

Muñoz, Paula, Martín Monsalve, Yamilé Guibert, César Guadalupe, and Javier Torres. 2016. *Élites Regionales En El Perú (2000-2014) En Un Contexto Del Boom Fiscal: Los Casos de Arequipa, Cusco, Piura Y San Martín*. Lima: Fondo Editorial de la Universidad del Pacífico.

Murakami, Yusuke. 2007. *Perú En La Era Del Chino: La Política No Institucionalizada y El Pueblo En Busca De Un Salvador*. 1st edn. Serie Ideología y Política27. Lima: IEP.

National Democratic Institute, Acción Ciudadana, and University of Notre Dame. 2012. *Aproximación a Las Percepciones de La Ciudadanía Sobre La Compra de Votos Y La Intimidación de Votantes En El Régimen Político Electoral Guatemalteco*. Ciudad de Guatemala: NDI Guatemala/ University of Notre Dame/AC. Available at: www.ndi.org and http://accionciudadana .org.gt/.

Nichter, Simeon. 2008. "Vote Buying or Turnout Buying? Machine Politics and the Secret Ballot." *American Political Science Review* 102 (01). doi:10.1017/ S0003055408080106.

2009. "Declared Choice: Citizen Strategies and Dual Commitment Problems in Clientelism." *SSRN eLibrary*. Available at: http://papers.ssrn.com/sol3/ papers.cfm?abstract_id=1449058.

2010. "*Politics and Poverty: Electoral Clientelism in Latin America*." Ph.D., Political Science, United States, California: University of California, Berkeley.

2014. "Conceptualizing vote buying." *Electoral Studies* 35: 315–327. doi: https://doi.org/10.1016/j.electstud.2014.02.008

Nichter, Simeon and Michael Peress. 2017. "Request Fulfilling: When Citizens Demand Clientelist Benefits." *Comparative Political Studies* 50 (8): 1086–117.

Nielsen, Rasmus Kleis. 2012. *Ground Wars: Personalized Communication in Political Campaigns*. Princeton: Princeton University Press.

Norris, Pippa. 2000. *A Virtuous Circle: Political Communications in Postindustrial Societies. Communication, Society, and Politics*. Cambridge, UK; New York, NY: Cambridge University Press.

Nugent, Paul. 2007. "Banknotes and Symbolic Capital: Ghana's Election under the Dourth Republic." In *Votes, Money and Violence: Political Parties and Elections in Sub-Saharan Africa*, Mathias Basedau, Gero Erdman and Andres Mehler, eds. Uppsala: Nordic African Institute Press, 252–75.

O'Donnell, Guillermo. 2002. "Las poliarquías y la (in)efectividad de la ley en América Latina." In *La (in)efectividad de la ley y la exclusión en América latina*, Juan Méndez, Guillermo O'Donnell, and Paula de Moraes, eds. Buenos Aires: Paidós, 305–36.

Oliveros, Virginia. 2012. "Public Employees as Political Workers. Evidence from an Original Survey in Argentina." Paper for Delivery at the Congress of the Latin America Studies Association. San Francisco, California, May 23–26, 2012.

2013. "A Working Machine: Patronage Jobs and Political Services in Argentina." PhD Dissertation, Political Science. New York: Columbia University. Available at: http://academiccommons.columbia.edu/catalog/ac%3A161503.

2016. "Making It Personal. Clientelism, Favors, and the Personalization of Public Administration in Argentina." *Comparative Politics* 48 (3): 373–91.

Ospina, Pablo. 2006. "La Crisis Del Clientelismo En Ecuador (Tema Central)." In *Ecuador Debate. Elecciones 2006*. Clientelismo y política (69). Quito: Centro Andino de Acción Popular CAAP, 57–76.

Ostiguy, Pierre. 2009. The High and the Low in Politics: A two-dimensional political space for comparative analysis and electoral studies. Working Paper 360. The Helen Kellog Institute for International Studies.

Pachano, Simón. 2001. "Partidos Y Clientelismo En Ecuador." *Quórum: Revista de Pensamiento Iberoamericano* 2: 21–39.

Parodi Trece, Carlos. 2000. *Peru, 1960-2000: Políticas Económicas y Sociales En Entornos Cambiantes*. 1st edn. Lima, Perú: Universidad del Pacífico, Centro de Investigación.

Payne, J. Mark, G. Daniel Zovatto, and Mercedes Mateo Díaz. 2007. Democracies in Development: Politics and Reform in Latin America. Washington: Inter-American Development Bank/International Institute for Democracy and Electoral Assistance/David Rockefeller Center for Latin American Studies.

Persson, Torsten, Guido Tabellini, Francesco Trebbi. 2003. "Electoral Rules and Corruption." *Journal of the European Economic Association* 1 (4): 958–89.

Peterson, David. 2005. "Heterogeneity and certainty in candidate evaluations." *Political Behavior* 27: 1–24.

Piattoni, Simona, ed. 2001. *Clientelism, Interests, and Democratic Representation: The European Experience in Historical and Comparative Perspective. Cambridge Studies in Comparative Politics*. Cambridge; New York: Cambridge University Press.

Planas, Pedro. 1998. *La Descentralización En El Perú Republicano (1821-1998)*. Lima: Municipalidad Metropolitana de Lima.

Plasser, Fritz, and Gunda Plasser. 2002. *Global Political Campaigning—A Worldwide Analysis of Campaign Professionals and Their Practices*. Westport, CT: Praeger.

PNUD. 2009. *Informe Sobre Desarrollo Humano Perú 2009: Por Una Densidad Del Estado Al Servicio de La Gente*. Lima: Programa de las Naciones Unidas para el Desarrollo. Available at: www.pe.undp.org/content/peru/es/home/library/poverty/InformeDesarrolloHumano2009.html.

Popkin, Samuel L. 1991. *The Reasoning Voter: Communication and Persuasion in Presidential Campaigns*. Chicago: University of Chicago Press.

Powell, John Duncan. 1970. "Peasant Society and Clientelist Politics." *The American Political Science Review* 64 (2): 411–25. doi:10.2307/1953841.

Pro Descentralización. 2006. *Proceso De Descentralización 2005–Abril 2006. Balance y Desafíos*. Lima: PRODES/USAID.

Quirós, Julieta. 2006. "Movimientos Piqueteros, Formas de Trabajo Y Circulación de Valor En El Sur Del Gran Buenos Aires." *Anuario de Estudios de Antropología Social*: 151–59.

Roberts, Kenneth M. 1995. "Neoliberalism and the Transformation of Populism in Latin America: The Peruvian Case." *World Politics* 48 (1): 82–116. doi:10.1353/wp.1995.0004.

2002. "Social Inequalities without Class Cleavages in Latin America's Neoliberal Era." *Studies in Comparative International Development* 36 (4): 3–33. doi:10.1007/BF02686331

2006. "Populism, Political Conflict, and Grass-Roots Organization in Latin America." *Comparative Politics* 38 (2): 127–48. doi:10.2307/20433986.

2015. *Changing Course in Latin America. Party Systems in the Neoliberal Era*. New York: Cambridge University Press.

Roberts, Kenneth M., and Moisés Arce. 1998. "Neoliberalism and Lower-Class Voting Behavior in Peru." *Comparative Political Studies* 31 (2): 217–46. doi: 10.1177/0010414098031002004.

Robinson, James A., and Thierry Verdier. 2003. "The Political Economy of Clientelism." *Scandinavian Journal of Economics* 115 (2), 260–91.

Roniger, Luis. 1990. *Hierarchy and Trust in Modern Mexico and Brazil*. New York: Praeger.

Rosenblatt, Fernando. Forthcoming. *Party Vibrancy and Democracy in Latin America*. Oxford: Oxford University Press.

Rottinghaus, Brandon, and Irina Alberro. 2005. "Rivaling the pri: The Image Management of Vicente Fox and the Use of Public Opinion Polling in the 2000 Mexican Election." *Latin American Politics and Society* 47 (2): 143–58.

Rousseau, Stéphanie. 2009. *Women's Citizenship in Peru: The Paradoxes of Neopopulism in Latin America*. 1st edn. New York: Palgrave Macmillan.

Sachs, Jeffrey. 1989. Social Conflict and Populist Policies in Latin America. NBER Working Paper No. w2897.

Samuels, David. 2002. "Pork Barrel Politics Is Not Credit-Claiming or Advertising: Campaign Finance and the Sources of the Personal Vote in Brazil." *Journal of Politics* 64: 845–63

Sánchez, Omar. 2009. "Party Non-Systems A Conceptual Innovation." *Party Politics* 15 (4): 487–520. doi:10.1177/1354068809334566.

Sartori, Giovanni. 1976. *Parties and Party Systems: A Framework for Analysis*. Cambridge; New York: Cambridge University Press.

1968. *Political Development and Political Engineering. Public Policy XVII. Cambridge Mass.* Massachusetts: Harvard University Press, 261–98

Schady, Norbert R. 2000. "The Political Economy of Expenditures by the Peruvian Social Fund (FONCODES), 1991–95." *The American Political Science Review* 94 (2) (June): 289–304. doi:10.2307/2586013.

Schaffer, Frederic Charles. 2007. *Elections for Sale: The Causes and Consequences of Vote Buying*. Boulder, Colo: Lynne Rienner Publishers.

Schaffer, Frederic Charles, and Andreas Schedler. 2007. "What Is Vote Buying?" In *Elections for Sale: The Causes and Consequences of Vote Buying*, Frederic Charles Schaffer, ed. Boulder, Colo: Lynne Rienner Publishers, 17–30.

Schaffer, Joby and Andy Baker. 2015. "Clientelism as Persuasion-Buying Evidence from Latin America" *Comparative Political Studies* 48 (9): 1093–126. doi: https://doi.org/10.1177/0010414015574881

Schedler, Andreas, and Laura Manríquez. 2004. "'El Voto Es Nuestro'. Cómo Los Ciudadanos Mexicanos Perciben El Clientelismo Electoral." *Revista Mexicana de Sociología* (1): 57–97

Scheiner, Ethan. 2007. "Clientelism in Japan: The Importance and Limits of Institutional Explanations." In *Patrons, Clients, and Policies: Patterns of Democratic Accountability and Political Competition*, Herbert Kitschelt and Steven Wilkinson, eds. Cambridge, UK: Cambridge University Press, 276–97.

Scherlis, Gerardo. 2010. "Patronage and Party Organization in Argentina: the Emergence of the Patronage-based Network Party." PhD Dissertation. Netherlands-Leiden: Leiden University. Available at: https://openaccess .leidenuniv.nl/handle/1887/14598.

2013. "The Contours of Party Patronage in Argentina." *Latin American Research Review* 48 (3): 63–84.

Scott, James C. 1969. "Corruption, Machine Politics, and Political Change." *The American Political Science Review* 63 (4): 1142–58.

1972. "Patron-Client Politics and Political Change in Southeast Asia." *The American Political Science Review* 66 (1): 91–113.

1976. *The Moral Economy of the Peasant: Rebellion and Subsistence in Southeast Asia*. New Haven: Yale University Press.

Seawright, Jason Woodland. 2006. "Crisis of Representation: Voters, Party Organizations, and Party-System Collapse in South America." PhD Dissertation. Berkeley: University of California.

2012. *Party-System Collapse: The Roots of Crisis in Peru and Venezuela*. Stanford University Press.

Shaw, Daron R. 2006. *The Race to 270: The Electoral College and the Campaign Strategies of 2000 and 2004*. Chicago: University of Chicago Press.

Shefter, Martin. 1994. *Political Parties and the State: The American Historical Experience*. Princeton, NJ: Princeton University Press.

1997. "Party and Patronage: Germany, England and Italy." *Politics & Society* 7(4): 403–51.

Silva, Patricio. 2001. "Towards Technocratic Mass Politics in Chile? The 1999–2000 Elections and the 'Lavín Phenomenon.'" *European Review of Latin American and Caribbean Studies* 70: 25–39.

Singer, Matthew. 2009. "Buying Voters with Dirty Money: The Relationship Between Clientelism and Corruption". SSRN Scholarly Paper ID 1449001. Rochester, NY: Social Science Research Network. Available at: http://papers .ssrn.com/abstract=1449001.

Skocpol, Theda, and Margaret Somers. 1980. "The Uses of Comparative History in Macrosocial Inquiry." *Comparative Studies in Society and History* 22 (2): 174–97.

Slosar, Mary Catherine. 2011. "The power of personality: candidate-centered voting in comparative perspective." PhD Dissertation. Austin, TX: University of Texas at Austin.

Soifer, Hillel D. 2015. *State Building in Latin America*. New York: Cambridge University Press.

Stokes, Susan. 1995. *Cultures in Conflict: Social Movements and the State in Peru*. Berkeley: University of California Press.

2005. "Perverse Accountability: A Formal Model of Machine Politics with Evidence from Argentina." *The American Political Science Review* 99 (3): 315–25.

2007a. "Political Clientelism." In *Oxford University Press Handbook of Comparative Politics*, Carles Boix and Susan C. Stokes, eds. Oxford; New York: Oxford University Press, 604–27.

2007b. "Is Vote Buying Undemocratic?" In *Elections for Sale: The Causes and Consequences of Vote Buying*, Frederic Charles Schaffer, eds. Boulder, Colorado: Lynne Rienner, 81–99.

Stokes, Susan, Thad Dunning, Marcelo Nazareno, and Valeria Brusco. 2013. *Brokers, Voters, and Clientelism: The Puzzle of Distributive Politics*. Cambridge, MA: Cambridge University Press.

Suárez Bustamante, Miguel. 2003. *Caracterización Del Programa Vaso De Leche*. Lima: Dirección de General de Asuntos Económicos y Sociales del Ministerio de Economía y Finanzas. Available at: www.mef.gob.pe/contenidos/pol_econ/documentos/carac_vaso.pdf.

Swanson, David and Paolo Mancini. 1996. "Patterns of Modern Electoral Campaigning and Their Consequences." In *Politics, Media, and Modern Democracy*, David Swanson and Paolo Mancini, eds. London: Praeger, 247–76

Szwarcberg, Mariela. 2009. "Making Local Democracy: Political Machines, Clientelism, and Social Networks in Argentina." PhD Dissertation. Illinois: The University of Chicago.

2011. "The Microfoundations of Political Clientelism: Lessons from the Argentine Case." The Kellogg Institute Working Papers, #377. Available at: http://kellogg.nd.edu/publications/workingpapers/WPS/377.pdf.

2012a. "Political Parties and Rallies in Latin America." *Party Politics* 20 (3): 456–66

2012b. "Uncertainty, Political Clientelism, and Voter Turnout in Latin America: Why Parties Conduct Rallies in Argentina." *Comparative Politics* 45 (1): 88–106.

2015. *Mobilizing Poor Voters: Machine Politics, Clientelism, and Social Networks in Argentina. Structural Analysis in the Social Sciences*. New York: Cambridge University Press.

Tanaka, Martín. 1998. *Los espejismos de la democracia. El colapso del sistema de partidos en el Perú, 1980-1995, en perspectiva comparada*. Lima: Instituto de Estudios Peruanos.

1999. "La Participación Social y Política De Los Pobladores Populares Urbanos: ¿del Movimentismo a Una Política De Ciudadanos? El Caso De El Agustino." In *El Poder Visto Desde Abajo: Democracia, Educación y Ciudadanía En Espacios Locales*, Martin Tanaka, ed. Serie Urbanización, Migraciones y Cambios En La Sociedad Peruana 14. Lima: IEP, 103–153.

2001. "¿Crónica De Una Muerte Anunciada? Determinismo, Voluntarismo, Actores y Poderes Estructurales En El Perú 1980-2000." In *Lecciones Del Final Del Fujimorismo. La Legitimidad Presidencial y La Acción Política*, Jane Markus-Delgado and Martín Tanaka, eds. Colección Mínima 47. Lima: IEP, 57–112.

2005a. *Democracia Sin Partidos, Perú, 2000-2005: Los Problemas De Representación Y Las Propuestas De Reforma Política*. 1st edn. Colección Mínima 57. Lima: Instituto de Estudios Peruanos.

2005b. "La Estructura de La Oportunidad Política de La Corrupción En El Perú: Una Hipótesis de Trabajo." In *El Pacto Infame. Red para el Desarrollo de las Ciencias Sociales en el Perú*, 355–75.

2002c. *La Dinámica De Los Actores Regionales y El Proceso De Descentralización*. Lima: IEP.

Tanaka, Martin, and Carlos Melendez. 2014. "The Future of Peru's Brokered Democracy. Clientelism, Social Policy, and the Quality of Democracy." In *Clientelism, Social Policy, and the Quality of Democracy*, Diego Abente and Larry Diamond, eds. Baltimore, Maryland: Johns Hopkins University Press, 65–87.

Tanaka, Martín, and Rodrigo Barrenechea. 2011. "Evaluando la oferta de Partidos: ¿cuál es el perfil de los candidatos al próximo Parlamento?" Revista Argumentos, 5(1). Available at: http://revistaargumentos.iep.org.pe/articulos/evaluando-la-oferta-de-los-partidos-cual-es-el-perfil-de-los-candidatos-al-proximo-parlamento/

Tanaka, Martín, and Yamilé Guibert. 2011. "Entre La Evaporación de Los Partidos Y La Debilidad de Los Movimientos Regionales Una Mirada a Las Elecciones Regionales Y Municipales Desde Las Provincias, 2002–2006–2010." In *El Nuevo Poder En Las Regiones. Análisis de Las Elecciones Regionales Y Municipales 2010*. Departamento de Ciencias Sociales – PUCP, 18–28.

Thachil, Tariq. 2014. "Elite Parties and Poor Voters: Theory and Evidence from India." *American Political Science Review* 108: 454–77.

Tironi, Eugenio. 2002. "El cambio está aquí. Santiago, Chile: La Tercera-Mondadori." In *La Campaña Política: Técnicas Eficaces*, Ventura Egoávil, José, ed. Lima: Escuela Mayor de Gestión Municipal.

Transparencia Paraguay and Alter Vida. 2005. "Recolección De Fondos y Gastos Electorales En Las Elecciones Municipales. Informe Final De Investigación. Proyecto Piloto Financiamiento De Los Partidos Políticos y Campañas Electorales." Manuscript.

Uribe, José. 2014. *El mercado del oro en Colombia*. Bogotá: Banco de la República. Available at: www.banrep.gov.co/es/revista-1035

Van de Walle, Nicolas. 2007. "Meet the New Boss, Same as the Old Boss? The Evolution of Political Clientelism in Africa." In *Patrons, Clients, and Policies: Patterns of Democratic Accountability and Political Competition*, Herbert Kitschelt and Steven Wilkinson, eds. Cambridge, UK: Cambridge University Press, 50–67.

Vera, Sofía. 2010. "Radiografía a La Política En Las Regiones: Tendencias a Partir de La Evidencia de Tres Procesos Electorales (2002, 2006 Y 2010)." *Revista Argumentos* 4 (5). Available at: www.revistargumentos.org.pe/index .php?fp_cont=916.

2014. "What Motivates Politicians to Build Legislative Careers?" Paper presented at the Annual Meeting of the American Political Science Association (APSA), Washington, DC, August 28–31.

2017. "Conditional Corruption Costs." Paper presented at the XXIX Congress of the Latin American Studies Association (LASA), Lima, Peru May 21–24.

Vergara, Alberto. 2012. "United by Discord, Divided by Consensus: National and Sub-National Articulation in Bolivia and Peru, 2000–2010." *Journal of Politics in Latin America* 3 (3): 65–93.

Vergara, Alberto, and Daniel Encinas. 2016. "Continuity by Surprise. Explaining Institutional Stability in Contemporary Peru." *Latin American Research Review* 51 (1): 159–80.

Vicente, Pedro 2014. "Is Vote-Buying Effective? Evidence from a Field Experiment in West Africa." *Economic Journal*, 124(574): F356–F387.

Vommaro, Gabriel, and Julieta Quirós. 2011. "'Usted Vino Por Su Decisión': Repensar El Clientelismo En Clave Etnográfica." *Desacatos. Revista de Antropología Social* 36: 65–84.

Waisbord, Silvio R. 1996. "Secular Politics: The Modernization of Argentine Electioneering." In *Politics, Media, and Modern Democracy: An International Study of Innovations in Electoral Campaigning and Their Consequences*, Swanson, David and Paulo Mancini, eds. Westport, Conn.: Praeger, 207–226.

Wang, Chin-Shou, and Charles Kurzman. 2007. "The Logistics: How to Buy Votes." In *Elections for Sale: The Causes and Consequences of Vote Buying*, Frederic Charles Schaffer, ed. Boulder, CO: Lynner Rienner, 61–80.

Wantchekon, Leonard. 2003. Clientelism and Voting Behavior: Evidence from a Field Experiment in Benin. *World Politics* 55 (3): 399–422.

Wattenberg, Martin. 2009. *The Decline of American Political Parties 1952–1996*. Cambridge, MA: Harvard University Press.

Weaver, Julie Anne. 2017a. The Breakdown of Local Electoral Accountability: Evidence from an Original Survey in Peru. Manuscript

2017b. Voting, Citizen Engagement and Political Accountability in Municipal Politics: The Case of Peru. Manuscript.

Weingrod, Alex. 1968. "Patrons, Patronage, and Political Parties." *Comparative Studies in Society and History* 10 (4): 377–400.

Weitz-Shapiro, Rebecca. 2008. *Choosing Clientelism: Political Competition, Poverty, and Social Welfare Policy in Argentina*. New York: Columbia University.

2012. "What Wins Votes: Why Some Politicians Opt Out of Clientelism." *American Journal of Political Science* 56 (3): 568–83.

2014. *Curbing Clientelism in Argentina: Politics, Poverty, and Social Policy*. Cambridge. New York: Cambridge University Press.

Weyland, Kurt. 1996. "Neoliberal Populism in Latin America: Unexpected affinities." *Studies in Comparative International Development* 31 (3): 3–31.

1998. "Swallowing the Bitter Pill Sources of Popular Support for Neoliberal Reform in Latin America." *Comparative Political Studies* 31 (5): 539–68.

1999. "Neoliberal Populism in Latin America and Eastern Europe." *Comparative Politics* 31 (4): 79–401

2001. "Clarifying a Contested Concept: Populism in the Study of Latin American Politics." *Comparative Politics* 34 (1): 1–22.

2002. *The Politics of Market Reform in Fragile Democracies: Argentina, Brazil, Peru, and Venezuela*. Princeton: Princeton University Press.

Wilkinson Magaloni, Beatriz. 2006. *Voting for Autocracy: Hegemonic Party Survival and Its Demise in Mexico. Cambridge Studies in Comparative Politics*. Leiden: Cambridge University Press.

Winters, Matthew and Rebecca Weitz-Shapiro. 2013. "Lacking information or condoning corruption: When will voters support corrupt politicians?" *Comparative Politics* 45 (4): 418–36.

Wise, Carol. 2002. *Reinventing the State: Economic Strategy and Institutional Change in Peru*. Ann Arbor: University of Michigan Press.

Wolfinger, Raymond E. 1972. "Why Political Machines Have Not Withered Away and Other Revisionist Thoughts." *The Journal of Politics* 34 (2): 365–98.

Young, Lisa, and Bill Cross. 2015. "Personalization of Campaigns in an SMP System: the Canadian Case." *Electoral Studies* 39 (3): 306–15.

Zarazaga, Rodrigo. 2011. "Vote-Buying and Asymmetric Information: A Model with Applications to Argentina." Paper presented in the annual APSA meeting. Seattle, Washington.

2012. "Brokers Beyond Clientelism: The Case of the Peronist Hegemony." Manuscript.

2014. "Brokers beyond Clientelism: A New Perspective through the Argentine Case." *Latin American Politics and Society* 56 (3): 23–45.

2016. "Party machines and voter-customized rewards strategies." *Journal of Theoretical Politics* 28 (4): 678–701.

Zas Fris, Johnny. 2005. *La Insistencia De La Voluntad. El Actual Proceso De Descentralización Política y Sus Antecedentes Inmediatos (1980–2004)*. Lima: Defensoría del Pueblo/SER.

Zavaleta, Mauricio. 2012. "*La Competencia Política Post-Fujimori. Partidos Regionales Y Coaliciones de Independientes En Los Espacios Subnacionales Peruanos.*" Thesis for the Degree in Political Science and Government. Lima: Pontificia Universidad Católica del Perú.

2014. *Coaliciones de Independientes. Las Reglas No Escritas de La Política Electoral. Ideología Y Política*. Lima: IEP.

Zhen, Tian, Matthew Salganik, and Andrew Gelman. 2006. "How Many People Do You Know in Prison?: Using Overdispersion in Count Data to Estimate Social Structure in Networks." *Journal of the American Statistical Association* 101: 409–23.

Index